D1552879

ETHNIC CONFLICT IN
THE WESTERN WORLD

Also by Milton J. Esman

Administration and Development in Malaysia: Institution Building and Reform in a Plural Society

The Common Aid Effort: The Development Assistance Committee of the Organization for Economic Cooperation and Development (with Daniel S. Cheever)

ETHNIC CONFLICT IN THE WESTERN WORLD

edited by **MILTON J. ESMAN**

CORNELL UNIVERSITY PRESS   Ithaca and London

First published 1977 by Cornell University Press.
Published in the United Kingdom by Cornell University Press Ltd., 2–4 Brook Street, London W1Y 1AA.

International Standard Book Number 0–8014–1016–9
Library of Congress Catalog Card Number 76–28012
Printed in the United States of America by Vail-Ballou Press, Inc.
Librarians: Library of Congress cataloging information appears on the last page of the book.

TO JANICE

who puts it all together

.

Preface

The essays in this book were presented originally at the Conference on Ethnic Pluralism and Conflict in Contemporary Western Europe and Canada, held in Ithaca, New York, from 21 May through 24 May 1975. The conference was sponsored by the Western Societies Program of the Center for International Studies at Cornell University. The Ford Foundation contributed financial support through its grant to the Western Societies Program for the study of center-periphery relations in contemporary Europe. Though numerous case studies were available, the renewed salience of ethnic solidarity in the politics of Western societies had not yet been treated in comparative terms. The conference provided the opportunity to bring together leading specialists in ethnic pluralism and in the politics of contemporary Europe and Canada to explore the utility of the center-periphery metaphor in explaining the recent intensification of ethnic conflict. This book is the result.

In addition to those whose essays appear in this volume, I am grateful to Peter Gourevitch, Michael Hechter, Val Lorwin, Donald MacKay, Sidney Tarrow, and Pierre van den Berghe, who enriched the conference by their participation. Conference arrangements were handled flawlessly by Renée Pierce and Andreas Svrakov, who joined James Jacob as conference rapporteurs. With the help of Sean Killeen and Susan Spencer, Allen Miller performed valuable editorial service in moving this multi-authored manuscript toward publication. The editorial work of the staff of the Cornell University Press has been, as usual, superb.

MILTON J. ESMAN

Ithaca, New York

Contents

Maps

Introduction

This book examines the reinvigoration of communal and ethnic solidarities and their emergence in recent years as important political movements in the industrialized and affluent societies of Western Europe and Canada. The essays deal only with ethnic groups that claim a traditional homeland; the political role of recent immigrants who now constitute a substantial proportion of the urban labor force in several Western countries is not discussed in this book, since the problems of these peoples differ in many respects from those encountered by peoples who have long been established in their own territories.[1]

Though national sentiment among minority peoples in Western countries never disappeared, it seemed, with few exceptions, to be quiescent and even declining during the two decades following World War II. Then, unexpectedly, in the late 1960's, the protests and demands of ethnic minorities—Scots and Welsh, Corsicans, Bretons and Alsatians, Basques and Catalans, Québécois, Flemings and Walloons, Croats and Macedonians, Jurassians and Ulster Irish—began to be asserted with new vigor, confidence, and sometimes violence. The intensity of their activities, the scope of their demands, the base of their popular support, and their legitimacy, especially among young people, increased dramatically—sufficiently to annoy and at times to preoccupy the leaders of governments and of established political parties.

Rapid economic growth, the spread of state-provided welfare services, and expanded educational opportunities have undermined the ideologies of class conflict and of religious authority that for three generations had

1. The absence of a territorial homeland for its largest minority, the blacks, and the complexity of its ethnic pluralism account for the exclusion of the United States from this volume. For a brief review of the problems of migrant workers in contemporary Europe, see Jonathan Power (in collaboration with Ann Hardman), *Western Europe's Migrant Workers,* Minority Rights Group Report no. 28 (London, 1976).

oriented much of the political organization and activity in industrialized countries. Their loss of appeal has been reinforced by erosion of the once powerful ideologies of liberal individualism and state-associated nationalism, which together had illegitimatized ethnic particularism and relegated it to the status of backwardness and even subversiveness. Among ethnic minorities this ideological vacuum is being filled by an energetic reaffirmation of the populist right of self-determination, by a renewal of ethnic pride, and by the association of the ethnic community in its homeland with a higher quality of life than is presumed to be possible in a bureaucratized and homogenized mass society. This development represents not the end of ideology, as proclaimed by some liberal and technocratic heralds of the postindustrial age, but the emergence of a competing ideology. While this ideology has limited appeal among ethnic majorities, it commands much more respectful attention among them than did similar claims a generation ago.

Ideological change, however, is only one element that helps to explain the activation of ethnic political movements. Coincident economic and social changes, including the rationalization of economic activity, the expanding regulatory and service functions of increasingly centralized governments, the uneven distribution among regions of the benefits and costs of modern industry and government, the penetration of electronic mass communications media into peripheral regions that are the homelands of many of the ethnic minorities—all contribute to this phenomenon. So do international developments, including the decline of European empires and the emergence from colonial status of independent states successfully asserting the right of national self-determination.

The interplay of these factors and their impact on the mobilization and politicization of ethnic solidarities in Western societies are the focus of the theoretical explorations and case studies of ethnic politics in this book. The theoretical pieces represent early efforts at systematic treatment of a complex and in many ways new subject. The case studies not only provide well-informed descriptions, analyses, and interpretations of recent events, but also attempt to state, test, and criticize specific propositions. The absence of agreed-upon concepts and even of standard terminology reflects the current state of scholarship on this subject.

The theoretical task is complicated by the variety of historical and institutional circumstances affecting ethnic political movements in industrialized countries. Some of these movements have emerged within highly centralized, unitary states, such as France, Spain, and Great Britain, while others, including those in Canada, Switzerland, and Yugoslavia, occur within federal systems. Some of the grievances that fuel these movements are primarily economic, as in Scotland, while others are mainly cultural, as is the case with the Basques. Still other movements, such as in Quebec, are motivated by both types of grievances. Some ethnic homelands, including Croatia and Catalonia, are relatively rich; others, such as Brittany and Corsica, are relatively poor. Some have substantial populations in relation to the total in their countries (Flanders and Quebec); the populations in others are relatively small (Wales and South Tyrol). Some function within such highly consensual polities as Belgium and Great Britain; others must attempt to mobilize support in authoritarian systems, as in Spain and Yugoslavia. In all cases, as Daniel Bell has observed, the erosion of the prestige of established institutions provides the opportunity for groups that feel deprived or disadvantaged to organize and propound grievances and demands through fresh symbols and idioms. Ethnicity is particularly effective for this purpose, since it has the capacity to "combine an interest with an affective tie." [2]

Processes of ethnic mobilization, attempts by central government elites to manage the ensuing conflicts, and eventual outcomes are affected by the many possible combinations of the factors just mentioned and by others as well. But here a caution is in order. Though ethnicity has become a more compelling mobilizing principle and cleavage in many Western societies, loyalties and cleavages based on class, occupation, religion, region, and ideology have by no means disappeared. On some issues they continue to exert greater influence than ethnic loyalties. Moreover, no ethnic community is monolithic; within a single community there may be serious cleavages and differences in judgment among individuals and groups on the value they attach to ethnicity, on the definition of issues, and on how the interests of their community can best be served. What has happened is that the ethnic theme, usually under the influence of new leaders, has assumed a more prominent but by no means exclusive role in orienting political attitudes, behavior, and organization.

Because of this complexity and variety, and in the absence of a convincing taxonomy of conflict situations, propositions that appear to explain one situation are often insufficient or irrelevant for others. The "internal colonialism" hypothesis may help to explain the grievances of the

2. Daniel Bell, "Ethnicity and Social Change," in *Ethnicity, Theory and Experience,* ed. Nathan Glazer and Daniel P. Moynihan (Cambridge: Harvard University Press, 1975), p. 169.

Breton minority in France, but it does little to illuminate the current anxieties of the Walloons in Belgium. The problem of developing general theory is further complicated by the dynamic quality of identity and solidarity in contemporary ethnic movements. One example is the recent shift in self-perception among Francophone Canadians in Quebec: for two centuries they struggled as "French Canadians" to survive first as a conquered people, then as a disadvantaged minority; today as "Québécois" they demand a dominant cultural and economic role in their homeland and insist on increased autonomy, not excluding the possibility of independence. As Nathan Glazer and Daniel P. Moynihan have observed in the introduction to their book *Ethnicity,* in efforts to theorize on this complex and dynamic subject, "we are all beginners." [3]

Repeatedly in these essays the reader will encounter the concept of *consociationalism.* This influential model of democratic conflict management in segmented societies was originally formulated by Arend Lijphart, one of the contributors to this volume.[4] Consociationalism is an alternative to majoritarian politics. In majoritarian systems the individual citizen is the significant unit of value and of action. Political movements or parties that achieve and maintain majority support earn the legitimate right to shape and enforce public policy. By contrast, the consociational model is group focused, the relevant actors being the solidarity communities, ethnic, racial, or religious, into which the society is fragmented. Consociational governance involves the organization of politics by parties or movements, each representing one of the constituent solidarity groups. The leaders of all the communities form an elite cartel that governs the polity and distributes the benefits and costs of government among the component groups. Each leader asserts the interests of his community and negotiates differences with colleagues who represent parallel communal

3. Glazer and Moynihan, p. 25.
4. See Arend Lijphart, *The Politics of Accommodation: Pluralism and Democracy in the Netherlands* (Berkeley: University of California Press, 1968); and Lijphart, "Consociational Democracy," *World Politics,* 21 (January 1969): 207–225. For subsequent treatment of the consociational concept, see Jürg Steiner, *Amicable Agreement versus Majority Rule: Conflict Resolution in Switzerland* (Chapel Hill: University of North Carolina Press, 1974); Kenneth McRae, ed., *Consociational Democracy: Political Accommodation in Segmented Societies* (Toronto: McClelland & Stewart, 1974); Milton J. Esman, *Administration and Development in Malaysia: Institution Building and Reform in a Plural Society* (Ithaca: Cornell University Press, 1972), pp. 16–66; and Eric A. Nordlinger, *Conflict Regulation in Divided Societies,* Harvard University Center for International Affairs, Occasional Paper no. 29 (Cambridge, January 1972). For a critique of the consociational model, see Alvin Rabushka and Kenneth A. Shepsle, *Politics in Plural Societies: A Theory of Democratic Instability* (Columbus: Charles Merrill, 1972).

constituencies in the elite cartel. Every group is prepared to take seriously the expressed needs and interests of every other participating group. Because all are committed to the maintenance of the polity, they settle their differences by "amicable agreement." This requires elite accommodation and depends on the capacity of leaders simultaneously to promote the interests of their constituents and to persuade them to accept the outcomes of compromise agreements. The rules of the game are antimajoritarian. They explicitly legitimatize politics based on communal pluralism and the attempt to strike accommodative bargains that will leave no group a winner at the expense of another. The emphasis is on peaceful communal coexistence and the maintenance of communally plural societies on a consensual basis, rather than on reduction or elimination of politically significant communal solidarities or domination of minorities by majorities.

In this volume data have been assembled and analyzed by leading students of ethnic politics in industrialized societies. The essays reflect quite faithfully the current state of knowledge and theory on this subject. The authors expect that this volume will facilitate further research, analysis, and theory building which will help to explain more fully one of the most interesting and important phenomena of contemporary politics.

I

HISTORICAL AND
THEORETICAL EXPLORATIONS

1

Ethnonationalism in the First World: The Present in Historical Perspective

WALKER CONNOR

Until quite recently, the conventional view of scholars concerning the vitality of ethnonationalism within the region known as Western Europe rested upon two pillars. The first was a conviction that World War II had impressed upon the peoples of the region the realization that modern technology had made nationalism an unaffordable luxury. For an amalgam of both positive and negative reasons, the prewar tendency to ascribe primary significance to being "British," French, or German was alleged to have been succeeded by an emphasis upon a supranational consciousness of being European, with an attendant willingness to accept radical alterations in traditional political structures so as to bring the latter into line with the new European identity. In the words of Stanley Hoffmann: "If there was one part of the world in which men of good will thought that the nation-state could be superseded, it was Western Europe. The conditions seemed ideal. On the one hand, nationalism seemed at its lowest ebb; on the other, an adequate formula and method for building a substitute had apparently been devised." [1]

In identifying this first pillar, Hoffmann here quite unintentionally also

1. Stanley Hoffmann, "Obstinate or Obsolete? The Fate of the Nation-State," in *Conditions of World Order,* ed. Stanley Hoffmann (New York: Simon & Schuster, 1966), p. 110. See also Charles Lerche and Abdul Said, *Concepts of International Politics,* 2d ed. (Englewood Cliffs, N.J.: Prentice-Hall, 1970), p. 274; "Postwar Europe provided a particularly fertile field for experimentation with new forms of international organization. The European peoples needed to escape from the destructive nationalism which had led to the devastation of two world wars within a half-century." The broad acceptance this view received is also indicated by its endorsement in Dankwart Rustow's essay "Nation" in the *International Encyclopedia of the Social Sciences* (New York: Crowell, Collier, and Macmillan, 1968), 11: 10: "Since World War II, common European loyalties have begun to compete with the national allegiances of the past, and to that extent the European countries are losing their character as nations; if the process should continue, our descendants may one day be able to speak of a European nation."

bears testimony to the prevalence of the second, namely, the assumption that Western Europe was devoid of significant national minorities. States of the region were (and, all too often, still are) described indiscriminately as nation-states, that relatively rare phenomenon, characterizing less than 10 percent of all states, in which the political borders of the state contain a single ethnic group. This commonly propagated image of Western Europe held that the individual states had either successfully assimilated their disparate peoples (for example, in Belgium, France, Spain, Switzerland, or the United Kingdom) or were themselves the product of the political consolidation of a nationally conscious people (as in Germany or Italy).[2]

The assumption that those Western European states that contained more than one ethnic group had successfully solved their national problems through assimilation was particularly consequential for the collective academic endeavor known as *nation building*. Surveying with one eye the problems of sociopolitical integration faced by the ethnically complex states in Africa and Asia, while perceiving with the other an uninterrupted pattern of successfully assimilated states within the industrially advanced region of Western Europe, the "nation builders" concluded that the experience of the latter had precedential value for predicting the political future of Africa and Asia.[3] If Cornishmen, Scots, and Welsh had

2. The states said to have assimilated their populations quite evidently displayed two distinct methods for attaining this end. While all were seen as pursuing (and achieving) psychological assimilation, some, such as Britain, France, and Spain, had fostered cultural assimilation, while others, such as Belgium and Switzerland (and Canada), had tolerated cultural, particularly linguistic, diversity.

3. Easily the most prominent and influential member of the nation-building school has been Karl Deutsch. For a relatively early exposition of this thesis, see his "Nation-Building and National Development" in *Nation-Building,* ed. Karl Deutsch and William Foltz (New York: Atherton, 1966), particularly pp. 1–8. For a later statement concerning the successful assimilation experience of Western Europe, see his *Nationalism and Its Alternatives* (New York: Knopf, 1969), chap. 1, entitled "The Experience of Western Europe." In this chapter, Italy, Spain, and Switzerland (as well as Canada and the United States) are cited as examples of states with a single national consciousness. Specific references to the successful assimilation of Bretons, Cornishmen, and Scots are also made. In both editions of his earlier *Nationalism and Social Communication: An Inquiry into the Foundations of Nationality* (Cambridge: MIT Press, 1953 and 1956), Deutsch cites Bretons, Flemings, French Canadians, the French- and German-speaking Swiss, Scots, and Welsh as examples of totally assimilated peoples. The impact that this image of successful assimilation had upon Deutsch's vision of the future of the Afro-Asian states is apparent in his description of a four-stage process leading to successful assimilation. After enumerating the four stages, he inquires: "How long might it take for tribes or other ethnic groups in a developing country to pass

become thoroughly British; if Basques, Catalans, and Galicians had become Spanish; if Flemings and Walloons had become Belgian; if Alsatians, Bretons, and Corsicans had become French, then why should not Ibo, Hausa, and Yoruba become Nigerian; or Baluchi, Bengali, Pashtun, and Sindhi become Pakistani?

This thesis that the process of building nation-states, presumably undergone by Western Europe, was destined to be repeated within the Third World was not predicated upon simple chronological determinism, that is, the notion that newer states must necessarily follow the sequential evolution undergone by older counterparts. Afghanistan, Ethiopia, Iran, and Thailand, for example, could boast of being created prior to all or most of the Western European states; yet they were not held up as likely models for the future. Indeed, they were grouped with other Third World states that were thought to be about to embark on the Western European route. The key element was held to be not chronology but modernization, the term applied to that amalgam of subprocesses including industrialization, urbanization, increasing literacy, intensified communication and transportation networks, and the like. These processes and the "social mobilization" of the more isolated and inert masses that the pro-

----

through such a sequence of stages? We do not know but European history offers at least a few suggestions" ("Nation-Building and National Development," p. 324).

Another example of the linking of Europe's "assimilationist" experience with the future of the Afro-Asian states is offered by Benjamin Akzin, *State and Nation* (London: Hutchinson University Library, 1964). Having noted the dissolving political significance of groups such as the "Welsh, Scots, Lapps, Frisians, Bretons, Savoyards, [and] Corsicans" (p. 63), the author continues: "If we look at the modern nation-States of Europe we shall see that, except perhaps for those of the Scandinavian peninsula, the population of each of them is largely the product of pre-existing ethnic groups which have integrated into the nations we know today. This is true of the French nation, consolidated from fairly heterogeneous elements between the seventh and the twelfth centuries. . . . Germans, Italians, Poles, Russians, and Spaniards have all become the well defined nations we know within a century or two of one another. . . . Under pre-modern conditions the process required a fairly long period of gestation. . . . Put into the pot of physical proximity, covered by the lid of a common political system, exposed to the heat of cultural and social interchange, the various elements will change after a fairly long time—it took a few centuries in the past, but may take less in the future—into a brew. The brew will not be quite homogeneous. You can still point to a grain of rice, to a leaf of onion, to a chunk of meat, to a splinter of bone. But it will manifestly be one brew, with its distinct flavor and taste" (pp. 83–84). A more succinct avowal of this same linkage doctrine is offered by Donald Puchala, *International Politics Today* (New York: Dodd, Mead, 1972), pp. 200–201. After defining the nation-state as one in which "the political perimeters of the state and the ethnic perimeters of the nation coincide," he concludes that "processes similar to those that produced nation-states in Europe during the last two centuries, are producing new nation-states in Africa and Asia today."

cesses heralded were considered to be at the root of successful assimilation within the First World.[4] Since modernization must also infect the
Third World, a series of nation-states was the predictable outcome. But
what would be left of this linkage theory and the prognostications based
thereon, should the states of Europe prove not to be successfully assimilated?

As is now generally recognized, both of the scholarly pillars that I have
described (a postnational Europe and a Europe of nation-states) rest upon
shaky foundations. The notion of an intuitive sense of ''Europeanness''
that transcends national consciousness was challenged by, among other
things, (1) the defeat of the European Defense Community as a result of
French distrust of German militarism, (2) the broad-scale toleration with
which President Charles de Gaulle's insistence on a *Europe des patries*
was greeted both within and without France, a toleration suggesting substantial though unarticulated support, (3) the rejection of European Economic Community (EEC) membership by the Norwegian electorate and a
general lack of interest in membership displayed by the people within a
number of other states, (4) the sporadically demonstrated proclivity for
each state to look out for itself, as occurred when Arab oil-producing
states elected to pursue a policy of selective embargoes, and (5) the negative responses, often bordering on xenophobia, which were accorded to
migrant workers throughout Western Europe.[5] Meanwhile, the increasing
manifestations of ethnic unrest throughout the area drew attention to the
mirage-nature of that second pillar, a Europe composed of uninational
states. Among the more well publicized cases were the revitalization of
the Scottish and Welsh nationalist movements, and the frictions generated
between Flemings and Walloons, between the South Tyrolean Germans
and Rome, between the Basques and Madrid, between the Irish and non-
Irish of Northern Ireland, and between the French- and German-speaking
elements of the canton Berne in Switzerland. Less advertised, but no less

4. The First World here refers to the industrialized states of Canada and the United
States, as well as to those of Western Europe. Though unquestionably also a member of the
First World, Japan was usually ignored in the general, theoretic treatises on nation building,
perhaps because of its ethnic homogeneity, which long antedated modernization.

5. A well-known American sociologist, Arnold Rose, tested the strength of supranational
sentiment (''Europeanness'') by studying the willingness of host populations to accept the
alien workers as compatriots. Although noting some variations among host populations, he
recorded a high incidence of xenophobia throughout Western Europe and failed to find substantial willingness anywhere to accept the foreigner as a fellow citizen. See his *Migrants in
Europe* (Minneapolis: University of Minnesota Press, 1969). Since publication of the book,
ethnic prejudice and attempts to expel foreigners have become more flagrant.

pertinent, was the growing ethnonational assertiveness among the Catalans and Galicians of Spain; the Alsatians, Basques, Bretons, Corsicans, and Occitanians of France; the Slovenes and the Val D'Aostans of Italy; the Croats and Slovenes of Austria; the Norse-descendent inhabitants of the Danish-controlled Faroe Islands; and the Eskimo population of Danish-controlled Greenland.[6] Even this listing does not exhaust all of the region's groups who retain a sense of ethnic distinctiveness from their state's dominant element (see Map 1).[7]

The first few manifestations of ethnonationalism within postwar Europe (among the South Tyroleans, for example) could be explained away as vestigial or unique. But as ethnonationalism has become unmistakably evident on the part of several peoples whose ethnic consciousness had hitherto been considered nonexistent or, at the least, politically inconsequential, scholars have proffered a variety of theories to explain this unanticipated transsocietal phenomenon. Among the more popular explanations have been (1) the theory of relative (economic, cultural, and/or political) deprivation; (2) anomie, resulting from a growing feeling of alienation from the depersonalized and dehumanizing modern mass society, leading, in turn, to what is alternately described as a reversion to "tribalism" or as a new, more relevant alternative; (3) a "center-periphery" series of relationships in which these newly assertive ethnic

6. The lack of publicity accorded to some of these movements is, in turn, reflected in a low level of public awareness concerning their existence. For example, at the annual meeting of the Northeastern Political Science Association in November 1973, I was criticized for a reference to ethnonational stirrings within France, and particularly for references to the Bretons. The critic (a specialist in French affairs) insisted that his many sojourns in Brittany had failed to uncover any such sentiment. Yet, only two months later, the French government felt compelled to outlaw four national liberation movements, two of which were Breton (the others being Basque and Corsican). For a reference to France as a case in which ethnicity and state are "synonomous," and where "culture and nationality coincide," see Myron Weiner, "National Integration vs. Nationalism," *Comparative Studies in Society and History*, 15 (March 1973): 253. See also Collette Guillaumin, "The Popular Press and Ethnic Pluralism: The Situation in France," *International Social Sciences Journal*, 22 (1971): 576–593. The author presumably believes that ethnic minorities within France are limited to Jews, Gypsies, and peoples from overseas departments; she is apparently oblivious to the Alsatian, Basque, Breton, Catalan, Corsican, Flemish, and Occitanian communities within her own state.

7. The mid-1970's witnessed a series of conferences of European minority groups. One held at Trieste in July 1974 was attended by representatives of, among others, Alsatians, Basques, Bretons, Catalans, Corsicans, Croats, Flemings, Frisians (of the Netherlands), Galicians, Irish, Occitanians, Piedmontese (of Italy), Sardinians, Scots, and Welsh. The Celtic League Conference held on the Isle of Man during September 1975 included representatives from "Alba," "Breizh," "Cymru," "Eire," "Kernow," and "Manin" (i.e., Scotland, Brittany, Wales, Ireland, Cornwall, and the Isle of Man).

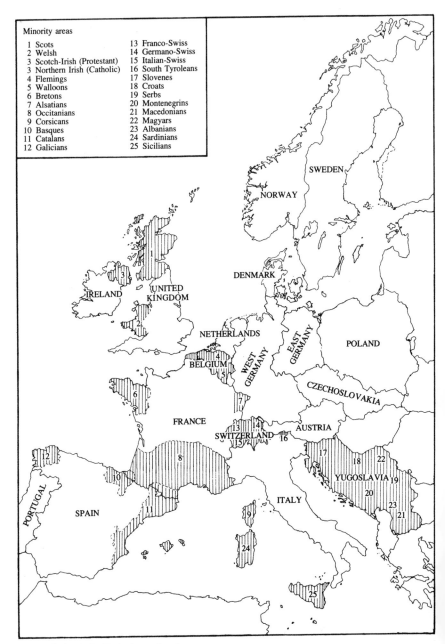

Minority areas

1 Scots	13 Franco-Swiss
2 Welsh	14 Germano-Swiss
3 Scotch-Irish (Protestant)	15 Italian-Swiss
3 Northern Irish (Catholic)	16 South Tyroleans
4 Flemings	17 Slovenes
5 Walloons	18 Croats
6 Bretons	19 Serbs
7 Alsatians	20 Montenegrins
8 Occitanians	21 Macedonians
9 Corsicans	22 Magyars
10 Basques	23 Albanians
11 Catalans	24 Sardinians
12 Galicians	25 Sicilians

Map 1. Selected ethnic homelands.

groups (the peripheral peoples) are viewed as having remained essentially outside or at the edge of the dominant society and have, therefore, been only marginally influenced by that society's principal currents; [8] and (4) the loss of global prestige suffered by individual European states, as contrasted with their eminence in the prewar period, and a corresponding loss of pride in being viewed as British rather than Scottish, or French rather than Breton. [9]

One explanation that has been overlooked is that the surge of ethnonationalism among Basques, Bretons, Welsh, and other such groups reflects a quite natural and perhaps even predictable stage in a process that has been underway for approximately two centuries. Ever since the abstract philosophical notion that the right to rule is vested in *the people* was first linked in popular fancy to a particular, ethnically defined people—a development which first occurred at the time of the French Revolution—the conviction that one's own people should *not,* by the very nature of things, be ruled by those deemed aliens has proved a potent challenger to the legitimacy of multinational structures. As a consequence of this wedding of popular sovereignty to ethnicity (a marriage that during its history would come to be known as national self-determination), the political legitimacy of any state falling short of actual nation-statehood would become suspect to a segment or segments of its population. [10] Since 1789, the dogma that

8. The center-periphery model can vary among devotees. In some hands, it is essentially a spatial or geographic concept, connoting that a Brittany or Scotland has been physically remote from the state's sociopolitical ecumene and is, as a result, not part of the state's intensive communication and transportation network. In other hands, the notion of a peripheral people is essentially social, denoting those who are least socially mobilized and who are, for example, among the lowest income and education levels.

9. Further reference to some of these theses will be made below. It is worth noting here, however, that while some of the explanations overlap and reinforce one another, others appear to be at least somewhat contradictory (e.g., the anomic reaction to being engulfed by the mass society compared to the peripheral argument of remoteness from it). Moreover, some theories apply to certain states only (e.g., Denmark and Spain were hardly world powers in the prewar period).

10. This notion of popular sovereignty should be seen as a principle of state legitimacy rather than of governmental legitimacy. As such, it does not presuppose democracy, but only that the political elites acknowledge that they rule in the name of the people. Thus, spake the Emperor Napoleon, "We have been guided at all times by this great truth: that the sovereignty resides in the French people in the sense that everything, everything without exception, must be done for its best interests, for its well being, and for its glory." Message to the Senate, 1804, as reprinted in *The Mind of Napoleon: A Selection from His Written and Spoken Words,* ed. and trans. J. Christopher Herold (New York: Columbia University Press, 1955), p. 72. In a similar vein, Hitler described his "folkish state": "We, as Aryans, are therefore able to imagine a State only to be the living organism of a nationality

"alien rule is illegitimate rule" has been infecting ethnically aware peoples in an ever-broadening pattern. Indeed, as far as Europe is concerned, the region's subsequent history has been largely a tale of national liberation movements.[11] Ethnonational sentiments undergirded the struggle of the Greeks for independence in the 1820's; the liberation struggle of the Walloons and Flemings in 1830; the abortive revolutions of 1848 (particularly among the Germans, Italians, and Hungarians); the political consolidation of Germany and of Italy in the 1860's and very early 1870's; and the creation of Romania (1878), Serbia (1878), Norway (1905), Bulgaria (1908), Albania (1912), Finland (1917), Czechoslovakia, Estonia, Hungary, Latvia, Lithuania, Poland, Yugoslavia (all in 1918), Ireland (1921), and Iceland (1944).[12] Thus, by the end of World War II, all but three of the states of Europe either were the result of ethnonational aspirations or had lost substantial territory because of them.[13]

Consonant with my earlier comments concerning the scarcity of true nation-states within Western Europe, it is clear that many of the entities created or modified in response to ethnonational aspirations did not represent a completion of the self-determination process. Multiethnic structures remained the rule both within and without Europe.[14] But just as a host of secessionist movements throughout Africa and Asia (including the

---

which not only safeguards the preservation of that nationality, but which, by a further training of its spiritual and ideal abilities, leads it to the highest freedom." *Mein Kampf* (New York: Reynal and Hitchcock, 1940), p. 595.

11. For a more detailed account of the historic growth of ethnonationalism within Europe, see Walker Connor, "The Politics of Ethnonationalism," *Journal of International Affairs,* 27, no. 1 (1973), particularly pp. 5–11.

12. In addition to the Finns, Estonians, Letts, and Lithuanians, at least nine other groups seceded from Russia during 1917 and 1918 and created separate states. With the exception of the above four, and the peoples of Bessarabia and what had been Russian Poland, the Soviet government succeeded in reabsorbing all of the groups within a few years. Moreover, as a result of World War II, it reabsorbed all of the remaining peoples with the exception of the Finns and Poles.

13. Of the three exceptions (Portugal, Spain, and Switzerland), one (Portugal) was an ethnically homogeneous state. Technically, Spain was not an exception, for during the short-lived Spanish Republic of the 1930's, the Basques, Catalans, and Galicians had voted themselves very abbreviated periods of autonomy before being reincorporated by Franco's forces. Switzerland too was not without its ethnic problems during the Franco-Prussian War (1871) and World Wars I and II. See Walker Connor, "Self-Determination: The New Phase," *World Politics,* 20 (October 1967), particularly pp. 40–43.

14. From the Serbian viewpoint, the formation in 1918 of the Kingdom of Serbs, Croats, and Slovenes, later renamed Yugoslavia, might even be seen as a stride in the other direction. However, it brought the Croats and Slovenes a step closer to self-determination than they had been as part of the far larger Austro-Hungarian Empire.

aborted Ibo and the successful Bengali secessions) serve to remind us that attempts to stop short of fulfilling self-determination for all ethnically conscious elements are not apt to go long unchallenged, so too should developments in Eastern Europe.[15] Although the designers of the peace treaties following World War I believed that they could prescribe limits to ethnonational aspirations, stopping short of balkanization, unsatisfied ethnonational demands plague the area more than fifty years later. The case is little different in Western Europe. The rationale for the independence of Cyprus in 1960 and for that of Malta in 1964 was the illegitimacy of alien rule.[16] And the surge of nationalism among Basques, Catalans, Scots, and other ethnic groups can be viewed as merely the most recent step in a process that has been unfolding since the late eighteenth century.

Perceiving this recent surge as part of a long-range process does not preclude acknowledging catalytic roles for other phenomena. To return to the matter of modernization and the intensification of communications, for example, while it may trouble many whose lives straddle World War II to hear the prewar period characterized as "primitive," there does appear to be a substantial difference in the nature and intensity of contacts between groups during the prewar and postwar periods. As I have noted elsewhere:

The recent upsurge in ethnic conflict within the more industrialized, multiethnic states of Europe and North America seriously challenges the contention that modernization dissipates ethnic consciousness. But does not this upsurge also run counter to the assertion that modernization increases ethnic consciousness? Given the fact that the Industrial Revolution was introduced into each of these states more than a century ago, should not the high-tide mark of ethnic consciousness have appeared long ago? Part of the answer may be found in what Marxists term "The Law of the Transformation of Quantity into Quality," a paraphrase of which might read "enough of a quantitative difference makes a qualitative difference." The processes of modernization prior to World War II did not necessitate or bring about the same measure of international contacts as have developments in the postwar period. With fewer and poorer roads, far fewer and less efficient private cars, local radio rather than state-wide television as the primary

15. The tensions between Croat and Serb, Slovak and Czech, Magyar and Romanian have been most publicized, but numerous other groups (Albanians, Slovenes, Macedonians, Bulgars, and Bessarabian Romanians) are also involved. For a recent broad-brush treatment of many of these ethnic struggles, see Robert King, *Minorities under Communism: Nationalities as a Source of Tension among Balkan Communist States* (Cambridge: Harvard University Press, 1973).

16. The subsequent de facto division of Cyprus into Turkish and Greek territories during 1974 can be seen as analogous to the Biafran and Bangla Desh movements, i.e., a further step toward national self-determination.

channel of non-written mass communications, lower levels of education and of knowledge of events beyond one's own experience, and lower general income levels that kept people close to home, ethnic complacency could be maintained: Brittany's culture appeared safe from French encroachment, Edinburgh felt remote and isolated from London, most Walloons and Flemings seldom came into contact (including artificial contact through media such as television) with members of the other group. In short, the situation of ethnic groups within these states was not totally dissimilar from that which was described earlier with regard to non-industrialized societies. The difference was only one of degree until that point was reached at which a qualitative change occurred. However, the point at which a significant number of people perceived that the cumulative impact of the quantitative increases in the intensity of intergroup contacts now constituted a threat to their ethnicity represented, in political terms, a qualitative transformation.[17]

One author has noted with regard to the Bretons: "Indeed the sense of ethnic identity grew sharper as contacts and communications increased between Brittany and the rest of France. It was only after World War I, the first opportunity for most young Bretons to see 'France' and live among 'Frenchmen,' that regional ethnic organizations with political demands were created."[18] There is little question that mass support for these movements underwent a quantum jump during the late 1950's and 1960's.[19]

This perception of the impact of modernization upon social relations differs appreciably from Karl Deutsch's assimilationist model mentioned in note 3 above. The tendency to perceive contacts as encouraging assimilation apparently rests upon two situations in which at least one of the parties is not an ethnically conscious group. For example, Deutsch's model apparently does hold true for sectionalism. Indices to sectional attitudes within the United States have indicated a growing, countrywide uniformity as intersectional contacts increase. But while increased sectional contacts tend to dissipate sectional differences among a people,

17. Walker Connor, "Nation-Building or Nation-Destroying?" *World Politics,* 24 (April 1972): 330–331.

18. Suzanne Berger, "Bretons, Basques, Scots, and Other European Nations," *Journal of Interdisciplinary History,* 3 (Summer 1972): 170–171. A bit farther on (p. 174), the author notes, "Once conscious only of belonging to their own small region and to their administrative unit, the department, many Bretons discovered from radio and television that they were part of Brittany."

19. For a concise history of the Breton movement, see David Fortier, "Between Nationalism and Modern France: The Permanent Revolution," in *The Limits of Integration: Ethnicity and Nationalism in Modern Europe,* ed. Oriol Pi-Sunyer (Amherst: The University of Massachusetts Department of Anthropology, 1971), pp. 77–109.

increased contacts among diverse ethnonationally conscious groups appear more apt to cement and reinforce the divisive sense of uniqueness.[20] Therefore, while "nationalism and social communication" may indeed be linked within a crucible containing only a single ethnonational element, "nationalism and *unsocial* communication" is a more apt description of the relationship when the crucible contains two or more ethnonational elements.

The second situation in which contacts have had an assimilationist impact occurred when one or both parties were still in a prenational stage. Thus, prior to the Age of Nationalism, the trend was toward amalgamation into larger groups. Angles, Picts, Saxons, Vandals, and Visigoths were among those who traded group identities. Since the advent of the Age of Nationalism, however, contacts between groups, each of whom possesses even a dim sense of a separate ethnic heritage, have tended to cement and reinforce the sense of uniqueness. The quite common practice of employing cases of successful assimilation that were culminated prior to the eighteenth century as precedent for cases today involving self-conscious ethnic groups is therefore analogically spurious.

In yet another way, modernization and more effective communications have acted as catalysts for ethnonationally inspired demands. As formal education and globe-girdling communications have spread, the likelihood of people becoming cognizant of historic and contemporary self-determination movements has also spread. The quite common reaction to such cognition is, "If that people has a self-evident and inalienable right of national self-determination, then why not we?" What social scientists term the "demonstration effect" has had a very discernible, chain-reaction im-

20. I first expressed this position in "Self-Determination: The New Phase," and Arend Lijphart, after citing it with favor in his stimulating and influential article "Consociational Democracy," *World Politics,* 21 (January 1969): 220, went on to add, "This proposition can be refined further by stating both the degree of homogeneity and the extent of mutual contacts in terms of continua rather than dichotomies." From what has been said above concerning the difference in intensity of contacts between the prewar and postwar eras, it is evident that we agree that both the intensity *and the nature* of contacts can affect the level of conflict among ethnic groups. The matter of relative cultural similarity between two groups may be another matter, however. One of the oddities of our period (in large part a response to increases in the quantity and quality of communications networks) is that the cultures of various groups are becoming more resemblant of one another, while the saliency of feelings of ethnic distinction is also growing. What would seem to be involved here, then, is not the degree of cultural similarity. It is psychological and not cultural assimilation with which we are dealing, and whether or not one intuitively feels that he is a member of this or that ethnonational group is, for the mass of mankind, ultimately a matter of yes or no, rather than more or less.

pact upon the evolution of nationalism.[21] Each claim to national self-determination has tended to trigger still others. Through their cooperative efforts with one another and through sporadic precedential references to peoples who have successfully obtained and retained political independence, the most recent leaders of self-determination movements within Europe have indicated a strong role for the demonstration effect. Needless to say, the intensity of the effect exerted by a particular model upon a given ethnic group will depend upon a number of variables, for example, (1) chronological time (in general the more recent the illustration, the more graphic its analogical impact),[22] (2) proximity,[23] (3) comparability of size of population and territorial extent, (4) myths involving ancestral relationships,[24] and (5) whether or not the two groups were once ruled from the same capital.[25] Such factors can, of course, overlap in a reinforcing pattern. Thus, the pertinence of an independent Ireland partakes of all five elements for the Scots and the Welsh, of all but the fifth for the Bretons, and of only the first and the second for the Basques.[26]

21. The leaders of multiethnic states have quite consistently indicated their nervousness of this phenomenon. African political leaders, for example, have adamantly refused to recognize the legitimacy of secessionist ethnic movements within any of the black African states. India's intractability on the Kashmiri issue is also inspired in part by the fissiparous impact that Kashmiri independence might exert upon other ethnic segments of the population.

22. A noteworthy exception is the case where a prosecessionist is arguing against the often heard statement that the proposed state could not become an economically viable entity. In such a case, the longevity of the selected model may be the key to its utility.

23. To take some non–Western European examples, the Biafran episode was clearly seen as a greater threat by African leaders than by those of Asia. Similarly, the creation of Bangla Desh was viewed by the leaders of India and Pakistan, quite rightly as it turned out, to hold the greatest significance for the subcontinent itself. And, one of the reasons underlying the Soviet decision to intervene in Czechoslovakin in 1968 was the fear of the effect that the Slovak movement for autonomy would have upon the already restive Ukrainians residing immediately across the Soviet border.

24. It is perhaps to risk accentuating the apparent to note that the closer the relationship is perceived to be, the more vivid the demonstration effect is apt to be. Thus, the creation of each independent Arab state incited demands that *all* Arabs be free. While less poignant, the notion of common Slavism made the creation of each Slavic state a matter of special interest to those Slavic peoples still under alien rule.

25. For example, when an overseas possession gains its freedom, the event is of greater significance to minorities within the mother country than would be the case had the overseas territory been owned by another state. Still more significance would be attached to the successful severance of part of the "home territory," that is, of a portion of the state itself.

26. See, for example, Kenneth Morgan, "Welsh Nationalism: The Historical Background," *Contemporary History,* 6 (1971): 172, in which it is noted that the Welsh national movement "clearly owed a little to nationalism everywhere, to Hungarian nationalism, and most of all to Irish." The common Celtic ancestry is what principally accounts for the influ-

Two developments have proved to be particularly significant for the demonstration effect they exerted upon the postwar self-determination movements within Western Europe. One is the general, though irregular, trend in the historical evolution of nationalism within Western Europe from larger to smaller ethnic elements. The political independence of Norway in 1905, for example, represented an important milestone because the Norse number less than either the Catalans or the Scots.[27] Ireland's emancipation was a further step in this direction, and Iceland's decision to acquire separate status during World War II offered existent proof that size was no barrier whatsoever to independence. The contrary notion that insubstantial size posed an insurmountable barrier to political independence had long been treated as a truism by scholars and statesmen and also must have exerted its impact upon the masses. Otherwise, it is difficult to account for the great stress that the leaders of the new movements have placed upon the examples of still smaller communities in their quest for converts.[28] In any event, there were few ethnic elements in Western Europe, which harbored potential leaders with dreams of independence, whose numbers did not exceed that of Icelanders. As late as 1944, Alfred Cobban, as a means of ridiculing the logical extension of the national self-determination principle, raised the image of an Iceland

---

ence of the Irish struggle upon the Bretons; there are no common historic or political bonds. The influence of common celticity is more problematic in the case of the Scots and the Irish because traditional animosities exist between the two due to the predominance of people of Scottish ancestry among the non-Irish of Northern Ireland. George Malcolm Thomas, after first noting that the Scots "are nearer to the Irish in race and temperament than they like to admit," went on to note that "the truth is that Ulster is both Irish (geographically) and British. Or to be more exact, Scottish (culturally)." *Christian Science Monitor,* 6 July 1974. But see Owen Dudley Edwards et al., *Celtic Nationalism* (London: Routledge & Kegan Paul, 1968), for contributions by Irish, Scottish, and Welsh nationalists, each of whom stresses the Celtic bond. See also the Scottish National party's publication *100 Home Rule Questions Answered by Sandy M'Intosh,* 2d rev. ed. (Forfar: Oliver McPherson, 1968), p. 15: "Where there is compulsory integration and discontent in one or more of the integrated countries, there is no real unity, as Irish history has well shown." And on page 28, there is a reference to "proud and patriotic nations like Eire." Contemporary Pan-Celtic organizations, such as the Celtic Congress and the Celtic League, though of unknown influence at the grass-roots level, are recent indications of political consequences flowing from pan- ethnicties.

27. The Scottish National party often makes use of Norway for comparative purposes when insisting that Scotland can "go it alone." See, for example, *100 Home Rule Questions Answered by Sandy M'Intosh,* particularly pp. 27 and 45.

28. Welsh nationalists, for example, point out that thirty-nine states have fewer people than Wales, and they particularly emphasize that Iceland, Luxembourg, and New Zealand are included among them. See the *Christian Science Monitor,* 2 August 1974.

or a Malta someday achieving independence.[29] The fact that Iceland achieved independence the same year as the publication of Cobban's comments and that Malta followed suit in 1964 illustrates how the formerly potent psychological restraint of meager size had been effectively exorcised from political axioms inherited from an earlier age.

A second development of great import was the ending of the colonial era due to the infectious spread throughout the overseas possessions of the notion that "alien rule is illegitimate rule." As noted, the demonstration effect produced by the obtaining of political independence by a specific state varied in the impact that it exerted among different Western European ethnic groups. Thus, the freeing of India could be expected to have its maximal impact upon groups within the United Kingdom, and the freeing of Algeria, upon groups within France. But the total effect of this spectacle of a global parade toward independence could be expected to have a broad impact upon all ethnically conscious European peoples without regard to state borders. In the words of Pierre Fougeyrollas: "The decolonialization of Asia and Africa incites the oppressed minorities of Europe to subsequently undertake their own decolonialization. . . . Why should not the ideas and the inclinations which had asserted themselves at Dakar, Brazzaville, Algiers, and even Montreal, irresistibly develop at Brest, Strasbourg, Dunkirk?"[30] Even had decolonialization not occurred, there is no apparent reason to believe that the ethnonational virus would not in time have afflicted all of the ethnically distinct peoples of Western Europe, just as it had the Germans, the Norse, and the Irish at an earlier time. Indeed, the post–World War II movements did not, Athene-like, suddenly appear in fully developed form; their developmental history straddles World War II and, in many cases, World War I. But the manner in which so many movements suddenly became prominent in the late 1950's and 1960's indicates the presence of powerful catalysts, one of which unquestionably was the demonstration effect produced by global decolonialization. Ethnonationalism, which the post–World War I leaders of France, the United Kingdom, and the United States had believed they could quarantine within Eastern Europe, had

29. Alfred Cobban, *National Self-Determination* (London: Oxford University Press, 1944), pp. 131–132. On page 173, the author makes similar comments concerning Wales, White Russia (Belorussia), Alsace, Flanders, and French Canada.

30. Pierre Fougeyrollas, *Pour une France fédérale: Vers l'unité européenne par la révolution régionale* (Paris: Editions Denoël, 1968), p. 12.

for its substance.[32] It helps to explain the ever-accelerating pace at which the idea of national self-determination has infected peoples. It has increased the impact of the demonstration effect. But while the media have undergone revolutionary changes, the disarmingly simple message that ethnicity and state legitimacy are linked has remained remarkably unembellished since put forth in the Declaration of the Rights of Man and of the Citizen in 1789: "The source of all sovereignty resides essentially in the nation; no group, no individual, may exercise authority not emanating expressly therefrom."

But if the emergence of national sentiment among the still dependent ethnic groups of Western Europe represented a sequential step in a historical evolution, why did it occasion so much surprise among scholars, particularly among scholars of nationalism? For many, one suspects, the answer is a general disregard for historical perspective. If, for example, one credits the rise of nationalism within a particular ethnic community solely to economic discrimination (the theory of relative economic deprivation), then there is little need to search history for antecedents or for the germination and development of an abstract notion of a kindred people. Similarly, what I have described as the first pillar of conventional postwar scholarship on Western Europe (the image of the region's inhabitants as sophisticated cosmopolites who had come to recognize that nationalism is a dangerous anachronism in the current era) reflected a view of nationalism as an ephemeral, easily discarded phenomenon. This view is quite at odds with both political and intellectual history since the late eighteenth century.

For others, the total lack of anticipation of recent events is not so much a case of no history as of poor history. Those who perceived the surge of ethnonational demands throughout Western Europe in the late 1960's as without forerunners were overlooking numerous, well-advertised portents. Among them were the previously mentioned autonomy voted by the Basques, Catalans, and Galicians of Spain during the 1930's; the unrest among South Tyrolean Germans almost from the commencement of their incorporation into Italy after World War I, the well-publicized plebiscite ordered by Hitler to protect the Rome-Berlin Axis from the reverberations of this unrest (and in which an astonishing number indicated their willingness to leave their homes and settle within the Third Reich

32. Tempo itself can, of course, exert a substantive impact: the more intense the contacts among groups, the more likely a militant ethnonational response. See Connor, "Nation-Building or Nation-Destroying?" pp. 351–352.

spread to all non-European regions, from which it exerted a bacl
effect upon Western Europe's nonindependent peoples.

Modernization and increased communications have indeed had a
pact upon contemporary ethnonational movements, though not the t;
impact perceived by the "modernization promotes assimilation" s
In an extraordinary anticipation of that school's erroneous thesis, C
Hayes warned nearly a half-century ago:

Many optimists of the present day are convinced that the Industrial Revo
fundamentally anti-nationalist. . . . The scope of communication is be
well as within the frontiers of any particular nation. Each country, each
ity, is becoming more closely linked to others by railways, steamshi;
cars, automobiles, aircraft, postal service, telegraph, telephone, radio, a
sion. Travel is becoming more international. Information for newspape
press is being gathered and distributed more internationally. Intellect
ments in one country ramify more and more speedily into other coun'
We do know that there has been an astounding improvement in the ;
arts during the past hundred and forty years, involving a veritable indu
lution. . . . But it is, or should be, apparent also that there have beer
same hundred and forty years . . . a parallel diffusion and intensific
tionalism. . . . It seems paradoxical that political nationalism s
stronger and more virulent as economic internationalism increases.
understanding of the paradox, it is important to bear in mind that t
Revolution is not necessarily an intellectual revolution. Of itself it
tionalist nor internationalist. It is essentially mechanical and ma
merely provided improved means and greater opportunities for the
of any ideas. . . . Now it so happened that when the Industri
began, nationalism was becoming a significant intellectual moveme
significant than internationalism. Consequently, while the newer
chinery has been utilized for international ends, it has also been
more, for nationalist purposes. The obvious international fruits o
Revolution must not blind our eyes to its intensely nationalist cc
implications.[31]

In short, the principal impact of modernization has been c
than causal. It has held greater import for the tempo of n;

31. Carlton Hayes, *The Historical Evolution of Modern Nationalism*
millan, 1931), pp. 234–237. Hayes's analysis of the relationship betwee
ization and nationalism was markedly different from that of Karl]
Engels, as witnessed by the following passage from the Communist N
differences and antagonisms between peoples are daily more and more
the development of the bourgeoisie, to freedom of commerce, to t
uniformity in the mode of production and in condition of life corresp(

rather than to become Italian citizens), and the very early resumption of antistate activities within South Tyrol following World War II; Hitler's successes in appealing to the ethnonationalism of the Flemings and Bretons in order to get their collaboration; Mussolini's similar appeal to the Corsicans; and the separatist movements that were active in Sardinia and Sicily during World War II and among French-speaking Val D'Aostans both during and immediately following that same struggle.[33] Considering the historical pattern of the national *idea*—its infection, beginning with the French, of an ever-greater number of peoples—it is particularly perplexing to encounter Konstantin Symons-Symonolewicz's statement that "one can hardly discern any clear evolutionary trend with respect to the growth of the principle of nationality—to claim that it is steadily advancing would be no less foolhardy than to conclude that its dynamics had been spent completely." [34] Moreover, considering the path of ethnonationalism throughout Europe traced above (a path that has left the borders of only three states unaltered in its wake), it is disquieting to read in Arnold Toynbee's monumental work:

Nationalism was comparatively innocuous in its West European birthplace, where, for the most part, it took the political map as it found it, and was content to utilize the existing parochial states, within their established frontiers, as its crucibles for the decoction of its intoxicating political brew of psychic energy. Its noxious potentialities revealed themselves on alien ground where, so far from consecrating the frontiers which it found on the map, this aggressive exotic political ideology denounced them in the name of the explosive political proposition that all persons who happened to be speakers of this or that vernacular language had a natural right to be united politically with one another in a single sovereign independent national state and therefore had a moral obligation to sacrifice their own and their neighbours' welfare, happiness, and life itself in the pursuit of this pedantic political programme. This linguistic interpretation—or caricature—of the West European ideology of Nationalism was never taken on pied de la lettre in the West European countries themselves, since here the external bond provided by community of speech was always recognized as being merely one among

33. A Canadian analogy would be the reaction of the French Canadians to proposals to draft them during World War I and World War II to fight what they perceived as "English wars." Little different is the case of Eastern Europe where Hitler gained a measure of Slovak and Croatian collaboration by offering them autonomy from the Czechs and the Serbs, respectively. The early positive response of Ukrainians, Crimean Tartars, and other non-Russian ethnic elements to the German invasion of the Soviet Union has also been heavily publicized.

34. Konstantin Symons-Symonolewicz, *Nationalist-Movements: A Comparative View* (Meadville, Penna.: Maplewood Press, 1970), p. 4.

divers outward signs of an inward sense of political solidarity springing from common political experiences, institutions, and ideals.[35]

All of the foregoing is not to deny that praiseworthy histories of a number of these ethnic movements existed prior to the 1960's.[36] Nor is it to deny that country specialists have often shown awareness of ethnic diversity within their respective countries.[37] All too frequently, however, these histories and specialists have suffered from too narrow a focus: the tendency to see the movement as sui generis, to look only within the state for the source of its nourishment, and not to perceive it as part of a broader intellectual movement. As Hans Kohn has opined: ''A study of nationalism must follow a comparative method, it cannot remain confined to one of its manifestations; only the comparison of the different nationalisms all over the earth will enable the student to see what they have in common and what is peculiar to each, and thus allow a just evaluation. An understanding of nationalism can be gained only by a world history of the age of nationalism.'' [38] Elsewhere, Kohn again underlined this need for both historic perspective and a broad comparative framework: ''Only a study of the historical growth of nationalism and a comparative study of its different forms can make us understand the impact of nationalism

35. Arnold J. Toynbee, *A Study of History* (London: Oxford University Press, 1954), 8: 536.

36. Two noteworthy illustrations in the English language are Shepard Clough, *A History of the Flemish Movement in Belgium: A Study in Nationalism* (New York: Farrar & Rinehart, 1930); and Reginald Coupland, *Welsh and Scottish Nationalism: A Study* (London: Collins, 1954).

37. It should not, however, be assumed that country specialists have been more attuned to such diversity than have generalists. Specialists on the United Kingdom, for example, had long emphasized the unusually high degree of homogeneity of what was called the British (or even the English) society. Richard Rose lists L. S. Amery, Samuel Beer, Harry Eckstein, Jean Blondel, and S. E. Finer as examples of some of the many authorities on the United Kingdom who have slighted ethnic considerations; see Richard Rose, *The United Kingdom as a Multi-National State* (Glasgow: University of Strathclyde Survey Research Center, 1970). He might have added himself to the list, for in his own work he has stated: ''Today politics in the United Kingdom is greatly simplified by the absence of major cleavages along the lines of ethnic groups, language, or religion.'' *Politics in England* (Boston: Little, Brown, 1964), p. 10. Monographs on France also indicate an amazing disregard of ethnic cleavages.

38. Hans Kohn, *The Idea of Nationalism: A Study of Its Origins and Background* (New York: Macmillan, 1944), pp. ix–x. For an interesting discussion of the strengths and limitations of the comparative method (though not specifically applied to the study of nationalism), see Arend Lijphart, ''Comparative Politics and the Comparative Method,'' *American Political Science Review,* 65 (September 1971): 682–693.

today." [39] Kohn was not arguing against the necessity for case studies. During his lifetime, he produced several monographs dealing with the rise of ethnonationalism within a single environment. Rather, his contention was that the student of a particular movement or movements should first observe the manner in which nationalism evolved in a number of other societies. [40]

His advice would appear to be relevant to much of the recent scholarly work on Western Europe. It is likely, for example, that the theory of relative economic deprivation is less compelling to those who are aware that the Basques and Catalans are financially better off than the Castilians; that Croats and Slovenes are financially ahead of Serbs; that Flanders received a disproportionately large share of Belgian-wise investments between 1958 and 1968, a period of growing Flemish intransigence; that ethnic movements in Western Europe and Canada have not received their major support from the poor, but, while cutting across income lines, have tended to attract a disproportionately large number of professional people; that during 1974 more than one-third of the voters of Switzerland voted yes on a referendum drawn up by the National Movement against Foreign Domination of People and Homeland, which would have deported huge numbers of foreign workers, despite overwhelming opposition to the referendum by both houses of Parliament (157 to 3 and 42 to 0), by political parties from left to right, as well as by labor, management, and religious leaders, and despite the fact that implementation would have caused serious economic dislocation and a drop in living standards; and that a number of ethnic groups within the Soviet Union have indicated opposition to additional investment within their ethnic homeland because of the conviction that greater industrialization brings with it more Russians, a price deemed too high to pay for increased living standards.

Similarly, those who feel that the explanation for the recent surge in nationalism is to be found in cultural deprivation should be aware that the Basques, who have been the most militantly nationalist element within Spain, are also the *least* interested in using their own language in every-

39. Hans Kohn, *Nationalism: Its Meaning and History,* rev. ed. (Princeton: Van Nostrand, 1965), p. 4.
40. In a most stimulating essay, Milton da Silva used the Basque movement to illustrate weaknesses in several theories concerning the nature and causes of ethnonationalism. In doing so, he evidenced a remarkable breadth of knowledge. See his "Modernization and Ethnic Conflict: The Case of the Basques," *Comparative Politics,* 7 (January 1975): 227–251.

day conversation, as well as the least interested in having their children taught to speak it; [41] that one of the factors that animated Flemish nationalists was *not* cultural deprivation but cultural freedom under which Flemish parents had been increasingly opting to have their children learn French as their primary tongue; [42] that Plaid Cymru (the National party of Wales) acknowledges that a majority of its members cannot speak Welsh and indirectly acknowledges that many have no interest in doing so, by promising that learning the language will not become compulsory; that polls have quite consistently indicated that a higher percentage of Scots than of Welsh are desirous of "going it alone," despite the fact that very few can speak the Scottish language and that the resuscitation of the language has not been a prominent element in the Scottish nationalist movement; and that the Irish vernacular, whose revitalization and reinstitution once occupied a prominent place in the programs of Irish liberation movements, has little support for its adoption (or even its learning as a secondary language) in the postindependence period. Those who maintain that the surge of nationalism is due to alienation from the modern, mass society should be perplexed by its concomitant vitality in such less-modernized societies as those of Baluchistan, Eritrea, Kurdistan, Mizoland, or Nagaland.

There are several other elements, in addition to a lack of historical and comparative perspective, which help to account for the surprise engendered by the recent surge of ethnonationalism within Europe. Elsewhere, I have suggested twelve possible pitfalls in the study of nationalism, four of which would seem to have particular application to the European experience: [43]

1. Confusing terminology leading to a tendency not to recognize ethnonationalism for what it is. The literature on Western Europe, as elsewhere, has tended to employ the terms *nation* and *state* interchangeably. By extension, *nationalism* is employed (and is therefore perceived) as

41. See Juan Linz, "Early State-Building and Late Peripheral Nationalisms against the State: The Case of Spain" (paper presented at the UNESCO Conference on Nation-Building, Cérisy, Normandy, August 1970), pp. 85–86.

42. Joseph Rudolph, "The Belgian Front Democratique des Bruxellois Francophones–Rassemblement Wallon (F.D.F.-R.W.) and the Politics of Sub-National Institution-Building" (paper presented at the Annual Meeting of the Northeastern Political Science Association, 9 November 1973), p. 3.

43. For a fuller explanation and examples of each of the four categories, see Connor, "Nation-Building or Nation-Destroying?" particularly pp. 332–355. Subject to the omission of eight categories listed in the above-mentioned text, the four categories listed here are in the order in which they were first presented.

describing loyalty to the state, rather than to the ethnonational group. The need to find a term other than nationalism to describe loyalty to a Basque, Breton, or Flemish nation has led to a number of substitutes, for example, *subnational loyalties, ethnic pluralism, regionalism,* and the like. Such terminology can naturally hamper analysis. Since nationalism is perceived as in the service of the state, it is assumed that these other phenomena pose no serious, long-term competition for the loyalty of citizens; the newer movements are not seen as analogous to the nationalist movements of such state-controlling nations as the Germans, Poles, or Norse.[44] The description of ethnonational movements as "regionalism" is particularly pernicious because, as I have noted, regionalism (in the sense of sectionalism) has tended to disappear as modernization has linked the segments of a state more closely.[45] He who views the ethnonationalism of a people as regionalism is therefore preconditioned to perceive its demise as modernization progresses; but I have noted that modernization tends to exert an opposite reaction where ethnonational groups are involved.[46] Moreover, *region* and *section* imply the existence of a

44. See, for example, the quote from Dankwart Rustow in note 1 above, in which "nation" clearly refers to "state." In the previous sentence, he links the experiences of the German nation to a "British" (and an also-questionable "Italian") nation, noting that "in Britain today no serious conflict is generally felt between a wider British and a more particular English, Welsh, or Scottish nationality."

45. *Regionalism* is also an unfortunate term in that it can mean either intrastate sectionalism or suprastate integration within a major area, such as Western Europe or Latin America.

46. For an article grouping ethnonational movements (such as those in Brittany, Corsica, Scotland, and Wales) with localism (such as that evidenced within a number of German Laender) under the single rubric of "subnational regionalism," see Werner Feld, "Subnational Regionalism and the European Community" in *Orbis,* 18 (Winter 1975): 1176–1192. The result is a confusing comparison of different phenomena. For a description of Scottish nationalism as regionalism (and a corresponding underevaluation of its potency), see John Schwartz, "The Scottish National Party," *World Politics, 22 (July 1970): 496–517,* and particularly page 515, where the author speaks of a "regional identity." See also Jack Haywood, *The One and Indivisible French Republic* (New York: Norton, 1973), pp. 38 and 56, where the movement within Brittany is referred to as regionalism. No reference to ethnonationalism is made, nor are there any references to France's other ethnic minorities. Since the term *region* implies a larger whole, the indivisibility of France (as indicated by the title) is assured. The propensity to refer to ethnonational movements within France and Italy as regionalism has probably been heightened in recent years by "regionalization" plans to decentralize authority. In both cases, the borders of the new regions often closely correspond with the distribution of ethnic groups. For more details, see my chapter on Western Europe in Abdul Said and Luiz Simmons, eds., *Ethnicity in an International Context* (Edison, N.J.: Transaction Books, 1976). *Periphery,* as used in the center-periphery concept, often means region, and as a result the above reservations concerning the use of *regionalism* to connote ethnonationalism would pertain to a like use of *periphery* as well.

larger whole; thus, even prior to its demise, regionalism is not mutually incompatible with loyalty to the state. By contrast, the ethnonational presumption that state legitimacy and ethnicity are linked is incompatible with loyalty to a state viewed as dominated by nonmembers of the group.

2. *The tendency to discern national strife as predicated principally upon language, religion, customs, economic inequity, or some other tangible element.* The classic contemporary case of this tendency is the strife in Northern Ireland, regularly depicted as a religious struggle. The compulsion to perceive and to report the struggle in terms of the handy, readily discernible element of religion, rather than to probe or to try to convey to one's audience the abstract notion of Irish identity on the one side versus the various national identities on the other is reflected in the following two illustrations. In an article in the *New York Times* reporting on an interview with Glenn Barr, a member of the non-Irish community, he is quoted as noting: "I don't know what I am. People say I'm British. The British treat me as a second class citizen. I am not Irish. I am an Ulsterman." [47] Despite this colloquy, Barr is introduced to the reader as a "Protestant leader" (though he holds no religious office), and the entire article discusses the conflict in terms of a religious struggle. Similarly, an Associated Press dispatch dated 30 January 1975 indicates that arms are being shipped to the Irish Republican Army "by Breton separatist Catholics who want to free Brittany from France." Why the need to draw attention to the Catholic faith of the Bretons who are citizens of an overwhelmingly Catholic state? Reference to the Celtic dimension would, of course, have introduced abstract notions of ancestral ties and ethnonational consciousness, notions extremely difficult to convey to both readers and editors. However, the tendency to describe the nature of the struggle as religious is encountering an increasing amount of contrary evidence. For example, a statement of policy released by the Social Democratic and Labour party of Northern Ireland (a somewhat moderate party whose base of support is in the Irish segment of the community) employs such expressions as "more than one-third of [the country's] population regard themselves as part of the wider Irish Community. . . . [The government] must take account of the divisions within Northern Ireland, the conflicting *national identities* and the special relations that Northern Ireland will always have with Great Britain and the Republic of Ireland. . . . *The two*

47. *New York Times,* 16 November 1974.

national identities must be recognized in Northern Ireland's relations with Great Britain and the Republic of Ireland.'' [48] References to religion are noteworthy by their absence.

While the most dramatic illustration of the tendency to mistake tangible characteristics for essence, Northern Ireland is not the only Western European illustration of this phenomenon. As my earlier comments concerning theories of relative deprivation make clear, there have been many who have perceived ethnic restiveness in terms of a group's choice of battlefields, that is, in terms of economic statistics or an aspect of culture such as language. [49]

3. *An unwarranted exaggeration of the influence of materialism upon human affairs.* Enough has previously been said concerning the theory of relative economic deprivation to document the prevalence of this tendency in the pertinent scholarship on Western Europe.

4. *The tendency to interpret the absence of ethnic strife as evidence of the presence of a single nation.* With the South Tyroleans constituting the most noteworthy exception, the years immediately following World War II constituted a period of relative quiescence as far as ethnonationalism is concerned. The reasons for this respite are understandable. The area was still recuperating from a holocaust whose principal cause was ethnonationalism in its most extreme form. The extravagant activities carried out in the name of the *Volksdeutsch* (the German people) and the *razza italica* (the Italian race), made ethnonationalism per se suspect. This period of ethnonational apathy temporarily interrupted the continuity of a number of movements which antedated the war. Interruption was interpreted as demise, and reappearance was therefore viewed as something startling, if not totally original. Latent attitudes had been ignored, as scholars concentrated on the more overt opinions of the day.

A number of movements faced particular problems, in addition to the general fear of the destructive capacity of ethnonationalism, which had

48. *Keesing's Contemporary Archives,* 23–29 September 1974, p. 26732. Emphasis added.

49. After repeatedly encountering the religious explanation for the strife in Northern Ireland, I was gratified to hear Professor John Whyte of Queen's University (Belfast) say in a conversation at the Harvard Center for International Affairs (October 1974) that the conflict was certainly ethnic and not religious. A few minutes later, however, my comment to a representative of the Belgian government to the effect that I should enjoy the opportunity to speak with him concerning his country's ethnic problem brought forth the rejoinder that the issue was definitely not ethnic but linguistic.

been engendered by the excesses of ethnic fascism. The recent equating of German nationalism and Naziism caused the feeling of a German heritage, in particular, to lose much of its luster. The impact of this phenomenon upon Germanic people such as the Alsatians was evident. Whereas the three political parties who favored autonomy for Alsace had garnered more than 40 percent of the Alsatian vote in 1928, ethnonationalism apparently declined among these people after the rise to power of Adolph Hitler, and seemingly disappeared during the immediate postwar era. Nevertheless, the resiliency of ethnonational motivation was indicated by the creation in 1970 of a Regional Movement of Alsace-Lorraine.[50] In a somewhat similar vein, the Flemish and Breton movements had become tainted by the collaboration of some of their leaders with the Nazis. In addition to needing time to permit memories of such activities to fade, the movements also needed time to find new leaders to replace the tainted elite, many of whom had fled, been killed by the underground, or incarcerated in the postwar period.

The postwar reaction to ethnic fascism was not restricted to minorities. Its behavioral impact upon Frenchmen, Dutchmen, Danes, and others in the war's immediate afterglow lulled scholars into believing that Europeans had left nationalism behind (that syndrome which we have labeled the first pillar of conventional postwar thinking on Western Europe). Reaction could be expected to be most intense in the case of the people who had been most fanatically caught up in the ethnonational, nightmarish crusade, the Germans. Armed by the fresh memories of the unbridled passions proved to lurk in that Pandora's box of German nationalism, embarrassed by if not remorseful for the excesses carried out in its name, realistically appraising postwar power realities and aware that all non-German Europeans were vigilantly watching for the slightest symptom of a revitalization of German nationalism, Germans held their ethnonational proclivities in tight rein. But as memories recede, as the realization grows that Naziism and German nationalism are not inevitably synonymous, as pride of postwar material and cultural achievements takes on the hue of pride in German achievements, as older Germans come to believe that

---

50. *Le Figaro,* 5 July 1971. The selection of Strasbourg as the seat of the Council of Europe unquestionably has had significant, if immeasurable, impact upon recent Alsatian ethnonationalism. The international role of this Alsatian city serves as a constant reminder that the Franco-German border no longer represents the same barrier to relations with transborder Germans that it did in the prewar era.

Germany's period of atonement and parole has lasted long enough, and as a postwar generation that believes it cannot be held in any way culpable for the mistakes of its parents comes into power, German nationalism manifests commensurate signs of recovery.[51] Throughout Europe, then, the obituaries for ethnonationalism have proved premature.

The theme of this essay has been that recent ethnonational developments within Western Europe can be viewed as a sequential, evolutionary step in the extension of the force field of nationalism. Recalling again the surprise occasioned by the factual undermining of those two postwar pillars of scholarship on Western Europe (the obsolescence of nationalism and the absence of multinational states), consider the following passage by Carlton Hayes: "One striking feature of the period's nationalist agitation, obviously, was that it affected and widely publicized a number of European peoples that had not previously been supposed to have national consciousness or political aspirations. Another of its features, even more startling, was its quickened tempo and fiercer manifestation among . . . peoples already known to be nationalist." By peoples "not previously been supposed to have national consciousness," Hayes was indeed referring to Basque, Breton, Catalan, Flemish, and the like. The passage, however, was written not in the 1970's but in 1941; not to describe West-

---

51. In the 1972 elections, for example, the victorious Social Democratic party phrased its appeals in terms of national pride and consciousness. See, for example, the *New York Times,* 17 November 1972. Basing their case principally on the interpretation of opinion surveys, several individuals have recently contended that the notion of a single German nation is a thing of the past, having been replaced by a coalescence of identity around the notions of Austria, East Germany, and West Germany, respectively. See, for example, William Bluhm, *Building an Austrian Nation* (New Haven: Yale University Press, 1973); Gordon Munro, "Two Germanies: A Lasting Solution to the German Question" (Ph.D. diss., Claremont Graduate School, 1972); and Gebhard Schweigler, "National Consciousness in Divided Germany" (Ph.D. diss., Harvard University, 1972). The survey data are not uncontradictory, however, and run counter to other data (e.g., the decision of the East German authorities in early 1975 to backtrack temporarily on their attempt to purge the notion that the peoples of East and West Germany are part of the same German nation). Moreover, given the many psychological and political forces at work in postwar Germany (as described above), it is at least questionable whether a valid opinion survey on nationalism can be conducted in that environment. There is also the matter of latent attitudes versus overt opinions. Finally, there is the question of whether, even under the best of circumstances, an opinion survey is an effective vehicle for determining ethnic attitudes. For two studies that contend it is not, see Arnold Rose, p. 100, and John Wahlke and Milton Lodge, "Psychological Measures of Change in Political Attitudes" (paper presented at the Annual Meeting of the Midwest Political Science Association, 1971), particularly pp. 2–3.

ern Europe of the 1960's and 1970's, but of the 1870's, 1880's, and 1890's.[52] The point is that the more sensitive literature on nationalism written in the prewar period did contain valuable clues to what might be expected to occur within Western Europe as nationalism further evolved. As early as 1926, for example, Hayes warned of troubles between ethnonational groups within Belgium and Switzerland, "despite the artificial attempts to promote a sense of social solidarity, akin to nationality, among all the Swiss and among all the Belgians." [53] He also referred to "the budding little nationalisms" of Icelanders, Catalans, Provençals, Basques, Wends, White Russians (Belorussians), Manx, and Maltese.[54] Similarly, the famous 1939 report on nationalism by the Royal Institute of International Affairs painted a more insightful portrait of the Northern Ireland conflict than do most current writers:

But in the minds of the Irish nationalists independence had become bound up with the idea of the geographical unity of Ireland, the territory which had formed the free, though slightly legendary, Kingdom of Ireland before the Anglo-Saxon invaders made their appearance. Not only must those who feel themselves to be members of the Irish nation be free to govern themselves, but the whole of Ireland must be united. The Irish question has thus created a second clash between the claims of two rival nationalisms.[55]

Elsewhere the report warned that "Great Britain herself is not immune from this problem, as it may be rash to assume that the present solution of the relationship between the English, Scottish, and Welsh must necessarily be permanent." [56]

Sensitive and perspicacious though these works are, many of their predictions proved fallacious.[57] The past need not be prologue. History—including the history of nationalism—does not operate independently of the whims and caprices of events and individuals. Even a proper regard for the historical development of nationalism does not, therefore, elimi-

52. Carlton Hayes, *A Generation of Materialism: 1870–1900* (New York: Harper & Row, 1941), p. 280.
53. Carlton Hayes, *Essays on Nationalism* (New York: Macmillan, 1926), p. 15.
54. *Ibid.,* p. 59.
55. *Nationalism: A Report by a Study Group of Members of the Royal Institute of International Affairs* (London: Oxford University Press, 1939), p. 111.
56. *Ibid.,* p. 137.
57. See, for example, Hayes's overly optimistic comments concerning the ability of Switzerland, Canada, the Republic of South Africa, and the British Empire to accommodate divergent nationalisms, in his *Essays on Nationalism,* pp. 21, 22, and 270. The report of the Royal Institute is the work of nine scholars, and inconsistencies, therefore, abound. While some of the essays indicate a keen understanding of the national phenomena, others do not.

nate the hazards inherent in predicting future political developments. But, as the cited passages by Hayes and the Royal Institute indicate, an appreciation of the pattern of nationalism's development will perhaps increase the chances of making accurate predictions; at least it will reduce the likelihood of being totally surprised when confronted with nationalism's most recent manifestations.

2

Political Theories and the Explanation of Ethnic Conflict in the Western World: Falsified Predictions and Plausible Postdictions *

AREND LIJPHART

The recent reemergence and intensification of subnational ethnic conflict in Western Europe and North America have come as a surprise to most scholarly observers. In contrast to the many plural societies of the Third World, frequently rent by ethnic strife, the states of the First World were considered to be not only mature and well-integrated "nation-states" but also participants in far-reaching ventures of supranational unification.

This assumption of domestic integration seldom has been stated explicitly. A striking exception occurs in *Political Community and the North Atlantic Area,* published in 1957, in which Karl W. Deutsch and his collaborators pose the question "Are nationalistic conflicts increasing or decreasing in the mid-twentieth century within the North Atlantic area?" The authors see only a slight decline of nationalism at the state level, but argue that, "as far as minority groups *within* states are concerned, these appear not to be at all dangerous." Citing the examples of the Alsatians, the Flemings, the South Tyroleans, and the French Canadians, they state that the political activities of ethnic and linguistic minorities are "of minor importance," and conclude that "most of the area seems to have settled down in this respect, and only at its fringes, in Algiers and Cyprus, do we meet exceptions." [1]

* I should like to express my gratitude to the Netherlands Institute for Advanced Study in the Humanities and the Social Sciences (NIAS) in Wassenaar, where I was a Fellow in 1974–75, for the opportunity it gave me to prepare the first draft of this essay.

1. Karl W. Deutsch et al., *Political Community and the North Atlantic Area: International Organization in the Light of Historical Experience* (Princeton, N.J.: Princeton University Press, 1957), p. 159.

The view that ethnic feelings and tensions are on the wane is usually implicit in treatments of political and social developments in the Western world. The most remarkable examples of this view are found in two books, both published in the early 1960's, that analyze the "new Europe." [2] In *A New Europe?*—a multiauthored volume with contributions from such American and European luminaries as Raymond Aron, Ernst B. Haas, Ralf Dahrendorf, Seymour Martin Lipset, and Michel Crozier—and in George Lichtheim's *The New Europe,* the phenomenon of subnational ethnic groups was evidently regarded as so insignificant that it was utterly ignored. The indexes of these books do not contain any references either to ethnic groups, ethnic conflicts, separatism, and nationalism, or—with one important exception to be discussed later—to any of the specific ethnic minorities in Europe. The term *integration* is used exclusively in the sense of integration at the international level.

The explanation of the unexpected resurgence of ethnic conflict in the Western world requires answers to two separate, or at least separable, questions: how can this resurgence be accounted for, and why was it so unexpected? This essay is organized according to a scheme prompted by these questions. It explores eight theoretical reasons for the expectation of declining ethnic conflict, and it suggests eight explanations of the fact that ethnic conflict not only failed to decrease but actually intensified.

The Decline of Ethnic Conflict: Falsified Predictions

Among the reasons—not all of them of equal theoretical weight and respectability—for the faulty diagnosis of increasing subnational integration in the states of the Western world are: the application of the leading theories of modernization to the Western experience, the perceived sharp contrast between the First and Third Worlds, the analogy of the theory of the "end of ideology," the analogy of the theory and practice of supranational integration in Europe, liberal wishful thinking, the "domino theory" of separatism and secession, the quasi-Marxist assumption of economic determinism, and the exaggerations inherent in future-oriented theorizing.

1. Theories of Modernization. An important proposition of modernization theories is that the various processes of modernization—industrialization, urbanization, increases in transportation and com-

2. George Lichtheim, *The New Europe: Today—and Tomorrow,* 2d ed. (New York: Praeger, 1964); Stephen R. Graubard, ed., *A New Europe?* (Boston: Houghton Mifflin, 1964).

munication, the growth of mass education, and so on—lead to national integration. This is certainly the major message of Karl Deutsch's writings on social mobilization and national assimilation, although Deutsch himself, unlike some of his readers, was careful to attach a number of qualifications to it. In his theory, the growth of large networks of transaction and communication are of decisive importance: "When several population clusters are united through more communications or more economic activity, then people begin to think of themselves as a country." [3] C. E. Black takes this proposition to its logical conclusion by stating that as a result of growing interdependence the world is moving "toward an ultimate integration of societies." In fact, he says, this development may lead to a stage "at which the various societies are so homogeneous as to be capable of forming a world state." [4] This image leaves little room for the activities of ethnic minorities in Western countries. Ethnic conflict in already highly "modernized" societies also appears as an anachronism in Samuel P. Huntington's effort to synthesize the most prevalent themes in treatments of the concept of modernization. He distinguishes a series of characteristics, two of which are significant in this context: modernization is not only a *homogenizing* process, it is also an *irreversible* process.[5]

This obviously inaccurate thesis of modernization inexorably leading to assimilation can be blamed partly on inadequacies of the theory but also partly on oversimplified interpretations of it. In the first place, modernization may have an assimilative effect in the earliest stage of development but not in later stages. In the first phase of development, it encourages the merger of exclusively local identities into more encompassing ones to which the label of "ethnic group" is commonly attached. But the next step of aggregating different ethnic groups into a single assimilated entity will encounter strong resistance. Only the first step belongs to what Clifford Geertz calls the "integrative revolution," and it "does not do away with ethnocentrism; it merely modernizes it." [6]

Second, national assimilation is an extremely slow process. This means

3. Karl W. Deutsch, *Nationalism and Its Alternatives* (New York: Knopf, 1969), p. 6.
4. C. E. Black, *The Dynamics of Modernization: A Study in Comparative History* (New York: Harper & Row, 1966), pp. 155, 174.
5. Samuel P. Huntington, "The Change to Change: Modernization, Development, and Politics," *Comparative Politics,* 3 (April 1971): 289–290. *See also* Michael Hechter, "Towards a Theory of Ethnic Change," *Politics and Society,* 2 (Fall 1971): 21–22.
6. Clifford Geertz, "The Integrative Revolution: Primordial Sentiments and Civil Liberties in the New States," in *Old Societies and New States: The Quest for Modernity in Asia and Africa,* ed. Geertz (New York: Free Press of Glencoe, 1963), p. 154.

that social mobilization is conducive to assimilation but only up to a certain point; when mobilization is rapid, assimilation will lag behind. Deutsch has made himself perfectly clear on this point, although it does not occupy a central place in his writings: "The more gradually the process of social mobilization moves, the more time there is for social and national assimilation to work." Conversely, when the processes of mobilization "have to be crowded into the lifetime of one or two generations, the chances for assimilation to work are much smaller. The likelihood is much greater that people will be precipitated into politics with their old languages, their old outlook on the world and their old tribal loyalties still largely unchanged; and it becomes far more difficult to have them think of themselves as members of one new nation." He adds that it is unrealistic to expect variegated African tribes to become nations in one generation in view of the fact that "it took centuries to make Englishmen [note, incidentally, that he does not say Britons] and Frenchmen." [7]

The third qualification to modernization theory is closely related to the first two. To the extent that social mobilization alone is insufficient to produce assimilation, one is tempted to believe that it can be assisted by a deliberate effort on the part of governments. This requires the eradication of ethnic loyalties and the artificial stimulation of national sentiments. Such efforts are not likely to be successful, however, especially in the short run, and may even be counterproductive.[8] As Walker Connor argues, "ethnonationalism appears to feed on adversity and denial." If national and ethnic groups are regarded as synonyms, one can say, again using Connor's suggestive terms, that "nation building" at the national or state level entails "nation destroying" at the subnational level.[9] But ethnic loyalties show remarkable resistance to efforts aimed at their destruction.

2. Comparisons with the Third World. Since World War II, the emphasis in comparative political research has been on the developing countries. This has led to the underestimation of the ethnic factor and to the exaggeration of national unity in Western countries in two ways: by the discovery of the relatively much greater ethnic differences in the Third

7. Deutsch, *Nationalism and Its Alternatives,* p. 73.
8. Eric A. Nordlinger, *Conflict Regulation in Divided Societies,* Harvard University Center for International Affairs, Occasional Paper no. 29 (Cambridge, January 1972), pp. 36–39.
9. Walker Connor, "The Politics of Ethnonationalism," *Journal of International Affairs,* 27, no. 1 (1973): 21; Connor, "Nation-Building or Nation-Destroying?" *World Politics,* 24 (April 1972): 319–355.

World and by the simultaneous neglect of developments in the First
World. For instance, in Lucian W. Pye's classic description of the non-
Western political process, he emphasizes the crucial role of communal, or
ethnic, ties. The first of his seventeen characteristics reads, "The fundamental framework of non-Western politics is a communal one, and all
political behavior is strongly colored by considerations of communal
identification." [10] If this is a distinguishing feature of non-Western politics, the strong implication is that communal identification is either not or
no longer important in the Western world. An earlier writer, J. S. Furnivall, adhered to a similar dichotomous view of highly homogeneous
Western societies and "plural" societies, that is, ethnically and communally divided societies, in the non-Western world. In his study of the
Netherlands Indies, published in 1939, Furnivall deviated from a strict dichotomy and stated that the plural society also occurred in the West, citing the racial cleavage in the United States, the linguistic division in
Canada, and the religious division in Ireland. But in his second major
work, published about a decade later, he drew a sharp "contrast between
the plural society of tropical dependencies and the unitary society that
western peoples take for granted." [11]

Moreover, the image of the Western countries as highly homogeneous,
based on comparisons with other parts of the world, antedates World War
II. In the interwar years, the contrast was not provided by the Third
World but by some of the countries in what was later called the Second
World. The states of Eastern Europe were forced to sign the Minority
Treaties, and when they protested against this unequal treatment and
demanded the application of the treaties to all the members of the League
of Nations, the Western states tended to "treat this demand *de haut en
bas,* and to assert that in their more fortunate countries, no minorities
problem existed." C. A. Macartney, writing in 1934, tried to controvert
this prevalent opinion: "Special historical conditions have led to a much
greater intermixture of population in the east than in the west, and to a
much livelier and more intransigent national feeling. . . . Nevertheless,
it is not possible to draw an absolute dividing line between east and west
as between the region where a minority problem exists and that where it

10. Lucian W. Pye, "The Non-Western Political Process," *Journal of Politics,* 20
(August 1958): 469.
11. J. S. Furnivall, *Netherlands India: A Study of Plural Economy* (Cambridge: At the
University Press, 1939), p. 446; Furnivall, *Colonial Policy and Practice: A Comparative
Study of Burma and Netherlands India* (Cambridge: At the University Press, 1948), p. 307.

is absent." In fact, he already detected the signs of "a remarkable national revival . . . among the minority races of western Europe." [12]

3. The "end of ideology." The end-of-ideology thesis implies not only the end of ideological politics but of all other types of politics, including ethnic politics, that are not purely pragmatic. In an age and in a world in which ideology is coming to an end, the resurgence of ethnic conflict seems unthinkable.

The end-of-ideology theory has been discussed so frequently and thoroughly, that all of its main arguments need not be repeated here. But because by implication the end-of-ideology theory appears to forecast the end of ethnic conflict in the Western world, it is important to emphasize its basically very restricted scope. For one thing, the phrase *"end* of ideology" is a misleading hyperbole and actually only means the *decline* of ideology. Second, it does not mean the gradual disappearance of ideology as such but the convergence of existing ideologies and the growth of an ideological consensus—that is, the appearance of a new, generally accepted ideology. Finally, the ideologies that the theory, at least in its original and most authoritative formulations, was concerned with were the radical weltanschauungen of the left and the right—Marxism and doctrinaire laissez-faire—instead of the whole range of value and belief systems that can be subsumed under the more or less loosely defined concept of ideology. Seymour Martin Lipset, one of the foremost end-of-ideology theorists, has made himself quite clear on all of these points: "The decline of . . . total ideologies does *not* mean the end of ideology. Clearly, commitment to the politics of pragmatism, to the rules of the game of collective bargaining, to gradual change whether in the direction favored by the left or the right, to opposition both to an all powerful central state and to laissez-faire constitute the component parts of an ideology. . . . And this ideological agreement, which might best be described as 'conservative socialism,' has become *the* ideology of the major parties in the developed states of Europe and America." [13]

It is tempting, of course, to broaden the scope of the end-of-ideology theory and to postulate a decline of ethnic conflict analogous to the

12. C. A. Macartney, *National States and National Minorities* (London: Oxford University Press, 1934), pp. 481–484.
13. Seymour Martin Lipset, "The Changing Class Structure and Contemporary European Politics," in Graubard, p. 362. See also Giuseppe Di Palma, *The Study of Conflict in Western Society: A Critique of the End of Ideology* (Morristown, N.J.: General Learning Press, 1973); and M. Rejai, ed., *Decline of Ideology?* (Chicago: Aldine-Atherton, 1971).

decline of the conflict between the total ideologies of left and right. And it is not implausible to deduce a decline of ethnic conflict from the perceived general trend toward political pragmatism. Nevertheless, these are logically independent phenomena, and an empirical relationship between them cannot be taken for granted. Analogizing is a valuable heuristic device, but it does not constitute evidence. Moreover, the end-of-ideology theory, even in its narrow formulation, failed in its predictions. The new ideology of "conservative socialism," which was the synthesis of the old antithetical ideologies, has not marked the end of the ideological dialectic. It has given rise to fresh antitheses that constitute formidable challenges to it.

4. *Supranational integration in Europe.* During the 1950's and 1960's, the nationalisms of the established Western European nation-states seemed to weaken, and some enthusiasts even hailed the birth of a "European nation." [14] The waning of subnational ethnic attachments appeared to be a foregone conclusion. In recent years, however, European integration has had a number of serious setbacks. The membership of the European Communities has expanded, but their supranational features have been eroded, and the old nationalisms have turned out to be far from dead or dying.

As a result, the integration theorists have been forced to reconsider some of their basic assumptions. The assumed trend toward pragmatic politics, noted above, was a crucial element in the leading neofunctional theories, too. For instance, Ernst B. Haas wrote in his *Uniting of Europe* in 1958 that integration was motivated primarily by pragmatic calculations of economic advantage on the part of politicians, bureaucrats, and interest groups. In a retrospective article nine years later, he conceded that his forecast of increasing integration had been wrong: "Pragmatic interests, simply because they are pragmatic and not reinforced with deep ideological or philosophical commitment, are ephemeral. Just because they are weakly held they can be readily scrapped. . . . Integrative decisions based on high politics and basic commitment are undoubtedly more durable than decisions based on converging pragmatic expectations." [15] Because such a basic commitment to Europe has not material-

14. See, e.g., Richard Coudenhove-Kalergi, *Die Europäische Nation* (Stuttgart: Deutsche Verlags-Anstalt, 1953).

15. Ernst B. Haas, *"The Uniting of Europe* and the Uniting of Latin America," *Journal of Common Market Studies,* 5 (June 1967): 327–328.

ized, the commitments to the national as well as to the subnational ethnic communities have not been seriously challenged.

5. *Liberal wishful thinking.* The expectation of declining ethnic conflict in the Western world has probably also been furthered by the liberal ideal of equality combined with liberal optimism. The liberal principle that people should be treated as individuals and not as members of racial, religious, and other groups, together with the liberal faith in progress, contribute to the unrealistic view that in the most advanced liberal democracies in the world, membership in ethnic groups must become increasingly irrelevant. Actual developments show that it is easier to change discriminatory laws than discriminatory, or merely self-differentiating, attitudes. Moreover, there are two ways to combat group discrimination: one regards group membership as irrelevant, but the other takes group membership explicitly into account. There are already clear signs of this contrary trend toward greater reliance on group membership in public policy, such as the use of ethnic quotas and preferential hiring. These ascriptive criteria are also advocated in the name of achieving equality. As Daniel Bell states: "The historic irony in the demand for representation on the basis of an ascriptive principle is its complete reversal of radical and humanist values. The liberal and radical attack on discrimination was based on its denial of a justly earned place to a person on the basis of an unjust group attribute. . . . But now it is being demanded that one must have a place primarily because one possesses a particular group attribute." [16] Instead of being progressively implemented, the old liberal ideal of equality, independent of group membership, may be in the process of being reversed.

6. *The "domino theory" of ethnic demands.* The hostility to ethnic demands for autonomy or secession is very strong in Third World countries. One of the reasons appears to be that the granting of such claims and especially a successful secession may be dangerous precedents. This fear is based on a new kind of domino theory, which predisposes political leaders to downgrade or ignore ethnic demands not only in their own country, but also in other states. It is possible that this domino theory is of some relevance in the Western world, too. The widespread condemnation of President Charles de Gaulle's endorsement of a "free Quebec"

---

16. Daniel Bell, *The Coming of Post-Industrial Society: A Venture in Social Forecasting* (New York: Basic Books, 1973), p. 419 (italics omitted).

was probably not based exclusively on the abstract principle of noninterference in the internal affairs of other states. Some striking examples of the shameless denial of the existence of ethnic minorities by representatives of Western states can be found in the debates in the League of Nations. On one occasion, the French representative made the astounding statement that ''France had not signed any Minorities Treaty because she had no minorities. To find minorities in France, they would have to be created in imagination.'' After dismissing any Breton claims to special treatment, he suggested as the height of absurdity ''some ill-humoured Welshman posing before the League of Nations as the champion of Wales,'' whereupon the British representative declared that ''he was not afraid of the obstreperous Welshman, because he did not exist.'' [17]

7. *Marxism and economic probabilism.* The prediction of declining ethnic conflict was also in accord with Karl Marx's forecast of increasing polarization between the social classes and the decreasing political relevance of noneconomic cleavages. Especially the Marxist doctrine of economic determinism has had a pervasive influence on non-Marxist social scientists, although usually in the diluted and merely quasi-Marxist form of economic probabilism instead of strict Marxist determinism. In the study of conflict, the question of economic advantage is likely to be among the first to be asked and to be translated into hypotheses. As Connor points out, this often entails ''an unwarranted exaggeration of the influence of materialism upon human affairs.'' Specifically, this presumption ''has had an evident impact upon much of the literature concerned with political integration. An ethnic minority, it is implicitly or explicitly held, will not secede from a state if its living standards are improving.'' And he adds, ''Such a prognosis . . . underestimates the power of ethnic feelings.'' [18] Economic probabilism also has influenced the assumption of a trend toward pragmatic politics which, as has been seen, underlies the theories of the end of ideology and of European integration, and has thus indirectly strengthened the image of declining ethnic conflict in the Western world.

8. *The hyperboles of future-oriented theorizing.* A final factor, which is not an independent one but which reinforces some of the factors enumerated above, is the tendency of forecasters to exaggerate the impact of the newest trends and developments. In Huntington's words: ''A model

17. Cited in Macartney, p. 482.
18. Connor, ''Nation-Building or Nation-Destroying?'' p. 342.

of a future society normally focuses on what is different from existing society and, in some measure, implies a break with that society. In fact, however, the slate is rarely, if ever, wiped clean. A model of a new society is only a partial model of future society. The new more often supplements, rather than supplants, the old." [19] Theorizing about the directions in which the Western world will develop has necessarily entailed the construction of such models, and their hyperboles have left no room for the persistence of ethnic conflict—already regarded as no more than a curious atavism in the early postwar years.

Postdicted Change: The Resurgence of Ethnic Conflict in the 1960's and 1970's

So far, the argument of this essay has been essentially negative. It has focused on the errors of commission and omission of a series of assumptions, analogies, theories, and interpretations of theories, all of which pointed to the waning of ethnic conflict in Western countries. The conclusion of this exercise is that there were no adequate theoretical grounds for the expectation that ethnic conflict would gradually disappear. In other words, in the absence of other relevant theoretical arguments, ethnic conflict should have been expected to continue at about the same level and not to decrease—but, of course, not to increase either. The next step is a positive one: it consists of trying to discover explanations for the increase in ethnic conflict which has, in fact, taken place in recent years. Such explanations are suggested by, or closely related to, elements of three of the theories discussed in the previous section: the theories of modernization, of the end of ideology, and of the domino effect.

1. The transaction-integration balance. The main thrust of the theories of modernization is that assimilation and integration are promoted by social mobilization—especially, as indicated earlier, in the first stage of political and economic development and especially if the processes of mobilization are not too rapid. However, these theories also concede that under certain circumstances the relationship may be reversed. When social communication, trade, and various other kinds of transactions increase at a rapid rate, assimilation may not only lag behind but may actually decrease. For instance, in Deutsch's first and most famous work on nationalism, he already hints not only that assimilation is slow and must

19. Samuel P. Huntington, "Postindustrial Politics: How Benign Will It Be?" *Comparative Politics,* 6 (January 1974): 191.

be "counted in decades and generations," but also that the comparatively faster growth of communications may have a negative effect on it: "linguistically and culturally . . . members of each group are outsiders for the other. Yet technological and economic processes are forcing them together, into acute recognition of their differences and their common, mutual experience of strangeness, and *more conspicuous differentiation and conflict may result.*" [20] Deutsch specifies two likely outcomes here: a reversal not only of the assimilation among groups, but even of their capacity to coexist peacefully.

This important theme is elaborated in Deutsch's subsequent publication, which is concerned with the conditions of integration, defined as "the attainment of a sense of community, accompanied by formal or informal institutions or practices, sufficiently strong and widespread to assure peaceful change." Deutsch argues that "the number of opportunities for violent conflict will increase with the volume and range of mutual transactions," because the various kinds of transactions throw "a burden upon the institutions for peaceful adjustment or change." Consequently, the prevention of conflict depends on the ability of integration to keep pace with the growth of transactions. How difficult it is to maintain this balance is indicated by Deutsch's description of it as a *race* between the two processes: "the race between the growing rate of transaction among populations in particular areas and the growth of integrative institutions and practices among them." [21]

If modernization leads to rapidly increasing social transactions and contacts among diverse groups, strain and conflict are more likely to ensue than greater mutual understanding. This explanation undoubtedly applies to much of the ethnic conflict that has taken place in Third World countries since their political and economic takeoff a few decades ago, but is it also valid for the First World? The difficulty is that, according to the analogy with the Third World, ethnic conflict in Western countries should have reached its high point in the wake of the Industrial Revolution more than a century ago instead of during the past decade. Connor attempts to resolve this problem by asserting that modernization in the West only led to intensive intrastate transactions and communications at a rather gradual pace, and that these quantitative increases did not add up to

20. Karl W. Deutsch, *Nationalism and Social Communication: An Inquiry into the Foundations of Nationality* (Cambridge: MIT Press, 1953), pp. 99–100 (italics added).

21. Karl W. Deutsch, *Political Community at the International Level: Problems of Definition and Measurement* (Garden City, N.Y.: Doubleday, 1954), pp. 33, 39–40.

a qualitative breakthrough until after World War II. This was "the point at which a significant number of people perceived that the cumulative impact of the quantitative increases in the intensity of intergroup contacts . . . constituted a threat to their ethnicity," and it "represented, in political terms, a qualitative transformation." [22]

2. *The "horizontalization" of vertical ethnic groups.* Whether or not Connor's claim is valid is an empirical question, but to the extent that the rapid multiplication and intensification of contacts do create interethnic tensions, these tensions are likely to be aggravated by the awareness of significant inequalities among the ethnic groups. Imbalances tend to foster feelings of superiority in the more-favored groups and of resentment and frustration among the less-favored groups.

It is useful in this connection to make a distinction between horizontal and vertical ethnic groups. Both are ideal types, and they correspond to Max Weber's concepts of "caste structures" and "ethnic coexistences." [23] They can be defined in terms of their relationship to the economic, status, and power dimensions: vertical groups (ethnic coexistences) cut across these dimensions at right angles, whereas the boundaries of horizontal groups (caste structures) coincide with them. Vertical groups are completely equal to each other in terms of class, status, and power; horizontal groups show the highest degree of inequality. In reality, ethnic groups are never purely vertical or purely horizontal, but may be said to approximate one or the other of the two ideal types.

The ethnic groups of the Western world are generally vertical rather than horizontal; the only major exceptions are the American Negroes and the recently immigrated groups of "guest workers." An important characteristic of vertical groups is that they are less likely to come into conflict with each other than horizontal groups. Their roughly equal position on the economic, status, and power scales precludes feelings of discrimination. They are also often regionally concentrated and their geographical separation from each other reduces the opportunities for conflict. A second feature of vertical groups is that as a result of their lower potential for conflict, they have a greater ability to survive as distinct units. [24] This means that ethnic conflict is comparatively less likely

22. Connor, "Nation-Building or Nation-Destroying?" pp. 330–331.
23. H. H. Gerth and C. Wright Mills, eds., *From Max Weber: Essays in Sociology* (New York: Oxford University Press, 1958), pp. 188–190.
24. Donald L. Horowitz, "Three Dimensions of Ethnic Politics," *World Politics,* 23 (January 1971): 236.

among vertical groups, but that they are more likely to persist as separate groups and that their relatively low potential for conflict also has considerable durability. This conflict potential, however, may be activated when the basically vertical groups become less equal, that is, when they become less vertical and more horizontal.

Modernization often leads to a degree of horizontalization because it tends to be a process that affects groups and regions unevenly. With regard to the Third World, Robert Melson and Howard Wolpe have stressed that modernization almost inevitably entails differential mobilization among ethnic groups and that the resulting inequalities "exacerbate communal conflict by multiplying coincident social cleavages." [25] Similar processes may have operated in the Western world, and especially in Western Europe, in the phase of high economic growth and prosperity of the 1950's and early 1960's. The only reference, brief but important, to ethnic conflict in *A New Europe?* concerns Alessandro Pizzorno's argument that industrialization and the resultant "economic inequalities among nations and among regions will very likely give rise to tendencies to territorial separatism, however anachronistic this may seem in these times of European integration. The Flemish-Walloon controversy is only the most striking of many we could mention." He adds that "tendencies to separatism and independence are a consequence of differentiations and discrepancies which inevitably become more marked during the course of development. Since the industrial revolution, Europe has known more struggles for independence than struggles for union." [26]

It is worth emphasizing again that this second explanation of the resurgence of ethnic conflict derives its strength from its close connection with the first explanation. Only in conjunction with the qualitative increase in social communication can the awareness of economic and other inequalities among ethnic groups be expected to become really acute.

3. The expanding scope of state intervention. The rapid growth in the scope and volume of state activities in the years since World War II has added to the problem of the perceived inequalities among ethnic groups. First of all, because hardly any public policy has a strictly equal impact

25. Robert Melson and Howard Wolpe, "Modernization and the Politics of Communalism: A Theoretical Perspective," *American Political Science Review,* 64 (December 1970): 1115. See also Anthony D. Smith, "Theories and Types of Nationalism," *European Journal of Sociology,* 10, no. 1 (1969): 130–131.

26. Alessandro Pizzorno, "The Individualistic Mobilization of Europe," in Graubard, p. 276.

on different groups and regions, the increase of state activities has also increased the possibility that unequal treatment will occur by chance. Second, if a governmental action is explicitly designed to counteract the uneven impact of the processes of modernization and if its purpose is, therefore, to equalize regional and group differences, it may paradoxically still be perceived as unequal and unfair treatment. The poorer regions and groups will feel relatively deprived to begin with, and may well regard remedial action by the government as inadequate—a tendency that is reinforced by the egalitarian expectations raised by the growth of state intervention. At the same time, their more prosperous counterparts will feel relatively deprived of governmental support and hence will also feel they are the victims of unfair discrimination. Especially in recent years, these problems have been aggravated by the general decline in the quality and effectiveness of governmental performance.

Another paradox is that the perception of inequalities, beyond calling forth claims for the redress of these inequalities, may also trigger ethnic demands for autonomy or secession—which are not very likely to bring greater equality! Inequalities tend to be greater among than within sovereign states, and in federal than in unitary states.[27]

4. *The decreasing displacement of ethnic conflict.* The previous arguments relied on a comparison of the relative *positions* of ethnic and socioeconomic cleavages. A closely related argument focuses on the comparison of the relative *salience* of ethnic and other cleavages. The point of departure is again that ethnic cleavages are primarily vertical, that socioeconomic cleavages can be depicted as horizontal, and that these cleavages, therefore, do not coincide. Other politically relevant cleavages, in particular the religious ones, generally do not coincide with ethnic cleavages either, although they tend to cut across each other at a more acute angle than the ethnic and socioeconomic cleavages. The previous argument was that ethnic conflict becomes more likely when the ethnic cleavage deviates from its vertical position. The present argument is that the probability of conflict along the ethnic cleavage increases when the horizontal socioeconomic cleavage and other relevant cleavages that do not coincide with the ethnic dividing line lose their salience.

This explanation follows E. E. Schattschneider's theory of the displacement of conflicts. Noncoinciding cleavages and the conflicts that

27. See David R. Cameron and Richard I. Hofferbert, "The Impact of Federalism on Education Finance: A Comparative Analysis," *European Journal of Political Research,* 2 (September 1974): 225–258.

arise along these cleavage lines compete with each other: "The more intense conflicts are likely to displace the less intense. What follows is a system of domination and subordination of conflicts." [28] During the first half of the twentieth century, the dominant cleavages in the Western world were the class and religious divisions; ethnic differences tended to be subordinated. This pattern of dominant and subordinate cleavages is clearly reflected in the history of Western party systems, which developed primarily along class and religious dimensions and which became frozen in the 1920's. [29] In their survey of the clienteles of the major Western political parties, Richard Rose and Derek Urwin found that, with only one exception, all parties showing some socially cohesive support were cohesive on religious or class grounds, or both. The few parties with ethnically or linguistically cohesive support either were of rather recent vintage or were parties for which the ethnic dimension was not foremost. The only exception was the Swedish People's party in Finland with a linguistically and regionally defined clientele. [30] An interesting example of the use of displacement theory is Hugh Seton-Watson's attempt to explain the relative moderation of Scottish nationalism. The Scots have frequently shown, he asserts, "that they want some form of self-government; yet at general elections they vote for the great national parties. This paradox is easily explained: Scottish home rule is not the most urgent demand of the Scottish voter, but this does not mean that he does not desire it." [31]

In this context, the end-of-ideology theory becomes relevant again. As was pointed out earlier, it was wrong to expect a decline of ethnic conflict analogous to the decline of the ideological conflict between the political left and right. We can now turn the argument around completely: it was as a *result* of the decreasing salience of ideological conflict along the horizontal left-right cleavage—and, to a lesser but still significant extent, the declining importance of religious differences—that ethnic conflicts have reemerged in recent years. The ethnic cleavages have long been less

28. E. E. Schattschneider, *The Semisovereign People: A Realist's View of Democracy in America* (New York: Holt, Rinehart & Winston, 1960), p. 67.

29. Seymour Martin Lipset and Stein Rokkan, "Cleavage Structures, Party Systems, and Voter Alignments: An Introduction," in *Party Systems and Voter Alignments: Cross-National Perspectives,* ed. Lipset and Rokkan (New York: Free Press, 1967), p. 50.

30. Richard Rose and Derek Urwin, "Social Cohesion, Political Parties and Strains in Regimes," *Comparative Political Studies,* 2 (April 1969): 12–20.

31. Hugh Seton-Watson, "Unsatisfied Nationalisms," *Journal of Contemporary History,* 6, no. 1 (1971): 6.

salient but more persistent than these competing cleavages. This explanation means that the wrong question was asked: it should not be Why has ethnic conflict suddenly reappeared? but Why has it been dormant for so long? The answer is that it was temporarily displaced by more salient conflicts.

5. *The new wave of democratization.* The theory of the end of ideology is important for an additional reason. If, as discussed earlier, the end of ideology is itself an ideology and does not constitute the end of the ideological dialectic, it suggests the question What do the new antitheses that challenge the ideology of conservative socialism consist of? One of these appears to be the ideology of participatory democracy, which rejects the kind of democratic regime that conservative socialism implies. Haas asserts that the new Europe is characterized by "a pragmatic synthesis of capitalism and socialism in the form of democratic planning," and he aptly describes its decision-making mechanism as follows: "It features the continuous participation of all major voluntary groups in European society through elaborate systems of committees and councils. The technical bureaucracies of trade unions, industrial associations, bankers and farmers sit down with the technocrats from the ministries of finance, labor and economics—or with central government planning offices—to shape the future." [32] This is the type of government that Robert A. Dahl has labeled the "new democratic Leviathan," as a reaction to which he predicted the emergence of "radical efforts (the shape of which we cannot foresee) to reconstruct the Leviathan to a more nearly human scale." [33]

The shape that the opposition to the new Leviathan has assumed, so far, borrows to a large extent from traditional democratic theory and does not represent a qualitative break with the past. What is important for the purposes of this essay is that all of the manifestations of the new wave of democratization encourage ethnic demands. First of all, it has entailed greater activity and a new stridency on the part of a variety of groups, including ethnic ones, that do not belong to the decision-making establishment. Second, these groups tend to be more concerned about minority rights than majority rule—in line with the priorities of ethnic groups. Third, their prescriptions for reconstructing the new Leviathan "to a more nearly human scale" are the rather traditional ones of decen-

32. Ernst B. Haas, "Technocracy, Pluralism and the New Europe," in Graubard, p. 68.
33. Robert A. Dahl, ed., *Political Oppositions in Western Democracies* (New Haven: Yale University Press, 1966), p. 400.

tralization, autonomy, regionalization, and grass-roots democracy. These general tendencies have given a powerful boost to specific ethnic demands. Finally, as Huntington has pointed out, the "expansion of participation could make postindustrial society extraordinarily difficult to govern." [34] Therefore, to the extent that widespread and relatively unstructured political participation increases governmental inefficiency and immobilism, demands for ethnic autonomy will be spurred even further.

The relationship between democratization and ethnic demands proposed here differs from the usual one. Ethnic pluralism is usually the independent variable and democracy the dependent variable, and the question is whether or not a society divided ethnically or otherwise can sustain a democratic regime. [35] The converse relationship links democracy as the independent variable with ethnic pluralism as the dependent variable, or more specifically, democratization with ethnic conflict. In Third World countries, the process of democratization and the encouragement of mass participation have undoubtedly strengthened ethnic feelings and demands. [36] During the first wave of democratization in Western countries in the late nineteenth and early twentieth centuries, the stimulation of ethnicity was much less pronounced. This may also explain the impetus belatedly given to it by the second wave of democratization.

6. *The growth of postbourgeois values.* The demands for democratization, decentralization, and autonomy may be said to represent the procedural antithesis to the end of ideology and to its institutional manifestation in the form of the new Leviathan. The substantive antithesis is a direct reaction to the values of conservative socialism. Economic determinism has always given a one-sided and distorted picture of developments in Western countries, which has become even more inaccurate in recent years, with a growing emphasis on the quality of life replacing the concern with economic growth and distributional problems. This is one of the issues that Martin O. Heisler considers to be typically dominant in his postindustrial "European polity" model. [37] It is also the main component of what Ronald Inglehart calls "postbourgeois values," which are in-

34. Huntington, "Postindustrial Politics," p. 177.

35. See Connor's summary of the views of John Stuart Mill, Lord Acton, Sir Ernest Barker, and Alfred Cobban in his "Self-Determination: The New Phase," *World Politics,* 20 (October 1967): 32–34.

36. Melson and Wolpe, p. 1122.

37. Martin O. Heisler, ed., *Politics in Europe: Structures and Processes in Some Postindustrial Democracies* (New York: McKay, 1974), pp. 24–25, 83–85.

creasingly prevalent in Western countries. These are the needs for belonging and for intellectual and aesthetic self-fulfillment.[38] For people who consciously see themselves as members of ethnic groups, these values can obviously best be realized within the framework of a self-governing ethnic community.

7. *The principle of self-determination.* Ethnic demands may have been further reinforced in recent years by the principle of self-determination. Connor attaches great significance to it and claims that, especially after World War II, the message of self-determination has received "wide acceptance as a universal truth," and "has induced minorities in Europe and North America . . . to question the validity of present political borders. It has therefore been more than a justification for ethnic movements; it has been a catalyst for them." [39] On the other hand, as Connor admits, most politicians only pay lip service to self-determination. Furthermore, although the United Nations Charter has explicitly and emphatically accorded it the status of an axiom of universal validity and applicability, it has in practice been interpreted rather narrowly. In Rupert Emerson's words, it has come to mean primarily "the UN-sanctioned right of every colonial people (assumed to constitute a single and indivisible whole) to achieve its independence as speedily and completely as possible." [40] The protection of national and ethnic minorities, which was a prominent concern of the League of Nations, has been virtually abandoned by the United Nations.

8. *The demonstration effect of ethnic demands.* Probably a more important factor than the abstract principle of self-determination is the concrete example set by a few of the more active ethnic minorities for the initially passive ones. Thus, there is more than just a grain of truth to the domino theory of ethnic demands discussed earlier. In addition, the conspicuously independent behavior of some of the smaller Western countries also provides an appealing model for ethnic minorities. For instance, the examples of tiny Iceland's defiance of the government of the United Kingdom in the intermittent cod war and Norway's refusal to join the European Communities are not lost on the nationalistic Scots. Here again,

38. Ronald Inglehart, "The Silent Revolution in Europe: Intergenerational Change in Post-Industrial Societies," *American Political Science Review,* 65 (December 1971): 991–1017.

39. Connor, "Nation-Building or Nation-Destroying?" p. 331.

40. Rupert Emerson, "The Fate of Human Rights in the Third World," *World Politics,* 27 (January 1975): 204.

the postwar qualitative transformation of not only intrastate but also interstate transactions and communications plays a crucial role. As the world, and the Western world in particular, becomes more unified by technology, it may—not only simultaneously but also consequently—grow more divided by ethnic loyalties.

Ethnic consciousness and potential ethnic conflict did not decline in the Western world, but were merely lying dormant for many years until, during the past decade, they were activated by a number of interrelated causes. A coherent explanation of this phenomenon, built upon a number of well-established theories and concepts in political science, has been attempted here. Idiosyncratic factors that may be of great importance in individual cases of ethnic conflict have not been taken into account. Moreover, the explanation is, however plausible, purely speculative and hypothetical. It should be tested against the empirical evidence, preferably derived not only from the most striking cases of ethnic conflict but also from the contrasting cases of less restive ethnic minorities, such as the Swedish Finns, Lapps, Frisians, and Alsatians. The result of such a test may well prove to be a forecast of future trends in ethnic relations in the Western world that is more accurate than the predictions of declining ethnic conflict made in the early postwar years.

3

The Interfaces of Regionalism in Western Europe: Brussels and the Peripheries

LAWRENCE SCHEINMAN

Part of the mythology surrounding the creation and evolution of the European Community predicts the progressive weakening of central authority and power in the state, an erosion of loyalties to central institutions, and the transference of authority and loyalty to new transnational centers of decision making.[1] A related prediction, derived from the mythology surrounding subnational regional movements in Europe today, is that the unification of a continent requires its decentralization as well, with the natural and logical beneficiaries of such decentralization being the regions;[2] that a natural accompaniment to the emergence of a united Europe is the emergence of a subnational regional dimension. As expressed by one advocate of regionalism: "At the moment when opinion is becoming conscious of the need to give a continental or European dimension to economic and financial markets, to scientific research, to diplomacy, defense and the production of civil or military goods, one observes the spread of the idea of the need for an administrative and even political regional dimension as well."[3] Thus, a relationship between suprana-

1. *European Community* (EC) refers to the nine Western European states that are working to achieve economic unity among themselves and that aspire to broadening that unity to the political sphere. The EC is based on the treaties of three organizations: the European Coal and Steel Community, the European Atomic Energy Community, and the European Economic Community (EEC). The terms *European Community* and *European Communities* as well as *Common Market* are used interchangeably in this essay.

The three organizations operate with a single administrative structure composed of four institutions: an executive consisting of the Commission responsble only to the Community as a whole, and the Council of Ministers, who represent the individual member states; a legislative body, the European Parliament, whose authority is limited and whose role is more advisory than legislative; and a judicial body, the Court of Justice.

2. Jean Buchmann, "Missions et structures des pouvoirs publics dans la démocratie européenne de demain," in *L'Europe en formation*, Nos. 91 and 92 (1967).

3. Hervé Lavenir, "Les perspectives régionales de l'Europe," in *Naissance de l'Europe des régions*, Bulletin 9 (1966), p. 4.

tional integration and subnational regionalism can be postulated: national territory is redefined in regional terms in conjunction with the progressive absorption of the state into European federal structures.

There are sound theoretical grounds for the asserted relationship between supranational integration and subnational regionalism. In the decades following World War II, the state in Western Europe was, as a principle of political organization, on the defensive, and the nationalism that sustained it was held in disrepute. The state-centered system was regarded as detrimental to the interests of peace and harmony on the continent. Further, the center of power had shifted from Europe to extracontinental powers, rendering the small and medium-sized states of Europe subjects rather than masters of their destiny. Hence, externally the state was visualized as increasingly incapable of performing its principal tasks of providing security and welfare to its citizenry, and strong arguments were mounted in favor of transcending the traditional state system in favor of subcontinental regional structures. Internally, reactions to the increasing centralization that accompanied modernization, industrialization, and expanding welfare activities—whereby central authority penetrated ever more deeply the social and cultural fabric in a homogenizing fashion—appeared to dictate solutions that entailed the dismantling of central state structures and the decentralization of political authority. There followed a logical juxtaposition of new European-wide authority structures with newly created or revitalized subnational structures at the expense of central state authority for meeting the social, economic, political, and security demands of the mid-twentieth century.

This essay examines the postulated relationship with particular reference to the perspective of the European Community on subnational regionalism. Salient aspects of subnational regional perspectives of the relationship are examined in the few cases where data are available. It is assumed that some relationship does exist between supranational integration and subnational regionalism. Also assumed are the a priori ideological harmony of these two forms of regionalism in attacking the state and the theoretical plausibility of their conjunction. But based on the actual experience of the European Community, the following hypotheses are made: the style, scope, and character of supranational integration that have dominated thus far generate disincentives to the postulated relationship; and the two levels of regionalism are, in fact, not a priori mutually reinforcing and are even potentially contradictory.

It is important at the outset to draw a distinction between *regionalism* and *regional policy* for it is only regarding the latter that the European Community has any formal (and limited) responsibility. By regionalism is meant the sum of subnational regional movements (such as of the Scottish or Breton nationalists, or of the linguistic separatists in Belgium) that are predicated on ethnic, cultural, social, economic, political, or other claims (or combinations of these) and that aim at some form of institutionalized recognition by central authority of the legitimacy of these claims. Regionalism reflects a set of beliefs concerning the distinctiveness of the group making the claims and seeks a framework within which these claims can be satisfied. Normally satisfaction of these claims entails the granting of an autonomous status (limited or broad, functional or federal) to the region in question.

Regional policy, on the other hand, can be defined in more explicitly economic terms as a mechanism contributing both to the optimization of the allocation of economic resources and to the promotion of greater economic rationality and efficiency in the provision of public services. In the words of the Commission of the European Communities, regional policy is a mechanism "to help improve the harmony of regional structures in the Community, firstly in order to combat the mechanical effects which tend to develop owing to the mere fact of opening internal frontiers, and secondly in order to permit the implementation of common policies and to create maximum external economies for each of the regions." [4] This economically oriented definition is adopted here.

Whereas regionalism appears to be pregnant with ideological and political considerations, regional policy, at least under the commission's definition, has a politically antiseptic quality. Subnational regional demands reflect a wide array of concerns. In one instance, relative economic deprivation may lie at the heart of a protest movement that takes advantage of ethnic identities to mobilize political support on behalf of its protest. This appears to be the case with Scottish nationalism.[5] In another instance, frankly political concerns may motivate a subnational movement as non-establishment elites seek a decentralization of political authority, transferring power to regional institutions either because of a loss of confidence in national leadership (such as in Italy) or because of a fundamental desire to more effectively control decisions affecting local

---

4. Commission of the European Communities, *A Regional Policy for the Community* (Brussels, 1969), p. 34.
5. See Milton Esman's essay in this volume entitled "Scottish Nationalism, North Sea Oil, and the British Response."

concerns (a justification offered, in some instances, in France). Occasionally these subnational movements will, as in the Scottish situation, capitalize on the presence of ethnic, cultural, or linguistic characteristics in order to more effectively press their case. With the exception of those situations where regional demands are heavily economic, the Commission of the European Communities has not been either accessible or available as an ally for local regional movements. Nor, from much of the available evidence, have subnational regional movements interpreted the supposedly common interest in disseising central institutions of authority in favor of a more rational or democratic distribution of power as facilitating an alliance with the communities.[6]

Congruity appears to vary according to how far beyond the boundaries of regional policy the demands of regionalism extend. At the extreme of exclusively political demands (for example, political autonomy or even increased local control over decisions affecting the area in question), regionalism and regional policy may be in contradiction and, hence, not mutually reinforcing but even mutually destructive. The reasons for this lie, as suggested in the first hypothesis, in the scope, style, and character of supranational integration.

The European communities were created for explicit economic and implicit political reasons. The economic reasons were to provide a framework in which to build a modern economy and to take advantage of the benefits that a large market could provide for establishing a competitive economic system. In the words of the treaty of Rome: "It shall be the aim of the Community, by establishing a common market and progressively approximating the economic policies of member states, to promote throughout the Community a harmonious development of economic activities, a continuous and balanced expansion, an increased stability, an accelerated raising of the standard of living and closer relations between its member states." [7] For many, of course, the European Economic Community (EEC) was not an end in itself, but rather a means by which to

6. Alliances may develop between community-level institutions and subnational regional elites, but thus far such relationships and linkages have been minimal and in some cases nonexistent because of national central-authority opposition or disapproval and because of the commission's sensitivity to the central authorities' views. In short, while the commission theoretically could be instrumental, it has not in fact been so.

7. Treaty Establishing the European Economic Community (Treaty of Rome) Article 2, 1957, as quoted by Leon Lindberg, *The Political Dynamics of European Economic Integration* (Stanford: Stanford University Press, 1963), p. 15.

achieve the unification of Western Europe.[8] Frontal assaults on sovereignty not being plausible (as evidenced by the debacle of the European Defense Community and the European Political Community in 1954), it was decided to try to induce political integration through economic integration, relying on the pressure of economic forces to bring about so close a coordination and harmonization of national policies that political integration would flow as a natural consequence.

The principal supranational structure created to implement this policy of back-door federation—the Commission of the European Communities—was kept largely devoid of political authority and deprived of a political base. Unlike the executive of the earlier-established European Coal and Steel Community, the commission was empowered to formulate and implement policy, but not to decide whether to adopt recommended policies. This latter responsibility was left in the hands of representatives of the member states sitting in the Council of Ministers. Nevertheless, the treaty, which the commission was responsible for implementing, potentially embraced the full range of national economic activity.

Hence, the EEC was fashioned along pragmatic, gradualist, and functional lines, wherein political choice remained the prerogative of the member states, and common interests could be forged into increased solidarity that would progressively constrain the decisional capabilities of the individual states.

This gives rise to the question of decisional scope and character. As conceived by the commission, economic integration was to be achieved largely through the consensus of economic interests built on a dialectical relationship between the Eurocracy in Brussels and the counterpart national bureaucracies, not through the establishment of a popular consensus and the crafting of political institutions. According to Altiero Spinelli, "In searching for the main key to the fulfillment of the mission confided to it the EEC Commission unhesitatingly sought out above all else the development of relations and collaboration with the national administrations." [9]

8. Leon Lindberg lists four main themes associated with the creation of the EEC-political unification, economic unification, economic and political cooperation, and free trade. He suggests that for the different supporters of the EEC, different themes dominated. *Ibid.*, pp. 108–109.

9. Altiero Spinelli, *The Eurocrats* (Baltimore: Johns Hopkins University Press, 1966), p. 71.

The building of Europe was to be a bureaucratic undertaking; supranationalism was an administrative system related to but not identical with the administrative state as it was known in Western Europe—similar in its bureaucratic and ultimately technocratic style; different in that the pluralistic democratic controls that have served to attenuate and ameliorate the national administrative state were lacking at the European level. As succinctly described by Ernst Haas:

The participants in the supranational decision-making process include of course "governments"; indeed governments theoretically dominate it because their representatives constitute the Council of Ministers which rules the three communities. But those representatives are for the most part high civil servants meeting in almost continuous confrontation with their opposite numbers and working out common policies on the basis of their perceptions of the technical possibilities inherent in whatever is being discussed. . . . Other participants include spokesmen for all major national and European interest groups, who confer almost all the time with the specialists in the Community executives.[10]

The New Europe has worked out a pragmatic synthesis of capitalism and socialism in the form of democratic planning. . . . The technical bureaucracies of trade unions, industrial associations, bankers and farmers sit down with the technocrats from the ministries of finance, labor and economics . . . to shape the future.[11]

The crux of the matter has been reached: the European communities are administrations without the state—a "pragmatic synthesis" of organized and established interests. The communities indeed aim at the rationalization of the economy and the maximization of welfare (for some), but do so within the framework of, and with a view to the maintenance of, the market economy and the prevailing political and social structures associated with that economy. The objective, declared or otherwise, is the reinforcement of existing structures and power relationships; change primarily entails making adjustments and improving efficiencies, not sundering established structures and lines of political authority.

The pattern of recruitment to the upper echelons of the commission bureaucracy ensures the perpetuation of these values. In 1970, more than 70 percent of all upper-echelon administrators in the commission came from public and parapublic bureaucracies and, to a much lesser extent, from private enterprise; in the highest ranks the percentages from these groups

10. Ernst Haas, "Technocracy, Pluralism and the New Europe," in *International Regionalism*, J. S. Nye, ed. (Boston: Little, Brown, 1968), p. 152.
11. *Ibid.*, p. 156.

ranged from 82 to 92.[12] Individuals from universities, trade unions and other international organizations, and within the community bureaucracies represented only a small proportion of the higher-level civil servants. The preferences among the technocrats of the liberal democratic states of rationalization of the economy rather than fundamental reform, of subordination of social action to economic modernization, and of emphasis on enlarging the "economic pie" rather than on its redistribution are faithfully reflected in the Commission of the European Communities.[13]

Hence, we have a community of experts, bureaucrats, and planners who represent an extension to the supranational level of values that dominate the state. As an administration without a political base the Community eschews political choice in favor of economic and technical approaches to the problems it confronts. It reflects an underlying consensus on economic, political, and social values and indeed retains its legitimacy by not challenging those fundamental premises. Its role is to optimize predetermined or politically negotiated goals and objectives, not to enter the dispute over the establishment of goals, which is what political choice is all about.

The definition of regional policy developed by the commission in its 1969 memorandum (quoted earlier) complies closely with the characteristics described above. Social, cultural, and human factors are not ignored. But although frequent reference is made to the need to satisfy human aspirations, personal needs, and cultural values, these goals are never clearly articulated and inevitably are subordinated to broader and more comprehensive system-level economic considerations. The commission's 1969 memorandum remains today, subject to slight modification, the basic document of the Community in this field. The Thomson report of May 1973 reaffirms the commission's definition of regional policy, noting that such policy should "give areas suffering from regional imbalances the means to correct them and to enable them to put themselves on

12. See Lawrence Scheinman and Werner Feld, "The European Economic Community and National Civil Servants of the Member States," *International Organization,* Winter 1972, pp. 121–135.
13. For an excellent review of these issues at the state level, see Michael Watson, "Conclusion," in Jack Hayward and Michael Watson, *Planning, Politics and Public Policy* (Cambridge: Cambridge University Press, 1975). The existence of reformist elements in the commission is not denied; but the prevailing situation is skewed toward making adjustments in the status quo rather than toward basic change.

a footing of more equal competitiveness." [14] Even more revealingly, the same report asserts that mitigation of the disparity in regional living conditions is a priority concern of the Community and that "it is unthinkable that the Community should only lead to an increase in the process whereby wealth is principally attracted to *places* where it exists already. Unless the Community's economic resources are moved where human resources are, thus sustaining living local communities, there is bound to be disenchantment over the idea of European unity." [15] There is nothing in the above statements or in any of the related commission material to suggest that redistribution of resources and wealth is interpreted as resource or income redistribution *among* social classes or as bringing about fundamental reform in social relationships. Rather the purpose appears to be a rationalization within the existing system to prevent regional disequilibria from undermining the progressive development of the Common Market. This objective conforms closely to the objective of regional policy at the national level.

By no means does a perfect symmetry on regional matters between the European Community and the national states exist. Differences have arisen in direct proportion to the degree that one moves away from purely market-oriented economic consideration. National governments use regional policy as political policy, that is, for purposes other than maintenance of the economic system. Thus, state policies have been devised in countries such as France and Great Britain to maintain nonproductive facilities in satisfaction of social policies or in response to organized political demands. Investment incentives have been employed in France and in the Netherlands to stem labor outflow from border regions (such as Alsace and Limburg) to German factories where higher wages are paid. Virtually all members of the Common Market, in fact, use a variety of tax-relief and subsidy programs to attract investment from outside sources. These policy objectives are not shared at the community level because they tend to intrude on the process of market rationalization by creating artificial barriers and conditions. Because the Rome treaty does not give a specific mandate to the Community to manage regional policy, but leaves this responsibility largely in the hands of the member states, the commission has had to try to mold a consensus on the value of concerting and coordinating national regional policy in the name of economic and mone-

14. Commission of the European Communities, *Report on the Regional Problems of the Enlarged Community* (Brussels, 3 May 1973), pp. 5–6.
15. *Ibid.*, p. 4.

tary union. The national governments, on the other hand, have tended to resist formalization of this effort because of the political value inherent in the ability to manipulate the flow of resources and the factors of production.

Differences also have arisen over the relationship between the commission and subnational regional authorities. In Germany there has been little problem. The federal structure facilitates a direct dialogue between the Laender and the commission, and the Bundesrat maintains an office in Brussels in order to keep in continuous contact with the commission. In Italy, however, where a constitutionally mandated devolution of authority has created a separate political base at the regional level, the situation is somewhat different. Rome is jealous of the relationship between the Italian regions and the Community with the result that, while direct contacts between Brussels and the regions are maintained, the commission, as a political reflex, informs Rome when contacts are made and frequently is accompanied into the field by a representative of the central bureaucracy.

France, on the other hand, reflects another type of relationship. Regionalization in France has been confined to administrative deconcentration, and Community-regional contacts are at an absolute minimum where they exist at all. In 1961 when the commission first mapped a strategy for regional policy, it asked for the right to communicate directly with regional personnel and local authorities in order to maximize information. This request was rejected, largely at French insistence. Despite its effort to eschew political controversy, the commission has recently reaffirmed its interest in establishing regional contacts in order to gather data on economic conditions in the community.[16]

A final difference between the national and the community-level authorities has developed over the concept of region. At the outset in 1961, the commission, for purposes of analysis, made a distinction between two regional concepts—one, socioeconomic regions as defined by the states in the context of their respective national regional policies; the other, macrosocioeconomic regions based on the commission's view of the economic logic of the Community territory. The commission recommended that France be envisaged as a country consisting of nine "macrosocioeconomic" regions. This plan was quickly rejected by Paris on the grounds that not only would it violate the French concept of regionaliza-

16. For an analytical overview of the Community's regional policy, see F. Massart Pierard, "La définition de la région au sein de la C.E.E.," in *La politique régionale du marche commun* (Brussels: Bruylant, 1971), pp. 127–141.

tion from an economic point of view, but further it would establish regions large enough to contemplate initiatives at the European level, and hence it would be a threat to national unity.[17]

Despite these differences between the national and community-level authorities regarding aspects of regional policy, the general compatability of interest between the dominant forces in the states and the bureaucrats in Brussels is sufficiently high, and the Community's understanding of the limits of its political capabilities is sufficiently clear, that regional policy issues are likely to be resolved "in-house" rather than by alliances of convenience between the Commission of the European Communities and dissident forces within the national political systems.

It becomes increasingly clear why subnational regional movements might find the European Community a questionable resource and a dubious ally in the quest for regional autonomy. Indeed, regional militants appear to be much more cognizant of the limitations than their armchair theorist confreres. Regionalism entails change: change in the prevailing economic and social structure (in the name of social justice); and/or change in the formal distribution of political authority (in the name of political self-determination). While most regional movements reflect a blend of interests and demands—some more frankly political, others more frankly socioeconomic—a distinction between the two basic types will be made here.

The socioeconomic viewpoint has been argued rather persistently in the preceding pages. Regionalism aimed at the fundamental redistribution of wealth and economic goods represents a challenge to the prevailing market economies of the member states of the Community. Public authority entered the economic realm in the postwar era to facilitate industrialization, investment, and the capitalist system, not necessarily at the expense of, but as a priority concern to the attainment of, full social justice. The public authority that promulgated this policy in countries such as France or Italy also promulgated the European communities. On the basis of this relationship, the charge has been made that Europe is a Europe of trusts, cartels, and capitalism in which "the battle against capitalism has only a secondary place when it is not simply ignored." [18]

One of the clearest expressions of this view from the perspective of a subnational regionalist is found in Robert Lafont's *La révolution régiona-*

---

17. See Robert Lafont, *La révolution régionaliste* (Paris: Gallimard, 1967), p. 214.
18. *Ibid.* p. 237.

liste. Lafont argues that France suffers from internal colonialism in the sense that the control of regional resources, levels of development, distribution of income, and ultimately life styles is dominated from outside the regions, largely by big capitalist agglomerations whose activities are facilitated by the centralization of the state. The solution to this situation, he contends, is a fundamental reorganization that would entail breaking the authoritarian-technocratic hold of the central authority on the population and establishing regional socialism under which basic resources would come under regional control, to be exploited according to the democratically expressed will of those who constitute the region.[19]

A self-declared "European," Lafont raises the question of the relationship between "regional revolution" and the European Community and concludes that not only is the Community not compatible with "regional revolution," but it is "its worst enemy, a sort of super-state which, despite all forms of decentralized administrative and political power, despite a federal or confederal statute, could only aggravate the colonizing factor."[20] This is so because of the capitalist-cartelist structure of the system. Even the federalization of Europe would be inadequate to change this judgment because as the state writ large the Community would still not attack the problem of socioeconomic relationships in European society, but rather would insure their perpetuation. An unfederalized Europe, a Europe of offices lacking political authority and access to a political base, is even less satisfactory for it would be only one step removed from a state technocracy—politically unaccountable, reflective of increased centralization (lacking political authority, it would not challenge state-established political structures), and even less accessible than central authority at the national level. This appears to be the lesson drawn by the Scottish nationalists.[21]

When the motivation for regionalism is fundamentally political (such as devolution of political authority to a regional dimension, increased regional-level participation in decisions affecting the quality of life, and achievement of autonomy in the name of ethnocultural considerations), the case for a mutual reinforcement between subnational regionalism and supranational community is even weaker. When possible, the European Community will eschew political controversy, especially when that controversy has only a marginal relationship to the exercise of the community's mandate. The Community is a creature of its member states: its

19. *Ibid.,* chap. 3.   20. *Ibid.,* p. 238.   21. See Esman, *op. cit.*

viability depends on their continued support; its credibility upon its essential noncontroversiality. Rarely has the commission ventured to beard the lion in its den. When it has, as in the controversy over community resources and the strengthening of the powers of the European Parliament in 1965–66, it has had to give its pound of flesh, but has received nothing in return. Political decentralization at the national level would be of value to the Community only insofar as the dismantling of central authority facilitates the reinforcement of supranational authority. It is difficult to see how this would occur in the case of ethnic regionalism, although it might be more plausible if devolution of political authority were in response to regional economic development. The Community thus suffers a dual deficiency: it is the creature of its constituents, and its institutional structure does not permit it to modify in any significant way the existing center-periphery relations in member states. It has little ability to affect regionalism per se.

Little direct attention has been paid here to the specific problem of ethnic regionalism. In part, this is because the ethnic factor has been subsumed under the socioeconomic and political categories. But it also reflects the low level of interest or concern in Brussels for explicitly ethnic problems. Perhaps the best evidence that can be offered in support of this is the list of macro- socio-economic regions devised by the commission in 1961. At that time one of the nine French regions designated included Pays-de-Loire, Basse-Normandy, and Britanny; another included Franche-Comté, Lorraine, and Alsace. Belgium was treated as a single region.[22] So much for the Bretons, Alsatians, Flemings, and Walloons! Brussels and the ethnic peripheries (and the other peripheries, for that matter) may well agree on the arbitrariness of boundaries and frontiers; there is far less agreement on how those boundaries should be altered.

If in the context of subnational regionalism the increasing remoteness of political man from political authority, of cultural man from control over his life style, or of economic man from social justice is the problem, technocratic Europe is not his salvation; political Europe might be. Are the two levels of regionalism, subnational and supranational, not only not presently mutually reinforcing but also condemned to remain so? It is difficult to give a definitive answer to this question, but several observations can be made which may serve as points of departure for further analysis.

---

22. The commission later amended its listing of regions to reflect the 1970 Belgian constitutional provision for three political regions—*not* the four linguistic regions also defined in the Constitution.

Where socioeconomic values of subnational regionalists are highly congruent with those of the Commission of the European Communities, and where national central authority is indifferent to interaction between these two regional levels, mutual reinforcement may occur. It remains difficult, however, to visualize the conditions in which this congruence would be anchored by ethnic demands, although economic demands that fall within the Community's mandate would appear to be a condition contributary to mutual reinforcement.

Customs unions, such as the EEC, generate economic problems, for example with respect to industrial location, new peripheries for revised economic centers, labor influx and emigration, and regional income differentials. Resolution of these problems, which initially are felt at the domestic level, require achieving balanced and harmonious economic development in the community and may augment domestic pressures for intensified regionalization policies. These pressures may include demands for the devolution of political authority and result in an intensified dialogue between the commission and regional spokesmen or authorities.

Regionalism has become a vogue in the Community states. Partial responses to regional problems, such as administrative deconcentration and the development of regional administrative structures (whether or not they do what they are supposed to do and whether or not they are given the necessary capacity to operate), can convert what started out as mythology and tokenism into a genuine political problem. Regionalism, once politicized (that is, accepted and treated as a relevant political issue by political elites), could lead to basic changes in political structure. In such an event, regional elites could interact more directly with Community technocrats, and each would become more available to the other as a potential supporter for mutually sought political and economic outcomes. With a more independent base for political action, the commission might become more attentive to the demands of regional activists.

There are, in short, persuasive reasons to speculate that the development of the Community may have substantial impact on subnational regionalism. It is quite plausible that economically generated discontent within national regions (whether stimulated by conditions of the Common Market or otherwise) may merge with more frankly political or cultural regional discontent in a drive toward increased local autonomy and the decentralization of political authority within the state; and, that a politically relevant liaison may develop between these subnational movements and community-level institutions.

But there is no certainty either that a systematic and meaningful interdependence of action of this sort will develop or that, having developed,
it will succeed. For against this possible evolution stands the powerful
structural resistance of political elites, the administrative apparatus, and
their client groups whose positions are threatened by change in the formal
political authority relations. The action of these groups may, as in the
past, serve to offset or minimize the potential political-structural consequences of the convergence of subnational and supranational regionalism.
Thus far the history of the European Community reveals the success of
national governments in using the Community for nationally defined purposes and goals and in warding off the devolution of authority to subnational institutions. Certainly this has been true in France where regionalism
is conceived primarily in functional rather than in political or institutional
terms. But even where subnational regionalism has more decentralist or
federalist connotations, as in Belgium or Italy, there is little evidence that
subnational elites have perceived their struggle against central authority
as necessarily compatible with the objectives of supranational actors. In
the end the management of subnational regional demands, including those
that are ethnically based, may be resolved within the framework of the
state with no visible advantage accruing to supranational institutions. The
latter may prefer to maintain their traditional relationships with central
national authorities even at the expense of leaving ultimate control over
the subnational-supranational regional dialogue with the national governments.

II

CASE STUDIES

4

Continuity in Change: Spanish Basque Ethnicity as a Historical Process *

DAVYDD J. GREENWOOD

When Admiral Carrero Blanco, his car, and Generalissimo Franco's plan for an orderly transfer of power were blown to bits on a boulevard in Madrid in 1973, no one was surprised that a Basque terrorist group claimed responsibility. Spanish Basque ethnic militancy and separatism are widely known. Less well known, however, is the diversity of political opinion among the Spanish Basques and the fact that Basque ethnic militancy long antedates the Franco regime. To understand the Basques, a wide range of information must be viewed—one's perspective must include nearly one thousand years of history and a remarkable variety of political regimes. This study examines Spanish Basque ethnic identity in this long-term perspective in search of answers to the questions of how and why the present conflict between the Basques and the Spanish government has come about. Specifically, the origin, development, and alterations of one concept basic to Basque ethnic identity, the concept of "collective nobility," are examined in the context of the changing relations between the Basques and the central government throughout the history of the Spanish state.[1]

The present study represents the findings of an investigation that has only begun. Major revisions will be required as more information is gathered. My own experience with the Spanish political scene is limited

* The research for this essay was undertaken with the support of a Ford Foundation grant for the study of center-periphery relations in Western Europe. Help with the documentary sources was provided by Julio Caro Baroja of the Spanish Royal Academy of History and by Jon Bilbao and William Douglass of the Basque Studies Program of the University of Nevada at Reno. Helpful criticism was provided by Milton J. Esman and by Pilar Fernandez-Cañadas de Greenwood.

1. On the subject of "collective nobility," I have been aided personally by Julio Caro Baroja and by his monumental study of Navarre: *Etnografía histórica de Navarra,* 3 vols. (Pamplona: Editorial Aranzadi, 1971–72).

to contact with Basque farmers and factory workers and to observation of their reactions to the combined impact of tourism and industrialization.[2] The Basque movement is both complex and fragmented, and a greater breadth of experience may be required to properly refine the contemporary implications of the material at hand. But my experience, in contradistinction to that of many observers of the Basque scene, is based on nearly two years of residence with families of Basque farmers and factory workers. What is real and meaningful to them about the Basque movement has escaped the journalists and other commentators who listen to the pronouncements of political groups vying for constituencies. The airy generalities that grace the pages of the *New York Times* or *Le Monde* appear to be generally mistaken. The sources for the historical portrait developed here consist exclusively of legal codes and political tracts. These are hardly adequate, however, for a genuine social history because the views of the large mass of the Basques, who never committed their thoughts to writing, are not included in them. Still they provide a new perspective on the Basque problem.

Four theoretical commitments underpin this study. First, it is inherent in the human condition that history, particularly a people's view of their own history, is an active force in determining present behavior. Second, ethnic identities are forged and altered through interactions within larger institutional systems which establish the bases for cooperation and conflict. Third, ethnic identities are formulated vis-à-vis other ethnic identities that compete with them. That is, an ethnic identity is as much a definition of who you are *not* as it is of who you are. Fourth, once ethnic identities have become sharply defined as a result of experience within particular institutional contexts, the combined force of group solidarity and remembered affronts may make institutional resolution of the conflicts difficult.

A working definition of ethnicity is also in order. Ethnicity is currently a topic of great interest among social scientists, and anthropologists have joined the bandwagon. A spate of recent books provides anthropological treatments of the subject.[3] Stimulating though these may be, they show

2. See Davydd Greenwood, *Unrewarding Wealth: The Commercialization and Collapse of Agriculture in a Spanish Basque Town* (Cambridge: At the University Press, 1976).
3. See, for example, Fredrik Barth, ed., *Ethnic Groups and Boundaries* (Boston: Little, Brown, 1969); Abner Cohen, ed., *Urban Ethnicity* (London: Tavistock, 1974); and George De Vos and Lola Romanucci-Ross, eds., *Ethnic Identity: Cultural Continuities and Change* (Palo Alto: Mayfield, 1975).

the imprecision that accompanies newness, especially with regard to basic definitions. This literature is particularly imprecise about the difference between ethnicity and culture. The word ethnicity is now frequently placed in contexts in which the words culture or subculture were put a few years ago; this is no help because anthropologists define culture very broadly. Culture, to them, is virtually everything that makes humans specifically different from other animals. Needless to say, the current tendency to treat ethnicity as just another word for culture will lead one into a hopeless morass. Thus, a restricted definition of ethnicity is likely to be more helpful than a broad one. In this spirit the following working definition is provided.

Ethnicity is that part of the culture of a group that accounts for its origin and character, thereby differentiating it from other groups within large-scale political units and setting the tone for its relationships with those groups and with the government. It is a useful concept only when applied to groups incorporated into large-scale institutional systems. Thus, the symbols of ethnic identity and the institutional contexts of intergroup relations must be studied together as they develop over time.

The Spanish Basque Country: A Brief Overview

What constitutes the Basque country is a matter of dispute. Ethnic militants argue that it comprises four Spanish provinces (Vizcaya, Guipúzcoa, Alava, and Navarre) and part of the French department, the Pyrénées-Atlantiques. The reason for the ambiguity is that during the last four centuries the Basque language has been spoken less and less in most of Navarre and Alava. The unambiguous core area of the Basque country, then, is Vizcaya, Guipúzcoa, and the mountainous northern zones of Navarre.

This is a relatively small section of the northeast corner of Spain. The four provinces together constitute only 3.5 percent of the area of Spain and as of 1970 contained 7 percent of its population (see Table 4.1). If the non-Basques living in these provinces were discounted, an ethnically Basque area containing between 5 and 6 percent of the population of Spain, or approximately one and a half million people as of 1970, would remain, located on land covering about 1.5 percent of Spain's total surface area.[4]

The core Basque area is largely mountainous. It has a temperate,

4. These figures are guesses because the recent census is not at my disposal and because the number of Basque speakers is such a political issue that most figures cannot be trusted.

Table 4.1. Population, area, and percent of GNP of the Basque provinces in Spain, 1969–70

Province	Population (1970)	% of population of Spain (1970)	% of area of Spain	Inhabitants per km² (1970)	% of GNP (1969)
Guipúzcoa	631,000	1.9	0.4	316	2.7
Vizcaya	1,043,300	3.1	0.4	471	4.1
Navarre	464,900	1.4	2.1	45	1.7
Alava	204,300	0.6	0.6	66	0.9
Total	2,343,500	7.0	3.5	225 *	9.4

Source: Jose Miguel de Azaola, Vasconia y su destino, vol. 1, La regionalización de España (Madrid: Revista de Occidente, 1972), tables between pp. 402 and 403.
* Average.

humid climate, with heavy snowfalls occurring only inland. One of the leading industrial regions of Spain, it has major shipyards, steel mills, and manufacturing centers, and it is an important resort area with a lovely coastline. By discounting Navarre and Alava, one can easily see that the core Basque area is of considerable economic importance. In 1969, Vizcaya and Guipúzcoa (0.8 percent of the area of Spain inhabited by 5 percent of the population) together produced a disproportionately large share of the gross national product (GNP), 6.8 percent (see Table 4.1).

One of the reasons that much attention has been focused on Basque ethnic uniqueness is that the Basque population has actual features that make them quite unusual in Europe. For one thing, they have the highest incidence of the Rh negative blood factor of any population in the world. For another, the Basque language is unrelated to any of the Indo-European languages and indeed to any known language stock in the world. Two hundred years of research have failed to turn up any language related to Basque, which makes the Basques unique among Western and Central European populations.

These characteristics are intriguing. The Rh negative factor suggests possible endogamy among the Basques and is occasionally used to support their claim for cultural autonomy. Linguistic uniqueness lends support to their claim that they are one of the oldest populations in Europe. This claim is generally accepted as fact because the currently reasonable explanation for the uniqueness of the Basque language is that it is the only remaining pre–Indo-European language in Europe, the rest having been wiped out.

Despite their obvious appeal and importance, these characteristics often have a negative effect on research. On the one hand, observers and reporters tend to stress the "mystery" and "enigma" of the Basques. On the other, these features of the Basques mislead many into thinking that Basque ethnic identity is both fixed and unproblematic and that it is simply a fact that is now being given political expression. This sort of approach ignores the historical vicissitudes of Basque ethnic identity and generally vitiates dynamic analysis.

Coincident with the general upsurge of ethnic militancy in Europe, some Spanish Basques have become politically active. Basque bookstores bulge with books on Basque ethnography, folklore, geography, art, music, and literature. Over the last two hundred years the bibliography of Basque materials has grown to over half a million references.

Basque political protests, bombings, assassinations, trials, and dissemination of propaganda are widely known and have even been subjected to novelistic treatment in English. The actions of the separatists in particular are often reported in the French- and English-language press and are generally given favorable treatment because of the strength of antifascist sentiment in Europe and in the United States. The Basque protest is compared to the Breton and Irish situations and is considered to be one of the classic cases of ethnic militancy.

Much of the reporting overlooks the considerable internal division among Basques over the desired political solution to their problem. There are at least five distinct views among the Basques that are compatible with a sense of Basque ethnic identity. The first consists of a desire for a high degree of provincial autonomy (in government and in administration of the civil code) within a federated state of semiautonomous provinces. This view is here referred to as *foralism* because the provincial form of government and the civil code desired by Basques holding this view are the same as the government and civil code existing in the Basque area until the late nineteenth century under the name *fueros* (local rights ratified by the central government). The foralists themselves consist of strange bedfellows, among them Carlists, who call for the return to the traditional monarchy under the heir of King Carlos, as well as antimonarchical republicans.

Those who hold the second point of view call for the withering away of the current European nation-states and the creation of a European community made up of true ethnic groups. Some of those who believe in this utopian solution look to the present European Economic Community with hope; others demand a total restructuring of European society. A third position is separatism. Supporters of this approach demand the unification of the Spanish Basque provinces and the French Basque department in a single, independent nation. The separatists have garnered the lion's share of the attention devoted to the Basque cause.

A great many Basques are united in a fourth view that is characterized by agnosticism and cynicism about the possibility of any political solution to their problems. This cynical view of the futility of the political process is the result of centuries of negative political experience.

Finally, there is a fifth important segment of the population that more or less favors the existing regime. Intolerance of fascism should not cause one to overlook this substantial body of opinion.

Any attempt to weigh the relative proportions of the Basque population favoring these various views is doomed to fail for lack of evidence, and to attempt to gather such evidence under current conditions would be a fool's errand. In my opinion, however, the agnostics dominate, followed closely by the sympathizers of the current regime; all the rest together bring up the rear. The reasons for believing that the cynics predominate will become clear as the history of the Basque area is presented.

The Spanish Basque Concept of "Collective Nobility"

An understanding of the concept of collective nobility is essential to an understanding of Basque history, since collective nobility was the moral core of the Basque sense of ethnic uniqueness, and since it was once the prime point of contention between the Basques and successive Spanish regimes in the endless negotiations over provincial autonomy and rights. The phenomenon of collective nobility seems to have few parallels elsewhere in Europe, a fact that distinguishes the Basques from other ethnic groups in conflict with central governments.

Collective nobility is a direct translation of the Spanish *hidalguía colectiva*. It refers to the fact that any Basque able to prove birth of Basque parents in Vizcaya, Guipúzcoa, or in certain valleys of Navarre and Alava was automatically recognized as noble by virtue of purity of blood. In a country that had been dominated by the Moors for seven centuries and that went to the extreme of expelling the Jews and subjecting an important part of its citizenry to inquisitorial trials for heresy, this automatic grant of nobility takes on great significance.

In the rest of Spain purity of blood (*limpieza de sangre*) had to be demonstrated by a meticulous process of genealogical investigation. This almost automatically made nobility a monopoly of the wealthy and literate classes, for the lower classes often lacked either the requisite documentation or the wealth needed to prove their claims to nobility. On the basis of proofs of nobility, people were eligible to hold high secular and religious offices. Thus, nobility was an important rung in the ladder of social ascent.

But among the Basques, to be born in the Basque country automatically conferred the right of nobility on them collectively, and this right was recognized by a long line of Spanish monarchs. Thus, a butcher, shoemaker, charcoal burner, scribe, or soldier—rich or poor—was noble. Of course, this did not mean that all exercised the prerogatives of the wealthy, for nobility without wealth did not lead directly to social ascent. Nonetheless this was an extremely unusual situation in such a nobility-conscious society.

Collective nobility was frequently cited by the Basques in support of their claims to unique status within the Spanish state. The codifications of customary law (fueros), by which the provinces ruled themselves and to which the Spanish monarchs swore allegiance, all contained long disquisitions on the subject. Whenever conflicts between the Basques and the government arose, collective nobility was sure to be mentioned and used as a claim in support of Basque legal and fiscal autonomy.

Because of its central importance to the Basque identity, collective nobility was an oft treated subject in Basque writings during the period from 1053, when a grant of collective nobility was first made to a Navarrese mountain valley (the Roncal), to the nineteenth century, when collective nobility ceased to be an important social force. As a result, one can examine the various elaborations and reinterpretations made of it and relate these to the development of the relationships between the Basques and the rest of Spain. One can also argue that vestiges of the concept of collective nobility presently manifest themselves in the equalitarian and democratic tone of Basque society.[5]

5. Most of the information that follows would apply to all of Guipúzcoa and Vizcaya and to a number of valleys of Alava and Navarre, but the documentation with which I am most familiar is that of Guipúzcoa. Thus, I am seeing the Basque problem largely through Guipuzcoan eyes. Similar studies will have to be done for Vizcaya and Alava, while for Navarre there is Caro Baroja's *Etnografia* to draw on.

European Ideas about Nobility and the Special Character of Collective Nobility

Though the Basques themselves argued, for reasons that will become clear later, that collective nobility dated from time immemorial and represented a continuation of the undefiled state of man, it is fundamentally important to recognize that Basque ideas about collective nobility were special developments of basic European concepts of nobility. They represented not independent inventions but special elaborations of very widespread ideas. This is important because it shows that Basque ethnic uniqueness is not an autonomous development, but a particular development from, and integration of, very widely used ideas. It also provides background for a more exact understanding of the peculiarly Basque flavor these ideas came to have. A proper disquisition on the concept of nobility in medieval Europe is not possible here, but a brief summary of Basque jurists' and writers' views of the subject will suffice.

Perhaps the most important single codification of Iberian ideas and laws is the famous *Código de las Siete Partidas* commissioned by King Alfonso el Sabio. It was begun in 1251 and finished around 1265. The seven books cover virtually all aspects of life during that period, describing practices then current, elaborating definitions, and setting norms for conduct. They were the basis for most legal definitions of the estates of society and their obligations.[6] In the second book the obligations of emperors, kings, and other great men are recorded. Title XXI deals with nobles. Society is described as composed of three estates: the clergy, the military, and the laborers. The military had to have the attributes of honor and humility and were called *fijosdalgo,* from which *hidalgo,* one of the two major Spanish terms for nobleman, was derived. The hidalgo is described as a man of honor, good customs, and manners, who can prove unstained descent from his father's father's father and so on, following the male line only. What is most interesting about the description of hidalgo is that it pertains entirely to military nobility. The concept of nobility was totally entwined with that of military protection of the kingdom and its subjects. The right to bear arms and the duty to serve the crown, in return for freedom from taxation and imprisonment, were part of the concept of nobility current at that time.

Subsequent to the *Siete Partidas,* there were many treatises that further

---

6. See *Código de las Siete Partidas,* vol. 1 (which contains the first and second books), in *Los códigos españoles* (Madrid: M. Rivadeneyra, 1848).

refined the concept of nobility. One of these was so influential that elements of it are found incorporated in the corpus of Basque customary law itself. This is *Discursos de la nobleza de España,* written in 1636 by Bernabé Moreno de Vargas.[7] Moreno de Vargas's discussion of nobility, however, stemmed directly from the ideas of a famous Italian jurist Bártulo de Sasso-Ferrato (1313–57).[8] Thus, Basque compilers who adopted Moreno de Vargas's ideas were actually using ideas taken from the Italian Bártulo. Whatever was Basque about these ideas, it was certainly not their origin.

Perhaps the most interesting aspect of Moreno de Vargas's treatment is his strong emphasis on the notion that all nobility was conceded to men by princes. This emphasis demonstrates a need to justify the ongoing process of political centralization by pointing to the monarch as the source of all justice and rewards. The Basques later contested this point.

Moreno de Vargas viewed the royal concession of nobility to men of proven worth as an act that returned them to the state of purity in which men lived at the beginning of the world before sin had stained human nature. Thus, he equated nobility with purity of blood and moral rectitude, and he based the hierarchy of society on a hierarchy of moral worth. This aspect of his argument was subsequently taken up by Basques, who argued that their moral purity was never stained and that thus no king could have conceded them nobility.

Moreno de Vargas also explicitly dealt with the collective nobility of the Basques. He argued that it was conceded by kings and princes because of the virtue and valor of the Basques and because of the services they rendered. He made special reference to their long occupation of the area they inhabit and to their many acts of military service to the crown. He wrote that by proving birth in the Basque country and native Basque ancestry in unbroken descent in the male line, Basques were declared *hidalgos de sangre* (noble by virtue of purity of blood). His statement is accurate since by 1636 many monarchs had already recognized in writing Basque collective nobility. He explicitly pointed out that Basques were noble only by virtue of cleanliness of blood and not by virtue of wealth or other sorts of preeminence.

He then went on to describe eighteen privileges that pertained solely to nobles, including freedom from embargo of property or imprisonment for

7. Bernabé Moreno de Vargas, *Discursos de la nobleza de España* (reprint ed., Madrid: Imprenta de Don Antonio Espinosa, 1636).
8. It was with Julio Caro Baroja's help that I discovered this fact.

debt and freedom from taxation except for significant public works in the common good. He also stressed the obligation of nobles to defend the land. Each one of these privileges eventually became a source of dispute between the Basques and the crown. Freedom from conscription and freedom from taxation have been the most hotly debated.

Going beyond Moreno de Vargas's tract, and others like it, it is necessary to point out that nobility was an extremely valuable acquisition for any citizen, even though it could not make him powerful if unaccompanied by personal wealth. For example, to enter the military orders—a dominant political, military, and economic force in Spain—one had to be a hidalgo de sangre. Extensive investigations were carried out when anyone applied for entrance to such orders; they were designed to test people's claims of purity of blood as well as the sufficiency of their personal wealth. The crown expended huge sums on these investigations, giving some idea of their importance as gatekeeping mechanisms in the competition for status and power. That the Basques collectively, by virtue of mere birth in a particular place, should obtain this coveted status is an anomaly that requires explanation.

The Initial Grants of Collective Nobility to the Basques in Historical Context: The Fifteenth and Sixteenth Centuries

Why were such far-reaching grants of nobility made to the Basques, and why were they made collectively rather than individually, especially since it was fairly clear that this collective conferral of nobility would give the Basques an opportunity to argue that they were exempt from taxation and conscription and that they were free to bear arms and even to make their own international trade treaties? The grants of collective nobility may be explained by two circumstances: the pattern of the Moorish domination of Spain, and the defense problems of the Spanish crown regarding the French border after the Reconquest.

One effect of seven centuries of Moorish domination in most of Spain was to make claims to purity of blood impossible to sustain without elaborate genealogical proof. As has already been noted, this made nobility an upper-class monopoly. But the Moors never entered the Basque country. The Basques, along with the Asturians, distinguished themselves as defenders of the last outposts of Christian Spain and as initiators of the Reconquest. Because the ideological support for nobility in the rest of Spain after the Reconquest was based on the notion that all who could not prove their cleanliness of blood were likely to have been contaminated by

Moorish influence, the Guipuzcoans were able to use the history of their province to support their contention that the entire population of the province was free of this mixture and thus free of heretical influence.[9] They made a similar argument regarding Jewish influence; although this argument was weak in comparison, it too was accepted by the Spanish crown.[10]

The second element that helps explain the grant of collective nobility is the border defense problem of the crown. Spain was first centralized as a state by the Catholic Kings in the fifteenth century. The Catholic Kings had very little coercive power at their disposal. They centralized control of the peninsula by a combination of dynastic marriage and personal charismatic leadership, reinforced by constant travels throughout the realm. They united the exceedingly diverse regions of the peninsula into a state in which a very high degree of regional autonomy was tolerated. In return for their support, the Kings permitted the regions to continue their customary practices. The Kings thus recognized Basque claims to collective nobility as a matter of military policy.

One of the earliest acts of Ferdinand and Isabella, the Catholic Kings, was to order the systematic strengthening of Spain's border defenses and major citadels. France constantly threatened to, and sometimes did, attack the northeast corner of Spain. The Basque country is mountainous, but near the coast the mountains are easily crossed, and further inland, there are a number of major corridors through which armies could pass easily. If the northeast mountains should be taken, the whole Ebro Valley and the rest of the peninsula would become fair game. Thus, a successful northeast border policy was a vital element in the survival of the Spnaish state.

Excepting the concessions to the Roncal Valley and the Lana Valley, the grants listed in Table 4.2 coincide with the first major thrust of Spanish centralization, a temporal relationship that is hardly accidental. Taken in the geographical context of Spain as a whole, these grants were all made in the vulnerable northeast corner of the peninsula. In return for the grants, the people swore to personally defend their area without recompense. By so doing, they served as the border garrisons of the Spanish state. When attacks were particularly severe, their resistance gave the

---

9. This interpretation needs considerable development.

10. See *Nueva recopilación de los fueros, privilegios, buenos usos y costumbres, leyes y órdenes de la M.N. y M.L.: Provincia de Guipúzcoa* (1697; reprint ed., San Sebastián: Imprenta de la Provincia, Diputación de Guipúzcoa, 1919).

time needed to bring the state's army into position, first to protect the Ebro Valley, and then to push the invaders out of the peninsula.

The political centralization of Spain around the Castilian meseta had thus created an immediate problem of vulnerability to border attack and increased the French motivation to step up their incursions. Unable to afford massive border defenses, the Catholic Kings and their successors were able to use grants of collective nobility to insure themselves a degree of border control. At the time, these grants cost only the amount of taxes that were foregone and the loss of a few conscripts. Later the cost rose considerably.

Table 4.2. Dates and locations of grants of collective nobility

Place	Date	Place	Date
Roncal	1053	Munarriz	1457
Lana	1271	Guipúzcoa	1491
Lumbier	1391	Betelu	1507
Aoiz	1424	Errazquin	1507
Larraún	1429	Inza	1507
Baztan	1440	Miranda de Arga	1512
Bertiz	1449	Salazar	1566
Iribas y Allí	1455		

Source: All place names except Guipúzcoa are from Navarre (grants in Vizcaya and Alava are not included here). The Navarrese dates and locations are taken from Caro Baroja, *Etnografía* 2: 55–56.

What then of the question of ethnic identity during this period? The Basque sense of ethnic uniqueness and their acceptance of the idea that they were Spanish were at the time easily compatible. But the seeds of future conflict had been sown.

One of the most famous tracts of the time, published in 1564, was Bachiller Juan Martínez de Zaldibia's *Suma de las cosas cantábricas y guipuzcoanas*.[11] Zaldibia was a compiler of Basque customary law, a fact important in itself. Though the Spanish monarchs had sworn to uphold the local and provincial rights (fueros) of the Basques, it soon became obvious that when disputes regarding those rights arose, unwritten customary law was a poor basis for defending them. When disputes broke out over taxation and military conscription, the Basques began to write down their laws and to collect and compile all correspondence with, and grants

11. Bachiller Juan Martínez de Zaldibia, *Suma de las cosas cantábricas y guipuzcoanas* (1564; reprint ed., San Sebastián: Excma, Diputación de Guipúzcoa, 1945).

made by, the Spanish monarchs. This developing body of documented customary law took the form of many different compilations, nearly all of which were incomplete. The Basques saw that they had to complete this documentation as much as possible and be sure that the monarchs swore to uphold not merely collective nobility, but the full range of customary (foral) rights they claimed. Thus the compilation of customary law took place as part of the politics of regional autonomy. The compilations are important documents in the history of Basque ethnicity.

Zaldibia had a broad experience of this process and realized that a coherent interpretation of the history of Guipúzcoa, which was his home, had to be written to support the Basque claims there. His *Suma* is just that. It contains chapters covering the following: a description of Guipúzcoa; the first inhabitants of the north coast; the origin of the Basque language; ancient toponyms; the economy of the area; a history of the great military exploits of the Basques; a thumbnail social history of the Basques; and a long section on collective nobility and privileges, and royal oaths to uphold them.

One point in Zaldibia's *Suma* must be related to what was said earlier about the *Siete Partidas* and Moreno de Vargas's tract. Zaldibia argued that the Basques had always been noble by virtue of their unique history. He combined the book of Genesis and a history of the Reconquest to prove the priority of Basque nobility over the existence of all governments. He thus repudiated the claim made by the crown and its supporters that all nobility was conceded by kings. From his point of view, the monarchs only recognized the nobility of the Basques; they did not confer it. By the same logic, what they did not confer, they could not take away. This argument became one of the cornerstones of the Basque defense of their rights. The date of the *Suma* indicates the rapidity with which the tension between the centralizing designs of the monarchy and the attempts to retain regional autonomy developed.

A second significant element in the *Suma* is Zaldibia's feeling that a perfect compatibility existed between being Basque and being Spanish. Zaldibia's notion was that the Basques were not only Spaniards but were the best Spaniards of all. They were pure in blood, strong in arms, and steadfast in the defense of the faith. By virtue of this, they could claim to be the highest representation of what it meant to be Spanish. Thus there was no conflict at this time between being Basque and being Spanish; in fact the best way to be truly Spanish was to be Basque. Later, such a notion became utterly unthinkable.

Government by Regional Customary Law (Foralism): The Seventeenth and Eighteenth Centuries

During the seventeenth and eighteenth centuries, the system of foral government based on the interplay of royal power and provincial rights became fully developed. Definitive compilations of provincial rights were made. Provincial governments were set up in accordance with these and were recognized as the legitimate representatives of the people. These provincial governments were called *diputaciones forales,* calling attention to their basis in recognized customary rights.

In Guipúzcoa the diputación foral was made up of elected representatives of the municipalities who met in provincial juntas to make policy, to settle disputes, and to plan public works. But perhaps the most important function of the diputación foral was to watch over and negotiate the ever more complex relationships with the crown and its representatives. The Guipuzcoans were extremely jealous of their rights and made sure that the province never complied with illegal requests, even though such requests were often made.

The documentation of these activities shows a complexity of negotiation and diplomacy in which the crown clearly wanted to achieve greater legal and fiscal regularization in the whole country, and the provinces continually fought to uphold their rights, using the compiled documents as proof of the precedents. There was continual conflict between the crown and the provinces. But significantly, each succeeding monarch swore to uphold and honor the customary rights of the Basques, a sign of the strength of the Basque position.

One of the influential tracts of the time was Baltazar de Echave's *Discursos de la antigüedad de la lengua cántabra bascongada,* written in 1607.[12] In allegorical fashion, Echave portrayed the Basque country as a mother speaking to her children. Though ostensibly about the history of the Basque language, Echave's tract contains many of the arguments of Zaldibia. Echave made perhaps the clearest statement of all regarding the degree to which the Basque and Spanish identities were felt to be compatible and mutually reinforcing, and he insisted on the historical priority of Basque nobility and fueros over the existence of kings.

One element in Echave that was new was an undertone of fear that

---

12. Baltazar de Echave, *Discursos de la antigüedad de la lengua cántabra bascongada* (Mexico City: Emprenta de Henrrico Martínez, 1607; facsimile ed., Bilbao: La Gran Enciclopedia Vasca, 1971).

because of the continual conflicts between the crown and the Basques, the Basque country might be abandoned to France. This curious idea needs to be investigated, but it conveys the sense of unease to which the continual conflicts between the Basques and the crown had given rise.

Perhaps the most remarkable document of the seventeenth and eighteenth centuries is the final compilation of Guipuzcoan customary law published by the diputación foral in 1697.[13] Written under the continuing pressure of the crown, which was eroding the rights of Guipúzcoa, it has been justly criticized for failing to document many important rights that the Guipuzcoans had long held. The crown swore to uphold only the rights noted in the compilation—no others. Thus it became the total legal foundation for all future relations with the crown.

The reader of the compilation is likely to be impressed by its scope. The reprinted edition contains over 645 pages, 41 titles, and 358 chapters, and the topical coverage is amazingly broad. It is at once a history, geography, ethnography, and civil and criminal code; it includes all of the oaths sworn to by Spanish kings, and it contains a great deal of correspondence relevant to the subjects it addresses. In it the views of Moreno de Vargas, Zaldibia, Echave, and many others are brought together in a comprehensive charter for Basque rights throughout Basque history.

On the subject of Basque nobility, it states that "nobility of blood . . . [is] inherited from the first fathers of mankind; although there are authors who assert with some basis that all nobility originated in grants from kings and other princes, this general proposition does not fit the true origin of Guipuzcoan nobility which . . . is general and uniform in all Guipuzcoans."[14] In swearing to uphold the rights represented in this document, the crown gave credence to this interpretation of Basque history.

There is no question that Guipuzcoan rights were extremely bothersome to the crown. Why then did it swear to uphold them? For one thing, the military importance of the Basque country had not waned. A number of invasion attempts marked this period, including major sieges on Basque citadels. In addition, the Basque shipbuilding industry had be-

13. *Nueva recopilación de los fueros.*
14. *Ibid.*, p. 18. The translation is mine. The original reads: "hidalguía de sangre . . . heredado de los primeros padres del género humano; pues aunque hay autores que con algunos fundamentos asientan que todas las hidalguías tuvieron principio en !a concessión de los Reyes y Señores naturales, no adapta bien esta proposición universal, al verdadero origen de la Nobleza Guipuzcoana, que . . . es general y uniforme en todos los descendientes de sus solares."

come a fundamental element in the Spanish European and colonial policies. Thus, the continuing military importance of the Basques quite likely
left the crown little choice. To abrogate these rights might have resulted
in the incorporation of the area into France, the breakdown of the defenses of the Ebro Valley, and the loss of the shipbuilding and ironwork-
ing industries on which the crown relied.

The Basque freedom from taxation and conscription was a continual
thorn in the side of the monarchy. It is not that taxes were never paid and
conscripts never gotten, but that the crown was forced to *request* them.
Its requests were granted in Guipúzcoa only by a favorable vote of the
diputación foral. Reference to Guipuzcoan rights frequently served as the
rationale or denial. Other provinces of Spain, which did not have these
rights, pressed the crown either to give similar rights to all or to abrogate
the Basque rights. The monarchy, however, was still an untidy confederation of provinces, many of which had special rights that they also defended. An abrogation of the Basque rights might well have broken the
back of the monarchy and occasioned its subdivision into a number of
smaller states.

In cultural terms, the continual debates and their hostile tone caused
the Basque ethnic identity to be ever more sharply defined. The Basque
tracts document differences between Basques and other Spaniards because so many of the writers were concerned with lending support to their
claims for provincial rights. Undoubtedly the crown came to be viewed
with considerable suspicion, and its activities were zealously watched.
Still, on the whole, the Basques retained a strong Spanish identity and
maintained their belief that they were the finest Spaniards of all. But the
issues of provincial rights and of Basque ethnic identity by this time had
become one. All acts of political centralization henceforth met with both
legal and moral resistance.

Centralization and the End of Customary Rights: The Eighteenth and Nineteenth Centuries

The military situation and the balance of power within the Spanish state
eventually began to undergo alterations that ultimately did away with
provincial rights. The monarchy's power grew ever greater as did its
desire for a completely uniform system of government within its borders.
The Basques began to lose ground. Soon the centralizing ideas that led to
the French Revolution swept across Spain.

The literature and documents of this long period show the Basques adopting a more defensive position with relation to their rights. The secure and even arrogant tone of the negotiations with the crown during the earlier period yielded to a more plaintive voice that resorted to moral rather than legal argument. But the complexity of dealings with the crown did not diminish; every single royal request was still processed through the diputaciones forales and was still subject to rejection, though the tone of the crown's arguments became much more strident. Tension was great and the Basques began to consider themselves an embattled ethnic minority.

Perhaps the most revealing tract written during the early part of this period was not published until much later, but the thoughts of its author gained considerable currency during his time. This is Padre Manuel de Larramendi's *Corografía de Guipúzcoa*.[15] The tone of Larramendi's tract, mirrored in many of his writings published at the time, is totally different from that previously encountered. It is sardonic and virulent, but above all the tract abandons many of the traditional arguments about Basque nobility in favor of a new rendering of this concept. Larramendi's alteration of the emphasis on nobility has since been incorporated into most Basque histories.

The importance of nobility was beginning to wane in Spanish society at the time Larramendi wrote his tract; the acquisition of high social standing and political power on the basis of wealth alone had become possible. But because collective nobility was such a fundamental element in the Basque identity, it did not disappear. Previously the claims of collective nobility centered on the notions of the purity of blood and the military virtue of the Basques. Now the emphasis began to shift to the *collective* aspect. Larramendi (as did many who came after him) argued that collective nobility implied that all men, regardless of social station, are equal. In support of his argument, he described Basque forms of local and provincial government, and pointed to the elected representatives who voted democratically. Thus, he began the process of revising Basque history to emphasize the uniquely "democratic" qualities. Equality and representative government were thereafter used to contrast the Basques with other Spaniards.

His prose vituperative, Larramendi argued that the Basques as good Christians recognized the fundamental equality of all men while the other

15. Padre Manuel de Larramendi, *Corografía de Guipúzcoa* (San Sebastián: Sociedad Guipuzcoana de Ediciones y Publicaciones, 1969; originally written in 1754).

Spaniards were continually building invidious distinctions between men. He developed extremely virulent ethnic slurs against the Castilians, singling them out as the worst of all Spaniards. His view of Basque superiority was founded on a reinterpretation of Basque history made to fit the declining importance of nobility and the rise of democratic philosophies of government. Larramendi viewed Spanishness and Basqueness as mutually exclusive and conflicting. Subsequent to Larramendi, and especially in the nineteenth century, a large number of tracts was written arguing various sides of this issue. Without exploring these in detail here, it seems fair to say that Basque sentiment had quite definitely been split between the moderate Zaldibia-Echave view and the more extreme Larramendi position.

Perhaps the most important change in the relationship between the Basque country and the rest of Spain, aside from the ideological ferment created by the French Revolution, was the declining military importance of the Basque area. The increased mobility of military manpower and the crown's establishment of permanent garrisons reduced the need for, and importance of, an armed civil population. As this military importance declined, the Basques found it more and more difficult to press their claims.

The fall of the Old Regime in Spain, the Carlist wars, the First Republic, and the Restoration all point to great ferment and internal division during the nineteenth century. One theme ran through the whole period: the definitive legal and political centralization of the state. Whether the proponents were those of the Old Regime, of the republic, or of the Restoration monarchy, they insisted that liberty and fraternity were only to be had in return for equality under uniform law and administration. So Guipuzcoan rights were suppressed in 1878. The system of provincial government and taxation was definitively reorganized to conform to the national model. The crown finally managed to have taxes and conscription shared equally among all Spaniards, and it refused to recognize different provincial rights on the basis of historical privileges. The republic, too, appears to have favored uniform though representative government. Since, as has been stated previously, provincial rights were intimately tied up with ethnic identity, the suppression of provincial rights set the stage for contemporary ethnic conflict.

The Contemporary Period [16]

That a people so conscious of their history should draw lessons from it is not surprising. The lessons the Basques have drawn from theirs seem fairly clear. Having lived through a sort of confederative monarchy, followed by an absolutist monarchy, then by a highly centralist republic, and finally by a restored constitutional monarchy, many Basques came to the conclusion that, regardless of the outward form of central governmental organization, the pressure for centralization and administrative uniformity was similar. Monarchy or republic, the attitude toward Basque rights seemed negative.

Conflicts over administrative centralization became ethnic conflicts as well. Royal oaths to uphold the Basque rights had signified to the Basques royal agreement with their definition of themselves. Rejection of these rights constituted more than a mere alteration in forms of administration; it meant, from the Basque point of view, a rejection of their claims to cultural dignity.

Basque reactions to this situation were diverse. The Carlists called for the re-creation of a traditional monarchy that would respect the rights of the provinces. Some—particularly those who had their eyes trained on Ireland and Hungary—dreamed of the creation of a Basque state and considered such a creation the only way to affirm their ethnic dignity and maintain their historic rights. Still others decided that all political solutions were impossible—no matter what the form of government, life would be no better for them. Finally others, perhaps a majority, accepted the central government's contention that the issue of provincial rights was separate from the question of being Basque, and hoped that they could continue to be Basque even without their traditional privileges.

Although the dominant tendency now is to distinguish the contemporary period from the past, the basic continuity of the Basque problem cannot be ignored. The Restoration ended in 1923 and was followed by Primo de Rivera's dictatorship, which lasted until 1931. Then the Second Republic came and went, and the civil war followed, after which Franco ruled until his death in 1975. None of these events fundamentally altered the relationships established in the nineteenth century.

During the Restoration, some Basques began to regroup culturally: ethnic symbols developed and were elaborated upon, scholarly research into

16. The best English-language analysis of this period is Stanley Payne, *Basque Nationalism* (Reno: University of Nevada Press, 1975).

Basque history flourished, and Basque festivals were regularly held to whip up ethnic sentiment. This florescence of interest provided a base on which many Basque intellectuals began to develop plans for a return to the regime of provincial rights.

Some of these intellectuals—among them Sabino Arana, founder of the Basque nationalist movement—watched the Irish and Magyar situations with interest and tried to draw lessons from them. They thought that the Basques, rather than trying to return directly to a regime based on traditional rights, could organize politically and press their claims in the new institutional context that had developed. Others developed differing programs covering the broad spectrum of approaches outlined at the beginning of this essay. The power of these various combinations of ethnic symbolism and political pressure engendered great fear in the central government, which was reeling from the loss of the colonies and from its passage from monarchy to dictatorship to republic. The instability of the government motivated many groups to strengthen their positions, and soon Spain dissolved into a hopeless civil war.

Still, in viewing the Spanish civil war, it is well to remember that, while the Basque nationalists fielded a small army, the majority of the Basques served the national government as conscripts. The Basque army itself was crushed, and the bombing of Guernica ushered in an era of unparalleled ethnic repression.

The bombing of Guernica was an act of savagery, for this market town was of little military moment. On the day of the bombing, in fact, it was filled with civilians. But Guernica was the location of the great hall in which the representatives of Vizcayan customary government had met, near a great oak tree, to carry out foral administration. In bombing the town, Franco's forces frontally attacked one of the most venerated symbols of Basque rights and ethnic identity.

After the war, the Basques, and particularly the Guipuzcoans, were singled out for blame. The national propaganda machine produced immense amounts of anti-Basque propaganda, which was widely circulated in Spain. Whenever terrorism occurred, the provincial newspapers cited it as further proof of the Basques' lack of respect for law and order. Many Basques remember being clubbed for speaking Basque on the streets in the years following the war, and Basque school children, often monolingual at the age of five, were punished for their poor Spanish.

Lessons from the Basque Case

The long-term historical experience of governmental institutions is an extremely important dimension in the genesis of the continuities in ethnic conflict in Spain. Over the centuries, the Basques have come to the conclusion that all forms of government—monarchies, republics, constitutional monarchies, dictatorships, and fascist states—consistently move against regional autonomy in favor of national centralization and administrative homogenization. Some have appeared more ideologically sympathetic to subnational identities, but in the end all have pressed for centralization and uniformity. The documented history of five hundred years of Basque political experience has led a great many contemporary Basques to conclude not only that all forms of government are equally bad but that politicians exist only to enrich themselves at the expense of others and even that many Basque movements that agitate for regional reform are not to be trusted.

The Basque case shows that ethnic identity and national government are inextricably fused. Basque ethnicity has always been politicized. In fact, it can be argued that the Basque ethnic identity is a product of the history of Basque interactions with the central government. The Basque identity originated in the concept of collective nobility, which summarized a set of political rights given to the Basques by the early monarchies in Spain in return for services. These rights were justified in terms of the special history of the Basques and were chartered with reference to the book of Genesis. Thus what originated as grants soon became the cornerstone of an ethnic identity that was held to predate all grants.

This fusion of provincial rights and Basque identity was developed further by tracts and by the continual oaths sworn by the monarchs. These oaths were taken not only to validate the specific rights of Basques but also to validate their sense of ethnic identity. As a result, when attempts were made administratively to centralize the Spanish state, they generated not only political conflict over specific rights but virulent ethnic reaction, which soon escalated to the extent that virtually all compromises with the central government were impossible. Once this escalation began, it soon became independent of the particular administrative problems that set it off; thus, it in itself became a problem.

This phenomenon is important for two reasons. First, it shows that ethnicity is highly malleable and responsive to the circumstances in which groups find themselves. Though this is not surprising, it needs to be stressed because of the common-sense notion that ethnicity is a sort of fixed attribute of a group of people. The form that Basque ethnic identity has taken and the justifications given for it alter greatly throughout the history of Spain.

Second, Basque ethnic identity has not altered randomly. It began in a specific historical context, and it altered in response to equally specific contexts and events. Its core symbol, collective nobility, was developed and elaborated and modified continually. But whether it is seen as cleanliness of blood or as equalitarianism and democracy, a basic symbolic consistency is maintained throughout. These changing versions of Basque ethnicity provided some of the major values by which eighteen generations of Basques lived their lives and in terms of which the Basques will have to construct their future. The naive hope that Basque ethnicity can be "depoliticized" is based on a misunderstanding of both Basque ethnicity and Spanish history. The genesis of Basque ethnicity is found in national political institutions and processes. The thorny problems of ethnic militancy and political reorganization in Spain will have to be faced together, for they are inseparable aspects of the same historical process.

5

Splitting the Difference: Federalization without Federalism in Belgium *

ARISTIDE R. ZOLBERG

Mirage or F-16? In Belgium, as in other European countries seeking to update their air defenses, this debate, which began in 1974, involved not only purely technological and financial considerations, but also the more general orientation of defense and foreign policy, the future of NATO, the future of Europe, the future of the local aviation industry, and unemployment. On 6 April 1975, the chairman of the Defense Committee of the Chamber, a French-speaking Socialist representative from Brussels, advocated the Mirage: "In our European capacity, we must buy the Mirage, which is not merely a French plane, since the aeronautical industries of several European countries, among them Belgium, participate in its construction. To buy American is not to construct Europe." [1] Speaking as a member of the Socialist party, "resting in opposition" after a long period of governmental responsibility, he was registering dissent against a coalition government headed by a Social Christian (Catholic) reportedly tilting toward the F-16. Although his remarks naturally evoked negative reactions among government supporters, it was among Dutch speakers that the reactions were sharpest. The leading newspaper of Ant-

* As this essay is based in part on earlier work, I am grateful to several institutions, whose support made my study of Belgium possible over the years: Social Science Research Council (1967–68); Committee for the Comparative Study of New Nations and Social Science Divisional Research, University of Chicago (1971, 1973–75); Institute for Advanced Study, Princeton (1972–73). Val Lorwin generously shared his extraordinary knowledge of Belgian politics and made numerous corrective suggestions of an earlier draft. Vera L. Zolberg read and listened to every paragraph many times over until each one met her standard of sociological clarity.

1. This and subsequent remarks were quoted in Le Monde, 8 April 1975. A full account of the airplane affair, at the end of which Belgium adopted the F-16, is contained in Courrier Hebdomadaire, no. 690 (Brussels: CRISP, 4 July 1975). The account suggests that Walloons in the government eventually accepted the American-Flemish F-16 in exchange for compensations in other spheres.

werp stated that the Brussels representative's remarks were misleading because "he is wrongly identifying France with Europe." Another Dutch-language newspaper editorialized that he was no longer qualified to chair the Defense Committee and added: "We'll end up taking the Mirage for the Walloons and the American F-16 for the Flemings. That would be consistent with the Belgian habit of splitting the difference."

This incident illustrates the extent to which Belgium's linguistic segmentation is part of the rational calculation of everyday political life, whether the matter under consideration pertains originally to the realm of culture or not. The wisecrack indicates how this is done. Belgian politicians have a propensity for identifying almost any choice as favoring one or the other of the two major communities; once an object is defined as valuable by one side, its opposite becomes valuable to the other, so that an American plane becomes "Flemish" because it is other-than-French. But the wisecrack also suggests that politicians do not view their game as terribly risky because a solution will usually be found. While accusing one another of jeopardizing the very survival of the country and of fueling the fires of communal hatred, Belgian politicians know that ever since communal issues once again moved to the fore at the beginning of the 1960's, the population at large has maintained a relatively low interest in such matters. As the Belgian fire is fueled mostly from within the political class rather than by inexorable forces without, it smolders on without conflagration. The politicians are both firebugs and firemen. It is indeed true that they are often able to transform issues considered in other countries to involve "either/or" choices, and hence "all or nothing" from the point of view of the antagonists, into issues that can be resolved by allocating to the contending parties shares proportional to their bargaining power.

Such considerations, evoked by an incident Belgians would consider typical, provide the starting point for an overall answer to the question: what is Belgium a case of today? Reading a configuration as one does a text, I shall argue that the interpretation presented here is more compatible with the details of political trends and events, as well as with contextual economic, social, and cultural factors, than are alternative ones. Because the character of the linguistic segmentation has changed in the course of Belgium's existence as a distinct and sovereign political unit, and its impact on political life has varied as well, a brief review of Belgium as a set of earlier cases will be presented in order to delineate more sharply what it is *not* a case of today.

Does contemporary Belgium illustrate how and why latent and dormant ethnic identities and solidarities become politicized, and hence does it belong in a category of political systems considered pathological by political scientists because they involve deep cleavages and unreconcilable subcultures? Or does it rather demonstrate how well-established, clearly defined cultural groups, whose members possess mutually exclusive identities, but also common ones, have sought in recent years to modify those parts of the established political framework that fostered the sort of communalist confrontation most Belgians would prefer to avoid? Rather than leading to an uncontrolled explosion of communal sentiment, Belgian politics during the most recent period has followed the path delineated above, as the result of a rational calculation by corporate political actors, old and new, on the basis of their interests within a specific situational logic. They are constrained to act not only within the limits imposed by earlier settlements of conflicts involving religion and class as well as language, but also according to certain principles defined by themselves as equitable and acknowledged as such by the more active segments of the population at large.

In particular, the constitutional settlement, which was aptly dubbed by one of its major engineers "federalization without federalism," resulted from an attempt by the network of consociational leaders to preserve their control over the political game in the face of challenges—less to the survival of Belgium as a political community, than to their cartel-like position.[2] These challenges were less the manifestation of a recrudescence of primordial sentiment than of the use by aspiring political actors of opportunities, generated by legitimate discontent among specific groups, to secure a place in the cartel. In order to achieve their respective goals, both established and aspiring political actors resorted to mechanisms so clearly recognizable that they might properly be said to constitute the central nexus of the Belgian culture of politics. Strikingly congruent with the historically bourgeois character of the country, the Belgian habit of "splitting the difference" is a mechanism for the transformation of a po-

2. Consociational democracy or "segmented pluralism" in Belgium was first presented by Val R. Lorwin in "Belgium: Religion, Class, and Language in National Politics," in *Political Oppositions in Western Democracies,* ed. Robert Dahl (New Haven: Yale University Press, 1966), pp. 147–184 and 409–416, and was further elaborated in subsequent publications. The best Belgian analysis is Luc Huyse, *Passiviteit, pacificatie en verzuiling in de Belgische politiek* (Antwerp: Standaard Wetenschappelijke Uitgeverij, 1970). My own interpretation of Belgium political development is forthcoming as a chapter in a book edited by Raymond Grew.

litical arena into a political marketplace in the most literal sense of the term. Consociational democracy might, therefore, be understood as a political trading club similar to a stock exchange; and the organizers of communal parties in contemporary Belgium might be viewed as traders who seek to amass sufficient goods to make a bid for membership in the club, for a seat on the exchange.

The recent political crisis, which is in the final stages of resolution, is the contemporary reenactment of several earlier ones concerning language and other major issues. That the resolution of important issues requires the uncovering of all possible assets and the mobilization by the traders of a variety of present resources, as well as of "futures," accounts for the vast extension of conflict into various hitherto unaffected—and largely irrelevant—spheres of societal existence. But once the process gets underway, it also provides reasonable assurance that at some time in the future the challengers will have either been driven into bankruptcy or become members of the trading club. All exchanges having been accomplished, a new acceptable equilibrium will emerge in which the surviving traders, as well as, perhaps, some hitherto disadvantaged Belgians, will somehow be better off. There is, beneath the acrimonious tone of Belgian crisis politics, a degree of collusion among the antagonists that serves to keep them in check.

The Politicization of Language in Belgium, 1750–1960

The linguistic segmentation of Belgium into two major groups of nearly equal size, of which those using mainly Flemish or Dutch somewhat outnumbered those using mostly French or Walloon, remained remarkably stable from the time it was recorded in the first postindependence census (1846) until the most recent count (1947). This stability was the result of an exchange between contradictory processes, which provide a key to an understanding of the political implications of the segmentation. In the course of that century, the population in the northern part of Belgium (for the present purpose, "Flemings" living in "Flanders") grew at a faster rate than did the population in the south ("Walloons" living in "Wallonia"). But while this occurred, many more Flemings than Walloons became bilingual, and eventually quite a few came to be recorded as members of the group using mostly French or Walloon. These transfers, which are hinted at by a comparison of the right-hand and left-hand sides of Table 5.1, occurred mostly in urban areas of the northern part of Belgium, and most prominently in and around the capital

Table 5.1. Languages spoken and/or used or preferred in Belgium, 1846–1947 *

Year	Percent who can speak				Percent who use or prefer		
	French/ Walloon	Flemish/ Dutch	German	Multilingual	French/ Walloon	Flemish/ Dutch	German
1846	. . .	. . .	. . .	. . .	42	57	1
1866	49	56	1	6	. . .	. . .	. . .
1880	52	56	2	9	. . .	. . .	. . .
1890	54	58	2	13	. . .	. . .	. . .
1900	55	58	2	14	. . .	. . .	. . .
1910	54	59	2	14	45	54	1
1920	55	59	2	15	46	53	1
1930	54	59	3	15	45	54	1
1947	56	63	5	20	44	55	1

Source: 1846–1930—Paul M. G. Levy, "La statistique des langues en Belgique," Revue de l'Institut de Sociologie, 18, no. 3 (July–September 1938): 566; 1947—Belgium, Ministry of the Interior, Annuaire Statistique de la Belgique, 1956 (Brussels, 1957), p. 50.
* Figures are rounded to the nearest percent. In 1846 individuals were asked to name the one language they "use mostly"; from 1866 on, they were asked which languages they "can speak"; from 1910 on, both questions were asked. No census ever distinguished between French and Walloon, a group of distinct Romance languages. The German-speaking minority is not discussed in this essay.

city, Brussels, to which many Flemings and Walloons migrated. Consequently, the groups, conceived of as ethnic or national, that were constituted by the distinction between Flemings and Walloons do not coincide with those constituted by the distinction between users of the two major languages. Whereas almost all those who use what is now properly called "Dutch" (nederlandsch) as their preferred language of public interaction are of Flemish origin, only a part of those who use French in that same sense can properly be called Walloons. The remainder are French-speaking Belgians whose roots lie in the northern part of Belgium.

The secular movement of Flemings into the French-speaking group occurred as a response to the hegemony of the French language and of its culture in Belgium.[3] This hegemony was firmly institutionalized in the middle of the eighteenth century when the Austrian Habsburgs used

3. The pre–World War I period is analyzed in considerable qualitative and quantitative detail in my article, "The Making of Flemings and Walloons: Belgium, 1830–1914," Journal of Interdisciplinary History, 5 (Fall 1974): 179–235, to which readers are referred for detailed evidence and appropriate references. I have sketched movements and their changing orientations (to the present) in "Transformation of Linguistic Ideologies: The Belgian Case," in Multilingual Political Systems: Problems and Solutions, ed. Jean-Guy Savard and Richard Vigneault (Quebec: Presses de l'Université Laval, 1975), pp. 445–472.

French as the vehicular language of enlightened despotism in their west-ernmost possession, a Catholic region which straddled the old boundary separating the Romance from the Germanic speech zones (see Map 2). French replaced Latin as the principal language of secondary education for indigenous elites who aspired to public office and to related profes-sions; concomitantly, Brussels became the seat of a more active political and economic center to which Flemings and Walloons were drawn. These processes were vastly reinforced during the subsequent period of French rule (1795–1814). By the time what had become nine French departments was subjected to Dutch rule (1814–30), French was the common lan-guage of Belgian elites and also the language of upward mobility for the middle classes. Most of them resisted attempts by the Netherlands to sub-stitute Dutch for French as the official language, especially in Brussels. The Catholic church also preferred education in French to education in Dutch, the language of a *Protestant* state. It was only among a segment of the Flemish middle classes that Dutch linguistic policies were wel-come, as these policies facilitated their ascent. The political class that founded Belgium in 1830–31, composed of Flemings as well as of Wal-loons, was uniformly French-speaking; it unhesitatingly legislated French as the sole official language throughout the country. The Netherlands's lack of interest in Belgium after the international settlement of 1839 and the power and prestige of France further reinforced the hegemony of French culture in Belgium well into the twentieth century. Flemish and Walloon became residual languages of the lower classes as well as of private and local affairs. When primary education was generalized, how-ever, it was dispensed in French to the Walloons but in Flemish to the Flemish masses. Since nearly all education above that level was in French, Flemish became in the nineteenth century the language of a regional ghetto.

The emergence of Flemish and Walloon communities in the latter part of the nineteenth century, far from constituting the revival of a non-Belgian political past, was a process concurrent with the formation of the Belgian national community itself. It was, at the beginning, the middle strata of Flanders who perceived most acutely the injustice of established language arrangements; it was, therefore, from their growing ranks that the aspiration for equity arose and through their efforts that, as the liberal regime became more formally democratic, linguistic issues became more prominent in Belgian politics. The most prominent demand voiced by those then known pejoratively as *Flamingants* was, from the 1840's on, for official recognition of the northern part of Belgium as a bilingual zone for the purposes of administration and education. That this remained a limited affair expressed in the form of associations and interest groups rather than of a nationalist movement or of a regional party was due to several factors. Although the condition of the Flemish masses in the middle third of the nineteenth century approximated that of the Irish masses, the middle classes of Flanders were incorporated into the regime at a very early stage along with their fellows elsewhere and hence gave it their political support in all but linguistic matters. This very incorporation also facilitated the precocious institutionalization of a stable two-party system founded on a Catholic-Liberal cleavage. As each party was genuinely national in scope, together they preempted the political space that otherwise might have been occupied by regional organizations.

After a generation of resistance to the Flamingants, the political class acknowledged the bilingual character of northern Belgium in the 1870's. After another generation, under the impact of further pressures by the Flamingants, now able to organize mass demonstrations on behalf of their program, Dutch was recognized as the second official language of Belgium in 1898. By this time, however, the Flamingants had extended their concerns to encompass the social and economic development of Flanders as a whole. Since previous victories did little to dam Francophonic assimilationist forces, the most militant among them advocated the removal of these forces from Flanders altogether by declaring the region unilingual as was Wallonia. It was particularly vital to transform the region's state university at Ghent into a Dutch-language institution where those who would replace the established French-speaking Flemish bourgeoisie would be trained.

Around the turn of the century, the implementation of earlier Flemish demands had already begun to alter the character of Belgium. The demographic growth of Flanders, itself an attribute of the region's backwardness in contrast with Wallonia, mattered more than ever since under universal male suffrage the region would soon contain a majority of the Belgian electorate. These considerations, in turn, provoked a reactive process of community formation among the Walloons.[4] On the eve of World War I, Flemish and Walloon vanguard groups formulated and propagandized ideologies concerned with the reorganization of Belgium

4. See, for example, the statement by Jules Destrée quoted in Shepard Clough, *A History of the Flemish Movement in Belgium: A Study in Nationalism* (New York: Richard R. Smith, 1930), p. 128.

to achieve congruence among language, territory, and ethnic group, a thrust that challenged, at least implicitly, the unitary organization of the Belgian political community.

As elsewhere, the tensions produced by World War I exacerbated preexisting cleavages. In occupied Belgium, some Flamingants collaborated with German authorities to secure the rapid achievement of their prewar program, including the conversion of the University of Ghent; the Germans themselves found it convenient to treat the linguistic zones as administrative units. A Flemish protest movement arose concurrently within the ranks of the Belgian army fighting on the Allied side on a corner of Belgian soil. Consequently, the Allied victory was interpreted as the victory of "patriotic" Belgians against "disloyal" Flemings. French was reinstated in Ghent, and there were widespread purges; any talk of federalism was tantamount to treason. Although loyalist Flemish leaders involved in the postwar political settlement, which ushered in the age of consociational democracy in Belgium, secured from their partners the promise of a new deal, including a Flemish University of Ghent, that part of the settlement evaporated in the pro-France atmosphere of the early postwar years.[5]

It is under these circumstances that there emerged for the first time in Belgian history a self-designated Flemish nationalist movement, which explicitly advocated self-government for Flanders, mostly by the transformation of Belgium into a federal state, and which contested parliamentary elections. Its progress in the late 1920's, in turn, brought about the delayed implementation of the promised new deal, founded on the prewar Flamingant program. A series of laws beginning in 1932 used the language boundary to define two unilingual zones for general administration, education, and adjudication. The University of Ghent finally became Flemish. The boroughs of the capital city were declared bilingual. However, the linguistic status of its suburbs—located mostly in the Flemish zone—and of villages and towns along the language boundary was to be

5. The most useful work on Belgian politics during the interwar period remains Carl-Henrik Hojer, *Le régime parlementaire belge de 1918 à 1940* (Uppsala: Alunquist and Wiksells, 1946; reprint ed., Brussels: CRISP, 1969). The wave of pro-France feeling is discussed in Jonathan Helmreich, "The Negotiation of the Franco-Belgian Military Accord of 1920," *French Historical Studies*, 3, no. 3 (Spring 1964): 360–378. The major works on the Flemish movement are in Dutch: A. W. Willemsen, *Het Vlaams-nationalisme: De geschiedenis van de jaren 1914–1940*, 2d ed. (Utrecht: Ambo, 1969); and J. H. Elias, *Vijfentwintig jaar Vlaamse Beweging, 1914–1939*, 4 vols. (Antwerp: Nederlandsche Boekhandel, 1969).

determined by the decennial census, a procedure that was likely to reflect the further progress of Francophonic assimilation. Subsequently, some steps were taken as well to divide the administrative services of the Ministry of Education into parallel linguistic segments.

In all but name, Belgium had taken a step toward the establishment of a territoriality principle for distinguishing Flemings from Walloons. Although this entailed, by implication, some movement away from a unitary state, the decision makers rejected federalism and concentrated instead on finding an eclectic solution acceptable to those who exercised actual power. That solution was reached when the established traders (Catholics, Socialists, Liberals) co-opted demands formulated by nonestablished entrepreneurs (Flemish nationalists) after the latter had built up support to a point where they jeopardized control of the political market by the former. It is also noteworthy that the goods traded to reach agreement were not limited to the "communal sector," but involved, as well, items valuable in terms of the secular-religious controversy, and that the linguistic laws of the early 1930's were passed with large majorities.[6]

Although the solution was successful, in the sense that it provided the basic legal framework within which bargaining over language arrangements in Belgium occurred for the next thirty years, it failed to contain communal tensions which involved matters other than language per se. In the circumstances of the Great Depression and of the European-wide challenges to parliamentary democracy, however, it is difficult to ascertain to what extent subsequent political upheavals in Belgium were communal, or were manifestations of other phenomena which merely flowed into preexisting communal channels. In the course of World War II and its aftermath, each community acquired a bad reputation in the eyes of the other: the Flemings collaborated; the Walloons exacted an unjust revenge. These antagonisms were injected into the "Royal Question" (concerning whether King Leopold III's wartime behavior made him unsuitable to rule), which dominated Belgian politics from 1945 to 1950 and transformed it into a conflict between Dutch-speaking Catholics and French-speaking Socialists, with the remainder of each of these parties and the Liberals less committed.[7] In the midst of this, the 1947 census in-

6. The trading patterns of 1932 emerge clearly in J. D. Rycx d'Huisnacht, "L'opinion parlementaire et la réforme du régime linguistique de l'enseignement en 1932," *Res Publica*, 12, no. 4 (1970): 543–590.

7. For the post–World War II period, see Jean Meynaud et al., *La décision politique en Belgique* (Paris: Armand Colin, 1965); and E. Ramon Arango, *Leopold III and the Belgian Royal Question* (Baltimore: Johns Hopkins University Press, 1961).

dicated that the Flemish region definitely contained a majority of the Belgian population, whereas the French language was making considerable progress along the linguistic border and in Brussels. The linguistic settlement of the 1930's was itself called into question. It is remarkable, therefore, that the parties succeeded in separating the Royal Question from the linguistic problem. Shelving the first in 1947, they negotiated in 1948 a ''treaty'' over the second whereby the existing language arrangements would be maintained for another ten-year period, at the end of which a study group would report alternative proposals. The Royal Question itself was stalemated in 1950, when the king's partisans obtained a majority in a referendum, but his opponents were able to mobilize mass support against resumption of his rule. The only way out was to ''split the difference'': having formally won the right to rule, the king refrained from doing so. By the time Leopold III formally abdicated in favor of his son a year later, the Royal Question had disappeared from Belgian politics. The entire episode demonstrates that the Belgian political parties emerged from the war with an even greater degree of control over the political process than before and, incidentally, provides confirming evidence that the course of communal conflict in Belgium cannot be analyzed solely in terms of variations in popular sentiment under the impact of raw sociological trends.

A Settlement That Failed

By the early 1960's, Belgium had fully recovered from the traumas of two generations of war and was in the course of resolving, with relatively little domestic political difficulty compared with its northern and southern neighbors, the process of relinquishing an empire. The country was, generally speaking, one of the world's most stable liberal democracies of the welfare state variety. The rate of growth of its capitalist economy, among the most vigorous in the world before World War I, had declined during the interwar period. A rapid postwar recovery was followed by a slow rate of growth during most of the 1950's, which subsequently accelerated.[8] As population growth was minimal throughout the period, however, per capita growth was greater than within countries with slow growth rates and expanding populations, such as the United States or Canada.[9]

8. Charles P. Kindleberger, *Europe's Post-War Growth* (Cambridge: Harvard University Press, 1967), p. 74.

9. Angus Maddison, *Economic Growth in the West* (New York: Norton, 1964), p. 30.

It was not so much overall changes in Belgian society as it was modifications in the relative circumstances of the linguistic regions that affected the logic of political issues and the rational calculation of the various actors concerned. As anticipated at the beginning of the century, the proportion of the population living in Flanders and in Brussels had continued to increase in relation to that in Wallonia. Between 1930 and 1947, the population in Flanders had become an absolute majority; in 1961, Flanders contained 51.3 percent of the Belgian population as against 33.1 percent in Wallonia and 15.6 in Brussels.[10] Flanders had undergone belated economic modernization between the two wars, as indicated by a decline in the proportion of its population engaged in agriculture to a level much closer to the national average, itself among the lowest in the world. Afterward, it experienced a genuine boom as a result of the revival of Antwerp as a major European port, the exploitation of new coal fields, and because of its excellent "European" location on the Paris-Amsterdam axis, with easy access both to the sea and to the Rhine. Flanders now attracted considerable Belgian and foreign investment, much of it in new, light industry. In 1966, its gross product per capita surpassed that of Wallonia for the first time in modern times.[11] From a strictly linguistic point of view, Flanders had also made much progress since the 1930's. The use of French among the urban upper- and middle-classes had dwindled considerably. "Standard, cultivated Dutch" (*algemeen beschaafd nederlandsch*) increasingly crowded out local Flemish speeches; regional unilingualism had become a reality in the public sector.

At the national level in Belgium, however, the situation was much more ambiguous. The status of Dutch as a language in relation to French benefited from the growing importance of English as the international language of business, science, and international affairs, as well as from Belgium's participation in Benelux and later in the multilingual European Economic Community, which also contained ten million Dutch-speaking Netherlanders. Yet in the uppermost spheres of the private and public sectors, French retained its preferred status and power of attraction. For example, whereas the proportion of school children through the secondary level whose language of instruction was Dutch equaled the proportion of Dutch-speaking children in the total population (57.8 percent at the sec-

10. Lorwin, p. 415.
11. Georges Goriély cites these figures and provides an excellent overview in "Rapport introductif sur Bruxelles et le fédéralisme," *Res Publica,* 13, no. 3–4 (1971): 396–422.

ondary level in 1960–61), the proportion enrolled in Dutch-language programs at the university level was lower than one would expect (45.8 percent). This could no longer be attributed to the general backwardness of the region.[12] The communities on the Flemish side of the linguistic border, where French was progressing, would constitute, according to the settlement of the 1930's, new incursions of bilingualism in Flemish soil. Much more serious, however, was the situation created by Brussels, whose growing population was also becoming more French-speaking. Even as Flanders triumphed as the majority region, Dutch speakers were reduced to minority status in the capital. Data from the 1947 census—not released by the government until 1950 to avoid controversy—indicated that only 27 percent of the capital's population spoke "Dutch mostly." Various independent estimates suggest that by the 1960's the population that characterized itself as French-speaking constituted between 80 and 85 percent of the total in the capital and its neighboring boroughs. Moreover, French was spreading beyond these limits into the surrounding Flemish countryside, where villages were being transformed into residential suburbs.

Overall, then, a very ambiguous situation had emerged. Dutch speakers in Flanders now exercised, for the most part, the right to life in their own language; and they took for granted, on the whole, a similar right for the Walloons in Wallonia. But they perceived two sources of inequity within Belgium. One was direct, in that bilingualism at the institutional center was far short of having become a reality, especially in the private sector. The other was indirect but perhaps more humiliating: ethnic Flemings who lived in the capital continued to absorb French along with upward mobility, thus disappearing into the Belgian Francophonic landscape, leaving identifiable Flemings as a backward residue, much as in the nineteenth century. This process, incidentally, accounts for the mistaken impression of many visitors that there is severe ethnic discrimination in Brussels. Flemings are not restricted to low positions, but rather most of those who do *not* occupy them speak French and, hence, appear to be Walloons to the uninitiated.

What of the Walloons proper? Not only had the regional population declined to one-third of the Belgian total, but Wallonia increasingly resembled northern England, with which it had shared a history of precocious industrialization, in that its industrial plants were obsolete, its

12. Lorwin, p. 416.

mines were depleted, and it was poorly located for new investments. Although there was very little concern with language—Wallonia, after all, has never been forced to become bilingual—there was growing concern that the demographic dominance of Flanders, inexorably reflected in the weight of Flemish representatives in Parliament and in governmental coalitions, would further accelerate the decline of Wallonia. Through the normal exercise of bargaining power at the center, Flemings would undoubtedly allocate public benefits preferentially to their own constituencies at the very time Wallonia needed compensatory redistribution. In this fashion, secularist, Socialist Wallonia would become the economic colony of a Catholic Flanders.

Under these circumstances, the Flemings had little interest in separatism. If things were allowed to take their course, the normal play of legislative reapportionment, based on a territorial headcount, would give Flemish constituencies a permanent majority in the Belgian Parliament. The only threat would come from the continued use of a linguistic headcount as the basis for legislation, since that might lead to an expansion of the area defined as bilingual at the expense of Flemish territory, and might even produce in the future a majority of Belgians who preferred to use French. Flemish interests were, therefore, threatened by the putative outcome of the census of 1960, which would provide data for the determination of the bilingual area around Brussels and along the linguistic frontier, as provided by law. Since the census would act as a referendum, the Flamingants threatened a boycott. The government first postponed the count to 1961 and then carried it out in ostrich fashion without language questions. The most satisfactory solution, from a Flemish point of view, would entail the freezing of regional boundaries to eliminate the play of assimilation and personal preference, coupled with a decentralization of cultural decision making to the regional level, as the "bilingual" center was unreliable. Some went further than that: the more regional autonomy there would be, the more that Flemings would retain their newly acquired wealth and be free to operate in an international context in which Amsterdam and Cologne, London or New York, and even Paris, mattered more than Brussels.

Although some Walloons, by contrast, dreamed of a reunion with France, President de Gaulle seemed more aware of oppressed "Frenchmen" in the New World than on his own doorstep. Short of that, Walloon spokesmen stressed economic and political guarantees for the smaller region, which might be obtained through the establishment of some form of parity of political arrangements at the center, such as is found in the representative assemblies of federal states (for example, in the United States Senate), possibly coupled with similar decentralization of *economic* decision making but with parity of resources (that is, redistribution). Brussels, of course, had a distinct interest of its own.

Its population generally would be harmed by the freezing of unilingual regional boundaries, since this would prevent the extension of bilingual facilities into the new suburbs; they also would oppose any move to prevent parents from choosing to educate in French children whose mother tongue was Flemish. Furthermore, Brussels calculated that any moves toward regional autonomy would lessen the status of the city and the tangible economic benefits it derived as the capital of a unitary state with a centralized administration.

The Belgian party system, however, provided a constraining framework within which the interplay of linguistic and regional groups and the settlement of issues related to their interests must necessarily occur. The party professionals and the quasi-public associational networks they controlled would generally oppose any moves toward decentralization since new arrangements were likely to lessen the control of established traders over a known political market. The extent of their control over political processes in Belgium was probably at an all-time high. Starting in 1920 with a total of nearly 91 percent of the valid votes under conditions of universal suffrage for males, proportional representation, and mandatory voting, the Catholic, Socialist, and Liberal parties maintained a remarkable degree of stability until 1936, when they fell to a low of 72.2 percent of the total (the rate of external mobility, which measures changes from one election to another, rose from a range of from 2.65 percent to 7.04 percent in previous elections to 16.85 percent).[13] Recovery, from their point of view, began in 1939 and continued after the war, when they benefited from the elimination of the extreme right. In spite of Communist gains, the three parties obtained 84.6 percent of the votes in 1946, the reinstating election (the external mobility rate was 21.6 percent). The threesome then reached a historical maximum of 95.3 percent in 1950 and nearly matched it with 95.2 percent in 1958 (see Table 5.2). As of

13. William Fraeys, "Les élections législatives du 10 mars 1974: Analyse des résultats," *Res Publica,* 16, no. 3–4 (1974): 523. The rate of external mobility is the half-sum of the absolute values of the percentages in relation to the valid votes obtained by the various parties (or groups of parties) in two successive elections. All such rates cited here are from Fraeys.

that year, there was even a possibility that the Liberals might be eliminated from the game, as the two large parties also reached their historical joint maximum of 84.2 percent, almost as much as the three had obtained together right after the war. The three-party system was institutionalized within each of the three informal linguistic regions, as seen in Table 5.4. Every study of the Belgian political system during this period confirmed the very great actual and reputational power of the leaders of the parties and related organizations.[14]

Table 5.2. Percent of valid popular votes in Belgium by party, 1958–74 general elections (Chamber) *

Year	Communist (1)	Socialist (2)	Catholic (3)	Liberal (4)	VU (5)	FDF/ RW (6)	Misc. (7)	Total of cols. 2 and 3	Total of cols. 2, 3, and 4
1958	1.9	37.7 †	46.5	11.0	2.0		0.9	84.2	95.2
1961	3.0	36.7	41.5	12.3	3.5		3.0	78.2	90.5
1965	4.6	28.3	34.4	21.6	6.7	2.3	2.1	62.7	84.3
1968	3.3	28.0	31.7	20.9	9.8	5.9	0.4	59.7	80.6
1971	3.1	27.3	30.0	16.4	11.1	11.3	0.8	57.3	73.7
1974	3.2	26.7	32.3	15.2	10.2	10.9	1.4	59.0	74.2

Source: Luc Rowies, "Les partis politiques en Belgique," *Dossiers du CRISP,* no. 7 (January 1975), Annex.
* Counts vary slightly in different sources because electoral alliances and dissidents can be categorized in various ways.
† Includes 1.9 Socialist-Liberal cartel.

However committed to the institutional status quo, these professionals had to face the possibility of losing support to political entrepreneurs in their own midst as well as to outsiders, who might emphasize communal and regional interests on the basis of principle or sheer opportunity. This dilemma affected each of the parties somewhat differently at the time linguistic issues returned to the fore (see Tables 5.2, 5.3, and 5.4). Under the impact of some stirrings to this effect, the three-party total declined to 90.5 percent in 1961. The Catholic party was most affected, losing five percentage points. Of its total national vote, it owed 66.2 percent to Flemish counties, among which it had an absolute majority. Faced with a revival of Flemish communal voting, together with pressures from its own Flemish-based segment, the party tended to be, as a whole, sympathetic to Flemish demands. Decentralization of cultural decision making

14. See, for example, Wilfried Dewachter, "De machtshiërarchie in de Belgische politiek," *Res Publica,* 13, no. 3–4 (1971): 533–549.

would, of course, redound to its benefit in Flanders; but, on the other hand, such decentralization would reduce the party to a permanent minority position in the Walloon region where it now had less than one-third of the votes. The very different situation of the party in the two regions provided the elements of growing tension between its component parts.

Table 5.3. Regional percentage distribution of electoral clientele of major parties in Belgium, popular vote, 1961 and 1974 general elections (Chamber)

	Flanders	Brussels	Wallonia
		1961	
Catholic	66.2	8.6	23.4
Socialist	44.1	14.4	41.3
Liberal	51.1	17.6	30.7
		1974	
Catholic	69.4	8.5	21.3
Socialist	46.9	9.3	43.4
Liberal	63.9	4.7	30.7

Source: 1961—Lorwin, p. 414; 1974—Rowies, Annex. Eastern counties not included.

With 36.7 percent of the national vote in 1961, the Socialist party held its own. Its regional clientele was more evenly balanced, with 44.1 percent from Flemish constituencies and 41.3 percent from Walloon constituencies. It viewed itself as a more clearly national party, an outlook which was also stressed by the leadership to maintain a middle-of-the-road policy between its more conservative Flemish and more militant Walloon components. The party was, therefore, strongly unitarist, albeit wary of a Communist revival and the activities of a federalist-minded regional splinter group in Wallonia.

As the Liberals drew a greater share of their clientele from Brussels than did the other two parties, they were most militant in the defense of unitary Belgium and of the specific interests of the capital city; yet it was to a slight gain in Flanders that they owed the beginnings of their recovery in 1961.

For the time being, the parties attempted to settle communal issues in the manner most congruent with their interests. Issues concerning reapportionment were held in abeyance; decentralization was avoided altogether; and the parties set to work toward a readjustment of the 1930's settlement to satisfy the most vociferous claimants. In the short run, they achieved a considerable degree of success. The Catholic-Socialist coalition formed in 1961 in an atmosphere of linguistic tension, compounded by an economic recession and the sequels of decolonization, undertook to implement the report issued by the study group constituted in 1948, and which contained the makings of a "pact" similar to that reached during the intervening period in education. Its main features included a permanent settlement of the linguistic boundary by means of an exchange of municipalities to render the existing provinces even more homogeneous linguistically, the establishment of a special status for Brussels, and provisions for special facilities for linguistic minorities (the resulting geographical arrangements are shown in Map 2). During the yearlong parliamentary deliberations on these subjects, each community often took to the streets to prevent "the stealing of territory" by the other, a process

Table 5.4. Percent of valid popular votes within regions of Belgium by party, 1958–74 general elections (Chamber) *

Year	Communist	Socialist	Catholic	Liberal	VU	FDF/RW	Misc.
			Flanders				
1958	0.1	29.2	56.6	10.6	3.4		0.1
1961	1.0	29.7	50.9	11.6	6.0		0.8
1965	1.7	24.7	43.8	16.6	11.6		1.6
1968	1.4	26.0	39.0	16.2	16.9		0.5
1971	1.6	24.5	37.8	16.4	18.8		0.9
1974	1.6	22.5	39.9	17.3	16.8		1.9
			Brussels				
1958	2.7	42.4	33.5	18.2	1.1		1.3
1961	3.6	41.6	28.0	17.0	1.6		9.2
1965	4.1	26.3	19.6	33.4	2.4	10.0	4.2
1968	2.4	20.0	27.6	26.3	4.3	18.6	0.8
1971	2.8	20.6	20.1	13.5	5.6	34.5	2.9
1974	4.0	20.5	22.7	5.9	5.9	. 39.6	1.4
			Wallonia †				
1958	4.6	48.5	34.2	11.5			1.2
1961	6.5	47.1	30.1	11.8			4.5
1965	9.8	36.7	23.3	25.8		3.3	1.1
1968	7.0	35.1	20.3	26.5		10.6	0.5
1971	6.0	35.0	20.1	17.3		21.2	0.7
1974	5.9	37.4	22.2	15.0		18.8	1.7

Source: 1958—Meynaud et al., pp. 84–85; 1961–74—Rowies, Annex.
* Counts vary slightly in different sources because electoral alliances and dissidents can be categorized in various ways.
† Not including German-speaking counties.

which strengthened the bargaining power of their representatives in Parliament. The bill organizing the territorial exchange among the provinces was passed in October 1962 with a comfortable majority (130 to 56, with 12 abstentions, in the lower house).

The Brussels problem emerged as the most difficult. French speakers wanted to add eleven residential suburbs located in the unilingual Flemish zone (see Map 2) to the nineteen already bilingual municipalities of Brussels; but in the face of adamant Flemish resistance to this extension, an elaborate compromise was worked out providing for six municipalities (in addition to the nineteen already bilingual ones) with *limited* bilingual fa-

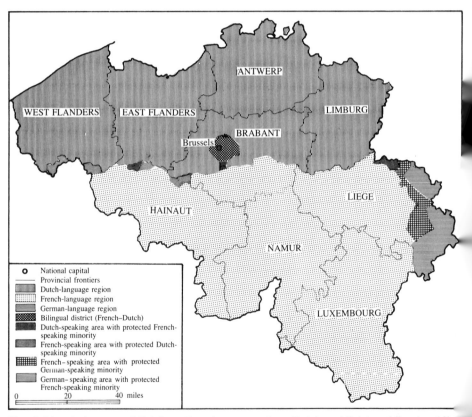

Map 2. Linguistic areas of Belgium. Based on a map from Belgium, Ministry of Foreign Affairs and External Trade, *Memo from Belgium,* no. 122–124 (March–April–May 1970), pp. 40–41.

cilities, precluding in particular French-language secondary schools. To secure Flemish acquiescence, however, it was necessary to institutionalize a procedure for official inspection of Brussels households in cases where parental declaration of their children's mother tongue was suspect. In other words, parental preference, already eliminated from the unilingual zones delineated in the 1930's, was now formally eliminated from Brussels as well. The law was approved in July 1963 with an even greater majority (157 to 33 in the Chamber).

In Brussels—the area most concerned—these measures probably had very little material impact, as French-speaking families in residential suburbs deprived of the right to have a French-language secondary school could easily, and in fact did, send their children a few miles away where such schools were available. "Language inspection" of Brussels households remained a threat rather than a reality. Nevertheless, however satisfactory the settlement of 1962–63 was from the point of view of parliamentary bargaining and coalition making, it was perceived by many as victimizing various groups of Belgians merely to facilitate the task of party politicians. The settlement reflected, in addition to particular grievances, the application of a sort of inexorable logic which, were the country France rather than Belgium, would undoubtedly be considered by analysts a typical example of the Cartesian political mentality. This application of logic, in turn, revealed all sorts of anomalies, now automatically defined by activists as "violations of equity," whether or not they were perceived as such by the individuals involved. Given the Belgian political process, such anomalies were valuable goods available for trading on the political marketplace.

Finally, the legislation failed to exhaust the agenda of regional grievances as interpreted by the political entrepreneurs active in the regional movements to whose growth the process of parliamentary bargaining over these issues had itself contributed. For them, the various compromises consisted of a set of discrete losses rather than a collective set of gains. They correctly perceived the settlement as a preemptive move *against* decentralization and, therefore, renewed their agitation.

The issue of legislative reapportionment remained unresolved. On the basis of the 1961 census, according to the constitutionally established formula, both the Flemish districts and the bilingual area in Brussels would gain more seats than would Wallonia. Faced with the prospects of a significant shift of regional power in Parliament, the major parties sought to mitigate its effects while also preempting federalist positions. In late 1963, the Socialists proposed that communal issues be designated "protected parliamentary questions," for which a majority vote among the representatives of each region would be required; the Catholics proposed administrative deconcentration of state services to the regional level, some form of cultural autonomy, and the requirement of two-thirds majorities for all communal questions in Parliament. The implementation of such proposals, however, required constitutional amendment, a process that begins with the passage of a law specifying the articles to be amended, and which automatically brings about a dissolution of Parliament. The subsequently elected parliament then becomes a constituent assembly with respect to the items specified, and the substitute constitutional provisions—which are *not* specified in advance—require a majority of two-thirds of the members present in each house for passage. The amending process is thus very risky: not only must the parties face an election, but the outcome might not be as originally intended. In the situation of the 1960's, the amending process might well have opened up a Pandora's box from which the evils of federalism would escape.

The bill of intent was passed in April 1965. The subsequent elections confirmed the Catholic and Socialist coalition partners' worst fears, as their share of the national vote dropped nearly sixteen points to about 63 percent (see Table 5.2), a postwar low and only slightly above the all-time low in 1936. Quite unexpectedly, however, the election was a triumph for the Liberals who had recently reorganized themselves to overcome their image as an anticlerical, Freemason party, in order to broaden their appeal to the middle class as a whole. Campaigning as the "Party for Freedom and Progress" (PLP), they obtained 21.6 percent, an all-time maximum. The election also witnessed the further growth of the Flemish Popular Union (VU) as well as the appearance of new regional parties among French speakers, the Francophonic Democratic Front (FDF) in Brussels and the Walloon Rally (RW) in Wallonia. A rate of external mobility of nearly 17 percent, the highest since the reinstating election of 1946, indicated that an electoral realignment might be in the making. In Flanders, both the Catholics and the Socialists lost votes to the Liberals, and the Catholics to the VU as well (see Table 5.4). Still the regional leader, the Catholic party no longer retained its absolute majority in that region. In Wallonia, both the Socialists and the Catholics lost even more votes to the Liberals, who now surpassed the Catholics; and the Socialist position as regional leader was further weakened by losses to the Communist party and to the RW. Similar shifts on a somewhat larger

scale occurred in Brussels, where the Liberals now emerged as the leading party, and the FDF, campaigning for the first time, obtained 10 percent of the votes. Most ominously, in the capital the country's two major
parties combined fell short of a majority, as had occurred only once
before, in 1936.

As clear victors, the Liberals were invited into a coalition by the
Catholics. Although the presence in the government of this "unitarist"
party would block the process of constitutional amendment envisaged by
the outgoing coalition, this state of affairs was, of course, not unwelcome
by the French-speaking wing of the Catholic party nor, on the whole, by
the Socialists. The prime minister designate was, therefore, able to negotiate a "linguistic truce" among the established parties and devote his
government to other matters, including questions on which there was no
division, such as the establishment, for the first time, of an official
Dutch-language text of the Constitution. In spite of his consummate skill
as a negotiator, however, he was unable to resolve one of the anomalies
found in higher education.

Ever since the 1830's, the Belgian system of higher education had been
organized to reflect parity of political forces: two state universities (Liège
and Ghent) and two private ones (Catholic Louvain and freethinking
Brussels) reflected each of the ideological camps. The conversion of the
University of Ghent into a Dutch-language institution had established
linguistic parity between the state universities, and subsequently the universities at Brussels and Louvain (in Dutch, Leuven) each became bilingual. This might do for the University of Brussels, located in a bilingual
zone, but obviously not for the other, located a few miles north of the
line on Flemish soil. An attempt by the government to divide the University of Louvain/Leuven into two linguistically separate sections was
deemed unsatisfactory by militant students and faculty members, whose
fervor probably owed as much to the worldwide malaise in higher education in 1967–68, and to local antiepiscopal feeling, as to linguistic sentiment. It was on that stumbling block that the unusually long-lived government fell in early 1968. After it proved impossible to organize another
coalition, Parliament passed another bill of intent concerning constitutional amendment, and new elections were held.

The relative stability of the new elections in comparison with those of
1965 confirmed that an electoral realignment had taken place (see Table
5.2). The Liberals declined slightly from their very high level, the Socialists experienced small losses, and the Catholics slightly greater ones.

These losses (as well as those of the Communist party) benefited, of
course, the regional parties, whose total rose to nearly 16 percent; with
32 out of 212 seats in the Chamber, they now constituted a troublesome
presence. The VU now surpassed the Liberals in the Flemish districts; the
RW tripled its share in the south; and the FDF obtained 18.6 percent of
the votes in the capital (see Table 5.4). In short, Belgium retained at the
national level a weakened two-and-a-half-party system. Moreover, at the
level of what might become relevant political units under an amended
constitution, three significantly different four-party systems had emerged.

These changes dramatically altered the rational calculation of interest
that shapes the course of Belgian politics, the consequences of which are
discussed below. It is much easier to analyze these consequences, however, than to account for the changes themselves. The clues available
from a postelectoral survey conducted in 1968, which sought to reconstruct changes since 1961, do not add very much to what is already visible from a more ad hoc analysis of electoral data and from the manifest
appeals of the parties.[15] In short, the realignment of 1965–68 involved a
desertion of the Catholic party by voters in all three regions, and of the
Socialist party, especially in Brussels and Wallonia. Most voters did not
wander very far in ideological terms. Many moved toward the renovated
Liberals; others toward the new parties, often called "antisystem" by
Belgians and foreign observers, but which were not that at all in terms of
the system as a whole. Not one of them deviated significantly from the
range of variation of the three established parties on two major ideological dimensions: secular versus religious orientation, and economic liberalism versus state intervention. On communal issues, not one of them was
genuinely "separatist," although they were normally called that by their
opponents. They deviated from the other parties only with respect to two
issues: (1) they advocated some form of decentralization of the decision-
making process; and (2) they challenged the oligopolistic political process
that gave established parties and their associated networks exclusive
power in Belgian politics. With respect to the first of these, they were, in
fact, not very far from the appropriate regional wings of the established
parties. Indeed, the 1968 survey suggests that the Catholic votes that
were lost in Flanders after 1958 benefited the VU and the Liberals, in that
order; and votes lost by the Socialists benefited the Liberals and, second,

15. Nicole Delruelle et al., *Le comportement politique des électeurs belges* (Brussels:
Editions de l'Institut de Sociologie, 1970).

the communal parties. Support for communal parties in 1968 also came disproportionately from first-time voters. These dramatic electoral changes should, therefore, not be taken as an indication of dramatic changes in the dispositions of Belgian voters.

Why did these changes occur when they did? Were they attributable to tensions generated by linguistic issues themselves? Another survey carried out in 1966 on the "Problems of Concern to Belgians" provides some clues on this subject.[16] It indicates, somewhat surprisingly, that in the very midst of the period of electoral realignment, concern over language questions ranked only sixth in a list of eighteen items, below inflation, taxes, and miscellaneous welfare issues, such as pensions. However, linguistic concerns ranked higher among certain categories: voters under thirty (fourth), white-collar workers (fourth), managers and professionals (second), residents of large cities (fifth), inhabitants of the Brussels region (third). As the above categories overlap to a considerable extent, the emerging pattern showed Flemish and Walloon workers, farmers, inhabitants of small towns, and elderly citizens, who constitute the bulk of the population of Belgium, standing by quite unconcerned while small numbers of young middle- and upper-middle-class compatriots, located mostly in Brussels, attempted to remodel some features of their common environment in the midst of a great show of upheaval. Yet even for those most concerned and probably accounting for most of the realignment, language issues were seldom cited as a prime concern. Moreover, constitutional reform, which was ranked last overall, was ignored by these groups as well.

These limited findings are compatible with a somewhat paradoxical interpretation put forth by some Belgian social scientists as well as with the overall analysis presented here.[17] The recent electoral shifts can be considered a protest vote against the traditional political game in Belgium, a local manifestation of the process of *ontzuiling* noted in the Netherlands and other hitherto rigidly organized consociational democracies. Its bearers are the younger, more educated, new middle classes, who display

16. Nicole Delruelle et al., "Les problèmes qui préoccupent les Belges: Février–Mars 1966," *Revue de l'Institut de Sociologie,* 46, no. 1 (1966), 291–342.

17. Luc Huyse, as cited in Nicole Delruelle-Vosswinkel, "L'évolution de l'opinion publique belge: 1971–1974," *Res Publica,* 16, no. 3–4 (1974): 348–349. Delruelle also points out that in late 1973–early 1974, when asked "What constitute the most urgent problems for the forthcoming government?" 56.8 percent of those interviewed cited "fight against the cost of living" as their first choice, while only 16.8 percent chose "regionalization."

increasing autonomy vis-à-vis traditional cleavages on which the established system rests. To them, the specter of federalism agitated by traditional leaders is attractive rather than frightening. The appeal of the new communal parties is perhaps less to "primordial sentiments," that is, attachments to language and ethnic identity per se, than it is in the *use* of these referents in the acquisition by citizens of greater control over political affairs. Thus the movement toward federalism, which originated in Belgium in the course of bargaining over linguistic equity, provided an opportunity for the expression of a generalized striving for the establishment of a new framework, which would allow for greater participation in decision making concerning cultural and economic life and for the distribution of resources to implement these decisions. It is the specifically Belgian expression of a phenomenon generally observed in liberal capitalist democracies. In Belgium, as elsewhere, it is not the more traditional but the most modern who are striving hardest to loosen the iron cage of modernity; and it is not surprising that in Belgium these strivings are expressed with reference to communities and regions much as different strivings were expressed through these channels in the 1930's. Rather than leading to the deplorable end of a certain kind of Belgium, the transformation might constitute the prelude to participation in a new Europe, in which the new generations might overcome the constraints of living in a small, self-centered country.

Federalization without Federalism

That was possibly how things looked from the vantage point of 1968. Following the elections, Belgium experienced its longest period of governmental crisis since World War II. Constitutional revision required a two-thirds majority in each house, which could no longer be produced by a coalition of the two large parties alone; a three-party coalition was possible, but required prior agreement on too many issues. Furthermore, as the parties' regional wings had become further differentiated in the course of the campaign, the coalition game was more complex than ever. For over two months Belgium had nothing but a caretaker government. It is remarkable, however, that after several years during which the country's communal conflict attracted unprecedented attention from foreign observers, Belgium remained strangely peaceful, even while next door, in France, what was initially a minor clash among extremist student minigroups erupted into a crisis of regime, if not into a crisis of civilization. It was, therefore, in a relaxed atmosphere that the next government, another Catholic-Socialist coalition, undertook to revise the Belgian Constitution. That things henceforth moved very fast suggests that much of the preceding period had been devoted to "lifting the mortgage" constituted by the preservation of the status quo.[18] The way was now clear to pursue the course intended all along. Although the new political actors were not included, it was as a clear concession to their point of view and in an attempt to reclaim the votes they had gained that the government declared, "The unitary state . . . has now been outpaced by events," and "the communities and the regions must take their place among the renovated structures of the state." [19]

The new prime minister refused to allow his coalition also to founder on the Louvain/Leuven rock; declaring that "there will be no Trojan War," he worked out a compromise solution to the "unsolvable" issue by simultaneously launching the construction of a new Francophonic University of Louvain on the proper side of the language line and of a new Dutch-language university in Brussels. Toward the end of 1969, he organized a "last chance" conference, whose twenty-eight participants came from *all* parties represented in Parliament, including the Liberal opposition and the communal parties, who, in keeping with established Belgian practice, had demonstrated their staying power after taking to the streets, and were now ready to be considered for membership in the trading club. By the end of the year, agreement had been reached on major provisions concerning cultural autonomy and regionalization, except as pertaining to Brussels. The twenty-eight participants decided to proceed without agreement on Brussels, and the tentative agreement they reached—distinct from a full treaty, but a possible prelude to one— served as the basis for proposals submitted to Parliament in February 1970. By December 1970, the Constitution had been thoroughly revised for the first time since its inception. This tour de force resulted in a system characterized by Leo Tindemans, who later became prime minister, as "federalization without federalism." The idiosyncratic reorganization of Belgium, which now includes three sets of units in addition to the preexisting provinces and municipalities, was praised by its creators as congruent with Belgian realities, but was deplored by others as "Leba-

18. Nathan Leites, *The Game of Politics in France* (Palo Alto: Stanford University Press, 1959), p. 82. In some respects, the Belgian parliamentary process resembles that which might be found in France or in Italy in the absence of a major communist party.

19. Governmental declaration of 25 June 1968, *Documents—CEPESS*, 7, no. 2–3 (1968): 147 ff.

nese," that is, as enhancing communal identities and interests at the expense of those that cut across language groups.[20]

First, the amended Constitution divides Belgium into *four linguistic regions* (Dutch, French, German, and Brussels-bilingual), each a separate territorial entity, for the application of rules concerning language usage; all municipalities must belong to one of them, and they may not have governing bodies of their own. Second, the Constitution specifies that Belgium includes *three cultural communities:* French, Dutch, and German. It provides only the French and Dutch communities with cultural councils, each composed of members from the appropriate linguistic group in the two houses of Parliament; German-speaking members are included in the French community in this arrangement. (In 1973, however, a law created a directly elected council for the German cultural community.) The councils constitute assemblies without an executive of their own and are empowered to issue decrees with the force of law that are applicable to the appropriate cultural community and that concern certain aspects of cultural and educational policies. Third, the Constitution creates *three political and administrative regions:* Flanders, Wallonia, and Brussels. It specifies only that their governmental bodies be elected and that their responsibilities not overlap those entrusted to the cultural councils, leaving all other matters to be decided by law. The exact powers and functions of Brussels as a region will also be decided by law.

The implementing legislation, as well as other laws pertaining to cultural and regional matters, must be passed by special majorities defined by the Constitution as follows: a majority vote of the representatives of each of the two language communities (Dutch and French) in Parliament, and a two-thirds overall majority in each of its two houses. For elected members of Parliament, except those from Brussels, membership in a language community is indicated by the language of their constituency; for elected members from Brussels, as well as for indirectly elected or co-

20. Tindemans made his statement in the course of a colloquium held by the Belgian Institute for Political Science on 31 January and 1 February 1970. The proceedings, which constitute an excellent source for understanding the constitutional changes of 1970, were published in *Res Publica,* 13, no. 3–4 (1971): 395–516; the quote on "federalization without federalism" appears on page 434. For details of the Constitution, the process of amendment, and so forth, see Robert Senelle, "The Revision of the Constitution, 1967–1970," published by the Ministry of Foreign Affairs and External Trade in *Memo from Belgium,* no. 128–129 (September–October 1970), and no. 132–133 (January–February 1971). Changes through 1974 are set forth in "Les institutions politiques de la Belgique régionalisée," *Dossiers du CRISP,* no. 6 (1975). The summary that follows is based on the latter two sources.

opted senators, membership in a language community is indicated by the language in which they take the oath of office in a given legislature. Moreover, an elaborate system of "alarm bells" enables the parliamentary representatives of a community to demand an additional reading of any legislative matter not covered by the special majority provision (except for budgetary legislation) which they believe affects their rights. As for the executive branch, the preexisting representation of the communities on a parity basis in the cabinet is codified in the amended Constitution. Whatever coalition might be constituted, the cabinet must consist of an even number of Dutch and French speakers; if included, a German-speaking member is not counted as French; and the prime minister is not necessarily counted at all, thus becoming in Belgian political parlance a "linguistic neuter" (in French, *un asexué linguistique*). Finally, the Constitution includes various provisions to protect minorities.

Underlying the settlement was an exchange process very much akin to the process of international bargaining, including procedures guiding the sequence in which concessions would be made. The Walloons, who feared minority status, obtained the institutionalization of a sort of parity principle; the Flemings secured the maintenance of the "iron collar" (*carcan*) established around the nineteen municipalities of the capital in the 1930's; in compensation, the inhabitants of Brussels secured the *promise* of a reinstatement of the freedom to educate their children in the language of their choice ("parental freedom"). Dutch speakers, the national majority, granted the French-speaking national minority parity in the cabinet in exchange for a grant of parity at the level of the municipal executive in Brussels, where the Dutch speakers, in turn, constituted a minority. Parity was also established within the national civil service, where Dutch speakers were underrepresented.

The process of reaching this equilibrium was marked by deadlocks and crises throughout the year. After several months of immobilism, the first breakthrough occurred in June, when Parliament, by a vote of 142 to 22, established the "alarm-bell" procedure cited earlier. Although the other measures mentioned above passed the Senate, not as affected yet by the electoral realignment, they could not make it through the Chamber, where the various traders simply stayed away in anticipation of the forthcoming municipal elections, which might clarify the distribution of power. Considered the most important municipal elections in the country's history, the October 1970 contest indicated overwhelming opposition to the proposed compromise concerning Brussels, where the FDF obtained 26 percent of the votes (as against 18.6 percent in the 1968 general elections). The Liberals were now the greatest losers. Elsewhere, communal parties also made further gains as did the Socialist party.

The progress of the communal parties now provided the other parties with an incentive to preempt any movement toward genuine federalism by carrying out the program agreed upon by the twenty-eight nearly a year earlier. The Walloon Catholics, fearing minority status in a double sense—as Walloons in Belgium and as Catholics in Wallonia—unless some form of insurance was institutionalized, addressed an ultimatum to the prime minister (a Flemish Catholic) that they would withdraw from the governmental coalition unless he acted. The various items mentioned above then became law within a few weeks on the basis of overwhelming majorities. The "iron collar" was maintained by a vote of 157 to 49 in exchange for the pledge to reinstate the freedom of parents in Brussels to choose the language in which their children would be educated, effective at the beginning of the 1971–72 school year. Viewed as a governmental coup at the expense of the capital, this compromise triggered demonstrations in Brussels, which signaled that further trades were needed before an equilibrium could be reached.

The newly amended Constitution provided a framework, for which implementing laws would now have to be passed; and the new requirement of special majorities gave the groups most affected a veto over all decisions. Far from a clarification, the changes had produced greater ambiguity. As one Belgian analyst put it, there was now "a state which did not become federal but which appears to be very broadly decentralized; communities and regions whose autonomy has been recognized but whose dependence on the center has been insured." [21] If all went well, not only would members of Parliament man the cultural and regional councils (except in Brussels, where the twenty-eight had provided for the inclusion of municipal representatives as well), but Parliament as a whole would retain control over the purse strings. As of early 1971, the traditional leaders remained faced with the same dilemma: would further delays or rather preemptive actions be the best way to protect their interests? A similar dilemma affected the newcomers: should they settle for

21. For a detailed account and the quotation itself, see Maurits Boeynaems, "Les années 1970 et 1971 sur le plan communautaire et linguistique," *Res Publica*, 15, no. 5 (1973): 881–914, as well as Wladimir S. Plavsic, "Les régions, les provinces et les communes en quête d'autonomie," in *ibid.*, pp. 915–946.

what they could get now, or hold out for more on the expectation of further electoral support?

In order to act, the coalition needed to broaden its parliamentary base. Since the VU had the largest number of seats among the communalist opposition, it made sense to begin with measures they favored and thus associate them with the settlement as a whole. On 23 June 1971, the Senate unanimously (eight abstentions) passed a law specifying the membership and powers of the cultural councils for the French- and Dutch-language groups. The Chamber followed suit on 1 July (Communists against; forty-two abstentions). In the course of marathon sessions held in the midst of an almost unprecedented European heat wave, further measures, including the reinstatement of "parental freedom" in Brussels were agreed upon in the next two weeks. Significantly the VU contributed its support to the government at a crucial point in this process, signaling a second step toward admission of the newcomers into the club. The major question now remaining concerned the status of the regions.

By the beginning of the 1971 summer recess, Prime Minister Gaston Eyskens was being hailed as the "Eddy Merckx of the Belgian politics," a signal tribute, which compared his record to the one achieved by the greatest contemporary bicycle champion. The government leader's performance was so remarkable, indeed, that one politician suggested that Eddy Merckx be called instead the "Gaston Eyskens of the bicycle world." With only another year to go in the present legislative term, however, the members of his coalition were beginning to jockey for electoral positions. When the coalition tottered in September over the Fourons/Voeren, a handful of villages whose linguistic status had remained unsettled since 1963—a minor but spectacular issue that could be raised whenever a stumbling block was useful—the prime minister resigned to hold elections before the coalition fell apart and to spring a surprise on the opposition.

The Catholic and Socialist coalition partners campaigned on their remarkable achievement of a federalization sui generis, as well as on their staying power. The communal parties advocated making the regions into genuine federal units, but differed significantly on the issue of Brussels: French speakers wanted it to be like Flanders and Wallonia, whereas the VU objected to a system that might allow for a coalition of Wallonia and Brussels against Flanders, and, therefore, campaigned to downgrade the regional status of Brussels. Torn by internal dissension under the impact of their great losses to the FDF, the Liberals fell apart in Brussels, where they sponsored competing tickets, some of which established alliances with the FDF, itself campaigning in alliance with the RW (see Table 5.4).

It was now the French-speaking communalists who emerged as the great victors, doubling their proportion of the national vote and surpassing the achievements of the VU (see Table 5.2). Their triumph occurred mostly at the expense of the Liberals, but also of the Catholics. With 34.5 percent of the votes in Brussels, the FDF with Liberal defectors who campaigned with it now constituted the leading party there; in Wallonia, the RW replaced the Liberals as the second largest party. The situation was much more stable in Flanders. In the Chamber, the Socialists gained two seats, the Catholics lost two, the Liberals lost seven, the FDF and RW combined doubled their representation from twelve to twenty-four, and the VU gained one.

The three-party national total now decreased to 73.7 percent, nearly equaling the 1936 low. Among them, with 16.4 percent of the votes, the Liberals still remained above their pre-realignment level. It is, therefore, quite clear that the consequences of the various electoral shifts of the previous decade occurred at a net cost to the two major parties, whose total of 57.3 percent now fell definitely below the previous historical low of 59.8 percent in 1936. The VU, with 11.1 percent, and the combined FDF/RW, with 11.3 percent, now came within the Liberal range. At the national level, Belgium had thus moved from a stable two-and-a-half-party system to a system of two medium-sized parties (themselves divided into autonomous regional organizations) and three small ones. Three of the parties remained national, in that, as in the past, they drew a substantial proportion of their votes from each of the regions. Because of the demographic weight of Flanders, all three parties drew more votes from that region than from Wallonia or Brussels, ranging from 70 percent for the Catholics to 50 percent for the Socialists. However, since the proportion of Brussels voters had declined among all three, the national parties actually could be viewed as two-region coalitions. The 1971 results also confirmed that the most dramatic changes had occurred at the level of the regions, where newcomers had in each case surpassed one or more of the traditional parties; as none of the older parties had been eliminated, however, each region constituted a four-party system of some sort.

Although the process of coalition making, modified as well by new institutional constraints, was beginning to reflect these changes, it was not yet clear whether the newcomers would definitely wish to become or would be accepted as ordinary members of the Belgian political trading club. These questions were, in turn, intimately linked with the issue of the manner in which regionalization would be implemented in subsequent years.

The formation of a new government was delayed briefly by yet another election, for the newly created council of Greater Brussels, which took place under conditions guaranteeing linguistic parity of its executive branch regardless of outcome. Campaigning on a rejection of this constraint, the FDF obtained forty-three out of eighty-three seats, an absolute majority (with 49.2 percent of the votes). It was only two and a half months after this election that a new government was formed. Headed once again by Gaston Eyskens, it was also once again a Catholic-Socialist coalition in which balance was achieved among twenty-nine members through a very intricate system. Aside from the "linguistically neuter" prime minister (who was in fact Flemish), there were nine ministers from each of the two language groups; but the Flemish demographic majority was reflected in the allocation of six of the ten secretaryships of state (junior ministries) to that group. There were two ministers of education and two of culture, reflecting the splitting of these ministries along linguistic lines some time earlier. Flanders and Wallonia each obtained secretaryships for local government and town planning, as well as for economy (but Brussels did not, as the issue of whether it was a region like the others remained in abeyance). As for party balance, there were ten Catholic ministers (including the prime minister) to nine Socialist ones (including the deputy prime minister), and five secretaries of state from each of the two parties. Among the Catholics, the Flemish wing had a total of nine posts to the Francophonic wing's six, reflecting the relative distribution of the Catholic voters; on the same principle, among the Socialists, each of the two language components was represented by seven members. Balance also existed within specific governmental sectors. The Catholics had the two ministries of culture, but the Socialists had the two ministries of education; and each region had one secretary of state from each of the two parties.

Pledged first to settle the remaining issues pertaining to cultural autonomy and then to launch the process of regional decentralization, the coalition lost its momentum. Not only did Brussels remain a stumbling block, but the fact that the new cultural councils dealt with matters pertaining to education reopened the secular-religious settlement achieved by the 1958 school pact. Equally important was a growing desire on the part of Belgian politicians to eliminate Eyskens, whose longevity in office was now disturbing. This proved easier to do than to beat Eddy Merckx. It was opportune to bring up, once again, the issue of the Fourons/Voeren. It was for these reasons rather than, as the *New York Times* put it in an editorial, because of a revival of " 'Tribalism' in Belgium" that Eyskens fell at the end of the year.[22]

Two months later, all three traditional parties joined a coalition headed by the Walloon Socialist deputy prime minister under Eyskens, M. Edmond Leburton. It was the first time since 1958 that a Socialist headed the executive, and the first time in years that the prime minister was a genuine Walloon, rather than a mere French speaker. The prime minister's "linguistic neutrality" notwithstanding, the Flemish Catholics objected to his inability to speak any Dutch at all. Although M. Leburton might easily have overcome his deficiency by taking a Berlitz course during the period of his ascent to power, the issue was settled instead by granting Flemings more important cabinet posts—which was, of course, the point they had sought to achieve by raising the issue in the first place. The Francophonic Walloon prime minister was "balanced" by granting each of the coalition partners a Flemish deputy prime minister, as well as by allocating, for the first time in Belgian history, the Ministry of Foreign Affairs to a Fleming. Balance was so complicated by the presence of three rather than two parties that the number of coalition members went up from twenty-nine to thirty-six.

The new coalition was necessarily unwieldy and wore itself out very rapidly, as it was vulnerable to a very broad range of controversial issues. There were now open skirmishes in the "school war," and tensions between the religious- and secular-minded components of the coalition were further exacerbated by the appearance of the abortion issue. The Catholics "betrayed" the Socialists by supporting a Liberal candidate as head of the Walloon Cultural Council. Catholics and Liberals were also close to each other on defending the tradition of free enterprise against a Socialist plan for state participation in the creation of a new refinery, which would be located in Wallonia. The Flemish Cultural Council's decision to

22. *New York Times,* 26 November 1972.

enforce regional unilingualism in the *private* sector (large firms), an action similar to that being taken in Quebec at about the same time, seemed to extend the powers of the new bodies beyond the intended range and stimulated further apprehension concerning the consequences of the still impending regionalization. On that score, no progress was made concerning Brussels, where the FDF—not a member of the coalition—now ruled almost supreme. The coalition's sole progress in implementing the amended Constitution was to create a cultural council for the hitherto neglected German-speaking community. All of this occurred in the face of a mounting recession, which drove the Socialists somewhat to the left where, influenced by developments in France, they initiated a rapprochement with the Communist party. After a government reshuffle, which reduced the weight of Flemish Catholics and of Walloon Socialists in the coalition, the prime minister, further weakened by a corruption scandal, decided in January 1974 to resign in order to provide his party with an opportunity to recover while in opposition.

The residual Catholic-Liberal partners did not constitute a majority coalition. Appointed *formateur* (prime minister designate) in late January, the leader of the Flemish Catholics, Leo Tindemans, sought to organize a minority Catholic-Liberal coalition, with assurances of neutrality from the regional parties, a situation that would give them for the first time a power of life and death over a government and that also would further test their suitability for club membership. The regional parties demanded a very high price for the deal: the government must limit itself to the completion of matters already pending and pass a bill of intent concerning further constitutional revision in a genuinely federal direction. Unwilling to pay it, Tindemans then sought to detach the Flemish Socialists from their party's adamant opposition; but this move, in turn, antagonized the French speakers in his own Catholic camp. Although he was eventually able to convert to his views the left wing of the French-speaking Catholic parliamentary group (nine out of twenty French-speaking Catholic deputies)—a categorization that illustrates the fragmentation of the Belgian political process—the coalition did not materialize. Parliament was then dissolved and new elections called. The most important event, however, was one that did *not* happen: in the absence of a bill of intent, the new Parliament would not be a constituent assembly. By failing, the man who had coined the formula "federalization without federalism" several years earlier achieved his greatest success.

Gambling on electoral futures, Tindemans emerged as the great victor of 1974. Not only did he achieve a personal triumph in his own constituency, which contributed to an overall Catholic gain of two percentage points in Flanders, but the collective total obtained by the regional parties declined for the first time since they had begun their ascent in the early 1960's (see Table 5.2). The Liberals also lost some votes. Among the two major parties, a very slight Socialist decline was more than compensated for by a Catholic victory of over two points, bringing their combined total up to 59 percent. At the national level, the overall return to electoral stability was clearly indicated by a rate of external mobility of 3.5 percent, the lowest since World War II.

In Flanders, the Liberals beat the VU for third place for the first time since 1965. In Wallonia, however, they declined further; as both the Socialists and especially the Catholics consolidated their positions, the RW was now the third party rather than the second. In Brussels, the situation was confused by the shifting position of the splinters among Francophonic Liberals. Support for the FDF and its Liberal allies (whose total is shown in the FDF/RW column of Table 5.4) rose over that generated in the last general election (1971) but declined in comparison with their maximum strength during the intervening period. With 39.6 percent, the alliance remained in the lead, but was now far short of achieving an absolute majority in the capital.

The regional distribution of the electoral clienteles of the major parties in 1974 can be compared with the pre-realignment distribution in Table 5.3. The weight of the Flemish region remained about the same within the Catholic and Socialist camps, but became much greater within the Liberal one; Brussels contributed less to the national total of Socialists and Liberals; and the Socialist electorate was uniquely balanced between Flanders and Wallonia. Under the amended Constitution, as already mentioned, general elections also constitute "community elections" in which parliamentary candidates—who will constitute future members of the cultural councils—have to indicate their community membership. It is therefore possible to estimate voting patterns of the cultural communities as against the regions by allocating Brussels voters to the appropriate community. Of the electorate as a whole in 1974, 58.4 percent voted for Dutch-speaking candidates. Among the parties, their proportion varied as follows: Catholic, 75.0 percent; Liberals, 66.4 percent; but Socialists, only 47.9 percent. This confirms the unique character of the Socialist party and helps account for some of the choices it has made in recent years. The regional parties draw, of course, from their own language group. It is noteworthy that in 1974, the FDF/RW and their allies captured 26 percent of the French-speaking community's votes, whereas the VU obtained only 17 percent of the Dutch.

Altogether, then, as of early 1974 it appeared that a new pattern of electoral stability had been achieved, based either on six parties (including the Communists), or on ten, if the now largely autonomous wings of some parties are counted separately. The electoral realignment seemed to have accomplished what such processes often achieve—a containment of popular upheavals. On the other hand, it had contributed to bringing about a very great change in the membership and in the procedures of the political trading club. That there was to be a single club seemed to be assured; but it was also to be a club engaging in different, but intricately related, exchanges in distinct national and subnational markets.

Whether or not observers can make sense of the Belgian system, the ingenious indigenous traders seem to have experienced little difficulty in managing it so far. The implications of the 1974 outcome quickly came to light. The established parties publicly exulted in their victory over the regionalists, a spectacle that led the *New York Times* to report that a coalition with the regionalists seemed unlikely. In fact, the established parties were in the course of doing exactly the opposite. Four general elections in less than a decade had clarified the resources available to each of the actors. After a whole decade of change, there was a stable stalemate, in which the established parties had failed to stem the tide but could resist the imposition of federalism, and the newcomers had ceased to grow but could effectively veto any settlement that contained features they rejected.

The process of coalition making, which had begun prior to the elections with the failure to constitute a minority government, resumed in the light of these outcomes with a declaration by the president of the federalist RW that the future prime minister—who was most likely to be the Flemish Catholic advocate of federalization—would have his party's support on behalf of a fundamental law on regionalization. Appointed formateur on 15 March, Leo Tindemans sought to organize another coalition of the three national parties—an attempt which foundered on Socialist opposition to his proposals concerning executives for the future regional councils. Was this not a willful ''design for failure'' on the part of a man who had earlier advocated a minority government and evoked the possibility of "new allies"? In any case, it was toward the latter solution that he now moved.[23]

It turned out to require a two-step process. Calling a conference of all parties represented in Parliament (except the Socialists), Tindemans was able to secure from them commitment to his formula for the regional executives. They would consist of *ministerial committees,* thus binding the political process of the regions to the national one. Although a deadlock was reached on Brussels, Tindemans was able to form in late April a minority Catholic-Liberal government, which pledged itself to immediate regionalization. The new regional councils—not to be confused with the cultural councils already formed—would consist of the senators from each region except in Brussels, where they would be supplemented by one-half of the members of the local (agglomeration) council. The executives of these organs would be *within the government;* and their budgets would be allocated by Parliament to the regions on the basis of a formula giving equal weight to their proportion of the total population, their proportion of the national territory, and the proportion they contributed to the total personal taxes collected. Tindemans had thus publicly made his pledge, and the regionalist parties reciprocated by *abstaining* in the subsequent vote of confidence, leaving the Socialists and Communists alone in opposition. These mutual indications of good faith enabled the traders to resume private negotiations in mid-May, during which they hammered out a preliminary agreement on Brussels, providing for the maintenance of the "iron collar" around the nineteen municipalities for purposes of creating a region, but retaining the limited bilingual facilities established in 1963 in six others, to which another twelve were now added. The latter entailed a violation of the principle of regional unilingualism, which was papered over by granting to the French-speaking residents of these municipalities the ability to maintain a fictitious legal residence elsewhere.

Judging the concessions to be insufficient, the Brussels FDF refused to enter the government; it agreed, however, to let its RW partner do so and to remain neutral on the condition that the VU not be invited. It is on the basis of this entente that Tindemans proceeded, insuring governmental stability by exacting from the future ministers a pledge not to take individual action to create a ministerial crisis and making that pledge *public* when the government appeared before Parliament. It was in this fashion that, in

23. My account of the period 1973–74 (other than the elections themselves) is based on *Documents—CEPESS,* 13, no. 4–5 (1974); *Keesing's Contemporary Archives;* and daily reports in *Le Monde.*

July, Article 107, Paragraph 4 of the Belgian Constitution was implemented, and that Belgium was transformed into a unitary state divided into cultural communities, linguistic regions, and economic regions, all governed by the same political personnel wearing different hats. One of the "antisystem" parties (RW) had accepted responsibility for bringing about this solution; another (FDF) accepted it tacitly; and the oldest of them all (VU), by now considered to be the most reasonable among them, had merely decided for the time being to oppose an ordinary Belgian government.

Conclusions

If the interpretation presented here of Belgian politics during the most recent decades is reasonable, then there is some question as to what extent ethnic solidarities properly speaking—as against the differentiated interests of groups identifiable on the basis of language, but also on the basis of region, and especially of political and economic power—have provided the driving force for political transformation in Belgium. One major theme of the present essay is that in Belgium, as in other societies that contain a significant language segmentation, this segmentation will always provide some difficult items for the political agenda. It is not, however, because compromises between subcultures are impossible, as was suggested by Robert Dahl on the basis of American pluralist theory.[24] It is rather because many different compromises are possible, and because the equilibrium of forces is constantly shifting, that language remains on the agenda forever. The question becomes, in Harold Lasswell's phrase, "who gets what, when, and how" in the area of linguistic arrangements. In order to analyze the political process of countries with language segmentation, it is, therefore, necessary to understand the dynamics of language itself.

Although this has not been discussed in the present essay, the very properties of language insure that the impact of the differentiations it forms will differ significantly from those of other cultural or ethnic segmentations. Liberal solutions to inequities stemming from religious differences, for example, take two basic forms: removal from the public sector altogether (by way of separation of church and state, as in the United States or in France in the twentieth century), or formalization of equity in the public sector (as in Belgium and other consociational democracies).

24. See Dahl, p. 357.

Language issues, however, cannot be processed by separation from the state, since the state can make itself "blind" but not "deaf-mute." Language has a prominently *instrumental* aspect in addition to the expressive ones it shares with other attributes by which groups are differentiated, such as religion or even ethnicity and race. Furthermore, the very trends that have reduced the importance of religion in modern societies have enhanced the importance of language. There cannot be a linguistic equivalent of the process usually known as "secularization."

Certain properties of language—such as the fact that it does not lend itself to the constitution of mutually exclusive groups, since individuals can learn more than one language and ultimately exercise some choice over their "identity" or that of their children—contribute to the emergence of further differences between the processes of language politics and those related to other cultural and social differentiations. For example, language differences tend to produce, in the long term, areal patterns of the "regional" rather than of the "mosaic" variety since, under ordinary conditions, low-status minorities tend to get absorbed (such as Dutch speakers in Wallonia, or French speakers in Canada outside of Quebec). For this reason, among others, language segmentations seldom give rise to lasting patterns of communal violence but often do give rise to political separatism. Similar sociolinguistic factors help one to understand why "bilingualization"—often advocated by political elites as a solution—tends to be highly unstable, as it either leads to more rapid assimilation of the subjected group into the dominant one, or, alternatively, to the enhanced power of the subjected group and, hence, to its demands for unilingual autonomy. As opposite trends can occur concurrently in the same society—for example, the "Flemishization" of Flanders and the "Francization" of Flemings in Brussels—it is usually impossible to find, at any one time, a single equitable formula to regulate all situations encountered in a given country. Deviations, in turn, can become sources of new demands.

The impact of the linguistic segmentation on Belgium politics has varied considerably over time, not only because of the dynamics of language itself, but also because of the changing socioeconomic context within which the dynamics of language proceed. Since political settlements themselves affect these factors, it is quite obvious that sociolinguistics must be accompanied by political linguistics, a form of analysis that is not yet very well developed in the social sciences. Moreover, such an analysis cannot be limited to a consideration of factors internal to the society under consideration.

I have suggested that the impact of language differences in Belgium was most severe during the period 1914–50, because of the links that came to be established between internal differentiations and world politics as they affected the Western European region. This involved both macronationalisms (the clash of French and German civilizations) and ideology (regime orientation). During the more recent period, Belgium has been relatively unaffected by the ideological dimension of world politics, and there has been relatively little macronationalism in the Western European region. Hence, although some of the new communal and regional parties have been characterized as antisystem, they are hardly antisystem in comparison with their predecessors in the 1930's. On the whole, Belgian elites and the middle strata have welcomed the new Europe; but some of them have viewed its emergence as an opportunity to achieve membership in a political community with a much broader horizon than Belgium can provide. Hence, it is not surprising to find that some of the "federalists" in Belgium, far from being "parochial," are rather to be ranked among "cosmopolitans." Furthermore, it may well be that the fate of Belgium as a political community will be determined more in the long run by the fate of Europe than by internal forces. Movement toward European political unification is likely to revive separatism in Belgium. The present stagnation of Europe, following the flurry of hope that followed de Gaulle's departure from the scene, has perhaps contributed to the willingness of separatists to accept seats in the Belgian political exchange.

The achievement of "federalization without federalism" represents the political institutionalization of a specific social, economic, and cultural equilibrium, which had been in the making during preceding decades. In bringing about "a solution sui generis," which can be quite easily deciphered by anyone who has learned to "read" Belgium, there is no doubt that the Belgian habit of "splitting the difference," which is founded on an avoidance of distinctions between the necessary and the contingent, between the sacred and the profane, has played an important part. However important, the acquisition by the political class of this habit is but one factor in accounting for the relative absence of severe conflict in Belgium in the last decade and a half. As a consequence of earlier changes, intended and unintended, there was no longer any significant social or political inequality between cultural or ethnic groups in Belgium. Concurrently, the international situation—over which Belgium exercises little control—evolved in a favorable direction from the point of view of internal relationships. It is, therefore, not only misleading, from the point of view of social science, but cruel from the point of view of those affected, to propose this habit as a recipe for conflict management in societies where ethnic tensions are founded on injustice.[25] Under conditions similar to those found in contemporary Belgium, the habit works. It is uninspiring; it makes for little political beauty or heroism; but it does make a certain kind of life possible.

25. The most flagrant instance is provided by Eric A. Nordlinger, *Conflict Regulation in Divided Societies,* Harvard University Center for International Affairs, Occasional Paper no. 29 (Cambridge, January 1972).

6

The Social Class of Ethnic Activists in Contemporary France *

WILLIAM R. BEER

Ethnic activism is on the rise again in France.[1] The royalist and fascist movements of before World War II, compromised by collaboration, had vanished by 1945, and from Liberation until 1960 there was very little indigenous ethnic political agitation. Since the near-revolution in May 1968, however, more than sixty ethnic activist groups have emerged. The appearance in the spring of 1974 of the first presidential candidates in French history whose aim was a Europe of federated ethnic groups is significant, even though they received only a total of fifty-eight thousand votes.

"Ethnic" here refers to the socially significant cultural characteristics of a group in a larger sociocultural context.[2] Ordinarily these characteristics comprise items of dress, diet, and especially language, so in this discussion a regionalist movement is not considered ethnic unless it addresses itself to a linguistic minority.[3] The regions with linguistic minori-

* The research for this essay was carried out during my Fulbright Junior Lectureship at the University of Strasbourg in 1974–75.

1. Ethnic activism, in this essay, refers to regionally based, indigenous ethnic groups in France. It, therefore, does not include regional movements that have no ethnically specific population, such as the Young Normandy Movement, Eklitra (in Picardy), and the Center for Regionalist Studies of Savoy. Immigrant ethnic minorities, such as Algerians, Turks, and Portuguese, are similarly excepted. Finally, indigenous ethnic groups with no fixed regional base, such as Jews and Gypsies, are also not considered.

2. This conception of ethnicity is based on the distinction between race and ethnicity made in Pierre Van Den Berghe, *Race and Ethnicity* (New York: Basic Books, 1970), p. 10. There is some ambiguity with the linguistic criterion, though, because numerous people who claim ethnic identity do not speak their ethnic languages. For instance, only eighty thousand Frenchmen speak Basque although some two hundred thousand claim to be Basque.

3. This does not mean that all ethnic groups are linguistically distinct. In France, because of the peculiar place that well-spoken French holds in that country's value system, language is a criterion of ethnic identity accepted by most people, as well as by ethnic activists them-

ties in France today are Alsace-Lorraine, Westhoek-Flanders, Brittany, the French Basque country, French Catalonia, Occitania, and Corsica.[4] In each of these regions movements of greatly varying vigor have appeared, but all share a sense of cultural uniqueness and a resentment of the French state and its linguistic vehicle, the French language.

One of the principal problems that these movements present is how and why latent ethnic conflicts become politically revived. Here, this question is explored by examining the social class of the leaders of these groups, based on the proposition that there is a relationship between social class and the choice of this particular kind of political activity. The leaders rather than the followers are studied because the followers tend to be an evanescent and informal group and because the leaders should provide a clue as to why the groups have reappeared.

Historical Background

The regions of France were more autonomous before the Revolution than after. The monarchy had been centralized more than any other in Europe, but each province had a special status based on the terms of its union with the crown. The Revolution abolished all these special statuses and replaced the provinces with departments, ruthlessly subjecting all of France to the rule of Paris. From 1789 to World War II, regionalist movements in France, both ethnically specific and not, were nearly universally opposed to the consequences of the Revolution. Except for the revolutionary Girondists and the federalism espoused by Proudhon, opposition to Parisian centralism was the preserve of provincial conservatives. Paris was supposed to be Jacobin and the provinces reactionary; the dialectic between the two was seemingly the motive force of French history from the Revolution to Liberation.

In actual fact, Parisian centralism far antedated the Jacobins, and pro-

---

selves. See Guy Héraud, *Peuples et langues d'Europe* (Paris: Denoël, 1966); and Paul Sérant, *La France des minorités* (Paris: Robert Laffont, 1965).

4. Corsica was not included in this study because I originally intended to visit all of the regions and could not plan on a visit to Corsica. The regions studied include the following departments: Alsace-Lorraine—Bas-Rhin, Haut-Rhin, Moselle, Meuse, Vosges, Meurthe-et-Moselle; Westhoek-Flanders—Nord, Pas-de-Calais; Brittany—Finistère, Côtes-du-Nord, Ille-et-Vilaine, Morbihan; the French Basque country—Pyrénées-Atlantiques; French Catalonis—Pyrénées-Orientales. Occitania includes nearly all of southern France, and there is some disagreement as to exactly what its boundaries are. As its etymology indicates, Occitania denotes that part of France where the word *oc* was used to mean "yes," as opposed to *oil* (*oui*) in the northern part of France.

vincial opposition was not always aristocratic and clerical. But provincial France did repeatedly show itself to be conservative, as in the 1848 election of Louis Napoleon and in the suppression of the Commune in 1871. As a result of the Law of Separation of Church and State in 1905, many country "fiefs" became bastions of devout opposition to the anticlerical republic. Before World War I, anticentralist opposition took the form of federalism, and René Charles-Brun, the best known of this school of thought, had been a member of the royalist Charles Maurras's circle. Finally, the interwar measures of Premier Edouard Herriot—significantly, a Radical Socialist—to stamp out vestiges of Breton, Basque, Catalan, and Alsatian in the French school system reinforced the union of the ethnic opposition with the right. In practical terms, this meant that the ethnic opposition tended to be royalist or fascist.

The notable exceptions to the pattern were the Basques and the Catalans. The former were antifascist because of the ethnic overtones of Franco's war against the Spanish Basques. But they were also devout and politically conservative. The anarchist tradition was strong in rural Catalonia, and the Catalans on the other side of the Pyrenees could not be unaffected by it, nor by the republican stance of Catalonia in the Spanish civil war. The struggle of these ethnic minorities against their formidable foe in Burgos made the prewar conservatism of their French counterparts much less pronounced than that of others in the province-versus-Paris strife.

The Occupation proved to be a short-term boon for many other ethnic activists. Vichy policy was favorable to susceptible *völker,* especially Bretons. Scores of Bretons collaborated with the Germans, and there were even Breton shock troops to aid the occupying forces. Alsatians were conscripted by the thousands, though most were reluctant soldiers. Nonetheless, in the reprisal massacre of civilians at Ouradour, Alsatian troops helped the Nazis. Liberation was followed by purges of collaborators who had taken advantage of German and Vichy policies favoring some ethnic minorities. For a decade or so after the war ethnic regionalism was dormant.

Ethnic regionalism in France today is different from any in the past in that it is—in rhetoric, at least—almost entirely left-wing. Marxist-Leninist jargon is widely used even by some activists who still have strongly fascist beliefs.[5] This pose of radicalism has come about prin-

5. A contemporary Breton journalist's description of his political past serves to illustrate why the term *fascist* is used precisely and correctly here. This activist belonged to a group

cipally because other "movements of national liberation," particularly in the Third World, use communist slogans. Since many of these other movements have been successful, it is fashionable to imitate them.

Two series of events paved the way for the present wave of ethnic activism. These are the Algerian war and its aftermath, and the events of May 1968. The Algerian war was important for raising the question of who was French and who was not, as well as for demonstrating that France was not really "one and indivisible." The non-Muslim Algerians argued that Algeria should be French and that they were French citizens, since they or their recent ancestors had come to North Africa from the metropole. Thus, for them, the measure of "Frenchness" was that one spoke French. Based on this reasoning, Basques, Catalans, and Alsatians could argue that they were no more legitimately subject to Parisian control than were Arabs or Berbers.

According to the Evian Accords of 1962 the *pieds-noirs,* as the French Algerians were called, were to be considered French citizens only if they left Algeria and returned to the metropole. If they stayed in Algeria they would cease to be French citizens even though they were still culturally and linguistically French. The essence of these measures was that a territory was not necessarily French just because there were French speakers there.

The argument of many ethnic activists was a continuation of this logic. Brittany had only become part of France in 1532, Alsace had been alternating between French and German rule for centuries, and Catalonia had become part of France after 1659. The Basque country had been joined to the French crown in 1589, and the whole southern portion of France where the "oc" dialects were spoken had been joined following the hideous Albigensian Crusades. These segments of France, it was argued, were just as artificially attached to Parisian control as had been Algeria. Territories joined to France by treaty or annexation, where at least some of the residents spoke a different language or a patois, had the same right to demand independence as had the National Liberation Front of Algeria. The success of the Muslim Algerians in detaching from France a territory

---

called Youth of New Europe, which was set up during the Occupation by the German authorities. "I left this group," he writes, "when it was dissolved in 1944, *following the defeat of the European armies* and my imprisonment by the French authorities" (emphasis added).

once considered an integral part of the country made it seem to the ethnic activists that they too might have some chance of success.[6]

The near-revolution of May 1968 had a similar "demonstration effect," showing that a small and dedicated group of revolutionaries could shake the Fifth Republic to its foundations. In addition, among those who wanted radical change in French society, there was a certain disillusionment with the traditional parties of the left. After 1968, dissent was channeled in a number of ways. Trotskyite and Maoist splinter groups, anarchism, communalism, natural foods, Jesus Christ, Oriental religions, feminism, soldiers' and prisoners' rights, pacifism, and drugs are a few of the causes embraced since then.[7] Many people sought solace from what they viewed as an inhuman and technocratic centralism by turning to the folklore of their ancestors or of the regions where they happened to be.

Today in Alsace-Lorraine there are nineteen ethnic-regionalist organizations, only one of which existed before 1968. The Flemish groups are far fewer in number, but all three were founded after 1968. Occitania shows the importance of 1968 most clearly. Before that date there had been eight groups in Occitania, while since 1968 at least twenty-six have been set up there. Brittany's groups are somewhat different, because Breton organizations have always been much more vigorous and numerous than those of other regions. Of the seventy-eight Breton organizations studied, eighteen existed before 1968 and sixteen are known to have been set up since then. As might be expected from their Spanish orientation, Basques and Catalans demonstrate less clearly the watershed of 1968. Of the seventeen Basque groups considered, at least two were set up after and one before 1968, while the dates for the others have not been established. In French Catalonia, two groups antedated the May days, and these evolved into six in the ensuing years.[8]

---

6. This polemic appears in Sérant and elsewhere.

7. Alain Jaubert et al., *Guide de la France des luttes* (Paris: Stock, 1974), is a catalog of contemporary dissident groups on the left; of the hundreds of groups listed, the vast majority were established after 1968.

8. The names and founding dates of ethnic activist groups in France established since 1945 include, by region: Alsace—Voice of Alsace-Lorraine (1953), René Schickele Circle (1968), Elsa (1969), Regionalist Movement of Alsace-Lorraine (1970), Committee for the Defense of the Interests of Alsace-Lorraine (1971), Council of Writers of Alsace (1971), Alsatian Information Agency (1971), European Federalist Movement—Alsatian Section (1971), Uss'm Follik (1971), Vroutsch (1971), Musauer Wäckes (1972), Klapperstei 68

Methods

The population under study included the personnel of all organizations whose collective purpose is the propagation and preservation of the language and culture of the six regional ethnic groups in metropolitan

---

(1972), Federalist party of Alsace-Lorraine (1972), Mulhouse Liberation Committee (1973), Strasbourg Liberation Committee (1973), Alsatian Liberation (1973), Peasants of Alsace (1973), Alsatian Cultural Front (1974), Federalist party of Lorraine (1974).

Flanders—New Flanders (1970), Lillie Mail (1971), Michiel de Swaen Circle (1972).

Brittany—Ar Falz (1945); Ar Skol Dre Lizer (1945); Bodadeg Ar Sonerion (1946); Kamp Etrekeltiek (1948); Kamp Yaouankiz Vreizh (1948); Kamp Al Leur Nevez (1948); Kamp Breuriezh Sant Erwan (1948); Bleun-Brug (1948); Committee for the Study and Liaison of Breton Interests (1950); Confederation of Breton Cultural, Artistic, and Folklore Societies (1950); Movement for the Organization of Brittany (1957); Breton Student Youth (1963); Breton Democratic Union (1964); The Call (1964); Committee of Free Brittany (1965); Breton National and European Federalist Movement (1966); College of Druids, Bards, and Ovates (1966); Breton Organizing Committee for Progressive and Regional Action (1967); Breton Front (1968); Youth of New Brittany (1968); Breton Liberation Front (1968); Office of Documentation and Information for Local Breton Officials (1969); Committee of Action for the Breton Language (1969); European Committee for the Defense of the Breton People (1969); Adsav 1532 (1971); Group for Breton and International Political Studies (1971); Breton Communist party (1971); Survival in Brittany (1972); Breton Action Committees (1972); Breton Cultural Centers (1973); For the Breton Language (1973); Party of the Land (1973); Presses of Breton Anger (1973); Breton Resistance (1974). In addition, there are approximately forty-four minor groups for which no dates of foundation have been established.

French Basque country—Enbata (1963), Seaska (1969), Basque Socialist party (1974). In addition, there are fourteen minor groups for which no dates of foundation have been established.

French Catalonia—Roussillon Groups for Catalan Studies (1960), Cultural Group of Catalan Youth (1967), Roussillon Institute for Catalan Studies (1968), Catalan Regionalist Action (1969), Catalan Youth Front (1969), Roussillon Committee of Study and Animation (1970), Catalan Workers' Left (1972), Roussillon Workers' and Peasants' Left (1973). There are three other minor parties for which founding dates have not been determined.

Occitania—Institute of Occitanian Studies (1945), Vida Nova (1953), Occitanian Nationalist party (1959), Occitanian Committee for Study and Action (1962), Per Noste (1966), Vida Nostra (1966), Christianity and Occitanian Reality (1966), Occitanian Socialist party (1967), Anarchist-Communist Federation of Occitania (1969), Occitanian Library (1969), Périgord Section of the Institute for Occitanian Studies (1969), New Occitania (1969), Aparamen (1970), Occitanian Dramatic Center (1970), Regional Center of Occitanian Studies (1970), Teatra de la Carriera (1970), Occitanian Poetry Action (1971), Limousin Circle of Occitanian Studies (1971), Occitanian Committee of Support for the Basque Revolution (1971), Bearn Review of Occitanian Action (1971), Lu Lugar (1971), Occitanian Struggle (1971), Atelier Occitan Peire d'Auvernha (1972), Lo Reveilh d'Oc (1972), Occitanian Cultural Center (1972), Occitanian Cinema (1972), Occitanian Committee of Popular Unity (1972), Le Rictus Occitan (1972), Occitanian Cultural Study of Etang de Berre (1973), People's Circle of Occitanian Culture (1973), Roquebrune Committee of Occitanian Studies (1973), Occitanian Front (1973), Occitanian Liberation (1973), Occitanian Popular Movement (1974). There are also twenty-five groups and periodicals for which no date of establishment has been found.

France. Personnel of organizations that demand some form of autonomy or federal or separate status for these regions were also among those questioned. The staffs of magazines and newspapers of the same orientation were included as well. Finally, folk singers, poets, and novelists who use an ethnic language in their art were studied. In short, the population was composed of the personnel of groups whose goals range from folklore preservation through federalism and autonomism to creation of a separate state. It was compiled on the basis of a study of periodicals published by or about ethnic activists and on the basis of consultation with informants. It was further expanded by the inclusion of people cited by respondents as regionalist activists (*militants régionalistes*).

Class was derived from categories of occupational groups. The French census bureau's classification system was adopted in order that comparisons of activists and of regional and state populations might be made. The census bureau's classes of actively employed persons are farmers (*agriculteurs exploitants* and *salariés agricoles*), businessmen (*patrons de l'industrie et du commerce*), professionals (*professions libérales et cadres supérieurs*), white-collar workers (*cadres moyens* and *employés*), blue-collar workers (*ouvriers*), service workers (*personnels de service*), and others (artists, clergy, military, and police).[9] The use of these categories precluded counting seventeen students and one housewife who were among the respondents.

A questionnaire was mailed to respondents requesting, among other things, that they indicate their occupation. Five hundred thirteen questionnaires were mailed, and 264 responses were received, representing a 52 percent return. The major weakness of such a survey is that those who responded may not be representative of the population of ethnic activists. For instance, a mailed questionnaire would seem to favor people who can express themselves in written form, even though the questionnaire called for very little eloquence. Unfortunately, no parameters of the population are known (besides the number), so statistical tests for the validity of the sample are impossible.

Illegal groups required some special measures. Three separatist organi-

9. These categories are regularly used by the National Institute for Statistics and Economic Studies (INSEE), the French census bureau. They are not satisfactory for social science research, particularly since they lump together artists, clergy, military, and police! The category "others" is obviously a statistical, residual category and has no operational validity in contrast to the rest. But these categories had to be adopted if any comparisons of activists and of regional and state populations were to be made.

zations were banned in January 1974. They are the Breton Liberation Front–Breton Republican Army (FLB-ARB), the Breton Liberation Front–For National Liberation and Socialism (FLB-LNS), and Enbata (a Basque word denoting a wind of freedom).[10] For obvious reasons the questionnaire could not be administered to officers of these groups, but a sense of their occupational structure was gained in other ways. Since 1969 there have been several waves of arrests of activists from these organizations; when the arrests were announced in the authoritative *Monde*, the occupations of those arrested were cited. This method of determining the professions of personnel has evident weaknesses, the most notable being that people arrested for bombings may not be among the officials of the organizations they belong to. The mere fact that they were notorious enough to be picked up by the police could serve to qualify them as activists, although not as activist is defined for the purpose of this study. On the other hand, such data may show important differences between legal and underground activists.

Data

Table 6.1 compares the occupational distribution of the activists who responded to the questionnaire to that of the total actively employed population in France. The salient aspect of the class of ethnic activists is that it is overwhelmingly professional. While only about 5 percent of the actively employed population in France are classed as professionals, more than 40 percent of the leaders studied fall into this category. The proportion of white-collar workers is abnormal, too, but this is because many of them are teachers.[11] This leads to another, more important point. Of the 115 professionals, 74 are professors, and of the 84 white-collar people, 24 are teachers (mostly in primary schools), which makes a total of 98 teachers of one sort or another. Teachers, then, constitute some 37 percent of the entire sample of activists.

As Table 6.2 suggests, the activists who are in the teaching professions are not confined to any one region in France. There is a rather higher

10. The Corsican Peasant Liberation Front was banned at the same time. The legal ground on which the interdictions were levied was the Law of 10 January 1936, which stipulates that "all associations will be banned whose aim is to attack the integrity of the nation's territory."

11. The professionals, or liberal professions and executives, include the following subcategories: liberal professions, professors, literary and scientific professions, engineers, and executives. The white-collar workers include teachers, other intellectual professions, medical and social specialists, technicians, and administrators.

proportion in Occitania and in Brittany, but the occupational group is represented in each of the six areas.

Comparison of the distribution of teachers in the different regions invites description of the class distribution in the sample and in the actively employed population by region. Table 6.3 makes a number of points. There is apparently little regional division of labor in France. Among professionals, businessmen, service workers, and "others" the differences between the regions and France are not very great. This is also true for white-collar jobs except in Brittany. The proportion of farmers in Brit-

Table 6.1. Occupational distribution of sample and of total actively employed population in France (in percent)

Occupations	Sample (N = 264)	Total actively employed (N = 20,398,000)
Farmers	2.3	14.9
Businessmen	8.3	9.6
Professionals	43.7	4.9
White-collar workers	31.8	24.5
Blue-collar workers	3.0	37.8
Service workers	0.0	5.7
Others	10.9	2.6

Source: For total actively employed—INSEE, Projet de loi de finances pour 1975: Régions françaises—statistiques et indicateurs (Paris, 1975); based on 1968 census.
Note: N = number in population.

Table 6.2. Regional distribution of teachers in sample and of responses in sample (in percent)

Regions	Teachers in sample (N = 103)	Responses in sample (N = 264)
French Catalonia *	1.9	2.7
Basque country †	11.7	11.7
Occitania	49.5	39.8
Alsace-Lorraine	6.8	6.4
Westhoek-Flanders	0.9	3.4
Brittany	29.2	36.0

Note: N = number in population.
* Includes Lozère, Gard, Hérault, and Aude, as well as Pyrénées-Orientales; and comprises the economic development region "Languedoc-Roussillon."
† Includes Dordogne, Gironde, Lot-et-Garonne, and Landes, as well as Pyrénées-Atlantiques; and comprises the economic development region "Aquitaine."

tany, in the Basque country, and in French Catalonia is above average. Westhoek-Flanders and Alsace-Lorraine have an inordinately high proportion of blue-collar workers. All that these disparities mean is that some regions are industrially less developed and others are more highly industrialized; the liberal sprinkling of people in other occupational categories shows that these variant regions are far from specialized in peasant or proletarian functions.

This observation is linked to the comparison of the occupational distribution by region of the actively employed population to that of the sample of activists. As might be expected from Table 6.1, the proportion of professionals among the activists in each region is vastly greater than that of professionals among the actively employed population in each region, as depicted in Table 6.3. The large percentage of professionals is

Table 6.3. Occupational distribution of sample by region and of actively employed population by region and in France (in percent)

Regions and France	Farmers	Busi-ness-men	Profes-sionals	White-collar workers	Blue-collar workers	Service workers	Others
Brittany							
Sample (N = 95)	1.1	12.6	40.0	29.5	3.2	0.0	13.6
Actively employed	33.0	10.8	2.9	16.2	29.3	4.3	3.5
Westhoek-Flanders							
Sample (N = 9)	0.0	0.0	11.1	55.6	22.2	0.0	12.0
Actively employed	7.8	9.6	3.6	22.4	50.4	4.1	2.1
Alsace-Lorraine							
Sample (N = 17)	5.8	11.8	41.2	29.4	0.0	0.0	11.8
Actively employed	9.5	7.3	4.3	23.9	47.4	4.4	3.2
Occitania							
Sample (N = 105)	3.8	4.8	49.5	32.4	2.9	0.0	6.6
Actively employed	18.5	11.2	4.4	22.4	35.8	5.1	2.6
Basque country *							
Sample (N = 31)	0.0	9.7	51.6	22.6	0.0	0.0	16.1
Actively employed	24.4	11.2	3.9	20.2	31.6	5.4	3.3
French Catalonia †							
Sample (N = 7)	0.0	0.0	14.2	71.6	0.0	0.0	14.2
Actively employed	21.9	11.7	4.5	21.9	31.9	4.6	3.5
France							
Total (N = 20,398,000)	14.9	9.6	4.9	24.5	37.8	5.7	2.

Source: For regional and state actively employed—INSEE, *Projet de loi de finances pour 197* based on 1968 census.
Note: N = number in population.
* Includes Dordogne, Gironde, Lot-et-Garonne, and Landes, as well as Pyrénées-Atlantiques; a comprises the economic development region "Aquitaine."
† Includes Lozère, Gard, Hérault, and Aude, as well as Pyrénées-Orientales; and comprises t economic development region "Languedoc-Roussillon."

consistent in every region's sample, and the proportion of the actively employed population who are professionals is evenly enough distributed among the regions (ranging from 2.9 percent in Brittany to 4.5 percent in French Catalonia) so that regional variation cannot explain the prevalence of professionals among the activists in each region.[12]

The disproportionate numbers among the regional samples make comparisons between the large and the small questionable. But one observation can be made: the total sample's proportion of professionals was 43.7 percent. Discarding French Catalonia and Westhoek-Flanders, where the numbers are small, the variation from the sample mode is no greater than 8 percent above and 4 percent below. So the strong representation shown by this class does not vary widely within the sample by region.

A characteristic of the research method may be partially responsible for the large proportion of professionals and of teachers. A written questionnaire, as the discussion on methods pointed out, would tend to favor those who can express themselves in written form. The literacy required of a respondent probably introduced bias into the sample toward professions requiring a relative facility with written language. In addition, the letterhead of the accompanying letter, as well as of the questionnaire, was that of the University of Strasbourg. It would seem that academic personnel would be more likely than others to respond to such a symbol. Unfortunately, this probable bias is impossible to quantify.

There are very few farmers in the regional samples, in contrast to the varying proportions of farmers in the regional actively employed populations. There are no farmers in the Flanders group, which is not surprising in view of the highly industrial nature of that region. What is more remarkable is the absence of farmers among the respondents in French Catalonia, the Basque country, and Brittany. Brittany's lack of farmers is especially remarkable because so many in the region's population are farmers. In fact, the only region where there is more than one farmer among the respondents is Occitania, a huge and heterogeneous area, which includes some of the most marginal and exhausted farming land in France. The conclusion is inescapable that even in areas where agriculture still occupies a substantial proportion of the labor force, ethnic activism is not an activity that attracts farmers.

Just as striking as the paucity of farmers is the absence of service per-

12. Of course, this proportion is not evenly distributed throughout the whole country. Of all the professionals in France, 38.9 percent are in the notoriously overcentralized Paris region.

sonnel. Among all the respondents there was not one who could be classified as service personnel. This is particularly interesting since these jobs are often held by people caught between farm and factory, temporarily out of work or otherwise uprooted. In spite of the potential unhappiness of such a precarious life, the class has without question not contributed to ethnic leadership.

In all of the regions, the class designated "others" is greater among the respondents than among the actively employed. This category, as noted above, includes clergy, artists, police, and military, and is really more a residual group than a class. Most of the sample's personnel who are in this group are clergy, which in another classification system could be considered a profession. In each region except Occitania the percentage is three or four times greater in the sample than in the actively employed population. Even though the Basque country and French Catalonia (where the samples are really too small for comparison) are in the southern portion of France, the long tradition of anticlericalism in the south may explain Occitania's disparity in this regard. The proverbial religiosity of the Basques and the Bretons contrasts with the weak position of the clergy in Occitanian leadership.

These data lead to some important inferences. The largest social class of activists does not vary greatly by region. Thus, even though some activists make a great deal of "internal colonialism" and of the antediluvian uniqueness of their ethnic regions, the evidence indicates that despite interregional differences (which exist, but are not nearly as great as they are depicted), the same kinds of people are preoccupied with ethnic politics, no matter what the region. They are mostly professionals and white-collar personnel, especially teachers. Ethnic activism appears, then, to be more related to certain characteristics of the professional and white-collar classes, particularly teachers, than to regions or regional differences.

Accused terrorists are occupationally different from the leaders of ethnic-regionalist organizations. There have been several waves of arrests among Enbata and FLB activists. There were too few arrests of Enbata personnel to analyze their class distribution, but Table 6.4 shows the occupational structure of suspected FLB activists arrested in 1969 and 1972. The figures for 1972 are less worthy of discussion since they represent such a small number of arrests. Also, half of those arrested in 1972 were farmers, which is a complete anomaly; since the number of arrests was so small, however, this fact probably does not indicate a new trend. The important comparisons, then, should be made between the 1969 arrestees and the Brittany sample.

The Breton leaders and the 1969 arrestees are fairly similar in three classes: "others," service personnel, and businessmen; "others" in both cases is comprised mostly of clergy. Where they are notably divergent is in the larger proportion of farmers, of white-collar workers, and of blue-collar workers, and in the smaller proportion of professionals among the suspected terrorists. The percentage of professionals is still far larger than

Table 6.4. Occupational distribution of FLB suspects and of Brittany sample (in percent)

Occupations	1969 FLB arrestees * (N = 49)	1972 FLB arrestees † (N = 10)	Brittany sample (N = 95)
Farmers	12.2	50.0	1.1
Businessmen	10.2	30.0	12.6
Professionals	14.3	10.0	40.0
White-collar workers	36.7	10.0	29.5
Blue-collar workers	14.3	0.0	3.2
Service workers	0.0	0.0	0.0
Others	12.3	0.0	13.6

Source: For 1969 and 1972 FLB arrestees—Le Monde, 8, 11, 15, 17, 23 January; 7 February; 27 March; 24 April 1969; and 4 October 1972.
Note: N = number in population.
* Does not include two students arrested in 1969.
† Does not include one student arrested in 1972.

that among the actively employed of the region or of France. But of the seven FLB professionals only three are teachers. It is hardly surprising that terrorism should be avoided by teachers, but these figures indicate that there is a distinct difference between the class of legal activists and that of illegal activists.

Though they were not included in the survey, the Corsican activists should be considered here for the purposes of comparison. As of the end of 1976, there were five legal autonomist groups in Corsica and seven underground groups.[13] From newspaper accounts little can be gleaned about

13. The legal groups are the Corsican People's Party for Autonomy, founded in 1974 from two other groups, the Corsican People's party (founded in 1966) and the Corsican Progress party (founded in 1970); the Corsican Socialist party (founded in 1973), a group of far-left socialists; the Union of the Fatherland (founded in 1970); the Association of Corsican Patriots (formed in February 1976 to replace the banned Action for the Corsican Renaissance); and the Corsican Front (created in March 1976). The clandestine groups are the Corsican Peasant Liberation Front (created in 1973 and banned in 1974), the Ghjustizia

the class composition of the leaders of these organizations. The founders of a recently dissolved group were two brothers who are doctors; another founding member is an optician. The various arrestees over the last seven years have been listed as a high-school teacher, a salesman, a bar owner, and a businessman. In contrast with the arrestees in Brittany, none was a blue-collar or an agricultural worker.

The data, then, indicate that a large plurality of the legal activists are teachers (service workers, blue-collar workers, and farmers are underrepresented in the legal-activist category); that teachers are overrepresented no matter what the ethnic region (this overrepresentation is not due to regional variations); and that most illegal activists are not teachers, but are farmers, blue-collar workers, and particularly white-collar workers. Beyond these inferences, explanations of ethnic activism must be discussed more tentatively.

The factors that make for the exceptionally high proportion of teachers among ethnic activists may lie less in the historical relations between ethnic minorities and Paris or in the rapidly diminishing differences between France's various regions than in the recent history of French politics and in the nature of the French educational system. The educational system is notorious for producing overqualified secondary-school teachers because of a severe lack of openings in universities. Often people will spend the ten to fifteen years required to prepare an advanaced doctoral dissertation teaching in a provincial secondary school. Even when one obtains a doctorate, a university position is not guaranteed because of the desperate competition for the limited number of spaces. Thus, the system guarantees an underemployed and overqualified army of provincial teachers, who are, therefore, almost certain to be discontented.

Whatever the source of the teachers' discontent, their role in ethnic activist groups must be understood in the broader context of this class of persons in *many* protest movements, in other countries as well as in France. Yet why have these teachers become involved in *ethnic* activist movements? One answer is suggested by the disenchantment since 1968 with the opposition parties of the traditional left. In French history, the primary-school teacher was the secular counterbalance to the village

---

Paolina (named after the founder of the seventeenth-century Corsican republic, and which claimed responsibility for blowing up a Caravelle jetliner in Bastia in 1974), the Committee of Support for the Pentecost Demonstration, the Committee of National Liberation, the Corsican Revolutionary Year, the Revolutionary Commandos, the National Liberation Front (created in May 1976 and including some of the foregoing illegal groups).

priest; primary-school, secondary-school, and university teachers have been inordinately active in the leadership of radical, socialist, and communist movements.[14] With the political bankruptcy of the traditional left in 1968, many concluded that the system could not effectively be opposed in that context, and they turned to other kinds of protest.

A complementary explanation of teachers' ethnic activism may be that these people are often the spearheads of "Frenchification." The extirpation of patois, regional dialects, and accents is to a very great extent the job of provincial school teachers. Most of them carry on this job assiduously, but it is inevitable that some, discontented with their lot in the system but unwilling to align themselves with the traditional opposition parties, should come to sympathize with regional linguistic minorities.

What of the class differences between legal leaders and suspected terrorists? Leaders of organizations in France tend to come from more educated backgrounds, while followers tend to be from different kinds of working class backgrounds, whether peasant, functionary, or worker. Additionally, there may be a qualitative difference in the sort of people who undertake legal political activity and those who gravitate toward terrorism. These explanations are complementary, in that professionals, especially teachers, will spend a lot of time studying and articulating discontent, though they may not be quick to undertake illegal or violent actions. Activists in other occupations—though not generally students, to judge by the paucity of students among arrestees—are more likely to translate slogans into explosions.

Conclusions

Present ethnic activism in France is unlike any in the past in that it appears to be radical or revolutionary, at least in its language, in contrast to the royalist and fascist tendencies of before the Occupation. But since many present-day activists are former collaborators, and since there is little evidence that the radicalism is more than rhetoric-deep, this aspect may not be so unique. The combined effects of the Algerian war and the events of May 1968 have given this wave of ethnic regionalism its un-

---

14. An example of teachers' participation in radical activism is provided in Roland Cayrol, "Histoire et sociologie d'un parti," introduction to Michel Rocard, *Le PSU et l'avenir socialiste de la France* (Paris: Seuil, 1969), pp. 38–39. Cayrol shows that of the dues-paying activists of the United Socialist party (PSU)—one of the most radical grassroots political parties in France—professors comprise 13.7 percent and teachers, 9.2 percent, making a total of 22.9 percent, or more than one-fifth of the activists.

usual strength. The former was as important for questioning the indivisibility of France as it was for making it stylish to imitate Third World "liberation" movements. The latter was important for driving many people, including those inclined to protest, away from the opposition parties of the traditional left, and some undoubtedly turned to ethnic activism.

The class makeup of the activist leaders, according to the data, indicates that the causes of this discontent lie less in regionally uneven development than in grievances felt by professional and white-collar classes, particularly teachers, throughout France. The unhappiness of people in the teaching professions can be explained at least partially by the fiercely competitive and bottom-heavy academic system. This explanation underlies the demands of Breton professors that the Treaty of 1532 be revoked, or the mourning of Provençal school teachers for the dead Cathari. Such displays should never be taken at their face value.

This conclusion only partially answers the question of how and why latent conflicts have become politically revived. The consequences of collaboration, the Algerian war, and the events of May 1968 provide an explanation for ethnic activism in France; the role of teachers in French economic, academic, and political life explains why that occupational group is so active in ethnic politics. These analyses, however, do not go beyond the French context, and further research must be aimed at cross-national explanations.

7

Bretons and Jacobins: Reflections on French Regional Ethnicity

SUZANNE BERGER

In misfortune and in pain
Duchess Anne became Queen,
Believing that the kingdom
Would save her good land.

(*Refrain a*)   That's what Anne would have wanted,
                  Koc'h ki gwenn ha koc'h ki du.

And then came the pillage
Of every town and every village;
The Breton had broad shoulders
To bear twice his share of taxes.

(*Refrain b*)   That's not what Anne had wanted,
                  Koc'h ki gwenn ha koc'h ki du.

Then came the missionaries,
The Jesuits, the good fathers;
No colonies without missions,
They are there to preach submission.

    (*Refrain b*)

To kill the Breton tongue
They picked on kids in school,
Caught speaking Breton,
A slap with a sabot.

    (*Refrain b*)

Bretons, Brittany is rich,
For five centuries they have robbed you
And hand back in charity a part of
What they've ripped off.

    (*Refrain b*)

In school they took away your sabots
And hung them round your neck;

Put them back on again and boot out
The bastards and the intruders.

(*Refrain a*) [1]

Almost five hundred years after the marriage of Duchess Anne to Charles VIII (1491) and the annexation of Brittany by France (1532), a regional ethnic movement with widespread popular support has arisen in Brittany. In an area where mass movements and mass gatherings have been rare, tens of thousands flock to listen to Gilles Servat, Glenmor, and Alain Stivell, whose songs, like the one quoted above, have become the medium of expression of Breton nationalism. Breton parties have been running candidates in national elections, and there has been an extraordinary multiplication of Breton organizations and an intensity of participation unusual in France. These organizations have diverse activities and goals: at one end of the spectrum are groups with purely cultural and linguistic activities; at the other, the Breton Liberation Front, a terrorist group. But underlying their vast differences and bitter conflicts over means and ends, these organizations share a set of beliefs that create an emotional coherence that binds these disparate groups into an ethnic movement. These elements of common feeling are well expressed in the song of Gilles Servat quoted above: that Brittany was a country with considerable economic and cultural riches that has been ruined by absorption into the French culture, economy, and polity; that this ruin was willed by France, which has systematically repressed Breton language and culture, exploited Breton resources, and impoverished the province by its economic policies; that the results have been underdevelopment, unemployment, exile for Breton children, and domination by the elites of the central state; and that the only path back to self-respect and prosperity lies through a restoration to Brittany of some measure of autonomy in culture, economics, and politics.

The first important ethnic political organizations appeared in Brittany in the interwar period. But the ethnic movement in Brittany today differs from them significantly, for it has developed an original synthesis of certain elements already expressed in the earlier movements with a new and far more radical interpretation of the situation of Brittany within France. The core beliefs about regionalism and ethnicity are present, but transformed. Where the earlier movements moved to the radical right, the con-

1. Verses from a song written in 1970 by André and Gilles Servat, in *Gilles Servat: Chansons* (Saint-Brieuc: Editions Kelenn, 1973). My translation.

temporary Breton ethnic movement has moved to a political identification with the left. What is striking is that the political trajectory covered by the Bretons in the postwar period has been retraced by both of the other major French ethnic movements: the Occitanians and the Corsicans. Regionalism, ethnicity, and a leftist orientation have emerged as the three constituent elements in a new French politics.

Regionalism has a long history in French political life. In the nineteenth century and during the first half of the twentieth century, regionalism usually figured in conservative programs alongside demands for functional representation and for the corporatist organization of professions. It was, in brief, one of various strategies advocated by the right for dismantling the Jacobin state and "returning" power to the hands of natural, local authorities. In the view of its proponents, such a redistribution of power would have the advantage not only of altering the balance of power between the central government and other units, but also of contributing to ending class war—for within regions and corporations a natural harmony of interests would emerge, and ideological parties would find no points on which to mobilize participants. In this view, party politics was class politics, and forms of representation that bypassed electoral and party channels and that reflected, instead, the "organic" forces of society would contribute to social stability. Seen in this light, regionalism, functional representation, and corporatism, however logically distinct and even contradictory, were in fact complementary strategies.

What is striking about the regional organizations that have emerged in Brittany since the war is the extent to which regionalist objectives have been separated from the rest of the corporatist program and, in a sense, liberated for use by parties and groups of both the left and the right. The history of the Committee for the Study and Liaison of Breton Interests (CELIB), the regional economic organization created in Brittany in 1950, is significant in this respect. The CELIB brought together elected officials (officials from approximately nine hundred municipal councils as well as most Breton deputies) and representatives from unions, trade associations, and official bodies like the chambers of commerce (about two hundred organizations by 1967) in an organization whose objective was regional economic development.[2] The considerable successes of the CELIB derived, first, from its willingness to use both traditional parlia-

---

2. On the CELIB from 1950 to 1967, see J. E. S. Hayward, "From Functional Regionalism to Functional Representation in France: The Battle of Brittany," *Political Studies,* March 1969.

mentary and bureaucratic modes of intervention and mass political demonstrations and strikes. Second, the CELIB proved able to get support from left-wing and right-wing parties, from the unions as well as business associations, and from ethnic groups with very different ideas about how Brittany should fit into France. From its founding in 1950 until 1972 when the left defected en masse, the CELIB managed to keep itself from shipwreck on the shoals of party politics and to operate as if regional programs were "above politics." It was able to achieve a remarkable measure of consensus from its constituent organizations in its defense of regional interests, in its elaboration of various plans for the industrialization of Brittany, and in its demands for state aid for railroads, highways, and transportation to reduce the geographic isolation of the area, despite the political nature of the stakes.[3]

Why this consensus survived so long, given the intensity of the conflicts that separated the CELIB's members when they met in other arenas, is difficult to understand. In part at least, the CELIB success seems to be due to the weakening of class and corporative ideologies and the possibility this creates for new categories of explanation to emerge. Here the example of the conversion to regionalist doctrines of the Breton farmers' unions is revealing, for these are organizations with old and deep attachments to an essentially corporatist view of the world. Interviews with militants in the cooperative movement and in agricultural syndicates in the early sixties showed that even when peasant leaders had a certain general sympathy with regional programs, it had thus far had little impact on their conceptions of how agriculture ought to be organized and defended.[4] First, the core meaning of regionalism—that a Breton farmer has more in common with other Bretons than with a farmer in the Beauce—was a notion that men who saw the world through glasses shaped by corporatism found difficult to accept. They recognized that certain critical problems of agriculture in their region resulted from Brittany's position on the underdeveloped periphery of an industrial nation. But from this they did not conclude that peasants might have as much or more in common with

3. One early important leftist defection should be noted: that of Michel Phlipponneau in 1967. Phlipponneau had played an important role in the organization and came to be disillusioned with the results of cooperating with the government. He urged CELIB support of the leftist presidential candidate in 1965 and ran on a leftist ticket for the Assembly in 1967. *Le Monde*, 10 May 1967. See Michel Phlipponneau, *La gauche et les régions* (Paris: Calmann-Levy, 1967).

4. See Suzanne Berger, *Peasants against Politics* (Cambridge: Harvard University Press, 1972).

other French social and economic groups in backward regions as they had in common with agricultural groups located in more privileged areas of the nation.

In particular, even though the departmental Federations of Farmers' Unions (the FDSEAs) participated in the CELIB, they had not accepted the notion that the fundamental cause of the problems of Breton peasants was the underdevelopment of the region and that their natural allies were, therefore, other Bretons—shopkeepers, businessmen, workers—and not peasants in other parts of France. On the contrary, the peasants interpreted the special problems that Breton agriculture faced because of its peripheral position in the country as exemplifying in the extreme the problems that all French agriculture faces in an industrial nation. In sum, for a long time regional arguments were used to bolster an old corporatist thesis about the weakness of agriculture in an industrial society.

By the middle and late sixties, however, regionalist doctrines had begun to make considerable headway in agricultural syndicalism. The case of the Finistère FDSEA is particularly interesting, since it had been the most militant of the peasant unions in the early sixties. In a speech at the 1967 congress of the Finistère FDSEA, the president, Michel Hemery, developed a new line about how farm incomes could be raised. He touched on the two main themes of previous years: prices and farm structures. Then he went on to argue that the critical cause of Finistère's peasants' problems was the fact that they live in a poor region. There are "regions that get rich and regions that become poor." [5] The former are industrial; the latter are regions like Brittany that are industrially underdeveloped and therefore provide no adequate road and rail facilities for exporting produce and no jobs for those who leave the farm. Without a solution for the region's problems, Finistère agriculture can never resolve its own. "How can we, Finistère farmers, escape when we are chained to a sinking ship? The sinking ship is the general economy of Finistère, which is in a state of deterioration." [6] For the overall economic development and prosperity of the region, the only solution is industrialization. "Without industry, our agriculture, our department are condemned," declared Michel Hemery at a special congress on problems of the region. "All together, present and united, farmers, fishermen, businessmen,

5. Michel Hemery, in xxième congrès fédéral, FDSEA, Quimper, Finistère, 10 May 1967, pp. 2–3 (mimeo).

6. Hervé Le Goff, "Compte-rendu," Assemblée générale extraordinaire, FDSEA, Quimper, Finistère, 16 February 1968, p. 10.

shopkeepers, workers, artisans, we refuse to be the victims, the losers. All together, present, united, we demand the industrialization of Finistère. Our program will be no list of demands; our program has only one point: industrialization with its economic justification.'' [7]

As this speech suggests, regionalist ideas for the first time forced the syndicalists to look for alliances beyond their class. Both the diagnosis of agriculture's troubles and the remedies the regionalists proposed implied policies that treated the region and not the peasantry exclusively. From this point, it was impossible to maintain the corporatist perspective of agriculture pitted against an outside world whose interests were so different in kind and so hostile to those of the countryside that no political coalitions were possible between the rural and urban worlds. On the contrary, the regionalists claimed that those social and economic groups that find themselves in the same region have more in common, and hence more reason to ally, than do agricultural groups located in different parts of France. The peasants came to believe that to force the state to industrialize Brittany, political alliances with other social groups would be necessary. In lesser degree, the trade unions in the region—the General Confederation of Labor (CGT), the Confederation of Democratic Forces of Labor (CFDT), and the Workers' Force (FO)—also experienced this "regionalist conversion" in the sixties. In each of these organizations, the new cognitive map hardly eradicated the old maps of class, but the superimposition on top of a class view of the political universe of a new orientation based on the region supported the emergence of new patterns of belief and behavior.

Erosion of old class and corporative ideologies does not, however, suffice to explain the success of the regionalists. Indeed, as the events of May–June 1968 and the subsequent radicalization of politics in Brittany were to demonstrate, the old categories still had considerable vitality. Rather, what made regionalist organization so successful was that it was supported, both directly and indirectly, by an enormous expansion of ethnic consciousness and ethnic organization. Ethnicity directly supported regionalism through the membership in the CELIB of Breton cultural associations. But the indirect support was far more important: the ethnic organizations provided, in effect, a mass base for the regionalist movement. In fact, the only regions in France where regionalism has acquired signifi-

7. Michel Hemery, ''Compte-rendu,'' Assemblée générale extraordinaire, FDSEA, Quimper, Finistère, 16 February 1968, p. 11.

cant mass support have been those like Corsica and Brittany, in which populations have a distinctive and common ethnic identity.

While evidence is difficult to provide, there seems to be, in France at least, a symbiotic relationship between regionalism and ethnicity. Though the leaders of the regional movement, and of the CELIB in particular, were careful to disassociate their objectives from those of the ethnic organizations—from the traditionalist, folkloric circles of the past, on the one hand, and from the nationalist movements of the present, on the other— they acknowledged their debts to the ethnic movements, in a sense, by not disowning them. It was striking that at the 1972 trial of eleven Breton Liberation Front (FLB) members accused of bombings, the most conservative of the regional leaders (Georges Lombard, centrist mayor of Brest and president of the CELIB) testified in favor of the accused, arguing that even though the end they sought (autonomy) and the violent means they employed were wrong, their actions had sprung from a legitimate and understandable despair about the state of Brittany.[8]

The Breton ethnic movement has two principal wings: cultural and political. One of the most interesting cultural aspects has been the revival of Breton literature and language in the postwar period.[9] This has, in part, been an elite phenomenon, but it reaches beyond intellectual circles into elementary and secondary schools. The number of students offering Breton in the baccalaureate examination in the Academy of Rennes rose from somewhere between 150 and 180 in 1969 to 744 in 1971, and to 788 in 1975, despite the difficulty, even for Breton speakers, of learning to read and write the language, and despite the paucity of state support.[10] At the beginning of 1975, for example, the Association for State Schools (Fédération des Œuvres Laïques) of Brest organized a Breton school for children aged six to fourteen for after-school hours and promptly enrolled two hundred students.[11] A mass popular base exists for the music, dance, and crafts groups that are flourishing not only in the cities but in the countryside. Two cultural federations alone (Bodadeg ar Sonerion and War'l Leur) have more than 120 organizations as members. The aspect of this cultural revival that has reached the largest numbers is the new gener-

8. *Le Monde*, 7 October 1972.
9. On contemporary Breton literature, see Yann-Ber Piriou, "Vingt ans de littérature bretonne," *Le Monde*, 6 March 1968.
10. The 1971 figure represents 7 percent of the students taking examinations at the Academy of Rennes that year. *Le Monde*, 16–17 May 1971.
11. *Le Monde*, 1 February 1975.

ation of Breton folk singers, who, in addition to performing traditional music compose their own songs. The concerts of men like Servat, Glenmor, and Stivell are more like mass rallies than performances. In an area where the Sunday-night dance has been the only form of organized leisure activity, mass culture has finally arrived in a Breton garb.

There are many who are interested in the cultural aspects of ethnicity but who reject any political projects for Breton autonomy. For example, Georges Dauphin, the past president of the Finistère FDSEA explained his opposition to Breton nationalism by the fact that the Algerian war had turned him against all nationalism, French included; but he then went on to express his enthusiasm for the revival of ethnic cultural activities and commented with astonishment on their impact. "This all began after May 1968. These Breton singers are mind-blowing [*epoustouflant*]. This business has a terrific strength, and it's hard to say how far it can go. The elites don't control this phenomenon, since the artists—their principal target—are now everywhere." [12]

For other Bretons, even the cultural manifestations of ethnicity are negative. In response to a question about Breton language and nationalism, one man interviewed said that although Breton was the language he used every day with family and friends— although he dreamt in Breton—he still thought that it was an "unnecessary language" and that it contributed to the humiliation and troubles of Bretons when they moved from their families into the wider society. This man's rejection of his own language (and the rejection by others) may in part be explained by the stigma that French schools and French society have attached to Breton culture. [13] During the Third Republic the inscription "No spitting and no Breton" figured on public buildings. Just as Little Black Sambo symbolized for Americans the happy, simple black, the cartoon figure of the servant girl Becassine symbolized for generations of Frenchmen the happy, stupid Breton. The Bretons were the servants, the prostitutes, the cannon fodder of France, and escape from Brittany into French civilization was held out by schools to Breton children as the only route to dignity and self-respect.

12. Interview with Georges Dauphin, June 1973.
13. On the ways in which the French denigrated Breton language and culture and distorted Breton history, see two excellent books: Morvan Lebesque, *Comment peut-on être breton?* (Paris: Seuil, 1970); and Pierre-Jakez Helias, *Le Cheval d'orgueil* (Paris: Plon, 1975). A general history of "Breton-French" relations is Paul Serant, *La Bretagne et la France* (Paris: Fayard, 1971).

There is, however, another reason for the rejection of cultural ethnicity. The Jacobin argument that regional languages and cultures necessarily lead to and support separatist movements and hence threaten the integrity of France is one which is widely accepted by both left-wing and right-wing elites in France and which finds a certain support even in Brittany. The Radical prime minister Combes who ordered in 1905 that no Breton be spoken in church—for the Bretons would be republican only when they spoke French—was only echoing his Jacobin ancestors who had proclaimed, "Citizens, let a sacred competition take place to banish from all parts of France those jargons which are the remains of feudalism and the monuments of slavery." [14] The Jacobin legacy has been appropriated by the right as well as by the left. It was a staunch Gaullist, Alexandre Sanguinetti, not a man of the left, who argued before the National Assembly: "It is no accident that for seven centuries monarchy, empire, and republics have all been centralizers. It is because France is not a natural construction. It is an artificial political construction, for which the central power has always strived. Without centralization, there could be no France. There might be a Germany or an Italy, for there is one German civilization and one Italian civilization. But in France there are several civilizations. And they haven't disappeared; you can take it from a deputy from Toulouse!" [15] When Breton autonomists collaborated with the Nazis during the Occupation and tried to get the Germans to establish Brittany as an independent state, they only confirmed what the Jacobins had always believed: that ethnic pluralism represents a danger to the survival of the state and that those groups seeking to preserve cultural values distinct from those common to all Frenchmen are seditious.

The leaders of the Breton cultural organizations have always denied that speaking Breton or participating in cultural activities has any necessary political consequences. But whatever the general links between cultural transformation and politics, it is true in the Breton case that the explicit political content in even the cultural activities has been increasing. When Servat concludes a song in praise of the Basque struggle in Spain with "Let Euzkadi be an example to us of how to live; / let the sea listen to the mountain; / suffering and bullets to be free; / and our love for you, Brittany," and when a federation of bagpipe groups votes a motion in 1961 condemning the policy of "cultural genocide and linguistic repression" practiced by the government of France, it is clear that the bounda-

14. Cited in Lebesque, p. 97.   15. Cited in *ibid.*, p. 127.

ries, however shifting and imprecise, between cultural activities and political ones have been crossed.

The great surprise is that although the Jacobins had always predicted
that the politics of ethnicity would be right-wing and reactionary, ethnic
politics in Brittany in the postwar period has been steadily moving left. In
this, the contemporary Breton political organizations break with their
predecessors. One need not go back to the Chouans to establish the right-
wing genealogy of Breton nationalism. Before World War I, the regionalist movement had been dominated by the Breton Regionalist Union, a
conservative Catholic organization of notables. The next efforts at organizing Breton nationalism were those of the Breton Autonomist party,
which published a paper called *Breiz Atao* ("Brittany Forever"), and
those of a secret terrorist organization called the White and the Black
(Gwenn ha Du), which modeled itself on the Irish Republican Army and
which first came to light in 1932 when it blew up a monument in Rennes
that commemorated the union of Brittany to France. Leaders of these organizations ended up in exile in Germany before the war and returned
with the invading German armies to urge a policy of active collabo-
rationism. At the end of the war, many of them fled to Ireland to escape
trial. Though there were figures on the left in the interwar period who
militated for recognition of Breton linguistic and cultural rights, they
remained isolated and were, by and large, disavowed by their own parties.[16]

The wartime role of the Breton autonomists threw such discredit on the
regional ethnic movement that, although various cultural groups resumed
after the war, it took twelve years before any organized political activity
began. The Movement for the Organization of Brittany (MOB) was
founded in 1957 to advocate a federal system in France and "home rule"
for the five Breton departments. The leaders of the MOB were a mix of
some of the interwar autonomists (principally Yann Fouéré) and of new
men. Alongside the political arguments for autonomy, the MOB urged
economic development of the area. The objectives and means it advocated virtually coincided with those the CELIB was defending during
the same period.[17] Although the CELIB refused to support the MOB's
autonomist politics, there was, in fact, a convergence of interests between

16. See Lebesque, pp. 169–170. On the Breton movement before World War II, see Jack
Reece's manuscript "The Bretons against France."

17. See quotations from the MOB newspaper, *L'Avenir de la Bretagne,* in *La Taupe bretonne,* no. 4 (May 1973), pp. 34–44.

the two organizations in the early sixties when the CELIB was organizing mass demonstrations and protests for its "Breton Plan." With the virtual co-optation of the CELIB into Brittany's Regional Economic Development Commission set up by the government in 1964, the former's interest in mass mobilization for the region disappeared, thus cutting the MOB off from an important group of its backers.[18]

At this point, a new organization was founded, the Breton Democratic Union (UDB), with a few defectors from the MOB, but largely drawing on a new reservoir of support: the Marxist, noncommunist left. By 1973 the UDB had about four-hundred members, was selling about sixty-five hundred copies of its newspaper, *Le Peuple Breton,* and was in general the best organized of what by now was a multiplying flock of Breton political organizations.[19] The UDB has focused on linking the economic difficulties of Brittany to its "colonized" status within France and on demonstrating the impossibility of solving Brittany's problems within the capitalist system. "The solution of the Breton problem requires socialism," reads the heading of one chapter in a 1972 UDB pamphlet entitled *Brittany = Colony: End This with the UDB.* However different the economic vision, the political relationship with France that the UDB proposes for Brittany is essentially the same as the MOB's: a federal France with internal autonomy for the five Breton departments, which would have an elected regional assembly.

To the left of the UDB have emerged organizations with Marxist-Leninist-Maoist attachments: the Breton Communist party and the Group for Breton and International Political Studies, which publishes *La Taupe bretonne.* For the latter, the UDB is a petit bourgeois nationalist organization whose socialist rhetoric masks its real intent: "to build capitalism in Brittany with the local bourgeoisie if possible, without it, if necessary, but to modify nothing in the existing relations of production." [20] They see the MOB as quite simply a fascist organization. The audience of these extreme-left groups is apparently very small and is restricted to intellectual circles. To the right of the UDB is a small Breton party, Strollad ar Vro (SAV), which has run candidates in the elections and has received a small proportion of the vote.

18. See Hayward, pp. 58–59.
19. Despite its bitter opposition to the UDB and the partisan tone of the article, *La Taupe bretonne's* long piece on the UDB (no. 4, May 1973) is extremely useful, for it lines up the various programs and declarations of the organization from its founding to 1973.
20. *La Taupe bretonne,* no. 4 (May 1973), p. 98.

To this field of multiplying and diversifying ethnic political organizations can be added a secret organization, the Breton Liberation Front (FLB). The first of its attacks on government buildings was carried out on 11 March 1966, and between that date and the rounding up of fifteen of its members by the police in January 1969, the group carried out about thirty bombings, mainly of tax offices and police stations. The group "signed" its attacks by leaving behind flyers with the message "Fight the abuses of French bureaucrats in Brittany with the FLB." Until the 1969 arrests, there was considerable confusion about the group and its objectives, and it was generally believed to be directed by Breton autonomists in exile in Ireland, who in fact took credit for the bombings. This was subsequently shown to be false. The FLB leaders were, in fact, all residents of Brittany and had only sporadic contact with the Irish exiles and little interest in their activities. The FLB activists turned out to be very different from the activists of the interwar autonomist movements. The latter had been mostly students and intellectuals, while the FLB represents a wide range of social categories and occupations. Several workers, an architect, a few white-collar workers, two students, peasants, and two priests were among those arrested in 1969.[21]

The confusion about the FLB existed not only in the minds of the public and the police: the FLB was, in fact, created by the fusion of four separate groups who discovered each other by accident when they learned of bombings that their own group had not carried out.[22] The final element of confusion stemmed from their doctrines, which called for both separatism and federalism, socialism and nationalism. A declaration in 1969 read:

Recent events in central Europe [Czechoslovakia] show that in Europe real socialism can only be independent and particular to each people. Our socialism . . . will be humanist, cooperative, federalist, and communitarian, respectful of all human freedoms. . . . If we are first and foremost nationalists and independentists, it is because we know that the construction of socialism requires the political liberation of Brittany and of the Breton people, by the creation of a Breton society free of any foreign hegemony. Those in Brittany who call themselves Socialists or Communists but reject independence are only hypocrites, fools, and traitors.[23]

What is known about the FLB has largely come out after the two waves of arrests of its activists—in 1969 and 1972. The movement was declared

21. *Le Monde,* 8 January 1969.   22. *Le Monde,* 28 January 1969.
23. *Le Monde,* 14 January 1969.

illegal by the government in January 1974, but a year later was reported still flourishing with substantial supplies of arms and explosives.[24]

The group of FLB activists rounded up by the police in 1969 was condemned by virtually all other Breton political groups—from the deputies of the majority, who likened their acts to those committed by the autonomists during the Occupation, to the UDB, who labeled them "adventurist and illusionary" and who charged that their political "infantilism" hid an "ideological vacuum with a 'socialist' vocabulary." [25] It is striking that by 1972, when the Court for State Security tried eleven FLB autonomists accused of eighteen bombings that had taken place since April 1971, the attitude of the other Breton groups toward the FLB had changed substantially.[26] Even the politically conservative regionalists of the CELIB (Georges Lombard and Joseph Martray), while condemning the acts of the accused, expressed a certain sympathy for their motives. On the left, Michel Phlipponneau testified that those responsible for the violence were the elites, who had betrayed their promises to obtain an economic development plan for Brittany; a United Socialist party (PSU) mayor of Côtes-du-Nord argued that those on trial stood for all those in Brittany who were fighting their "double exploitation": as proletarians and as Bretons. Others pointed out that the only way Brittany had ever gotten anything from the state was by violent action. A professor of history at the Sorbonne declared, "I am against violence, but isn't it violence to force a people to disappear?" Yet another professor appeared in court on behalf of the Catalans to argue that in a situation of "domestic colonialism" the response of the FLB was an act of legitimate defense.

There is no evidence that this shift in opinion about the FLB reflects any increase in support for that organization's goals or violent means. It seems rather to be one symptom among many of the progressive radicalization of the Breton ethnic movement. In the context of this radicalization and shift to the left, FLB violence, although still open to attack on a variety of moral and strategic grounds, can no longer be condemned as simply a continuation of the fascism of the interwar autonomist movement. In an atmosphere in which ethnic activism has moved to the left and

24. *Le Monde,* 22 January 1975.
25. *Le Monde,* 2 May 1968 and 14 January 1969.
26. It is claimed that between 1969 (when the police said they had entirely dismantled the FLB) and 1973 there were two hundred attacks. There have never been any victims. *Le Monde,* 19–20 August 1973. On the 1972 trials, see *Le Monde,* 5, 7, 11, 12 October 1972.

politicization is increasing around regional ethnic issues, the FLB has come to be perceived as merely the most extreme of the groups.

The problem to be explained is, then, a double one: why the shift to the left of regional ethnicity and why the increasing political salience of regional ethnic issues? For the first, there appear to be four critical factors at work. The long-term variable has been the Gaullist monopoly of power at the center since 1958. In the first decade of the Fifth Republic, the effect on the regional movement of stable right-wing rule at the center was by and large that discussed by J. E. S. Hayward in his study of regional institutions in France: to convince the regionalists in organizations like the CELIB that the best way to realize their designs was by cooperation and "concertation" with the government (see note 2 above). Since critical decisions affecting the region were being made in the Plan Commissariat and the Ministries of Finance, Agriculture, and Industry, and not in Parliament, the logical forum for the negotiation of regional interests was the bureaucracy. The logical vehicle for such action was an interest group, not parties. Even before 1968 the conviction that this kind of politics could produce significant results had begun to crumble; and it disappeared first among the more left-wing members of the CELIB, who began urging a strategy of alliance with the left during the 1965 presidential election and the 1967 legislative elections. The defection of these men from the CELIB and the founding of the UDB resulted from their frustration at having failed to achieve their goals with a strategy aimed at changing state policy by working within the system as an apolitical interest group.

For the same reason that the regionalists during this period began to discover the left, the left began to discover the regions. Excluded from power at the center, the left became more interested in signs of movement at the local and regional level. In an article on the FLB in the left-wing magazine *Nouvel Observateur,* the author observes "that in the past few years, the French left has been making a devastating critique of its views on regional problems. It realizes, with a certain astonishment, that the demand for a regionalist revolution may be the prerequisite for democracy, for socialism." [27] The process of ideological change in France during the Fifth Republic, which is leaving the Gaullists and the Communists

27. Yvon Le Vaillant, "Les fellagha breton," *Le Nouvel Observateur,* 24 April 1968, p. 6.

as the last two bastions of Jacobin strength, is important and deserves close analysis. Here, however, it need only be noted that seventeen years of stable right-wing governments at the center have helped the regionalists and the leftists to discover each other—and that this trend was well underway even before the events of May 1968.

The May-June student uprising was the catalyst that greatly accelerated the process. At the time, the demonstrations, strikes, and slogans in Brittany appeared once again to be nothing more than a provincial imitation of a Parisian event. Four years after the event, when virtually all traces of it had disappeared in Paris, the impact of it in Brittany was still producing shock waves. One of the reasons why the radicalization of opinion generated during the May-June events had so little permanent effect in national politics was that there were no organizations capable of channeling the waves of antistate feelings into political organization or even of attaching these feelings to more coherent and more stable systems of political belief. In Brittany, on the contrary, the ethnic organizations did succeed in capturing a certain part of the antistatism expressed in the May-June movements and in linking it to the symbols and doctrines they had been developing over the past decades. This appears to be the only explanation that can account for the otherwise paradoxical outcome of the May-June events in Brittany, which provided mass support for the regional ethnic movement and radicalized it. As one opponent of the ethnic political groups put it: "A certain part of the youth were taken up and exploited by the leftists. For them, the whole Breton movement is a way of not being French, a way of being revolutionary." [28] An admiring biography of Servat, with one of whose nationalist songs this essay begins, states simply, "Gilles Servat was born in the month of May 1968." [29]

The third set of events that pushed the regional ethnic movement toward the left was two bitter strikes in 1972: one, of workers in the Joint Français, a Saint-Brieuc branch of a firm with its principal headquarters and factories near Paris; the other, of dairy farmers against the cooperatives to which they sell their milk. The workers of the Joint Français went

28. Interview with a director of an agricultural cooperative, June 1973.
29. Alain Guel, in *Gilles Servat: Chansons,* p. 5. The piece continues: "He was one of the first of that Breton generation who rediscovered without knowing it, in the street fights of 1968, that Armoricain [Breton] liberty and sense of a free and generous life that animated Emsav [national reawakening]. Alas! Paris was to return to its submission, its false glories and its work flags. The Revolution took refuge in Brittany." P. 6.

out on strike to demand, among other items, wages comparable to those earned by workers doing the same kind of work at the Paris plant.[30] During the eight weeks the workers stayed out, the strike aroused an unprecedented wave of public sympathy, for the plight of the Joint Français workers seemed to exemplify the situation of all Bretons: they were being penalized for being Breton. Many towns voted to contribute to the strikers' fund, as did the departmental council of Côtes-du-Nord. The peasant organizations contributed large amounts of food. The unions, the parties of the left, every hue of Breton ethnic organization, the Breton folk singers—all poured into Saint-Brieuc to participate in demonstrations and to support the strikers. Delegations from all Breton departments arrived; one rally was attended by ten thousand persons. The government finally moved in to pressure the firm to settle the strike. The milk producers' strike had political consequences that were, from the point of view of the government, just as unsettling as the strike at the Joint Français.[31] For the first time in Brittany, groups of peasants were fighting each other; and the charges of the strikers against their own cooperatives were radical ones: that the cooperatives, like any capitalist firm, were exploiting the peasants who sold to them; that peasants are workers who deserve a living wage and that it should be paid to them by the firms for which they work, that is, the cooperatives. The combined impact of these two strikes produced the radically charged atmosphere in which the second trial of the FLB activists took place. At a public meeting at the Mutualité in support of them, the crowd chanted, "Joint, milk, FLB, the same battle." [32]

The fourth factor that has brought the regional ethnic movements and the left together is the growing interest, in some parts of the left, in environmental issues. The role of the environmentalists in the evolution of the Occitanian movement over the Larzac case, involving the expropriation of land by the army for a military camp, has been important. In Brittany, some groups have demonstrated against the proposed location of an oil refinery on the bay north of Brest, and there has been some protest over the army's use of coastal lands. But these issues have not yet mobilized public opinion. Many of the regionalists have been pushing for industrialization for years, and they see the environmental protection issue as

---

30. See Michel Phlipponneau, *Au Joint français, les ouvriers* (Saint-Brieuc: Presses Universitaires de Bretagne, 1972).

31. See Berger, "Postface," in *Les Paysans contre la politique* (Paris: Seuil, 1975).

32. *Le Monde*, 7 October 1972.

contributing to the government's reluctance to promote the development of the area. The arguments of the environmentalists are regarded, in fact, with a certain suspicion: when a national park was created in Brittany, there were regionalists who charged that the government was trying to turn the area into a kind of Indian reservation where Frenchmen on vacation would come to enjoy quaint Bretons. The environmental protection issue, however, might fuse with the ethnic issue if the government's recently announced plan to search for oil in the Mer d'Iroise off the Breton coast produces important results. The success of the Scottish National party in the past few years suggests that the combination of the promise of riches with the threats of serious environmental damage and social disruption is an issue that offers great leverage to a regional ethnic movement.

The most interesting question that all this raises is why regional ethnicity has become a political issue precisely at a time when ethnic minorities are least different from their fellow citizens.[33] Three reasons for the growing politicization of regional and ethnic questions in France may be suggested. First, there is substantial evidence of an erosion of the old ideological bases of French political life. In Brittany, interviews suggest that even over the past decade the intensity of feeling that divides the right and the left, churchgoers and public-school supporters, at the local level has greatly declined.[34] The results of the last legislative elections in Brittany confirm this fragmentary local evidence, since for the first time Socialists have begun to make significant inroads into the Catholic electorate. The same phenomenon of ideological erosion is visible in the behavior of voluntary associations, as the case of the Breton peasant union that shifted from corporatist to regionalist doctrines shows. The weakening of old class and corporatist ideologies has created a political space in which new ideas and explanations of the world have a better chance of survival than they had in the far more tightly integrated and structured ideological universes of the Third and Fourth Republics.

Why these new political categories should be regional ethnic ones requires explanation. One theory that the Breton case apparently confirms is developed by Edgar Morin in his study of a Breton village in the

33. I am following here an argument I previously developed in ''Bretons, Basques, Scots, and Other European Nations,'' *Journal of Interdisciplinary History,* 3 (Summer 1972).
34. Berger, ''Postface.''

1960's.[35] Morin argues that modernization has preserved and added new substance to archaism. The processes of centralization and modernization that produce cultural homogeneity and national political integration *also* produce ethnic consciousness and a growing desire for identification with and membership in a community less distant and impersonal than national society. As television, travel, education, and occupational mobility brought Bretons into greater contact with other Frenchmen, they became increasingly aware of their differences. The villager who in the past had identified only with others in the little region where his own dialect of Breton was spoken, and whose only contact with France was in regard to taxation, conscription, and education, has learned from the mass media that he is a *Breton*.

The third explanation for the heightened salience of regional ethnic issues lies in the growing set of grievances with objective regional bases and, just as important, in the increasing visibility of those problems that fall with uneven impact on citizens according to the regions in which they live. The existence of wide regional disparities in incomes, in the provision of public services, and in the balance of modern to traditional economic enterprises is, of course, no new fact in France.[36] Nor can these differences between rich and poor regions of France be explained merely by the predominance of industry in the former and of agriculture in the latter, since even workers in the same industry, performing comparable jobs in different regions, earn varying wages according to the location of the plants.[37] Although many of these inequalities are not new ones, they are being experienced by increasingly large proportions of the population in the peripheral regions. With the decline in agriculture in regions like Brittany, an expanding part of the population is employed in industrial jobs. While peasants find it difficult to calculate their incomes precisely enough to compare their earnings with those of peasants in other regions, the disparities in wages among industrial workers in different regions are far more transparent. The strike at the Joint Français is only the most

35. Edgar Morin, *Commune en France: La métamorphose de Plodémet* (Paris: Fayard, 1967), pp. 61, 276 ff.
36. See Kevin Allen and M. C. MacLennan, *Regional Problems and Policies in Italy and France* (Beverly Hills, Calif.: Sage, 1970), p. 125.
37. A National Institute for Statistics and Economic Studies (INSEE) study in 1968 showed that a Breton worker earned an average of 11,900 francs per year; a Paris worker, 19,700 francs per year; and a Lyons worker, 14,000 francs per year. *Le Monde,* 27 October 1970. See also Phlipponneau, *Au Joint français.*

prominent example of the growing awareness of inequalities that are distributed regionally as well as by class.

In the period of economic recession of the mid-1970's, a second form of regional inequality has also become both more prevalent and more visible. The poorer regions of France, which are also those with newer and weaker industries, have weathered the impact of credit restrictions and declining investment far less well than other areas. The Midi and the West of France, for example, had the highest increases in unemployment in 1974–75.[38] In Brittany, the increase in unemployment was 65 percent in 1974–75 in contrast to the national average of 57 percent. This represented 8.4 percent of the salaried population in Brittany in contrast to the national average of 5.5 percent.[39] The poorer regions probably always have suffered more in times of economic troubles. In the past, however, much of the population was cushioned by employment in agriculture and in traditional trades, which, because of their imperfect integration into the market economy, were relatively well sheltered against economic fluctuations. Today, the larger proportion of the population holding salaried jobs feels the impact of economic crisis far more directly.

Finally, a set of political changes in process in France has exacerbated the sense of powerlessness felt by citizens and groups living in the peripheral regions. With the shift of decision making in the Fifth Republic from Parliament to the bureaucracy, the access to power for the peripheral regions has become even more difficult. In the years of the parliamentary republics, Brittany, with its large population and substantial parliamentary representation, could translate at least a part of its electoral strength into political advantage at the center; in the Fourth Republic, the CELIB's successes derived in part from its skill in exploiting this asset. The shift of power to bureaucratic hands has meant a marked decline in the influence of Breton politicians and interest groups. Local resentment against technocratic rule is strengthened by the fact that recruitment to the higher bureaucracy is virtually the preserve of those born and educated in Paris.

In sum, what this analysis suggests is that the future of ethnicity in France depends not on the survival of linguistic and cultural differences but on the way that the changing relationships between center and periphery are perceived and politically interpreted. Ethnic symbols are a means

38. *Le Monde,* 28 January 1975.   39. *Le Monde,* 26 February 1975.

for expressing a revolt against inequalities, against loss of power, and against the impersonality and homogeneity of advanced industrial society. These grievances may, in fact, be experienced with as much force in parts of France that do not have distinctive ethnic traditions. But whether these issues will ever find alternative forms of political expression where ethnic symbols are unavailable is a question that leads beyond the range of this essay.

8

French-English Relations in Canada and Consociational Democracy

DONALD V. SMILEY

The consociational paradigm as developed by such contemporary scholars as Hans Daalder, Arend Lijphart, Val Lorwin, and Jürg Steiner has three related elements: [1]

First, a coincidence of the most politically salient societal cleavages exists; in Lorwin's terms, there is a condition of "segmented pluralism." Apart from the political elites, most citizens are in a sense encapsulated in institutions that separate them from those citizens who have other religious, ethnic, linguistic, or ideological affiliations.

Second, the major political processes consist of accommodations among the leaders of the respective subcultures. The characteristic outcome of such accommodations is that each recognized subculture gains something of value, and majoritarian and winner-take-all solutions are avoided.

Third, elites are able to elicit and retain the support of the members of their respective subcultures so that the results of their accommodation also receive support. A corollary would seem to be that elites strive to maintain the autonomy and relative isolation of their respective subcultures. In particular, they do not seek support among the masses of subcultures other than those of which they are the leaders, and they refrain from otherwise polarizing the whole of the political community on intersubcultural issues.

1. See Kenneth McRae, ed., *Consociational Democracy: Political Accommodation in Segmented Societies* (Toronto: McClelland & Stewart, 1974); Jürg Steiner, *Amicable Agreement versus Majority Rule: Conflict Resolution in Switzerland,* rev. and enl. ed. (Chapel Hill: University of North Carolina Press, 1974); and Arend Lijphart, *The Politics of Accommodation: Pluralism and Democracy in the Netherlands* (Berkeley: University of Calfornia Press, 1968). There are also informative articles on Belgium, the Netherlands, and Austria in Robert A. Dahl, ed., *Political Oppositions in Western Democracies* (New Haven: Yale University Press, 1966).

Because of the continuing existence in Canada of two major ethnolinguistic groups it is impossible to interpret the country's political stability or its long period of evolutionary constitutional development in
terms of the cross-cutting cleavages that are purported to explain the stability of other Anglo-American democracies. It is not immediately clear,
however, that the relations between English and French dominate Canadian politics as do subcultural relations between ethnic groups in such nations as Belgium and Switzerland. In Canada, there also exist crucial and
persisting cleavages of an economic nature, specifically differences between "have" and "have not" provinces and between, on the one hand,
the two central provinces of the industrial heartland and, on the other, the
regions to the east and west of the heartland. Consideration of these economic differences has led S. J. R. Noel to suggest somewhat tentatively
that the provinces rather than the English and French groups be considered as the operative subcultures in the Canadian variant of consociationalism.[2]

But even if one accepts that French-English relations are the central element of the Canadian political experience, one will note that these relations are carried on at three levels or sites: within the central government,
between the federal government and the provinces, and within the province of Quebec. Although the emphasis of this essay is on the relations
within the central government, the other two relations are also analyzed,
and an examination of the impact of each relation on the other two is
made.

The Circumstances of French-English Consociationalism
Demographic and Cultural Aspects

Linguistic and ethnic divisions. So far as the two official languages are
concerned, the 1971 census revealed that 67.1 percent of Canadians
speak English only; 18.0 percent, French only; 13.4 percent, both English and French; and 1.5 percent, neither language. Of bilinguals, 92.6
percent live in the provinces of New Brunswick, Quebec, and Ontario,
although these provinces together have 66.7 percent of the Canadian population; 67.5 percent of bilinguals have French as their mother tongue.
Despite the preoccupation with French-English relations in the 1960's,
the proportion of bilinguals in the Canadian population increased from
12.1 percent in 1961 to only 13.4 percent in 1971.

2. S. J. R. Noel, "Consociational Democracy and Canadian Federalism" in McRae, p.
265.

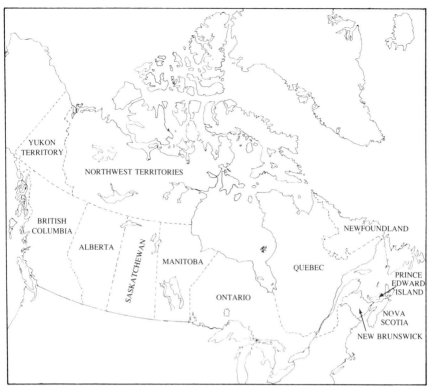

Map 3. Population and official-language distribution by province/territory in Canada, 1971. Population figures are taken from Susan Walters, ed., *Canadian Almanac & Directory* (Toronto: Pitman, 1975), p. 343. Language-distribution figures are taken from *Canada Year Book 1974* (Ottawa: Information Canada, 1974), p. 166.

Population and percentage distribution of English, French, and other mother tongues by province, 1971

Provinces	Population	English	Other mother tongues (%)	French
Newfoundland	522,105	98.5	0.8	0.7
Prince Edward Island	111,640	92.4	1.1	6.6
Nova Scotia	788,960	93.0	2.0	5.0
New Brunswick	634,560	64.7	1.3	34.0
Quebec	6,027,760	13.1	6.2	80.7
Ontario	7,703,105	77.5	16.2	6.3
Manitoba	988,245	67.1	26.8	6.1
Saskatchewan	926,245	74.1	22.5	3.4
Alberta	1,627,875	77.6	19.5	2.9
British Columbia	2,184,620	82.7	15.5	1.7
Yukon Territory	18,385	83.4	14.1	2.4
Northwest Territories	34,810	46.8	49.8	3.3
Total/percent of total	21,568,310	60.2	13.0	26.9

Source: Special Bulletin, 1971 Census of Canada, Population: Specified Mother Tongues for Census Divisions and Subdivisions (Ottawa: Statistics Canada, 1972). For census purposes "the concept of 'mother tongue' is defined as the language the person first learned and still understands. For infants, the language commonly spoken in the home is taken as mother tongue."

Until the 1960's the proportion of Canadians of French ethnic origin in the Canadian population as a whole was very stable.[3] It was 30.0 percent in 1881 and 30.4 percent in 1961, with a variation between 30.8 percent in 1951 and 27.9 percent in 1921, the latter figure representing the proportion after the highest immigration rate in the country's history. The fact that the French compensated for immigration with a higher rate of natural increase than the non-French accounts for the stability of the proportion. In the past decade, however, the convergence in fertility rates of Francophones and non-Francophones has resulted in a drop in the propotion to 28.6 percent in 1971.

With the decline of the Francophone rate of natural increase and the disposition of immigrants to assimilate into the Anglophone community, the proportion of Francophones is decreasing within the province of Quebec and in the Montreal metropolitan area.[4] This trend is likely to continue unless current efforts toward the assimilation of immigrants into the majority ethnic community are successful. The demographer Jacques Henripin has made two alternative projections, one based on a set of hypotheses favorable to the Francophones and the other unfavorable. According to the first, the proportion of those in the province with French as their mother tongue would decline from 82.3 percent in 1961 to 79.2 percent in 2000; according to the second, the decline would be to 71.6 percent in the same year. During the same period the proportion of those in the Montreal area with French as their mother tongue would decline from 66.4 percent to either 60.0 percent or 52.7 percent.[5]

Territorial separation of French and English. There has been a secular trend toward the concentration of Francophones within the territorial boundaries of Quebec and areas contiguous to Quebec in New Brunswick and Ontario. Richard Joy in a study published in 1967 describes this "linguistic separation" in these terms: "The pattern so common during the 19th century of English- and French-speaking communities intermingled within the same geographical region is now found only along the

---

3. The question Canadian census takers ask to determine ethnic origin is "To what ethnic or cultural group did you or your ancestor (on the male side) belong on coming to this continent?"

4. See generally Richard Arès, *Les positions—ethniques, linguistiques et religieuses—des canadiens français à la suite du recensement de 1971* (Montreal: Editions Bellarmin, 1975).

5. Jacques Henripin, "Quebec and the Demographic Dilemma of French-Canadian Society," in *Quebec Society and Politics: Views from the Inside,* ed., Dale C. Thomson (Toronto: McClelland & Stewart, 1973), pp. 161–162. *Mother tongue* is defined in the Canadian census as the language an individual first learned and still understands.

borders of Quebec province, with a zone of transition separating French-Canada from the English-speaking continent. This 'Bilingual Belt' includes Northern Ontario, the Ottawa Valley, Montreal, the Eastern Townships of Quebec and the northern counties of New Brunswick.'' [6] Outside what Joy calls the "Soo-Moncton line"—its extremities being Sault Ste. Marie at the eastern end of Lake Superior and Moncton in east-central New Brunswick—there is an ongoing assimilation of Francophones into Anglophone culture. The political dimension of the territorial separation of English and French can perhaps most easily be seen in terms of what one might loosely call units of political association. The 1971 census gives this breakdown:

Urban municipalities. There are fifty-two urban municipalities in Canada with populations of more than fifty thousand. Of these, only eight have official-language minorities of more than 10 percent. Five of these are in the Montreal metropolitan area while the others are Ottawa and Sudbury in Ontario, and Sherbrooke in Quebec.

Provinces. Only in Quebec and New Brunswick are there official-language minorities of more than 10 percent—13.3 percent English and 35.2 percent French, respectively. In the other provinces the proportion of the population with French as their mother tongue is: Newfoundland, 0.7 percent; Prince Edward Island, 7.6 percent; Nova Scotia, 5.4 percent; Ontario, 6.8 percent; Manitoba, 6.6 percent; Saskatchewan 3.9 percent; Alberta, 3.2 percent; and British Columbia, 1.6 percent.

Capital cities. Capital cities are the immediate working environments of elected and senior appointed officials of the federal and provincial governments, and the linguistic balances in these cities can be expected to have a significant though indeterminate effect on the politics of linguistic and cultural diversity. In Ottawa, the proportion of the population with French as their mother tongue is 20.6 percent, although if the Ottawa-Hull census region is included the proportion is 37.4 percent. In the provincial capital cities, the following proportions for the official-language minority prevail: St. John's, Newfoundland—0.3 percent; Charlottetown, Prince Edward Island—1.9 percent; Halifax, Nova Scotia—3.5 percent; Fredericton, New Brunswick—6.0 percent; Quebec, Quebec—3.4 percent; Toronto, Ontario—2.2 percent; Winnipeg, Manitoba—2.9 percent; Regina, Saskatchewan—1.6 percent; Edmonton, Al-

6. Richard Joy, *Languages in Conflict: The Canadian Experience* (Ottawa: published by the author, 1967), p. 5.

berta—3.2 percent; and Victoria, British Columbia—1.6 percent. Note that in New Brunswick and Quebec the proportion of the official-language minority in the capital cities is markedly below that in these provinces.

Federal constituencies. The House of Commons of Canada is elected from 266 single-member constituencies with an average population in 1971 of 81,054. Of these constituencies only 58, or 22.1 percent, have official-language minorities of more than 10 percent. Francophones are the minority in 24 of these ridings with a median strength of 21.3 percent; Anglophones, in 34 with a median strength of 25.0 percent. (In 4 of the constituencies where Francophones are in the minority—3 in the Toronto area and 1 in Manitoba—persons with a mother tongue other than English are more numerous than the French.)

Political culture. Only very recently have Canadian scholars come to study political culture and, more specifically, the differences between Anglophones and Francophones. Recent research has cast doubt on the largely unexamined premise of the 1960's that these differences are the most pronounced and salient ones in the Canadian political community. In focusing on feelings of political efficacy and political trust, Richard Simeon and David Elkins concluded the following from an examination of national surveys taken after the 1965 and 1968 general elections: "The polar regions are Ontario, British Columbia, and Manitoba, where we find high levels of trust and efficacy, and the Atlantic provinces, characterized by a pervasive disaffection from the political process. The other English-speaking groups fall close to the Ontario-B.C.-Manitoba pattern, although there are some differences between them. French-speaking Canadians fall nearer to the Maritime pattern." [7] John Wilson has claimed that there are ten political cultures in Canada, one for each of the provinces, and that such cultures are decisively determined by the stages of economic development that each culture has attained. In this formulation, the four Atlantic provinces are in the "underdeveloped" stage; Quebec, Ontario, Manitoba, and British Columbia, the "transitional" stage; and Alberta and Saskatchewan, the "advanced" stage. [8]

7. Richard Simeon and David Elkins, "Regional Political Cultures in Canada," *Canadian Journal of Political Science,* 7 (September 1974): 432–433, and more generally pp. 432–437.

8. John Wilson, "The Canadian Political Cultures: Towards a Redefinition of the Nature of the Canadian Political System," *Canadian Journal of Political Science,* 7 (September 1974): 438–483. Wilson's definition of political culture is idiosyncratic and relates to the

French and English in nongovernmental organizations. A study by John Meisel and Vincent Lemieux published in 1972 makes clear that there is no single dominant pattern of French-English relations in Canadian voluntary organizations.[9] Meisel and Lemieux devised a scheme of eight patterns ranging from "a single pan-Canadian structure composed of individual members" (the Royal College of Physicians and Surgeons of Canada) to "two parallel, pan-Canadian associations, one for each language group" (Boy Scouts of Canada and Catholic Scouts of Canada—French Section).[10] The varying kinds of ethnic relations arise from historical contingencies, individual personalities, and, of course, from the purposes such organizations serve. Because a relatively small proportion of Canadians are bilingual, one may assume that the ambience of these associations is dominated by one or the other of the official languages most of the time. In the 1960's there was a significant amount of French-English tension in organizations such as the Canadian Federation of Mayors and Municipalities, associations of university students, and labor unions, all of whose focus was largely on influencing governments. The Anglophones for the most part supported the national government, and the Francophones generally supported the demands of the Quebec authorities.[11]

Kenneth McRae has made an impressionistic attempt to designate the "degree of segmented pluralism" on linguistic lines in various aspects of Canadian life compared with the segmentation of subcultures in Austria, Belgium, the Netherlands, and Switzerland.[12] In general terms, linguistic segmentation was "high" in education at all levels and in the press and electronic mass media; it was "low" or "medium" in socioeconomic organizations, leisure activities, and government. Perhaps most significantly, linguistic segregation prevailed almost completely in postsecondary education, book publishing, newspapers and periodicals, and broadcasting.

---

nature of party competition, including the number of parties and their ideological commitments, rather than to the orientation of citizens toward their political system.

9. John Meisel and Vincent Lemieux, *Ethnic Relations in Canadian Voluntary Associations* (Ottawa: Information Canada, 1972).

10. *Ibid.,* chap. 13.

11. On the relations in labor and student groups, see David Kwavnick, "Interest Group Demands and the Federal Political System: Two Canadian Case Studies," in *Pressure Group Behavior in Canadian Politics,* ed., A. Paul Pross (Toronto: McGraw-Hill Ryerson, 1975), pp. 69–86.

12. See McRae, p. 246.

French-English Political Relations from the "Quiet Revolution" Onward

Current French-English political relations have been decisively shaped by the "Quiet Revolution" in Quebec, the beginnings of which are usually dated from the coming to power of Jean Lesage's Liberal government as a result of the Quebec general election of June 1960. Hubert Guindon's finding that the Quiet Revolution was a manifestation of modernization seems valid; urbanization and industrialization have brought into existence in Quebec a new Francophone middle class committed both by ideology and self-interest to secular, bureaucratic, and democratic values.[13] Recent developments in French-English political relations include the fragmentation of the political elite; the appeal of the Quebec political elites for Anglophone support, and the weakening of the insulation of Quebec provincial politics from external pressures; the breakdown of occupational segregation between English and French; and a weakening of the legitimacy among Quebeckers of the political institutions under which they are governed. A discussion of each of these developments follows.

The fragmentation of the political elite. The new political elites of Quebec are divided into three major groups, each of which espouses an approach that is fundamentally contradictory of the other two. The three groups are the federal Liberals, the Quebec Liberals, and the Parti Québécois.

The federal Liberals under the leadership of Pierre Elliott Trudeau, prime minister since 1968, have been committed to what I have called elsewhere the "bilingual and bicultural solution."[14] Proponents of this solution emphasize the linguistic and ethnic duality of Canada. They are dedicated to insuring equality of the French and English languages in the operations of federal political institutions, to strengthening the position of the Francophone minorities outside Quebec, and to encouraging the participation of Francophones at the senior levels of decision making in federal institutions.

---

13. See Hubert Guindon, "Social Unrest, Social Class and Quebec's Bureaucratic Revolution," *Queens Quarterly,* 81 (Summer 1964): 148–162; and Hubert Guindon, "Two Cultures: An Essay on Nationalism, Class and Ethnic Tension in Contemporary Canada," *Contemporary Canada,* ed. Richard H. Leach (Durham, N.C.: Duke University Press, 1967), pp. 33–59.

14. Donald V. Smiley, *Canada in Question: Federalism in the Seventies,* 2d ed. (Toronto: McGraw-Hill Ryerson, 1976), pp. 172–174.

The Quebec Liberals have adopted a policy of nonseparatist Quebec nationalism. Their current slogan is "[Quebec] cultural sovereignty within a Canadian common market." They have been uninterested in the bilingual and bicultural solution, and they are disposed to regard it as an irrelevant diversion. In domestic Quebec politics, their most controversial policy has been embodied in the Official Language Act, enacted by the National Assembly of Quebec in 1974 and popularly called Bill 22, which is directed toward establishing the primacy of the French language in government and in private business in Quebec. Significantly, the early 1960's saw an almost complete organizational separation of the federal Liberals and their Quebec counterparts.

The separatist Parti Québécois was formed in 1967. In the provincial general election of 1970 it received 23 percent of the popular vote, and in the succeeding election of 1973, 30 percent. Its social and economic policies are left of center, very similar to those of the New Democratic party in Anglophone Canada. To reassure the Quebec public, it has adopted the policy that after a Parti Québécois electoral victory the political independence of Quebec from Canada will not be effected unless and until a popular plebescite on this issue yields an affirmative verdict. Leaders of the Parti Québécois have spoken optimistically of the likelihood that Quebec's separation would be followed by some kind of continuing economic union with Canada.

The appeal of the Quebec political elites for Anglophone support and the weakening of the insulation of Quebec provincial politics from external pressures. In the 1960's, members of the contending Quebec elites were aggressive in communicating their respective positions to Anglophone Canadians and in seeking the latter's support. Trudeau became leader of the Liberal party in April 1968 and weeks later won his first general election on a highly personalized appeal emphasizing no substantive policy other than the bilingual and bicultural solution. During his campaign, Trudeau vigorously criticized the two major opposition parties for their support of the two-nations view of Canada. Significant numbers of Anglophones interpreted the Trudeau policies as being an effort to suppress Quebec nationalism. During the 1970's, however, members of the Quebec political elites have not confined their appeals for Anglophone support to federalists. Quebec nationalist leaders such as Michel Brunet, René Levesque, and Jacques-Yvan Morin have spent a significant amount of their time speaking to Canadian audiences outside the province. Paradoxically, the growth of Quebec nationalism has weakened the insulation of the province's politics from outside influence. Since the formation of the Parti Québécois and its rapid rise as a serious political force, successive Quebec elections have become, in effect, plebiscites on the continuance of Canada. Thus, Canadians outside the province, including of course the national political elites, have had strong incentives to become involved in the elections. Further, the increasing awareness among other Canadians of developments in Quebec has provided at least the potential for polarization outside the province on Quebec issues.

The breakdown of occupational segregation between English and French. The new Francophone middle class of Quebec has challenged the older patterns of occupational segregation. Those who have found their careers in private corporate business and in the federal public service have been less willing than were their predecessors to work in an environment that is wholly or almost wholly English and in which preferment is to varying degrees reserved for Anglo-Saxons. This new middle class perceives its individual and group interests largely in terms of the expansion of the public sphere in the province with the consequent creation of new occupational opportunities for professionally trained persons. An essential part of the bilingual and bicultural solution is to extend what Prime Minister Trudeau has inelegantly called "French power" in the federal public service, specifically in the professional and senior executive categories.

A weakening of the legitimacy among Quebeckers of the political institutions under which they are governed. The existence of a strong political party committed to separatism in a sense challenges the legitimacy of the existing political order, although the Parti Québécois has never encouraged Quebeckers to disobey federal law. The very speed of social and political change may have resulted in an even more fundamental challenge. One of Quebec's most respected political scientists, Vincent Lemieux, asserts that in the past the legitimacy of Quebec's political system was based largely on charisma. He contends that with the declining prestige of political leaders this kind of support has been weakened, and no commitment to new sources of rational-legal legitimacy (in a Weberian sense) has been established.[15] Such a loss of legitimacy in one of the subcultures would appear to attenuate one of the fundamental conditions of consociationalism.

15. Vincent Lemieux, "The Provincial Party System in Quebec," in Thomson, p. 113.

French-English Consociationalism within the Central Government

French-English consociationalism can be outlined in terms of three sets of national political institutions—the political parties, the cabinet, and the bureaucracy.[16]

The political parties. Since 1921 only the Liberal party has been able to gain consistent electoral support from both English-speaking and French-speaking Canada. In the seventeen federal general elections from 1921 to 1974 inclusive, the Conservatives have won as many as 20 percent of the Quebec seats on only two occasions (they won 24 of 65 seats in 1930, and 50 of 75 seats in 1958). The Cooperative Commonwealth Federation and its successor, the New Democratic party, have never gained a seat in Quebec. Social Credit has not elected any members from outside Quebec since 1965. Alan Cairns has argued cogently that the Canadian electoral system (election by pluralities in single-member districts) has influenced the tendency toward ethnic and regional polarization. In an article on the subject, he points out that "from 1921 to 1965 inclusive the Liberals gained 752 members from Quebec, and the Conservatives only 135. The ratio of 5.6 Liberals to each Conservative in the House of Commons contrasts sharply with the 1.9 to 1 ratio of Liberals to Conservatives at the level of voters." [17] In the 1974 federal general election only 6 of 95 Conservative seats were from constituencies where 10 percent or more of the population had French as their mother tongue, while 81 of the 141 Liberal seats, including 21 outside Quebec, were from constituencies with this percentage having French as their mother tongue.

The Liberal party is, thus, the major vehicle of French-English political accommodation. Since Confederation three of its leaders have been Francophone (Sir Wilfrid Laurier, 1887–1919; Louis St. Laurent, 1948–58; and Trudeau, 1968–). Survey research indicates that "French Canadians and Catholics support Liberals in larger proportion than they do the other parties (except the Ralliement des Créditistes). . . . The proportion of the Liberal vote from Francophones and Catholics is higher than the party's average vote. But, on the other hand, even allowing for this, no party is as broadly representative of the ethnic, religious, occupational or

---

16. For French-English relations in two other institutions of the central government, see Peter H. Russell, *The Supreme Court of Canada as a Bilingual and Bicultural Institution* (Ottawa: Queen's Printer, 1969); and David Hoffman and Norman Ward, *Bilingualism and Biculturalism in the Canadian House of Commons* (Ottawa: Queen's Printer, 1970).

17. Alan Cairns, "The Electoral System and the Party System in Canada, 1921–1965," *Canadian Journal of Political Science*, 1 (March 1968): 62.

any other kind of Canadian grouping, as the Liberal.'' [18] In terms of such demographic groupings each of the other parties appeals to a much less representative part of the electorate.

The federal cabinet. An essential element of the Confederation settlement was that there was to be a single prime minister for the Dominion and that his cabinet was to be constituted of ministers from the various provinces. According to the original agreement concluded in 1866, Ontario was to have the prime minister and four ministers; Quebec, four ministers; and Nova Scotia and New Brunswick, two each. Presently, the cabinet has twenty-nine members. The representative quality of this body has contributed to its growth and has frustrated the development of non-ministerial portfolios as has occurred in the United Kingdom.

Recent research indicates that between 1867 and 1965 Quebec held 30.4 percent of the portfolios in the federal cabinet, a proportion coinciding roughly with the proportion of Quebeckers in the population.[19] However, because of the widely varying significance of these posts the gross figures are not very meaningful. In the broad sweep, French Canadians have been overrepresented in portfolios that control large amounts of patronage but have limited policy-making functions. There have been few French Canadians in major economic portfolios, and there never has been a French Canadian minister of finance. Trudeau has overturned these older patterns since becoming prime minister in 1968. Under him, French Canadians hold or have held such important policy portfolios as minister of regional economic expansion; of transport; of communications; of national health and welfare; of industry, trade, and commerce; and president of the Treasury Board.

The secrecy of cabinet proceedings frustrates any definitive statements about this institution as a locus of French-English accommodation. Noel has said: ''If . . . the cabinet is viewed in the broad context of consociational theory, it can be seen as a mechanism of elite accommodation quite apart from the specific decisions it makes. Its importance, in other words, can be seen to be more in its function of bringing together political leaders from the provinces and maintaining their continuous involvement

18. John Meisel, *Working Papers on Canadian Politics* (Montreal: McGill-Queen's University Press, 1972), p. 35. Meisel's paper ''The Bases of Party Support in the 1968 Election'' is based on the most thorough investigation of Canadian voting behavior available. See pages 1–62.

19. Richard J. Van Loon and Michael S. Whittington, *The Canadian Political System* (Toronto: McGraw-Hill of Canada, 1971), pp. 349–350.

in the decision-making process than in the outputs of that process.[20] So far as these outputs are embodied in policies, legislative measures, regulations, and so forth, few are concerned in any direct way with French-English relations. Similarly, the activities of most of the departments and agencies of government are oriented toward clienteles, of which few are explicitly English or French. There is little on the public record about the partisan-political roles of ministers as these roles relate to the provinces from which these ministers come. That is to say that little is known of their activities in respect to patronage, to provincial and regional caucuses in Parliament, to provincial party organizations, and so on. It is, however, my impression that, less than in earlier periods of Canadian history, cabinet ministers today are politicians with bases of regional and provincial strength independent of the prime minister. It seems an exaggeration to imply, as one observer has done, that the representative nature of the cabinet is no more than a public-relations device aimed at convincing the public that the party in power is genuinely national.[21]

The federal public service. In the first half-century after Confederation the widespread use of party patronage in appointments to the federal public service and the representationalism in the cabinet together insured Francophones a significant access to preferment.[22] These conditions dramatically changed in 1918 when legislation was enacted to establish a merit bureaucracy. Merit, combined with the veterans' preference, which was awarded after both world wars, led to a rapid decline in the proportion of French-speaking civil servants—from 22 percent in 1918 to 13 percent in 1946—and this imbalance was most pronounced at the executive and professional levels. Although from 1938 onward some explicit recognition existed of the principle that, at the local level, French-speaking citizens, where they were concentrated, should be able to deal with the public service in their language, the working language of the bureaucracy in the national capital was almost exclusively English. In terms of salaries and career prospects, Francophones were disadvantaged when compared to Anglophones with the same credentials. Broadly speaking,

20. See Noel in McRae, p. 265.

21. Steven Muller, "Federalism and the Party System in Canada," in *Canadian Federalism: Myth or Reality,* ed. J. Peter Meekison (Toronto: Methuen of Canada, 1968), p. 126.

22. See generally *Report of the Royal Commission on Bilingualism and Biculturalism,* vol. 3, pt. 2 (Ottawa: Queen's Printer, 1969); and J. E. Hodgetts et al., *The Biography of an Institution: The Civil Service Commission of Canada, 1908–1967* (Montreal: McGill-Queen's University Press, 1972), pp. 473–482.

merit and efficiency criteria were so interpreted as to buttress unilingualism and Anglophone dominance.

As the Quiet Revolution progressed in the 1960's, the incumbent Liberal government in Ottawa "began to realize that a bilingual and bicultural civil service might be more than a generous gift to the Quebec minority and that it might be a political necessity to keep the nation together." [23] A new linguistic policy was announced by Prime Minister Lester Pearson in April 1966: as far as communications within the federal government were concerned, language would be at the option of the individual involved; communications with the public would normally be made in the language of the citizens involved. In June 1973, Parliament passed a resolution directing the government to identify the official-language requirements for all positions in the federal public service. The president of the Treasury Board reported in November 1974 that 281,664 positions had been so classified. Of these, English was essential in 60 percent and French in 13 percent, while 19 percent required bilingual competence, and for 8 percent, proficiency in either language was a qualification. [24] Of the 963 most senior positions designated as "executive," bilingualism was required in 93 percent. In the national capital region, 45 percent of all positions were to be occupied by bilinguals.

Since 1966, the government's policies regarding bilingualism in federal public service have reflected several not always compatible objectives. These policies are leading to increased tension between English and French. An explicitly stated aim of the government is to insure that Canadian citizens can communicate with their government and its agencies in the official language of their choice. A second objective is to create conditions under which federal employees, and specifically those of Francophone background, can work all or at least part of the time in the language with which they are most familiar. Another objective, however, is that of working toward a more representative bureaucracy along French-English lines and in particular of extending the number and influence of Francophones in senior positions in the public service. This trio of objectives has resulted in the co-optation of Francophones that were outside government into the middle and senior ranks and has led to Anglophone charges that the government is confusing bilingual competence with Francophone roots in giving preference to the latter.

23. Hodgetts et al., p. 479.
24. Communiqué, "Official Languages in the Public Service of Canada," 24 November 1974.

The Explicit Recognition of French-English Duality in the Central Government

There are several circumstances in which by law or convention explicit recognition of French-English duality exists in the national political institutions of Canada:

Constitutional and legislative recognition. Under Section 133 of the British North America Act of 1867, the French and English languages received limited constitutional recognition in the workings of both the national Parliament and the legislature of Quebec, and in the courts operating under their respective laws. The federal Official Languages Act of 1969 vastly extended this recognition in the operations of the government of Canada.

Rotation in office. Over the years, the leadership of the federal Liberal party has alternated between English and French: Laurier succeeded Edward Blake as national leader in 1887, William Lyon Mackenzie King succeeded Laurier in 1919, St. Laurent succeeded King in 1948, Pearson succeeded St. Laurent in 1958, and Trudeau succeeded Pearson in 1968. Since Vincent Massey became the first Canadian appointed governor-general in 1952, two Francophones have succeeded two Anglophones. Since the appointment of a Francophone as chief justice of the Supreme Court of Canada in 1944, there have been rotations between French and English in 1953, 1963, and 1973. The speakership of the House of Commons is frequently, though not invariably, rotated between Anglophones and Francophones, and by tradition the deputy speaker is from the group not holding the speakership.

The cochairmen device. Three modern inquiries into federalism and/or French-English relations have been cochaired by representatives from each of the two linguistic groups: these boards of inquiry include the Royal Commission on Dominion-Provincial Relations (1936), the Royal Commission on Bilingualism and Biculturalism (1963), and the Special Joint Committee of the Senate and House of Commons on the Constitution of Canada (1970).

Representation roughly in proportion to population. In aggregate terms over the period since Confederation, Francophones and Anglophones have held roughly the same number of cabinet portfolios as their respective populations would warrant. Under the Supreme Court Act of 1949 at least three of the nine justices must come from either the superior courts or the bar of Quebec.

Separation on linguistic lines. The French and English radio and television networks of the publicly owned Canadian Broadcasting Corporation are autonomous of each other. In 1971 the federal government began establishing "French-language units" in the federal public service to counterbalance the large number of units that were exclusively English-speaking; in 1974 it was reported that of 33,633 persons in these French-language units, 87 percent were in Quebec and 11 percent in the national capital region.[25]

The "Quebec lieutenant." The combination of John A. Macdonald and George-Etienne Cartier was decisive in carrying Confederation in Canada, and from 1867 to his death in 1873 Cartier was Prime Minister Macdonald's "Quebec lieutenant" in the new Dominion.[26] During King's administrations (1926–30 and 1935–48), Ernest Lapointe served as the "Quebec lieutenant," and after Lapointe's death Louis St. Laurent played the role. Although these Quebec leaders were by no means co–prime ministers, they were given much more control over Quebec politics (terra incognita, as far as the heads of government were concerned) than were other ministers over their various provinces and regions. With greater or lesser urgency, English Canadian leaders of the Conservative party have sought to fill this position, usually without success.

The panel device. The Supreme Court Act of 1949, discussed above, also determines that five judges constitute a quorum, and most cases other than those of a constitutional nature are decided by a five-man Court. In his study of the Court, Peter Russell found that in the period between 1949 and 1964 a preponderance of Quebec judges heard Quebec appeals and increasingly two or more of these judges usually sat on the majority.[27]

Several qualifications, however, must be made about the dualistic devices listed above:

The rotation of French and English leaders of the federal Liberal party has not been established as an unbreakable convention. Fifty-eight percent of the delegates at the Liberal leadership convention of 1968 rejected the tradition of alternation.[28] At this convention the two Francophone

25. *Ibid.*
26. See Frederick W. Gibson, ed., *Cabinet Formation and Bicultural Relations: Seven Case Studies* (Ottawa: Queen's Printer, 1970), particularly chap. 8 by Gibson.
27. Russell, pp. 146–152.
28. Peter Regenstreif, "Note on the 'Alternation' of French and English Leaders in the Liberal Party of Canada," *Canadian Journal of Political Science,* 2 (March 1969): 116.

candidates, Trudeau and Paul Martin, gained only 43.4 percent of the delegates' votes on the first ballot.[29]

Peter Russell has pointed out that although there have been four French-English alternations in the office of chief justice from 1944 to 1963, in each case the appointee was senior in years of service on the Court.[30] In 1973 an Anglophone was appointed to succeed a Francophone, but the senior justice at that time was also an Anglophone.

It is too early to regard French-English rotation in the office of governor-general as a firm convention. Prior to the appointment of a Francophone, there was informed speculation that the government would choose a person whose origins were neither English nor French.

Prime ministers have exercised much discretion in determining the representative composition of their cabinets. Canada's second French Canadian prime minister, Louis St. Laurent, in office from 1948 to 1957, chafed under the traditional conventions and appointed ministers on the basis of their assumed competence. As a result, French Canadians were appointed to several portfolios usually closed to them, and English Canadians were appointed to posts usually held by the French Canadians.[31] Although Quebec returned fifty of its seventy-five members of Parliament to the majority party in the Progressive Conservative victory of 1958, Prime Minister John Diefenbaker appointed only one French Canadian to an influential portfolio.[32]

In none of the circumstances mentioned above do the leaders of one or the other of the linguistic committees *as such* have a recognized influence over appointments. Political prudence and constitutional custom dictate that a prime minister, in choosing his cabinet, have several Francophone ministers, but he is free to choose from among the parliamentary members as he wishes. The prime minister and his cabinet have the same discretion in appointments to the offices of chief justice, governor-

29. Martin, although born of French Canadian parents, made his political base in Windsor, Ontario.

30. Russell, p. 69.

31. See Dale C. Thomson, "The Cabinet of 1948," in Gibson, particularly pp. 146–150.

32. From 1958 to the 1962 election, Prime Minister Diefenbaker had Francophones from Quebec in these portfolios: solicitor general, minister of transport, secretary of state, minister of mines and technical surveys, minister of defense production, associate minister of national defense, and minister without portfolio. Of these, only the ministry of transport, occupied by Leon Balcer between October 1960 and April 1963, could be considered an important cabinet post.

general, and speaker of the House of Commons. There is here a process of co-optation.

French-English Consociationalism and Federal-Provincial Relations [33]

The Dominion of Canada was formed as a federation in 1867 because the Francophone politicians of British North America so insisted. Most of the Anglophone leaders would have preferred a "legislative union," a system in which whatever powers were possessed by provincial or local governments would be held at the discretion of the central authorities. But political union was impossible on these terms.

Confederation was overwhelmingly an initiative of the politicians of the United Province of Canada, the present Ontario and Quebec. The Act of Union enacted by the Parliament of the United Kingdom in 1840 had provided for a legislative union of the previously separate colonies of Upper and Lower Canada with the explicit object of assimilating the Francophone community into the dominant Anglophone culture. This was quickly demonstrated to be impossible, and there developed in Canadian politics a number of consociational devices reflecting the ethnic duality of the colony. Among those devices were political parties whose memberships were exclusively or almost exclusively either Anglophone or Francophone; executive councils headed by leaders from each of the communities; the double-majority rule by which decisions affecting a section could be made only by the consent of a majority from that section; the legal recognition of the French and English languages in the operations of government; the bifurcation on sectional lines of several of the governmental departments and agencies; and, prior to 1857, the periodic perambulation of the capital of the province between Upper and Lower Canada.

A major impetus to Confederation was the desire of Canadian politicians to escape from the constraints of consociationalism. Federalism provided that escape. Legislative jurisdiction of matters over which the two ethnic communities markedly differed was conferred on the provinces, while jurisdiction over matters believed to have no ethnic incidence was conferred on the Dominion Parliament. Thus, the provinces were to control education, municipal government, property and civil rights (Quebec private law being based on the continental civil tradition; that of the other provinces on the English common law), the solemnization of mar-

33. For a more extended discussion, see Smiley, chap. 7.

riage, health and welfare matters, and so on. The Dominion was given jurisdiction over matters that involved the military defense of British North America and the establishment of an integrated national economy.

In a broad sense, the federal-provincial division of powers as agreed upon at Confederation afforded relative harmony between Anglophones and Francophones roughly during the period from 1867 to the 1930's. For the most part the Dominion authorities confined themselves to nation building in its economic dimension and did not intrude into activities regarded as having a direct ethnic incidence. Confederation did not end all French-English friction; conflicts over the treatment of French and Catholic minorities outside Quebec and over the external orientations of Canada as a member of the British Empire/Commonwealth still existed, but these were matters not directly related to the federal-provincial dimension.

By the beginning of the Quiet Revolution of the 1960's the division of powers between the central government and the provinces, which had provided for a modicum of harmony between English and French, had largely broken down. The Keynesian imperatives, as they were accepted in Ottawa at the end of World War II, assumed a high degree of centralization in fiscal matters. As in other federal nations, the central government had involved itself in many matters of provincial jurisdiction through the grant-in-aid device—technical and university education, health, welfare, and so on. The 1960's saw an intense conflict between the Quebec and federal governments over the scope of the activities of each. The Quebec objective was to roll back federal involvement in matters within provincial jurisdiction without financial penalties to the people or the government of the province. But beyond this, provincial leaders asserted a more influential role for Quebec in economic affairs, even in respect to matters mainly or exclusively within the constitutional jurisdiction of the central government in Ottawa. Quebec attained some success in both of these objectives.

The pattern of Quebec-Ottawa relations as it has evolved in the 1970's is more ambiguous than it was in the previous decade. Federal power and purpose have been reasserted in response to the energy crisis and inflation, and the Quebec government has not resisted Ottawa's action regarding either of these two problems. But where the federal government has attempted to become involved in matters traditionally outside its jurisdiction, it has been met with resistance not only from Quebec but from some or all of the other provinces. Thus, the specific federal-Quebec conflict has given way to a more general tension between the central government and the provinces.

To what extent do the processes of federal-provincial relations embody consociationalism, and to what extent does the government of Quebec express interests and attitudes that are explicitly Francophone? Throughout the 1960's Quebec pressures for autonomy and the preoccupation of other Canadians with French-English relations brought about a high degree of consociationalism on this axis. More recently, the somewhat more subdued quest of Quebec for autonomy, the enlistment of other provinces in the provincialist cause, and the renewed attention to economic issues have lessened the importance of ethnic dualism in federal-provincial relations. Further, these relations are ill-suited for consociationalism because the federal government itself has become a vehicle for Francophone attitudes and interests by virtue of the changes made during the past decade, and it is an increasingly effective vehicle.

French-English Consociationalism within Quebec

Until recently the politics and society of Quebec were characterized by a high degree of consociationalism.[34] There was occupational segregation along French-English lines. Anglophones were dominant in the corporate business sector, while members of the Francophone elite were drawn to the church, to the liberal professions, and to politics. The Catholic church was profoundly legitimist, and the clergy itself played an important role in consociational accommodation at all levels; the close link between religion and ethnicity that was forged by the church contributed also to the relative autonomy of the two societies. There developed effective channels of access to, and interaction between, the Anglo-Saxon business community and the Francophone political and ecclesiastical leadership.

Recent events within Quebec have weakened consociationalism; Francophones have begun to act in terms of majoritarian principles. These majoritarian currents are most explicitly embodied in Bill 22, discussed earlier, which declares that "French is the official language of the province of Québec" and it gives the executive sweeping powers to establish and sustain the primacy of French in public education, private business, and government. According to the act, children whose mother tongue is neither English nor French must receive their education in French, and the minister of education is given broad authority to determine the

34. These relations have never, to my knowledge, been analyzed in detail. However, Hugh MacLennan's well-known novel *Two Solitudes* is interesting here.

linguistic competence of pupils and to determine their language of instruction. French is to be the primary language of private business and labor relations, and the cabinet is empowered to issue certificates to firms who have "adopted and are applying a francization program." With specified exceptions, members of professions must have a working knowledge of French to receive professional certification.

The "Rules" of the Canadian Political Game and Consociationalism

In his analysis of the political system of the Netherlands, Arend Lijphart has written a stimulating essay on the "informal, unwritten rules" that "govern the political business in Holland." [35] Likewise, the "informal, unwritten rules" of Canadian politics as they impinge on French-English consociationalism are impressionistically described below.

The majoritarian principle. The majoritarian, winner-take-all principle permeates the operations of the Canadian political system as it does those of other nations who follow the British parliamentary tradition.[36] All members of the House of Commons are elected from single-member districts according to the plurality rule. The party that can command a legislative majority has the unshared right to govern. With a few exceptions, decisions of legislative chambers are made by simple majorities of their members. The majoritarian rule is also applied to other operations of the political system, that is, to decisions of courts composed of several judges and to the choices of party leaders by representative conventions at which delegates vote by successive secret ballots until one candidate has an absolute majority.

The majoritarian rule as it guides the operation of Canadian political institutions is a direct challenge to consociationalism. The double-majority procedure is not in evidence, and in a formal sense at least the ethnic composition of a majority is regarded as irrelevant to the legitimacy of the decisions made by it. Majoritarianism is, of course, a logical extension of the individualistic principle that "each is to count for one and no one for more than one." It is almost a truism to say that political systems in the Anglo-American tradition do not recognize group rights (although in Canada there is some such recognition related to denominational privileges in education) and that rights are held at the discretion of majorities as they are formed and re-formed.

35. *Politics of Accommodation.*
36. For an instructive analysis, see Allen Potter's essay "Great Britain: Opposition with a Capital 'O,' " in Dahl, pp. 5–33.

The obsession with national unity. The sociologist John Porter has spoken of national unity as "Canada's political obsession." [37] The operative belief is that the nation is in continual danger of being shattered into its disparate elements, which are almost invariably defined in terms of region or ethnic group rather than of class or some other kind of cleavage. While it is common for Americans to honor their purposeful and divisive presidents, Canadians honor (in one way or another) the three prime ministers who together headed the Canadian governments for a total of fifty-three years during the first century since Confederation and each of whom had rare talents for conciliation. [38]

The obsession of Canadian politicians with national unity need not and does not lead to accommodative behavior in their relations with each other or to conciliation between English and French. The operating rules of the British parliamentary system predispose these politicians to competition rather than to collaboration. Thus, it is the oldest and most cynical strategy in Canadian politics to claim that one's political opponents are disloyal to national unity and national consensus. For example, beginning in the 1920's the Liberals in Quebec perpetuated the divisions of World War I by depicting the Conservatives as the party of conscription, just as during the nineteenth century the Conservatives had questioned the Liberals' devotion to the empire. The persistent failure of the Conservatives to win effective electoral support in Quebec works against French-English accommodation since the party is under a continuing temptation to solidify and extend its support in Anglophone Canada by exploiting anti-French sentiments. On the other hand, Trudeau and the Quebec Liberals are so ardent in their pursuit of the bilingual and bicultural alternative that they have little sensitivity to English Canadians who, with different experiences and traditions, are unconvinced by this solution.

Instrumentalism. Canadian life and politics are permeated by a strain of instrumentalism. In institutional terms the instrumental principle directs that the assignment of tasks be based on actual or anticipated achievement rather than on ascription or patronage. Merit, however, is almost inevita-

37. John Porter, *The Vertical Mosaic: An Analysis of Class and Social Power in Canada* (Toronto: University of Toronto Press, 1965), pp. 368–369.

38. William Lyon Mackenzie King (prime minister: 1921–26, 1926–30, and 1935–48) was the most recent of these three, the others being, of course, Macdonald and Laurier. One of King's most influential advisers, J. W. Pickersgill, said, "Mackenzie King genuinely believed and frequently said that the real secret of political leadership was more in what was prevented than in what was accomplished." J. W. Pickersgill, *The Mackenzie King Record,* vol. 1, *1939–1944* (Toronto: University of Toronto Press, 1960), p. 10.

bly defined in terms of the norm of the dominant group. Thus, a reliance on this principle challenges consociational accommodation by assigning to the minority a very small share of the positions of influence. As was described earlier, the shift from patronage to merit in 1918 resulted in a decline in the proportion of Francophones in the Canadian public service, particularly in the executive and professional categories. Francophones have characteristically been regarded by Anglophones as deficient in economic leadership, and none of the ministers of finance since Confederation has been a French Canadian, nor has any Francophone been appointed deputy minister of finance or governor of the Bank of Canada. In succeeding to the leadership of the Liberal party, and thus to the prime ministership, neither St. Laurent nor Trudeau based his claim on the right to succeed an Anglophone leader. While English Canadians will accept French-English rotation in those offices they consider not crucial—the offices, for example, of the governor-general, of the chief justice of the Supreme Court, or of the speaker of the House of Commons—the rules of the political game do not allow rotation in less symbolic offices.

The desire for strong government dominated by the elected official. The dominant Canadian preferences are for strong governments carrying out an extensive range of activities under the dominance of elected officials. Each of the following dispositions works against consociationalism:

Most Canadians have a decided preference for majority governments, although in seven of the seventeen federal general elections from 1921 to 1974 majorities have not been returned. The operative belief is that it is the duty of governments to govern and that the party in power should not share this responsibility with other political parties or with private groups. In a more general sense, pressures for decisive public action often result in majoritarian solutions rather than solutions arrived at through the more dilatory processes of consociational accommodation.

The range of public activity is very extensive, and there is no consensus on the appropriate limits of such activity. The boundaries of the political, economic, and social spheres are ill-defined, and in many cases the boundaries of the latter have been deliberately established and sustained by government. This puts heavy loads on the governmental system in areas such as broadcasting, linguistic matters, and cultural development, which impinge directly on ethnic differentiation.

There is an overriding tradition that the most important decisions of the political system are to be made by, or subject to the discretion of, elected officials. Until now, Canadians have resisted extensive constitutional entrenchment of human rights, including linguistic rights, which would transfer discretion about these matters from legislative majorities to the courts. Whatever the relations between the elected officials constituting the cabinet and the appointed bureaucracy, the activities of government are carried out in the name of the former and the politicians are held accountable for the results. The more important decisions of administrative agencies are characteristically subject to final approval by or appeal to either individual ministers or the cabinet. These practices limit the possibility of consociational or other forms of political accommodation where they might more easily be achieved than at the political "summit."

In general, the dominant traditions and practices of the Canadian political system work against French-English consociationalism. To the extent that consociational devices exist they are not crucial to the system and, as has been seen, are not in some cases firmly established by law or convention. There are, however, countervailing forces:

The territorial separation of the two ethnic groups results in a situation in which the elected officials represent constituencies composed predominantly of one or the other group. This relative absence of mixed constituencies appears to be an important requisite of consociationalism.

Canadian society is relatively deferential and elitist and functions largely through elite accommodation, although the most important aspects of this process do not involve French and English elites as such. The historian W. L. Morton has stated, "Not life, liberty, and the pursuit of happiness but peace, order, and good government are what the national government of Canada guarantees." [39] In an essay entitled "Conservatism: The Deep Bond in an Embattled Marriage," John Porter has argued that "English and French Canadians are more alike [than either of them are like Americans] in their conservatism, traditionalism, religiosity, authoritarianism and elitist values." [40] Recent events may have weakened somewhat these conservative dispositions, not only more so in Quebec than elsewhere in Canada, but also where there is intense competition about fundamental issues among the political elites. However, Canadian political elites generally retain the capacity to persuade those whom they repre-

39. W. L. Morton, *The Canadian Identity* (Toronto: University of Toronto Press, 1962), p. 111.
40. William Kilbourn, ed., *Canada: A Guide to the Peaceable Kingdom* (Toronto: Macmillan of Canada, 1970), p. 267.

sent to accept solutions reached through elite bargaining and accommodation.

During the 1960's the most salient locus of French-English consociationalism and conflict was federal-provincial relations. In these relations the greatest resistance to Quebec demands came from those provinces and regions with the lowest proportion of Francophones. The most intense conflict is now found where large numbers of English and French coexist—in Quebec itself and in the national capital region. The majoritarian thrust of Bill 22 suggests a breakdown of the historic consociationalism within the province of Quebec. The policies of the Trudeau government in regard to the public service are more clearly recognized to be directed toward enhancing "French power" at the senior and middle levels of decision making, and this realization has given rise to increasing anxieties among Anglophones. As yet, however, neither the Anglophones of Quebec nor those in the federal public service have had any appreciable success in mobilizing other English-speaking Canadians to their respective causes.

Would consociationalism be more firmly established if Quebec were to leave the confederation? The program of the separatist Parti Québécois posits a continuing economic association between Quebec and Canada following independence for Quebec. Vehicles of interaction such as a customs union, monetary union, or common market would, of course, be regulated by bilateral institutions established for those purposes. It appears, however, unrealistic to believe that Anglophone Canadians would be more willing to support consociationalism under such new circumstances than they have been while both groups have been within one national political system.

9

Interethnic Relations and the Language Issue in Contemporary Canada: A General Appraisal *

JACQUES BRAZEAU and EDOUARD CLOUTIER

Linguistic dualism in Canada had necessitated governmental policy decisions for two centuries before 1960, but since then there have been new challenges on the ethnolinguistic front. This essay reviews some recent developments in linguistic matters and examines these developments in the more general perspective of social organization to reveal the complex web of social realities that have shaped interethnic relations in Canada with regard to private and public linguistic practices. This perspective will lead to an analytical examination of the critical issue of language use in the work situation in Quebec and of the intrinsic limitations to efficient political intervention in linguistic affairs.[1]

Recent Linguistic Developments

The Royal Commission on Bilingualism and Biculturalism, created by the federal government in 1963, defined the two major language groups in Canada—English and French—as being either a majority or a minority according to the ethnic composition of an area.[2] The novelty of this definition of official-language groups ought to be stressed. It led the commission to request that public services be offered in English and in French and that institutions of the central government be bilingual in the national

* We wish to thank Milton Esman and Daniel Latouche for their valuable advice in the preparation of the final version of this essay.

1. We have purposely refrained from setting our essay in any precise theoretical framework to be free to explore at will as many components of the linguistic situation that we deem relevant. Even though such freedom may seem to be exercised at the expense of scientific precision, we think that present-day research in linguistic matters should remain at the exploratory stage until the relevant variables have been successfully identified and measured to warrant the construction of realistic models and theories.

2. Royal Commission on Bilingualism and Biculturalism, *Preliminary Report* (Ottawa: Queen's Printer, 1965); and *Report,* bk. 1 (Ottawa: Queen's Printer, 1967).

capital and in bilingual districts throughout the land. It also led the commission to define in broad terms what ought to be the country's social organization in areas that were not directly under federal jurisdiction: provinces composed of significant English and French minorities were invited to declare themselves bilingual; parallel English and French educational systems were proposed; and private enterprises were invited to adopt linguistic procedures that would take account of the culture and language of the local population.

In 1969, the federal government accepted the recommendations of the commission on the status of English and French in federal matters, setting objectives to provide public services in both languages in the capital and in decentralized Federal institutions. It instituted a language training program for civil servants and created work groups in the capital that would function in French and allow French-speaking civil servants to use French as their primary language on the job. It named a permanent commissioner to watch over the program's progress and receive complaints from citizens who were not offered services in the official language of their choice.[3] Upon adopting the Official Languages Act of 1969 regarding bilingualism and the use of languages in federal administrative matters, however, the government disassociated language and culture by giving its support to bilingualism, on the one hand, and to multiculturalism, on the other. It allowed languages other than English and French to receive some public recognition, although not at the institutional level.

This gesture has been viewed by many French Canadians as a means of separating the issues of bilingualism and biculturalism. It can be said that giving culture a limited definition avoids the difficult issue of cultural inequalities linked to linguistic usage in daily activities of commerce for populations of different languages. Nonetheless, steps taken by Canada's government in the last decade have markedly affected the status of the French language in the federal public service, in the provinces that have significant French minorities, and within Quebec's non-French populations and institutions.

Why were these measures adopted at the particular time they were?

3. The commissioner's report for 1974 indicated that progress had been made in teaching French to civil servants but that after acquiring these language skills a high proportion of the civil servants did not use them. The report stressed as well the difficulty in having a sufficient proportion of positions that require French only. The commissioner noted the existence of goodwill but indicated that progress toward proportionality was being made very slowly.

The answer comes from Quebec rather than from Canada as a whole. Federal concern with bilingualism did not accidentally take a more mature form at the time it did. It evolved when industrial acceleration, secularization, ideological pluralism, and cultural nationalism had descended on Quebec, promoting an increase in schooling and in public expressions by the French Canadians of their privately felt subordination in the division of labor in Canada and in Quebec.

While the two-century-old ethnolinguistic issue was being defined differently at the federal level with the participation of French Canadians, it was simultaneously being redefined in Quebec. Many Québécois, that is, French-speaking Quebeckers, had become less interested in French minorities outside Quebec and less concerned to have bilingualism in the federal capital; in addition, they had begun to question the patterns of bilingualism that prevailed in Montreal and in Quebec's industrial enterprises.

After approximately 150 years of asking for "French also" in Quebec and in Canada, many Québécois had begun asking for "French only" within Quebec at the same time federal authorities were proclaiming bilingualism for a new Canada. During the 1960's, the French language received increasing consideration. Its use was seen to be related to occupational subordination in the face of inappropriate social mechanisms, and the survival of French became a matter of serious concern for Québécois. The decreasing birthrate among French Canadians, the small number of French-language immigrants to Quebec, and the assimilation of other immigrants into the English-speaking population appeared to seriously endanger the continued existence of the language.

Factors that have supported the French language include a rise in English-Canadian goodwill toward French Canadians, the above-mentioned federal measures, an increase in the participation of Québécois in public administration as well as in education and private endeavors and, lastly, some awareness on the part of French Canadians of the existence of a link between linguistic usage and popular culture. On the other hand, the effects of these factors have been in part negated by a time lag at the national level between majority actions and minority expectations.[4]

4. A time lag between French-Canadian demands and English-Canadian responses is practically a Canadian tradition. For instance, by the time the federal government acted on such measures as bilingual money, bilingual checks, and a distinctive national flag and anthem, French Canadians had generally lost interest in these matters. The federal government's Canadian-wide policy of bilingualism was likewise greeted with a relative lack of

Public policy at the provincial level also had to take account of the mutations just described. In 1968, Quebec established its own commission of inquiry to investigate the status of French and the rights of Quebec's minorities.[5] This points to the significance of the federal commission's definition of English and French Canadians as being either a majority or a minority depending on spatial location.

Which language policy alternatives were open to Quebec? One alternative was to proclaim the province bilingual and to identify within it a number of bilingual districts. This approach, recommended by the federal commission in order to benefit French minorities in New Brunswick, Ontario, and Manitoba, would have maintained the status quo in Quebec. It would have identified as bilingual the industrial southwest of the province, including Montreal and many cities where industry is implanted. It would have kept English and French services, including public schools, in these regions, and in Montreal it would have retained, in all likelihood, English as the administrative language of large enterprises for the professional benefit of persons of English mother tongue and of those who assimilate into the English language and culture. The bilingual proposals of the federal commission were not likely to have parallel consequences when applied to the different regions of Canada. Consequently, the bilingual-districts approach was not adopted by the Quebec government.

A second alternative was to define French as Quebec's first language and English as, primarily, a lingua franca for external communication and, secondarily, the mother tongue of a minority. It is largely in this direction that, following its own commission's report, the Quebec government has moved. In view of the novelty of defining an English-language group as a minority in Canada, it would seem that Quebec's second language is more the mother tongue of a group with rights than the language of communication with the outside. The Language Act of 1974, adopted by the National Assembly in Quebec, deals with language matters in public administration, public education, advertising, and labor.[6] Its

enthusiasm by most Quebec French Canadians who had gradually begun to concentrate on the Quebec territory since census statistics showed an unrelenting rate of assimilation of French Canadians by English Canadians outside of Quebec.

5. Commission d'enquête sur la situation de la langue française et sur les droits linguistiques au Québec, *Rapport,* bk. 1 (Quebec: Editeur officiel du Québec, 1972).

6. This law, popularly called Law 22, has attracted a great deal of attention in Quebec, in Canada, and in the United States. It abrogated Law 63, which had proclaimed, three years earlier, the bilingual character of Quebec and parents' rights to choose the language of schooling for their children. The adoption of these two laws within such a short period points to the rather sudden prominence of the language issue in Quebec.

methods of implementation have remained generally undefined, and the government's inability and unwillingness to state them are exemplified by the fact that most measures are left to ministerial discretion.

The law leaves intact two unilingual school systems. Attendance at English schools is permitted children of English mother tongue and children who, no matter what their origin, can demonstrate they know English well enough to benefit from schooling in English. Children who do not know English, children whose mother tongue is French, and children of immigrants who are without an adequate knowledge of English must attend French schools. In addition, the new language law proclaims French the official language of Quebec. But it also defines a variety of public matters and functions in which English has official use. Finally, the law attempts to control language use in private activity, labor relationships, public administration, and public schooling, but it does not aim to gradually change the language used in private activities by transforming the educational system and the population's dealings with public institutions.

This law has been criticized by all concerned because of the discretion it leaves to ministers; the English-speaking people of Quebec criticize it because it allegedly deprives them and immigrants of rights, and the French Canadians criticize it because it allegedly provides English-speaking people with the continuation of unwarranted privileges.

The difficulties involved in selecting either a bilingualism with two languages on an equal footing or a bilingualism with a primary and a secondary language give impetus to the possibility of adopting French unilingualism for Quebec. This alternative, which has the support of a sizable minority of the population, runs contrary to the federal and provincial commissions' recommendations and to present federal and provincial policies. While territorial unilingualsim has been adopted within certain multilingual countries, it has not been presented, outside Quebec, as a Canadian possibility. It is, however, among the feelings expressed by present-day cultural nationalists in Quebec in conjunction with political autonomy.

The language issue is not the only reason for the existence of a separatist party in Quebec. The reasons are many: reform of the economic system, changes in the ethnic division of labor, control of immigration, alienation, impatience with Canadian reforms, dissatisfaction with French-Canadian federalists in Ottawa and Quebec City, cultural and linguistic changes related to work activity and career, self-determination, and so forth. Language and culture constitute, in fact, an important aspect in these matters. Many separatists, of course, realize the role of English as the lingua franca to be maintained for relations within North America. On the other hand, they wonder, as do nonseparatists, whether the costs of restrictive language policies might not be higher than those of political autonomy itself.

A dilemma seems to face Québécois in language matters in unilingual North America that, in all likelihood, they would not face in polyglot Europe or Africa. Should they risk creating a barrier between themselves and Canadian and multinational enterprises over language demands? The risk would be worthwhile to have within Quebec a better share in employment possibilities and in work experience. The use of French, the language of the majority of the population, in administrative and technical functions would affect the division of responsibilities in Quebec and could lead to the sharing of industrial wealth, materially and culturally, in a new way. However, language demands might also stem industrial growth and deter private enterprise, accustomed to a free choice between English and French in Quebec, from choosing this region for its offices and plants.

This kind of dilemma, needless to say, favors the use of propaganda for the maintenance of present conditions and encourages the growth of dissatisfaction with the rate of progress of linguistic transformations. Why do ethnic groups get into such dilemmas? An analysis of some important aspects of communal life in Canada and Quebec provides some understanding of the relationship between the two linguistic groups and sheds some light on possibilities for the future of this relationship.

The Shaping of a Canadian Pattern of Interethnic Relations

Studies of interethnic relations in countries that have recognized minorities must take account of political history, economic organization, demographic changes, cultural evolution, and the worldwide context of intergroup relations. Consideration of broad internal realities and explanations drawn from external comparisons are required as well.[7]

In Canada, one is struck by the fact that recent French-Canadian expressions of dissatisfaction have come during a period of prosperity and

7. For a general study of these issues in a comparative perspective, see Royal Commission on Bilingualism and Biculturalism, *Report,* bk. 1, pp. 77–90, on Finland, Belgium, Switzerland, and South Africa; and Bernard Touret, *L'aménagement constitutionnel des Etats de peuplement composite* (Quebec: Presses de l'Université Laval, Centre international de recherche sur le bilinguisme, 1973).

within an industrial society in which French Canadians have had increased participation. Consequently, French Canadians suffer not from profound deprivation, but from deprivation relative to other groups in Canada or in the world. They have been aware of their minority status for centuries and have not often considered their problems to be solved adequately. What is now described as their new nationalism is a continuation of prior expressions of ethnic sentiment, even though some of its tenets are new and it is oriented to participation in industrial life rather than to isolation from it.

Canada did not begin in 1867; only the present federal political organization began then. Prior to 1867, within the history of British Canada there was first a long period in which French Canadians were a majority of the European settlers in the country. On the eve of the American Revolution, prior to the settlement of Quebec and Ontario by United Empire Loyalists and British immigrants, the French language and the Catholic religion were given official status in 1774.[8] When constitutional government came seventeen years later, central Canada was divided into two units, Lower and Upper Canada. Lower Canada was still demographically French, except in its two main cities, Montreal and Quebec City. The initial opening of these cities and of Upper Canada to American migration, and the extensive British settlement around 1815, gradually changed the ethnic balance. Shortly after 1840 and Union, demographic equality was reached, but when federalism brought into Canada newly settled Ontario and the Atlantic provinces, the population of British extraction was twice as large as that of French extraction.

During the nineteenth century, some attempt was made to assimilate French Canadians through the public educational system.[9] The attempt was unsuccessful primarily because English and French lived in different territories. Even today, most French Canadians occupy a contiguous area made up of Quebec province, adjacent eastern and northern Ontario, and a crescent in northern and eastern New Brunswick. It is in this area that

---

8. The second centenary of the Quebec Act, which, according to Michel Brunet, constitutes the Magna Carta of French-Canadian language rights granted them by the British crown, went almost unnoticed in French Canada.

9. The data accumulated by Canon Groulx on this matter have been presented in a summarized version in Albert Lévesque, *La dualité culturelle au Canada* (Montreal: Albert Lévesque, 1959). Educational laws adopted in the nineteenth century are discussed in Commission royale d'enquête sur l'enseignement dans la Province de Québec, *Rapport*, Tome 1 (Montreal: Pierre Desmarais, 1963). See also Marcel Rioux, *La question du Québec* (Paris: Seghers, 1969).

their group has maintained its distinctiveness. It has done so to a lesser extent and somewhat temporarily in some isolated rural settlements in other parts of Canada.

While Canada's economy was mercantile and preindustrial, the cities of the province of Quebec were the meeting places of English and French elements in local administration, the professions, and commerce. The English played a leadership role and gradually incorporated the French into matters of local government, local services, and commercial enterprise.[10] They also involved the French, but in more limited capacities, in the early industrial production aimed at developing western Canada from a Montreal base. In this task, however, recourse was made, to a great extent, to urban British settlers who were skilled workers and provided the cadres of enterprises located in southwestern Quebec.

Until the twentieth century, immigration into Canada was British and American and overwhelmingly English-speaking. The settlement of the Plains, while it still counted on this source of manpower, opened the country as well to other groups from northern and eastern Europe: Germans, Scandinavians, and Ukrainians, among others. Industrial development following settlement brought these same groups to Ontario's major industrial belt and northern mining regions, and to southwestern Quebec as well. After World War II, Toronto, Vancouver, and Montreal became the main cities for immigrants from Germany, Hungary, Italy, Greece, and Portugal, and, to a lesser extent, from Hong Kong, India, and the Caribbean. On the other hand, French Canadians migrated to New England rather than to western Canada as part of a Canadian-wide pattern of migration to the United States that was as important as foreign immigration into Canada.

While industrial concentration has meant a great deal of internal rural-urban migration, it has not led to a substantial crossing of the language barrier. French Canadians have not moved permanently to areas of

---

10. In the second half of the nineteenth century and at the beginning of the twentieth century, English-speaking Quebeckers played a large part in the provincial government and in the liberal professions in conjunction with the French rather than separately. Bilingual institutions, such as medical schools and hospitals, were more common then than at present. The history of Montreal shows that, prior to Confederation, the English-speaking population was bilingual in the city to a greater extent than it was between 1920 and 1960 when, apparently, the French population tended to learn English. A reversal of this trend has begun. These historical variations support the contentions of linguists that it is exceptional for two groups inhabiting the same area to be bilingual at the same time since communication does not require two-way bilingualism.

growth outside Quebec, and English-speaking Canadians have moved permanently only to Montreal where there is a large English-language community. Internal migration across a cultural barrier is akin, in some respects, to migration to another country, and it has not been practiced in Canada sufficiently to produce territorially mixed English-French populations except in border areas between the two groups' concentrations. In some of these areas outside Quebec, migration has meant the gradual assimilation of the French elements. In areas that are within Quebec, French invasion of English districts has been followed by a process of language succession through the departure of the offspring of early English settlers for English-speaking regions of Quebec, Canada, and the United States.

For Canada as a whole, immigration has reduced the percentage of Canadians of British origin; [11] it has not affected greatly the percentage of Canadians of French origin. Although the latter have not benefited from French immigration to the extent that British Canadians have benefited from British immigration, they had until recently a high birthrate, which kept their group at about 30 percent of the total population. On the other hand, immigration has had only temporary effects on the percentage of the Canadian population that is of English mother tongue, since most immigrant groups become fully Anglicized within one or two generations.

In Quebec, the situation is not different. For example, the immigrants who settled in Montreal in the past (few settled in rural Quebec) generally chose an English-language education for their children.[12] Accordingly, the English-speaking population of Montreal is made up about equally of persons of British origin and of persons of other origins who are assimilated into the English-language community.

The French-language group, on the other hand, maintains itself in Quebec while the most recent influx of immigrants are not yet assimilated. The defection of members of the French-language group to the English-speaking community is balanced by the assimilation into the French-speaking community of English-speaking peoples and of those

11. They comprised 60 percent of the population in 1871 and 45 percent in 1971. Today the percentage of the population of English mother tongue is still around 60 percent; that of French mother tongue, 27 percent. The remainder is high because of recent immigration. For statistics on immigration and emigration, in relation to origin and language, see Canada, Department of Manpower and Immigration, *Statistics on Immigration and Population* (Ottawa: Information Canada, 1974).

12. Gary Caldwell, *A Demographic Profile of the English-Speaking Population of Quebec* (Quebec: Université Laval, Centre international de recherche sur le bilinguisme, 1974).

whose mother tongue is other than French or English. The French-speaking group does not, however, incorporate into its membership a proportion of those with other mother tongues that is comparable to its own proportion of total population. In the whole of Canada, the English-Canadian communities assimilate a higher proportion of others than they represent. French-language isolates throughout Canada are decreasing in size due to the adoption of English by the younger generation.[13] Urbanization and industrialization have accelerated this process over the last two decades. Knowledge of these trends and of their accentuation has led Québécois to seek means of halting them locally, especially since Quebec's growth rate and the French community's relative size are declining. The Québécois' recent lack of interest in a Canadian-wide policy of bilingualism and their suspicion of the federal government's commitment to multiculturalism have resulted.

Patterns of Canadian growth through immigration have been ecologically rather than socially determined. The economic interdependence of Canadian regions is shaped by industrial concentrations in Canada and in the United States. Canada's industry is concentrated in a very small territorial area of southern Ontario and southwestern Quebec. This area, which is adjacent to an analogous area in the United States, makes Canada an industrial country at the production level. Like other industrial countries, Canada has been faced with regional inequalities and the need to effectuate some decentralization. It is the exploitation of the natural resources of other regions that has allowed the country to enter the postindustrial age as a consumer of industrial goods and industrially organized services.

A symbiosis exists between the industrial roles of Ontario and Quebec. The financial and industrial institutions of English-speaking Montreal had their heyday at the beginning of the century when western Canada was still being settled and Canada's transportation system had to be developed. Since the beginning of World War I, the Toronto region has be-

---

13. It is only in Ontario and Quebec that the percentages of persons of other mother tongues have increased appreciably between 1951 and 1971, from 10.9 to 16.2 percent and from 3.7 to 6.2 percent, respectively. Accordingly, in both these provinces, percentages for English and French mother tongues have decreased. In all other provinces, with the exception of British Columbia and Newfoundland where small French percentages have remained constant, the percentages of the populations of English mother tongue have increased and those of French have decreased. Statistics on language generally used at home emphasize this drift. For percentages of persons of English and French mother tongues in Canada, the provinces, and the territories in 1971, see Map 3, page 181.

come Canada's center for the production of manufactured durable goods. The Montreal region, on the other hand, has become Canada's center for the production of nondurable goods such as textiles, clothing, processed foods, and tobacco. Outside the Ontario-Quebec industrial basin, developments have taken place mainly in proximity to special natural resources: hydroelectric power in British Columbia and Quebec, gas and oil in Alberta, and mines in Nova Scotia. Over the last few years, some successful attempts have been made to decentralize industrial production: manufacture of electrical equipment, automobile assembly, and aircraft production and repairs take place in the vicinity of large population concentrations outside Ontario, such as Vancouver, Winnipeg, Montreal, and Halifax. It is, nonetheless, apparent that the regions presently undergoing expansion are those of southern Ontario, British Columbia, and Alberta. These now attract immigrants. Ontario's population is rapidly outdistancing Quebec's and may be twice as large as Quebec's in twenty-five years. British Columbia and Alberta together may become demographically as important as Quebec in about the same time. Thus, northern Ontario, Quebec, the maritime provinces, Manitoba, and Saskatchewan are becoming unfavored regions in terms of industrial production. They provide raw resources such as minerals, wood, cereals, and power.

These economic trends have had great influence on the ethnic and linguistic composition of Quebec. A small area of southwestern Quebec, from the Ontario border to Sorel along the Saint Lawrence River, has brought the province into the North American industrial production system. An increasing concentration of Quebec's English-speaking population is found in this area.[14] Elsewhere in Quebec, the proportion of English speakers is decreasing at every census. Bilingualism prevails in the industrial area. Enterprises, largely branches of American multinational organizations, use English in administration, technology, nonretail trade, and in the purchase of goods and services from other concerns. They use French in production (if in need of a large labor force), in personnel work, in local sales, and in public relations. This kind of arrangement favors the recruitment of English-speaking Quebeckers and of Canadian, American, British, and other itinerants as industrial, administrative, and technical cadres, without requiring them to know and use a great deal of French. It permits the overrepresentation of these personnel at the upper and middle levels of the occupational pyramid and results in the under-

14. See Caldwell.

representation of the French, who must have knowledge of English to be eligible for such employment. It points out to immigrants who have aspirations of economic mobility that they ought to identify with and assimilate into the English-language community.

In Quebec, French speakers constitute 80.7 percent of the population, control provincial and local public administration, have their own cultural institutions, and are now the majority of the skilled workers; as such, they experience both advantage and disadvantage in the division of labor. Upon examining, in Canada as a whole, class status according to origin, Bernard Blishen and John Porter have found that at the top of the status pyramid Canadians of French origin come between those of British origin and those of other origins. At the bottom of the pyramid, they are represented more than are those of British origin but less than are those of other origins. At the middle of the pyramid, however, they occupy the third rank. These findings were supported in research on Canadian income done for the federal commission on bilingualism. French Canadian income was found to be higher only than that of natives and of recent immigrants.[15]

The positions given the French in Canada's public administration, in Quebec's political and cultural institutions, and in enterprises in areas where the French are concentrated assure them of elitist representation. At the other extreme, recent immigrants' lack of such advantages and of acculturation overburden them with unskilled jobs that the local population will not readily engage in. The disadvantaged position of French Canadians at the intermediate level seems to come from two sources: regional specialization in the industrial system, which gives Quebec a complementary, rather than an identical, role to Ontario's; and the preference given in administrative functions in large enterprises, first, to persons of English mother tongue and, second, to those who have adopted English as their main language.

Studies have shown that bilingualism is not collectively advantageous: it allows institutions to function in one language at the top and in another language at the bottom with the help of intermediaries who can act as translators at low occupational levels in the office and the shop. There is

15. Bernard R. Blishen, ''A Socio-Economic Index for Occupations in Canada,'' Blishen, *et al.*, eds., *Canadian Society* (Toronto: Macmillan, 3rd Edition, 1968), chap. 48, pp. 741–53; John Porter, *The Vertical Mosaic* (Toronto: University of Toronto Press, 1965), esp. chap. 3, ''Ethnicity and Social Class,'' pp. 60–103; Royal Commission on Bilingualism and Biculturalism, *Report,* bk. 3, pt. 1 (Ottawa: Queen's Printer, 1969).

no doubt, however, that individuals do assure themselves of some promotion through bilingualism. It is likely, as well, that bilingualism has favored industrialization, that is, the installation of outside enterprises in Quebec.

It is felt now that bilingualism was instituted at a high cost in terms of the sharing of occupational opportunities between groups. Also, it is increasingly believed that bilingualism imposed on the local majority impedes its cultural development inasmuch as it curtails the use and development of the majority's language in important areas of activity in which the population is involved. Such bilingualism imposed on a population that is concentrated and large enough to insure its survival has the effect of inducing partial assimilation of each successive generation of its members into a culture other than its own. Thus, industrial participation by the local majority gives each generation something of immigrant status at home.[16]

The need for minority groups to be fluent in languages other than their own has been historically demonstrated. The consequences of such fluency in different types of societies, industrial and nonindustrial, have yet to be closely examined with respect to groups rather than persons. There are several types of bilingualism in industrial societies. At one extreme are the immigrants who, if they are not military or industrial conquerors, are expected to learn a local language, have their children schooled in it, and see their own language rapidly fall into disuse. At the other extreme are the national states that have languages that are not known to any extent by their neighbors and the world at large, such as Dutch in Holland. These societies encourage their highly educated nationals, and some specialists such as people in the tourist trades, to know outside languages, often more than one. At the same time, they see to it that as much as possible of societal activity, at all levels, takes place in their own language. They use other languages for external communication and to gain access to external knowledge, which they translate profusely into their own language.

It is not this latter type of multilingualism and bilingualism that, until the 1930's, the public authorities and entrepreneurs of Flanders were postulating for the Flemings who were becoming involved in the industrial process within the Dutch-speaking part of Belgium. It was bilingualism for lowly workers and low-level cadres, who, by being required to be

16. See Rioux, chap. 7.

bilingual, would be forced to use French.[17] It is this type of bilingualism that industrialization brought to Montreal, to Quebec's towns, and, until a short while ago, to Canada's public service. It is against this type of social arrangement that proponents of cultural nationalism have reacted without necessarily perceiving all of the implications of the economic colonialism that the arrangement represents.

The Linguistic Arrangements in Work Situations in Quebec

The state of linguistic use in work situations is well known in Quebec following an extensive survey carried out with the support of the commission of inquiry into the status of the French language.[18]

The primary finding of this survey is that Quebec's French population uses French during a large proportion of its working hours. It does so substantially less in Greater Montreal, however, than in the rest of the province. In Montreal, the French and the English have opposite patterns of linguistic usage: each group uses its mother tongue and the other language in a two-to-one ratio. The language patterns of those of other mother tongues are not the same: they use both official languages as well as their mother tongue. They employ English twice as much as French and they employ French just a little more than their mother tongue. The decline in the use of French by Montrealers is due to the increased use of English by the French and to the limited utilization of French by the English and by persons of other mother tongues.

If occupations are classified as manual, as nonmanual requiring oral communication, and as nonmanual requiring written communication, one finds that, among the French those who must communicate the most and

17. Jacques Brazeau, "Essai sur la question linguistique en Belgique," Rapport no. 13 soumis à la Commission royale d'enquête sur le bilinguisme et le biculturalisme, 1966, non publié, en dépôt aux Archives nationales à Ottawa.

18. See Commission d'enquête sur la situation de la langue française et sur les droits linguistiques au Québec, *Rapport,* bks. 1 & 2; and Serge Carlos, *L'utilisation du français dans le monde du travail au Québec,* Etude E 3 de la Commission (Quebec: Editeur officiel du Québec, 1973). The survey, carried out in 1971 by the Centre de sondage de l'Université de Montréal, yielded some 4,900 completed questionnaires from a random sample of 6,300 eligible households. It dealt mainly with the communication languages required of employees in the execution of work tasks, which demand reading, writing, or speaking to others. Information was also gathered on the linguistic identification of the main participants in interaction; on the language used in social intercourse in work and nonwork situations; on the social, cultural, and economic characteristics of the respondents; on their opinions and attitudes concerning the language issues; and on the respondents' occupational activities and hierarchical levels in the occupational structure.

those who must communicate in writing use the greatest amount of English. Conversely, persons of English mother tongue who employ French to the greatest extent are those whose work is manual; those who have communicative task requirements, on the other hand, use French orally rather than in reading or writing. The two languages and the two language groups are complementary in the sense that French is used most in material production and English is used largely in activities requiring greater communication with the public, with work peers, and with suppliers and administrators, especially if the communication is in written form.

Language use varies according to industrial sector. There are four sectors where French is dominant: the primary industries (agriculture, forestry, fishing, and mining), construction, public administration, and commerce. There are two sectors where English is dominant: finance and public utilities. In the French-dominated sectors, the French are overrepresented, and French and English speakers use more French than is average for their groups. Conversely, in the English-dominated sectors, the French are underrepresented, and less French is used by English and French speakers than is average for their groups. In manufacturing, which can be identified as a bilingual sector, the French use less French than the overall French labor force, while the English use more French than the overall English labor force. It is in this sector that one uses the other official language most. Each group uses its mother tongue in personal and social services more often than it does in any other work situation; this sector subdivides into two parallel linguistic subsectors. Conclusions drawn from data on the use of languages confirm the existence of vertical segregation between English- and French-speaking Canadians according to industrial sector. This segregation is also characterized by a greater use of English in durable written communication and by a tendency toward parity, instead of proportionality, of language use in manufacturing, the greatest source of employment.

Language use also varies according to characteristics of employment and qualities of employees. The least educated French laborers use French to the greatest extent at work; these are people of low status and income. The French who use French the least are those who have average education and income. The most educated French Canadians are in an in-between position: they comprise, on the one hand, those who are in personal and social services, commerce, and public administration, and, on the other hand, those who are in manufacturing, public utilities, and finance. The most educated represent a great dispersion of language patterns according to sector.

English Canadians with less than nine years of schooling use French the most at work. They are the group that can least depend solely on their mother tongue. English speakers who have more education, status, and income tend to use French less at work.

These findings show that English enjoys a position of strength and superiority relative to French and other languages in Quebec and, particularly, in Montreal. There is asymmetry in linguistic usage: if one is at the bottom of the occupational scale—whether one is of English, of French, or of another mother tongue—one has to use French more than other members of one's linguistic group. Among the English and the others, it is the workers who have to take into account that Quebec is 80 percent French. Social mobility allows them to escape paying this tribute. Upwardly mobile French speakers must use English increasingly unless they come to occupy a niche in the French-language parallel sectors of personal and social services and of nonfederal public administration.

In terms of a hierarchy of involvement in productive activities and of resulting social stratification in Quebec, and especially in Montreal, English is used at the top, French at the bottom, and both languages at the intermediate level. Besides a vertical segregation according to sector of activity, professional status within sectors implies a horizontal segregation as well.

Persons of English mother tongue, whether unilingual or bilingual, are overrepresented in managerial functions. They see some advantage to oral bilingualism in concession to the local work force and population. They interact with French-speaking colleagues and subordinates who practice a bilingualism of self-promotion and who use English orally and in written form. Persons of other mother tongues insert themselves as best they can in this complex system of relationships perceiving, on the one hand, the present supremacy of the English language and, on the other, the possibility that they may make a wrong choice at a time when consideration is being given to the redefinition of language requirements.

The two types of professional segregation just discussed, sectorial and hierarchical, permit a high level of use of one's mother tongue, be it English or French. Territorial segregation in the province and residential segregation in Greater Montreal have the same consequences. These patterns of segregation allow immigrants and their offspring to choose assimilation into the English culture, but to speak their own mother tongue in low-status work situations nearly as much as French Canadians speak French in comparable positions.

Professional segregation is accompanied by an etiquette of rapport between language groups and by norms regarding linguistic usage. Survey data show that English-speaking members of the labor force are largely impervious to linguistic pressures, whereas French and others are highly sensitive to them. Language choice is made mainly according to the individual or group addressed, but in an asymmetric fashion. The English-speaking person in authority uses English with his French and other subordinates more than the French person in authority uses French with his English and other subordinates. The same applies to communication with colleagues and to a mixed audience of colleagues and subordinates. These differences persist even in situations limited to the interaction of persons who can use both English and French. They are more marked in the case of written communication.

Thus, English speakers accept as a norm the present "bilingualism," which requires their knowing some French but functioning mainly in English, while French speakers, on the other hand, accept that their English-speaking superiors use English in communicating with them. On a personal basis, French speakers feel they cannot change their own use of languages in work situations: they see any effort they might individually make in this respect as likely to hinder their promotion and alter the climate of interpersonal relationships. They think, however, that the government as the representative of everyone's welfare should adopt legislative measures to change the situation. The English and others do not agree; they claim such legislation would deny their rights, limit industrial growth, and is not practically feasible. They foresee a gradual evolution, with more of them, particularly their offspring, learning French.[19] They have, however, rallied against the language law with respect to language of schooling.

Some Limitations to Political Intervention in Linguistic Affairs

An analytical summary of the Canadian case in the study of interethnic relations should highlight the continued occupation of somewhat distinct territories by French Canadians and English Canadians. It should stress

19. Such attitudes are generally corroborated by another survey: *Attitudes of the Anglophone Community of Montreal to Their Situation as a Linguistic Minority* (Toronto: Research Department, Canadian Broadcasting Corporation, 1972).

that prior to twentieth-century industrialization, while interdependence of regions was less pronounced, means had been found to assure within Quebec, but much less so in other parts of Canada, a certain cultural autonomy and self-maintenance for each ethnolinguistic group. The development of the country as a whole, in the face of emigration to the United States, required immigration of persons of British and other origins. Initially, French immigration was not sought and generally was not available. Settlers of diverse origins have not constituted, by and large, a political problem for Canada; they have become assimilated and have contributed to maintainance of the English-speaking population. The French have relied on a high birthrate to maintain their population and have not actively sought to assimilate newcomers. While there were, prior to industrialization, crises relating to French minorities outside Quebec and relating to Quebec's opposition to Canadian external policies, the French were, generally, a submissive minority who accepted their status within a country in which a major and a minor language and culture existed. An important majority of French Canadians continues to accept this condition. But this majority, together with a sizable minority of Québécois who seek other political arrangements, has noticed changes introduced by industrialization and feels the need for important social transformations. The two groups might disagree more on means than on ends.

Changes that have been perceived are, first, the involvement of Québécois, now largely urban, in the industrial process as producers and consumers and their consequent adoption of an urban-industrial way of life, lay in orientation, and requiring schooling; second, the existence of an ethnolinguistic barrier to their participation in the industrial process above the level of the skilled worker within most enterprises; third, a gradual decrease in the relative number of French Canadians outside Quebec; fourth, the continuation of a western movement of industrial development as a result of ecological and social forces, which will decrease Quebec's and Montreal's importance in relation to Ontario and Toronto; and fifth, a realization of the power of the local and central governments in the development of regions, enterprises, and, through them, people.

Québécois have also changed their attitudes toward the effects of industrialization on their group's survival and development. Whereas in the past they viewed this economic phenomenon as inevitably detrimental to the French Canadian way of life, largely structured by a preindustrial organization, they now see it as advantageous to the extent it can be harnessed to their own collective ends.[20] This would require the state to intervene not only in linguistic or cultural matters but in the overall social organization, as the survey on language use in the work situation, reviewed above, clearly demonstrates.

Governments, however, come very slowly to adopt important societal changes. Furthermore, they tend to adopt universal principles that give an appearance of symmetry rather than different modes in order to arrive at greater true social balance. One such principle, on which rests much of the inefficiency of governmental intervention regarding ethnic and linguistic problems, is that of individual equality. Liberal governments tend to view inequalities from an individualistic perspective, in terms of personal rights, and consequently they seek societal changes through interpersonal persuasion rather than through structural modifications.

In all societies, individuals who belong to favored groups (due to their age, sex, origin, or culture) are provided with more rewarding activities within institutions than are persons belonging to other groups that are considered amodal in terms of institutional functioning. Liberal governments view the groups that are different in individual rather than in institutional terms. They consider members of minority groups to be unable, for some reason or other, to compete with other members of societies for social and economic advantages. The solution lies in rendering the minorities more competitive.

But the division of labor in society creates interdependent relationships to satisfy the objectives of an impersonal productive system. It effectuates the distribution of responsibilities and rewards according to the selected modes of the system. These are culture-bound in the sense that they are but one possible way of organizing things to insure productive forms of interaction between different cultural groups. Even when prevailing modes are alleged to involve a merit system, it is evident that some types of knowledge and skills are considered more pertinent than others. It thus appears that rendering a different set of people more competitive consists of inculcating them with the culture-bound, socially pertinent qualities that they lack. In other words, the liberal solution to group inequalities rests on the gradual assimilation of the members of the minority groups into the existing system. Basically, the end result is the disappearance of

20. For a brief review of the multiple relationships between industrialization and French Canadian nationalism, see Edouard Cloutier, "Industrialization, Technology and Contemporary French Canadian Nationalism," in *Nationalism, Technology and the Future of Canada,* ed. Wallace Gagne (Toronto: Macmillan of Canada, 1976), pp. 147–166.

the group as such, because assimilation involves not only a sizable proportion of the individuals in the group but also the ever-expanding number of group activities of the social minority.

It thus appears that the liberal approach to a collective linguistic problem can hardly work. On the other hand, collective solutions are also problematic. Such solutions aim at guaranteeing that a given group will, in fact, be allotted a given share—most often a proportionate share—of jobs, language use, and so forth. In one way or another, these solutions imply the setting and attainment of quotas based not on the individual's capacity to compete within the system but on specific characteristics that permit group identification, such as sex, age, or ethnic origin. Consequently, any collective solution contradicts the liberal criterion of individual equality because it, in fact, strives for reverse discrimination.[21]

Two types of solutions were applied to the linguistic issue in work situations in Quebec. Before 1974, the government policy in Quebec was one of unrestricted liberalism: companies were free to set whatever internal linguistic rules and regulations they considered proper for their own functioning. Individual workers, on the other hand, were supposed to take into account the language used in the work situation when they chose an employer. As was shown earlier, in Quebec this linguistic liberalism resulted in a marked quantitative and qualitative advantage to the English language. This advantage was, in turn, closely related to a division of labor that coincided largely with the ethnic origin of employees, so that any mandatory linguistic realignment at work would have required either that some people in higher echelons start speaking a language they had no desire or inclination to speak or that French-speaking people be moved upward in the hierarchy.

Both solutions, which are clearly incompatible with the liberal equalitarian ideal, are implicitly included in Law 22, which provides for certificates to be issued by the government to business firms that adopt and apply a proper "Francization" program, requiring, among other things, that the management and personnel have knowledge of French and that Francophones be represented in management. Business firms must have

---

21. This contradiction is very clear between the equality-of-opportunity principle and the affirmative-action programs presently applied in the United States. See, in particular, Nina Totenbey, "Discrimination to End Discrimination," *New York Times Magazine,* 14 April 1974, pp. 9 ff.; "Affirmative Action," *Time,* 15 July 1974, p. 60; Marylin Bender, "Job Discrimination," *New York Times,* 10 November 1974, sec. 3, pp. 1 ff.; and Arthur Okun, *Equality and Efficiency: The Big Tradeoff* (Washington, D.C.: Brookings Institution, 1975).

these certificates "to be entitled to receive premiums, subsidies, concessions or benefits from the public administration . . . or to make with the government . . . contracts of purchase, service, lease or public works." [22] Such policies were correctly identified by English-speaking people as being antiequalitarian.

Social mobility used to be considered the classical nonmandatory answer to inequalities between ethnic or linguistic groups. It was believed to be attainable largely through raising the educational level of the disadvantaged group. However, such optimistic visions of overall social transformation proved unfounded: many studies have shown an extreme weakness in the relationship between educational level and social mobility in industrial societies [23] and, more specifically, between educational and occupational levels of French and English ethnic groups in Canada. [24] It is precisely the newly educated Québécois who have been demanding a realignment of job distribution along ethnic lines and a recognition of French as the language of work at all levels of production. Many authors even identify this group as the main force behind separatism. [25]

As pointed out earlier, the equalitarian mode of rewards distribution is but one possible form of social organization. Why is this mode considered so superior to others that it should not be tampered with? The answer is obvious. Equalitarianism produces a form of discrimination based on some socially pertinent qualities. The groups of people who possess these qualities are well served by the system and are, therefore, committed to its continued application. Ironically, the people who profit from equalitarianism have no qualms about relying on collective instruments, such as government, to protect the established mode of rewards distribution; thus, the orientation of liberal governments is, in general, toward the maintenance of administrative and productive functions based on individual

22. *Official Language Act* (1974), Editeur officiel du Québec, chap. 6, articles 26, 28, and 29.

23. C. Arnold Anderson, "A Skeptical Note on Education and Mobility," in *Education, Economy and Society,* ed. A. M. Halsey et al. (New York: Macmillan, 1961), pp. 164–179; Raymond Boudon, *L'inégalité des chances* (Paris: Armand Colin, 1973), pp. 23–48.

24. Lysiane Gagnon, "Les conclusions du rapport B.B.—de Durham à Laurendeau-Dunton: Variations sur le thème de la dualité canadienne," in *Economie Québécoise* (Montreal: Presses de l'Université du Québec, 1969), pp. 233–252.

25. Albert Breton, "The Economics of Nationalism," *Journal of Political Economy,* 72 (1964): 35–52; Pierre E. Trudeau, "Les séparatistes: Des contre-révolutionaires," *Cité Libre,* September 1964, pp. 2–6; Hubert Guindon, "Social Unrest, Social Class and Quebec's Bureaucratic Revolution," in *Party Politics in Canada,* ed. Hugh Thorburn (Scarborough, Ont.: Prentice-Hall of Canada, 1967), pp. 189–200.

equality of opportunity with minimal collective measures for the ame-
lioration of social inequality.

The establishment by the Quebec government of a policy with regard
to language of schooling illustrates this point. When public sentiment on
the language issue sought to make a scapegoat of a small Italian immigrant community for the decrease in enrollment in French schools, the
government created a commission to look into language matters. Through
Law 63 the bilingual character of the province and the right of parents to
choose the language of schooling for their children was still maintained,
however. A moratorium on the language-of-schooling policy in Saint-
Léonard would have been sufficient to keep matters under control until
the end of the commission's inquiry. Instead a law that was largely
disavowed by the French population because it maintained the linguistic
status quo was introduced. Discontentment with Law 63 was so widespread that in the summer of 1974 Law 22 was passed. Law 22 was
meant to effectuate social change without displeasing anyone, particularly
groups in power. It gave rights of schooling in their own language to
children of English mother tongue while denying the same privileges to
children of immigrants of other mother tongues unless they could qualify
in English through a language test. English-speaking and immigrant
groups set in motion legal procedures to question the constitutionality of
Law 22 and sought to circumvent it by teaching language-test English in
private kindergartens for the benefit of the children of immigrants whose
mother tongue was not English. French-speaking teachers as a consequence refused to administer the language tests. This episode underlines
the fact that Quebec's government, dependent on foreign finance and
multinational enterprises, is powerless to make decisions on matters that
have become a daily public issue. Needless to say, its dilemmas take
place in the context of diminishing rates of demographic and economic
development within Quebec in comparison to neighboring Ontario.
Hence, the Quebec government, unsupported as it is in many respects by
the central authority, is not ready to risk chasing corporate home offices
from Montreal by adopting cultural measures that would appear discriminatory to the privileged English-speaking group. It will not take the risk
of impoverishing the regional industrial economy.

Some people, however, are ready to take that risk. The official opposition in Quebec, the Parti Québécois, believes that democratically induced
changes will come soon and that they will involve the attainment of cultural and political autonomy within a common-market arrangement with

Canada. The party's leaders uphold the view that these changes will not be economically disastrous because of the need for interregional dependence within the industrial sector. They also maintain that the changes effected will not be directed against the groups that are privileged at present. Of this, they have been unable to convince English-speaking elements and immigrants, who remain overwhelmingly opposed to the party and what it stands for.

Thus, it appears that political action and power work both for and against social transformations in the economic and cultural realms. The Canadian Confederation, no doubt, laid the groundwork necessary to the development of Quebec society with a French-language public bureaucracy. A unitary form of central government might not have provided over the last century the same opportunities for this development. Organizational patterns, however, are not equally advantageous to all, and their reification prevents the definition of issues in terms of their objectives and consequences. The maturation of the aspirations and capabilities of populations have not been accompanied by the necessary transformations of patterns of relationships and of basic rules of social functioning. Thus, the English-speaking population of Quebec and the large enterprises that have joined English and French in a symbiosis are not ready to seek new modes of interaction, although these are considered necessary by many in the majority group of the Quebec population. Dissatisfactions and fears have become universally manifest. The central and local governments are not able to find solutions to the ills that they have diagnosed. Strong action on their part would endanger their publics' support, and it would not be in keeping with their valuation of the established order and of its traditions.

The course of the future is unpredictable. Caution must be exercised in the interpretation of political trends through electoral results. On the one hand, the strength of the Parti Québécois must not be underestimated: the small number of seats it won in 1973—six—could easily be multiplied by four or five in future elections with only a 5 percent increase in electoral support.[26] On the other hand, the 1973 election results cannot be interpreted as a clear-cut referendum on Quebec's independence since many

26. In the 1973 election, the Parti Québécois received slightly more than 30 percent of the votes. Given the present quasi two-party system in Quebec, the Cube law should handsomely reward the Parti Québécois in seats for each additional percentage point it gets in electoral support.

other issues obviously entered into the voters' calculations.[27] The interpretation of votes is further complicated by the fact that a great many voters apparently supported divergent ideologies with regard to French-Canadian nationalism at almost simultaneous federal, provincial, and municipal elections.[28]

Whatever interpretation is given to electoral results, however, it cannot be denied that demographic minorization, perception of a link between language and access to the culture of industrial life, increased schooling of the younger generation, and reliance on the provincial government will accentuate the demands of the Québécois for the "Francization" of their environment, including work activities. Will governments, intermediate bodies, and private concerns work for the realization of this objective within the present political framework? It is doubtful it will be done either immediately or during the next generation. If reforms that are substantial and that constitute a break with the past are not developed through the political system, support for cultural nationalism may well give way to general demands for secession.

27. In particular, Serge Carlos, Edouard Cloutier, and Daniel Latouche have shown that the independentist-federalist dichotomy is not by far in perfect relationship with the breakdown in votes between the Parti Québécois and the Liberal party. See "Autopsie du 29 octobre," in *La Presse,* 20 November 1973, p. B4.

28. For example, many French Canadian voters supported the Parti Québécois in October 1973, the Liberal party of Canada in July 1974, and an English-speaking candidate for the Rassemblement des Citoyens de Montréal in October 1974. Their electoral behavior is certainly not a clear indication of their feeling toward independence.

Note added in proof

Since this essay was written, in the spring of 1975, two important events have taken place which are bound to drastically alter both interethnic relations and the language situation in Quebec and in Canada. First, the November 1976 Quebec elections brought the Parti Québécois to power (it won 71 out of 110 seats with 41 percent of the popular vote). Second, the new Quebec government has made public its language policy paper entitled "The charter of the French language in Quebec." Its avowed aim is to make Quebec as French as the other Canadian provinces are English. It states, among other propositions, that all public affairs are to be conducted in French only, that the children of future immigrants of any origin are to be sent to French schools, that French is to be the language of work, that all private institutions are to be able to service their clients in French, and that all outdoor advertising is to be in French only. Bill 1, enacting these propositions, is scheduled to be debated in the Quebec National Assembly in the summer of 1977.

10

Ethnic Conflict in Northern Ireland: International Aspects of Conflict Management *

DAVID E. SCHMITT

This essay examines the principal dimensions of the conflict that has increasingly polarized Northern Ireland since 1968. Specifically, it briefly reviews the background to the present conflict and attempts to explain the emergence of the crisis at this particular time. Additionally, a discussion of governmental strategies for dealing with the evolving ethnic conflict is undertaken. The Northern Ireland case presents especially difficult problems of conflict resolution because of the international aspects of the situation. The governments of both the United Kingdom and the Republic of Ireland have been directly involved; moreover, there exists no sense of common national identity in Northern Ireland. Other nations such as the United States, as well as certain international organizations, also have had a bearing on the crisis.

Background

Anglo-Normans began invading Ireland in the twelfth century, but their invasion never resulted in England's complete political control of the country; the cultural and political assimilation of the Irish by the English proved to be an insurmountable task. In fact, during the early period of attempted conquest English colonizers and their offspring tended to acquire Irish cultural traits. The purposes and policies of English colonialism in Ireland went beyond economic gain. There had developed a realistic concern in England that Ireland, because of its location, could be a

* For their helpful suggestions on an earlier draft of this essay, I wish to thank Joseph Curran of Le Moyne College, Syracuse, New York; Sean Killeen of Cornell University, Ithaca, New York; and John Whyte of Queen's University, Belfast. The final draft of this essay has benefited from the article by Joseph M. Curran entitled "Ulster Repartition: A Possible Answer?" *America,* 134 (31 January 1976): 66–68.

means by which continental enemies such as France might outflank Britain and attack it from two sides. Indeed, unsuccessful French excursions to Ireland remain an interesting part of Irish revolutionary history.[1]

The northern province of Ulster was the last area to be politically and militarily subdued by the English. During the seventeenth century a "plantation" of settlers from England and Scotland was fostered by English authorities, largely as a means of establishing a loyal, politically stable population base. This plantation never completely displaced the indigenous Irish. They became dispossessed marginal tenants, beggars, or manual laborers, while the settlers from Britain, including a sizeable peasant and working class, enjoyed a privileged economic position. Economic disputes between the Irish and the settlers were at first essentially over land. Later, with the industrialization of Belfast, they centered more on urban concerns.[2] There were other, cultural differences between the settlers and the indigenous population. The natives spoke a distinct language, Irish, which survived as a living language well into the nineteenth century.[3] They tended to follow more clannish, personalistic forms of social organization, and they resented, distrusted, and were hostile toward the settlers, their language, and their culture.[4] The settlers, on the other hand, perceived the customs of the native Irish as barbaric.

Also of great significance is the fact that the native Irish were Catholic and that the settlers were Protestant. From a doctrinal point of view, each group tended to view the other as heathen. In more recent decades Catholics have come to view Protestants as religious unfortunates who have not found the true faith, while Protestants tend to consider Catholics simple-minded for accepting such notions as papal infallibility. Yet these views have not been unusual among Catholics and Protestants in other countries, where they have managed to coexist peacefully. The labels of *Catholic* or *Protestant* in Northern Ireland connote much more than con-

1. For a general history, consult Edmund Curtis, *A History of Ireland*, 6th ed. (New York: Barnes & Noble, 1950). An excellent discussion of the emergence of ethnonationalism in Europe is Walker Connor, "The Politics of Ethnonationalism," *Journal of International Affairs*, 27, no. 1 (1973): 1–21.

2. One of the better treatments emphasizing economics is Liam de Paor, *Divided Ulster* (Middlesex, Eng.: Penguin, 1970).

3. For an illustration of the politicizing impact of language in stimulating the twentieth-century Irish war of independence against England, see Padraic H. Pearse, "The Murder Machine," in his *Political Writings and Speeches* (Dublin: Talbot, 1952).

4. A useful account of cultural differences between the indigenous Irish and the settlers is Denis P. Barritt and Charles F. Carter, *The Northern Ireland Problem: A Study in Group Relations*, 2d ed. (London: Oxford University Press, 1972).

flicting doctrines or minor cultural distrust. These terms refer to profound ethnic differences.

The terms Catholic and Protestant have stood as important symbols of solidarity since the seventeenth century. Intermittent violence between the two groups has continued to reinforce the solidarity of each. The defeat of the Catholic James II by the Protestant William of Orange in 1690 still stands as a great victory in the minds of most contemporary Northern Irish Protestants. Catholics also have their ethnic heroes, among them Daniel O'Connell, the Great Liberator, who in the nineteenth century helped erase legal sanctions against Catholics.

Agrarian societies of Catholics and Protestants mounted recurring feuds, with one particular event, the Battle of the Diamond in 1795, resulting in the death of more than twenty Catholics and spawning the powerful Protestant Orange Order. In 1801 England and Ireland were politically linked as the United Kingdom of Great Britain and Ireland. The nineteenth-century quest for home rule—that is, for a local parliament for Ireland within the context of the United Kingdom—also triggered great hostility between Catholics and Protestants. Hundreds were injured during the 1886 and 1893 riots in Belfast, when home rule bills were before the London Parliament.[5] Protestants in the North feared creation of an all-Ireland parliament in which they would be heavily outnumbered by Catholics.

In sum, by the early twentieth century, ethnic solidarity under the ethnic labels of Protestant and Catholic had been reinforced by continuing economic grievances, cultural hostilities, political conflict, and centuries of violence. So terrified were northern Protestants of Catholic domination in an autonomous Ireland that an effort to implement home rule in 1912 through the United Kingdom Parliament led approximately five hundred thousand Protestant men and women to pledge that they would use "all means necessary to defeat the present conspiracy to set up a Home Rule Parliament in Ireland." [6] The more moderate efforts to attain Home Rule were displaced by the rising militancy of Irish nationalists, but World War I postponed and frustrated the nationalist cause.

    5. Andrew Boyd, *Holy War in Belfast: A History of the Troubles in Northern Ireland* (New York: Grove, 1969).
    6. A. T. Q. Stewart, *The Ulster Crisis* (London: Faber & Faber, 1967), p. 62. The Stewart volume contains a useful discussion of the period. See also F. S. L. Lyons, *Ireland since the Famine* (New York: Scribners, 1971).

Significantly, the independence movement contained a strong cultural component that emphasized the Irish language, Irish sports such as hurling, and Irish folk tradition. Cultural organizations such as the Gaelic League and the Irish Athletic Association provided much of the leadership for the war of independence. After the execution by the British of insurrectionist leaders of the 1916 Easter Rising and an abortive attempt to impose conscription in Ireland, the Anglo-Irish war of 1919–21 produced a settlement that led to the creation of the present border between North and South.

Following a complex series of events, the British Government of Ireland Act in 1920 partitioned off six of the nine counties of Ulster, forming a new political system, largely Protestant, known as Northern Ireland. It was to have its own parliament to control local affairs, while remaining within the United Kingdom. Although Protestant leaders had been against home rule for any of Ireland and especially for any of Ulster, they accepted the loss of the three Ulster counties with large Catholic populations in order to help guarantee a permanent Protestant majority in the region. A treaty between nationalist rebel forces and British leaders produced a separate political system, the Irish Free State, in the South, politically independent of the United Kingdom, but retaining Commonwealth status. Although the southern Constitution enacted in 1937 resulted in its de facto status as a republic and provided for an elected president, the country did not officially acquire the name "Republic of Ireland" until 1949.

A Unitary Political System

The partitioning of Ireland provided a vital new element in the ethnic identities of Protestants and Catholics in Northern Ireland. On the one hand, the existence of a viable Catholic nation in southern Ireland terrified and further solidified Protestants. Articles 2 and 3 of the 1937 Constitution of southern Ireland, in fact, claim the entire island as national territory. On the other hand, Catholics in the North, who comprised roughly one-third of the population, had a political system in the South with which to identify and a base from which to carry on Irish nationalistic activities against the state of Northern Ireland. In short, one of the most basic elements of viable democratic politics was missing from the political culture, namely, a common popular support for the new state. It can be argued, of course, that early efforts to establish a pattern of consociationalism within the regime might eventually have led to consensus among the political leadership and acquiescence or even support from the Catholic and Protestant publics.[7]

Among the most important variables precluding such evolution was the international dimension. Nationalist leaders (favoring a unified, independent Ireland) had little incentive to cooperate, given their hope in the early years of partition that unification might occur. Protestant Unionists had little incentive to attempt reconciliation, in part due to the hands-off policy of the British Parliament toward the Northern Irish state. The Government of Ireland Act had provided for a parliament on the Westminster model to be located at Stormont outside Belfast. The fifty-two-member House of Commons, elected on the basis of single-member districts after 1929, placed power largely in the hands of the prime minister of Northern Ireland and his cabinet through a system of party responsibility. Although the British Parliament in London maintained control of such key powers as external affairs, foreign trade, taxation of income, and defense, Stormont retained almost complete control of the internal state of Northern Ireland. Most government jobs, the police, most judicial posts, and the local governments, which controlled much public employment and public housing, were under the authority of the Stormont government.[8]

In situations of polarization into two hostile ethnic groups, majoritarian democratic processes can facilitate repression of the minority by the majority community. They can provide an aura of legitimacy to outside observers and a basis for rationalizing discrimination to those in the majority. Democratic structures in the small unitary state of Northern Ireland served the dominant Protestant Unionist party well. In the absence of federal controls from London, structural competition from other branches of government within Northern Ireland, and autonomous regions in which Catholics might have had a significant voice, control by the Protestant community was virtually complete. Because the society was divided over one central, ethnically based issue (the existence of the border), electoral contests were essentially meaningless since there was no chance of the minority gaining power.

7. For a classic discussion of the concept of consociationalism, consult Arend Lijphart, "Consociational Democracy," *World Politics,* 21 (January 1969): 207–225.

8. A basic source on Northern Ireland government is Nicholas Mansergh, *The Government of Northern Ireland: A Study in Devolution* (London: Allen and Unwin, 1936).

Not only did the Protestant leaders fail to attempt a consociational relationship with minority leaders, but they also followed discriminatory practices within government and encouraged discrimination in the private sector.[9] The franchise for local elections was stacked in favor of Protestants, gerrymandering further weakened the Catholic vote, and government jobs and other benefits were often awarded on the basis of ethnic ties, that is, mostly to Protestants. Furthermore, the system of criminal justice had many repressive and discriminatory features, including provisions for internment without trial, arrest without warrant, and an exclusively Protestant auxiliary police unit called the B-Specials. As Northern Ireland's first prime minister put it, Northern Ireland had "a Protestant Parliament and a Protestant state." [10]

Discrimination along ethnic lines within the private sector was also widespread. Although both sides favored their own members, Protestants controlled most of the economic base. The problem of job discrimination in both the public and private sectors was especially serious since Northern Ireland was faced with chronic unemployment and dying industries, such as shipbuilding and textile manufacturing. Further, in the more heavily Catholic areas west of the Bann River, unemployment figures were higher, and Catholic leaders complained of discrimination in industrial development on the basis of geographic area. With jobs scarce, the economic stakes of ethnic solidarity rose for Protestant workers, which helped prevent the coalition of Protestant and Catholic workers against the Protestant economic upper class.

The main factor helping to unify each side, however, was ethnonationalism. With southern claims of sovereignty over the North, Protestants remained terrified of "Rome rule" or domination by the Catholic church in a united Ireland, a concern only marginally based in fact.[11] From the Protestant perspective, most Catholics were disloyal, and southern Ireland was a priest-ridden society controlled by the Catholic church.

9. David E. Schmitt, *Violence in Northern Ireland: Ethnic Conflict and Radicalization in an International Setting* (Morristown, N.J.: General Learning Press, 1974).

10. Northern Ireland, *Parliamentary Debates* (Commons), 16 (1933–34): 1095.

11. It is, of course, a great overstatement to say that the Catholic church runs the Republic of Ireland or even that it determines most public policy. It has, however, intervened politically. For discussion, see John H. Whyte, *Church and State in Modern Ireland, 1923–1970* (Dublin: Gill and Macmillan, 1971). See also David E. Schmitt, "Catholicism and Democratic Political Development in Ireland," *Eire-Ireland: A Journal of Irish Studies,* 8 (Spring 1974): 59–72.

Especially in view of several small and unsuccessful Irish Republican Army (IRA) campaigns of terror against the North, there was enough rationality in these attitudes to help perpetuate Protestant antagonisms.[12]

Catholics, of course, had good reason to hate the Protestant system, given the discrimination noted earlier. But an increasing number of Catholics in the North, especially middle-class Catholics, favored the link with Britain for economic reasons: the North remained more economically advanced than southern Ireland and, because of its link with Britain, offered more and better welfare services. Thus, although Catholic ethnic loyalties after the Anglo-Irish war were strongly pro-Irish and although the Nationalist party—the major political party on the Catholic side— favored unification, no serious attempts were made to undermine the regime. The possibility of a consociational settlement leading eventually to a government based on consensus was at one time real. Given the history of violence and the fears of Protestants, however, speculation on consociational initiatives by Protestant leaders must be regarded as academic, even though they may well have worked given the milder Catholic ethnic mentality.[13]

The Breakdown of Order

One of the remarkable characteristics of the Northern Irish political system from the 1920's to the mid-1960's was its stability. Except for the residual violence from the Anglo-Irish war in the early 1920's and occasional minor flare-ups, such as activities by the small and popularly unsupported IRA, the Catholic population remained rather passive.[14] Since the mid-1960's, however, over thirteen hundred people have been killed and thousands more have been injured—this in a society of only about 1.5 million people. Bombs have exploded in Dublin and in British cities. American organizations have sent financial assistance to the Provisional IRA, which has been more militant than the Official wing. Thousands of British troops have been employed in an unsuccessful effort to maintain order. Why has ethnic conflict emerged in violent form so recently?

The civil rights movement in Northern Ireland originally began as an effort to terminate injustices suffered by the Catholic population. The

12. The IRA, of course, is not the army of the Republic of Ireland. Outlawed on both sides of the border, this nationalist organization has sought with varying degrees of vigor the unification of Ireland.

13. For a fine study of attitudes toward identity and violence, consult Richard Rose, *Governing without Consensus* (Boston: Beacon, 1971).

14. See J. Boyer Bell, *The Secret Army* (London: Blond, 1970).

Campaign for Social Justice, for example, was established in 1964 to investigate specific cases of discrimination against Catholic citizens. In large part, the leadership of the emergent civil rights campaign came from a new middle class. Social modernization in Britain had led to reforms in the British educational system allowing greater numbers of people to obtain university training. Increased educational opportunities in Britain and Northern Ireland stimulated the growth of the Catholic middle class, an obvious recruiting ground for civil rights activity. Also, the existence of modern mass media facilitated the dissemination of information on civil rights activities beyond Northern Ireland, and undoubtedly strengthened their impact. The media also became a useful means by which civil rights activists in Northern Ireland attempted to generate intervention by Great Britain and to elicit sympathies from abroad. In sum, technological and social modernization seems to have had significant impact on the present crisis.

The Civil Rights Association created in 1967 was a composite body with multiple aims. Yet it followed an official policy of not attempting to achieve unification nor of threatening the existence of the Northern Irish state. Rather, it sought to abolish the B-Specials and police powers such as internment without trial, to equalize voting privileges and establish fair electoral districts, and to terminate discrimination in employment and housing. Apparently some IRA figures were involved in this endeavor, attempting to use the civil rights movement as a means of uniting Protestant and Catholic working-class citizens and eventually breaking the link with Britain.[15] But the major thrust of the effort was for liberal, democratic reforms within the system.

The strategies of this moderate approach to solving ethnic grievances were nonviolent. They did not at this point even involve the civil disobedience that emerged later, such as refusal to pay rents and property taxes. Through publicity and peaceful demonstrations the movement sought to provoke British intervention that would force the Northern Irish government to liberalize. Indeed, there appears to have been a liberalization of some Protestant leaders. Terence O'Neill, prime minister of Northern Ireland, suggested that the danger of republicanism (the movement to seek a united, independent Ireland) would decrease with fair treatment of the Catholic community.

A key variable in generating the civil rights activity and reformism in

15. See Vincent E. Feeney, "The Civil Rights Movement in Northern Ireland," *Eire-Ireland: A Journal of Irish Studies,* 9 (Summer 1974): 30–40.

the 1960's appears to have been a complex international demonstration effect, encouraged by the previously noted impact of technological modernization. Following World War II a wave of liberalization swept the world, most noticeably among the colonized peoples of Asia and Africa struggling for independence. The liberalization also took the form of movements for equality within political systems and, in some cases, efforts toward separation. For Northern Ireland, perhaps the most significant movement was the civil rights struggle in the United States, portrayed by media throughout the world. Student protests in the United States, Britain, and France also provided organizational models. Of additional importance were the contemporary strategies of political activism developed in other countries: publicity campaigns, mass demonstrations, civil disobedience, and undoubtedly the deliberate provocation by some of police brutality as a means of politicizing and radicalizing the masses of citizens. All of these tactics were eventually employed by reformists in Northern Ireland.

One of the most significant and, by many, unintended outcomes of the civil rights movement was the radicalization of the Protestant community and the declining support for more moderate Unionists such as O'Neill. The Reverend Ian Paisley, a master political organizer, formed his own reactionary Free Presbyterian church and led counterdemonstrations against civil rights groups, which he claimed were forces of popery and republicanism. Paisley's tactics and those of other Protestant extremists contributed significantly to escalation of the ethnic conflict. A 1966 march organized by Paisley provoked a riot when it entered a Catholic area of Belfast. Protestant paramilitary organizations also emerged, employing such tactics as murder and bombings, occurring then on a rather limited scale.[16]

Marches of Protestant organizations, especially the Orange Order, had long been a traditional display of ethnic political solidarity in Ulster. However, with the escalating confrontations between civil rights activists, on the one hand, and government forces and extremist Protestants, on the other, these marches produced clashes that in August 1969 brought British troops directly into the crisis: objects thrown at marchers from along the periphery of the Catholic Bogside area of Londonderry produced police intervention; a Catholic counterattack and the birth of "Free

16. David Boulton, *The UVF, 1966–73: An Anatomy of Loyalist Rebellion* (Dublin: Gill and Macmillan, 1973).

Derry,'' from which security forces were excluded; and the introduction of British forces into Londonderry. Direct confrontations between Catholic and Protestant mobs in Belfast also brought British troops to that city where the soldiers were at first welcomed as protectors by minority Catholics.[17]

British forces sent in to restore order, however, acquired a status quo orientation in that they supported the survival of the Northern Irish government. Untrained in sensitive police work and employing tactics that penalized entire Catholic areas (such as curfews and CS gas), they gradually became viewed as the enemy by the Catholic working-class population. Indeed, in a massive August 1971 raid into Catholic areas to capture and intern IRA leaders, the British army radicalized even many middle-class individuals because of their indiscriminate and harsh treatment of Catholics. By this time the IRA, especially the Provisional wing, had become a significant offensive force seeking the ouster of Great Britain and unification with the Republic of Ireland.[18]

The Republic acquired an increasing role as the violence escalated. After Ireland and the United Kingdom entered the European Economic Community (EEC) or Common Market, the British government had to consider the Republic's political voice within that body. Cooperation of the Republic, essential in controlling activities of the IRA in southern Ireland, had direct bearing on any attempt at conflict management. Thus, the United Kingdom government was pressured repeatedly by the Republic to acknowledge an ''Irish dimension'' to the crisis even though Northern Ireland is within the United Kingdom's borders. The effect of this pressure, however, was multidimensional. It probably helped encourage Britain to hasten more equitable treatment of Catholics and to seek a settlement to the crisis. But the Republic's role served also to frighten Ulster's Protestants and to strengthen the position of Protestant extremist leaders at the expense of that of more moderate ones.[19]

17. For a more detailed account, see Northern Ireland, *Disturbances in Northern Ireland* (Cameron report), Cmd. 532 (Belfast: HMSO, 1969). Also helpful is the London Sunday Times Insight Team, *Northern Ireland: A Report on the Conflict* (New York: Random House, Vintage Books, 1972).

18. Among the useful analyses of the behavior of British security forces is United Kingdom, *Report of the Inquiry into Allegations against the Security Forces of Physical Brutality in Northern Ireland Arising Out of Events on the 19th of August, 1971* (Compton report), Cmnd. 4823 (London: HMSO, 1971).

19. See London Sunday Times Insight Team, chap. 11, for an account of probable involvement of certain government officials of the Republic in the establishment of the Provisional IRA.

Even without pressure from the Republic, a principal strategy by which the British government attempted to resolve the conflict was the initiation of various reforms. It pressured the Northern Irish government into initiating reforms that most Unionist politicians resisted. Among these were the phasing out of the reserve police force (the B-Specials) composed entirely of Protestants, the establishment of a commissioner for complaints, the institution of an equitable system for assigning public housing, and the abandonment of discriminatory voting restrictions for local elections. Some reforms, such as fair housing, however, were made unworkable by extremist groups. Other reforms, such as local electoral changes, could not be implemented immediately. In any event, none of the early reforms significantly altered Protestant control of the political system, which continued to be structured on the parliamentary principle that the majority Unionist party fill the position of prime minister as well as all cabinet posts.[20] The total benefits of the reforms for the Catholic community, moreover, were relatively small compared to the promises of British and Northern Irish officials for meaningful change. Furthermore, the reform effort helped to radicalize the Protestant community, which saw reforms as a threat to its survival.[21]

As the conflict progressed, the British government also attempted to stimulate economic growth, especially after the period of direct rule. It employed, in part, an international strategy, encouraging foreign investment in Ulster and seeking the use of EEC regional funds. It also supported failing Northern Irish industries and recently has put forward provincewide economic development plans rather than further developing industrial centers such as Belfast. In the long term these techniques could be important. With more jobs and greater prosperity, there is less rationality in discriminating against minorities. Also, the employed and better paid may be less violent in their assaults on the system than those with less to lose.

The British government also attempted to control the conflict through the application of force. Though British troops, and certainly top political and military officials, did not hold the bigoted and hostile stereotypes of

20. For a useful discussion of reforms prior to direct rule and for an analysis of their impact, consult *Commentary upon the White Paper (Command Paper 558) Entitled 'A Record of Constructive Change'* (Belfast: Irish News, 1971).

21. Henry Kelly, *How Stormont Fell* (Dublin: Gill and Macmillan, 1972). See also Thomas E. Hatchey, "One People or Two: The Origins of Partition and the Prospects for Unification in Ireland," *Journal of International Affairs,* 27, no. 2 (1973): 242–244.

the Catholic population that the Northern Irish security forces held, the dynamics of the situation eventually led to combat between the IRA and the British, with the vast majority of the Catholic working-class citizens growing to hate the British forces and officials. Under attack, army personnel became hostile toward the Catholic working-class communities, and British officials saw Catholics as harborers and supporters of terrorists who were killing their men. Internment without trial (officially terminated in late 1975) and other repressive measures, as well as instances of brutality by the British forces, infuriated the minority population. However necessary the maintenance of order and however well intended British military policy, it was often harsh and heavy-handed; especially during the early stages of confrontation, it was directed primarily at Catholics. The Protestant community, on the other hand, perceived the British as insufficiently forceful. The introduction of government force, then, compounded the negative impact of communal and terrorist violence in further polarizing the two ethnic communities.

Efforts toward an Externally Imposed Consociational Solution

The stage for an externally imposed consociational settlement was set when Britain took over direct rule of Northern Ireland in March 1972, suspending its Parliament. By this time it had become apparent that a solution within the context of majoritarian democracy was impossible. The list of casualties had mushroomed from IRA bombings and military operations, police and army actions, and other forms of violence. "Bloody Sunday," an incident in January 1972 in which thirteen civil rights activists were killed by British paratroopers, was probably the immediate cause of Stormont's demise.

Direct rule involved the superimposition of a British secretary of state and a few assistants on the Northern Irish bureaucracy. In other words, Northern Ireland's prime minister, cabinet, and parliament were replaced by a member of the British cabinet and his assistants. Not only did members of the British government lack the historical bigotries against Catholics and fears of a united Ireland, but they were also far less dependent upon the Protestant majority. The Conservative government of Edward Heath only marginally required the support of Unionist members of Parliament at Westminster. To be sure, paramilitary Protestant organizations constituted a greater ultimate threat than the IRA, and the British army certainly did not want to be engaged against both Catholic and Protestant extremists. Also, Protestants could bring the province to an economic halt, as extremist-led strikes have demonstrated. But British leaders were faced with a much larger national constituency. Remote Northern Ireland contained only about 3 percent of the total population of the United Kingdom, and the vast majority of British citizens quickly grew quite weary of hostilities, especially after the IRA began carrying its campaign of bombings to British cities.

The constituency of the British government leaders also included international actors, such as the Republic of Ireland, other EEC members, Commonwealth nations, and the United States. Additionally, the Irish Catholic population of Britain, which surpasses in number the Protestant population of Northern Ireland though their power is more diffuse, undoubtedly contributed indirectly to consociational efforts. Indeed, the Labour party has had a particular incentive to maintain its support from Irish voters in Britain.

In an effort to placate the Protestant majority, the British government held a referendum in March 1973 on the issue of retaining the border. Naturally, the overwhelming majority voted in favor of retaining the union with Britain. Many Catholics boycotted the referendum, with nationalist leaders arguing that the vote should include the electorate of the entire island, not just six counties of Ulster. Following this vote, constitutional proposals were set forth in a United Kingdom White Paper, which provided for a new assembly. Elections were to be on the basis of proportional representation (single-transferable-vote method, which allows voters to rank order their preferences) to encourage the election of moderate-party candidates, such as those of the Alliance party. Most significantly, there was to be a power-sharing executive (cabinet) of the Assembly. In the words of the United Kingdom government, "the Executive itself can no longer be solely based on any single party, if that party draws its support and its elected representation virtually entirely from only one section of a divided community." [22] The United Kingdom was to continue to provide for security as long as necessary, oversee the appointment of judges, attempt to prevent discrimination, and, in general, seek to insure the equitable treatment of all citizens and the maintenance of law and order. British officials pledged not to force unification without the consent of a majority and acknowledged an Irish dimension to the problem.

22. United Kingdom, *Northern Ireland Constitutional Proposals*, Cmnd. 5259 (London: HMSO March 1973), p. 13.

In May 1973 local elections were held under the reformed electoral system; the Assembly elections took place in June. These elections reflected the polarized ethnic character of Northern Irish politics, but they also suggested that the majority of Northern Irish citizens was not then determined to reject the proposed constitutional reforms out of hand. There was a total of seventy-eight Assembly seats. The Unionist party drew most of the Protestant votes, acquiring twenty-four seats for official Unionists and eight for other Unionists, while more extremist Protestant parties won eighteen seats. The Unionist party platform included modest proposals for power sharing (the Northern Irish term for consociationalism). For example, up to half of the Assembly committees, with greater policy-development roles, were to be chaired by opposition party members. Similarly, on the Catholic side, the Social Democratic and Labour party or SDLP (a more militant but nonviolent replacement of the Nationalist party) won nineteen seats. Nonsectarian parties won only nine places in the Assembly.

The "loyalist" members of the Assembly (Protestants opposed to power sharing) refused to take part in discussions on the formation of the executive. By November, leaders of the official Unionists, the SDLP, and the Alliance party, having worked out a power-sharing arrangement, had nominated an executive-designate. Significantly, as a concession to Catholic nationalist sentiment and SDLP demands, they announced the possible formation of a Council of Ireland, comprising members from both Northern Ireland and the Republic of Ireland. The details of this council, conceived as a weak advisory body, were to be established at a conference involving the executive-designate and the governments of the United Kingdom and the Republic of Ireland.

Loyalist members of the Assembly, who had refused to take part in forming a power-sharing government, were denied their request to attend the Sunningdale Conference of December. They were, however, invited to discuss their position with the United Kingdom's secretary of state for Northern Ireland and to attend the first session, at which they could present their views. They refused to do so. At the Sunningdale Conference the Irish government declared it would respect the wishes of the majority in the North concerning the constitutional status of Northern Ireland; the United Kingdom government pledged it would support the majority even if it should decide to unify with the Republic. Although details of the Council of Ireland were not established at Sunningdale, it was agreed that representation on the council should be limited to the two po-

litical divisions of Ireland, each with equal representation, and that safeguards for the financial and other interests of the British government
should be established. The Council of Ireland was to be comprised of
both a fourteen-member council of ministers made up of seven members
of each Irish government, with the chair rotating between North and
South, and a consultative assembly consisting of thirty members from
each of the Irish parliaments. Significantly, along the lines of Eric Nordlinger's "mutual veto" strategy of conflict regulation, the Council of
Ministers within the Council of Ireland was to be able to act only by
unanimous decision.[23] Also, no fundamental constitutional changes were
envisaged by the creation of the council, its suggested concerns being in
such areas as tourism, roads and transport, and economic cooperation.

A final aspect of the Sunningdale agreement was the establishment of a
commission on law enforcement, with four members each from the
United Kingdom (including Northern Ireland) and the Republic of Ireland. Commission members from the Northern Irish and British governments favored extradition measures, requiring the surrender of IRA and
other fugitives in the Republic to Northern Irish authorities. Commission
members from the Republic of Ireland advocated a system of extraterri-
torial jurisdiction by the Republic, which United Kingdom members ultimately accepted.

The new executive was appointed on 31 December 1973, thus formally
ending direct rule. But its life was short. The Sunningdale Conference
had generated intense debate in the North, and an increasingly radicalized
Protestant population displayed its support of loyalists in the 28 February
1974 general elections of the United Kingdom. Loyalist candidates polled
over 50 percent of the vote and won eleven of the twelve Northern Irish
seats to the United Kingdom Parliament in London. After this vote of
"no confidence" in the Protestant members of the executive, loyalist
members of the Assembly entered a resolution for renegotiation of the
original power-sharing constitutional amendments. An amendment offered by Brian Faulkner, chief executive, attempted to uphold the Sunningdale accord. The Assembly's rejection of this amendment helped produce a general strike by the Ulster Workers Council, a militant Protestant
organization supported by various Protestant paramilitary bodies. Lacking
the support of the Protestant majority and with the province at a virtual

    23. Eric A. Nordlinger, *Conflict Regulation in Divided Societies,* Harvard University
Center for International Affairs, Occasional Paper no. 29 (Cambridge, January 1972),
pp. 24–26.

economic standstill, Brian Faulkner and other Unionist members of the executive resigned. This led to the termination of the executive and the Assembly by the United Kingdom government on 29 May 1974. The consociational strategy imposed by the British government had failed.

A number of specific forces contributed to this failure. Continuing violence, such as IRA attacks and sectarian murders of Catholics, further polarized the population, facilitating the ability of loyalist leaders such as Ian Paisley to win additional mass support. A constant danger in consociational systems is that extremist leaders on both sides will appeal to their publics on ethnic themes claiming that moderate leaders are betraying them. Political leaders cannot operate without public support or at least acceptance. Indeed, the very existence of hostility may act as an independent variable blocking the possibility of successful consociational political structures.

The international dimension of ethnicity was again among the most significant explanatory variables. The proposed Council of Ireland, the functions of which had not been determined by the time of the general elections of February 1974, terrified the Protestant population, which viewed it as a move toward unification. The SDLP and some southerners contributed to this impression by indiscreet exaggerations of concessions to the minority and the hope of eventual unification. Also, moderate as well as extremist Protestant leaders felt betrayed by what they regarded as a failure by the Republic to adequately implement the law enforcement provisions of the Sunningdale agreement. In addition, imposition of a consociational settlement came from an external source, thus denying one of the basic tenets of the consociational principle—namely, an agreement among the relevant elites.

Other Avenues of Conflict Regulation

The British government again attempted to achieve a consociational settlement, but with significantly greater opportunity for Northern Irish elites themselves to shape new political institutions. Theoretically this seemed to be a logical step. Consociationalism requires agreement among salient political elites of the ethnically divided political system. This less directly imposed process involved Northern Irish elections called by the United Kingdom government in May 1975 for the purpose of choosing delegates to a constitutional convention. The convention delegates were "to consider what provisions for the government of Northern Ireland would be likely to command the most widespread acceptance throughout the community there." [24] The United Kingdom Parliament was then to be at liberty to accept or reject the proposals or to submit proposals to the Northern Irish electorate.

Using the proportional representation system employed in 1973, the convention elections produced a landslide victory for loyalist candidates of the United Ulster Unionist Coalition. These candidates captured forty-seven of the seventy-eight convention seats with 55 percent of the popular vote. The moderate Faulkner Unionists were the principal losers, winning only five seats with 7.7 percent of the vote. The SDLP took seventeen seats (two won by Protestants) with 23.7 percent of the vote. The nonsectarian Alliance party won only eight seats and captured about 10 percent of the vote. The remaining seat went to the Northern Ireland Labour party. The degree to which the Protestant majority rejected power sharing is reflected by the fact that loyalists acquired roughly five-sixths of Protestant votes. [25]

The likelihood of a common set of power-sharing proposals emerging from the convention seemed remote. Moreover, the loyalist parties had been able to educate their followers in the use of the single-transferable-vote system. Proportional representation benefited extremists, not moderates as originally intended by the British government. The power-sharing provisions of the report presented by the convention did, in fact, prove unacceptable to the British government, mainly because of the unwillingness of loyalists to allow for adequate minority representation in a new government. The British government responded by unsuccessfully reconvening the convention in February 1976 with a four-week deadline for developing acceptable proposals. Northern Ireland, however, still remains under direct British rule.

At this point, a successful long-term consociational agreement within the context of the United Kingdom must be regarded as possible but not probable. The present level of hostility and distrust will probably make it difficult to achieve. Of the potential outcomes, a unilateral declaration of independence by Protestant loyalists must still be considered possible, though such threats have been made in the past partly to pressure the United Kingdom government into acceptance of loyalist demands. A pos-

24. United Kingdom, *The Northern Ireland Constitution,* Cmnd. 5675 (London: HMSO, July 1974), p. 17.

25. For an analysis, see Richard Rose, "Ulster Speaks, Clearly and in Contradiction," *Times* (London), 5 May 1975, p. 14.

sible consequence of such a move would be all-out civil war and the establishment of a new border as members of the two communities retreat to safe areas. Civil war also could be precipitated by a unilateral British decision to withdraw from Northern Ireland.

There have been increasing calls for an independent Northern Ireland based upon agreement between the Catholic and Protestant communities.[26] Such proposals have the merit of being based upon a cooperative approach; political structures to emerge presumably would be of the consociational variety. The chances for the successful establishment and maintenance of a negotiated independent Ireland, however, must be regarded as problematic at best. Economically, the difficulties would be staggering. Linkages with the Common Market and economic agreements with the United Kingdom illustrate potential palliatives. Of far greater concern would be the continuing existence of two hostile subcultures. Some of the calls for a negotiated independent Northern Ireland appear to be little more than self-serving appeals for a new Protestant-dominated state. Even if an accommodation could be reached, chances of eventual breakdown would be high. Among other things, significant numbers of the minority would continue to identify with the Republic of Ireland, and Protestant reaction would probably again exclude meaningful participation by the minority. The control of law enforcement would constitute a particularly difficult problem in the event of flare-ups of ethnic violence.

The possibility of outright civil war must be considered real. The Ulster Army Council, for example, was established to marshal a force of twenty thousand paramilitary loyalists to secure Northern Ireland pending a negotiated settlement for independence from Britain. In a "doomsday situation," a phrase frequently employed to denote a mass Protestant assault on Catholic areas, the army of the Republic of Ireland, only about fifteen thousand strong, could at best help protect fleeing Catholics. It almost certainly could not occupy and control Belfast. Even at their highest levels, British troops were unable to maintain order in Ulster. Further, many of the Protestant paramilitary personnel are also government police auxiliaries or are otherwise situated to be formidable opponents. The IRA would be an additional force to protect Catholics in such

26. For example, see Kevin O'Neill's argument for an independent Ulster in the *Observer* (London), 20 October 1974, p. 12. For the dangers of independence, see Conor Cruise O'Brien, "Extremists: A Delusion," *Observer,* 14 April 1974, p. 12.

circumstances, but it again would be greatly outnumbered. The probable outcome of such circumstances would be a repartitioned Ireland, with predominantly Catholic areas accruing to the Republic.

Given the centuries of communal distrust and the small likelihood of an effective consociational settlement, government leaders in the Republic of Ireland and the United Kingdom might be wise to seriously consider as viable alternatives strategies for separating the two ethnic communities. Various plans have been suggested, including British withdrawal after a set interval of time, with compensation payments to Catholics and others wishing to leave Northern Ireland. It has also been suggested that various enclaves in Ulster opt for the national affiliation of their choice.[27]

A superior alternative might be a planned, strategic repartition aimed at minimizing the loss of life and creating a smaller, nearly homogeneous Protestant Northern Irish state.[28] This new state might opt for retaining its links to the United Kingdom or choose independence, perhaps within an EEC framework. Repartition would be expensive and it would entail some risk, but it would offer a more permanent solution than consociational alternatives. It is possible, moreover, that serious discussion of repartition might conceivably encourage consociational agreement between leaders of the two communities who now view it as unacceptable.

Repartition would provide a significant advantage from the Protestant perspective. If all or most Catholics lived outside a new Northern Irish political system, law enforcement would be much easier. There would be no significant hostile community to harbor fugitives within the border. Furthermore, a shorter border could be drawn along somewhat more defensible lines. Protestants could live with a sense of greater security. Northern Protestant groups could claim that the best areas, for example, industrialized Belfast, had been secured for Protestants and that the Catholics had been beaten once and for all in their quest for reunification. Just as Unionist leaders had agreed to cast off three Ulster counties in 1920 for purposes of political control, so leaders in the 1970's could maintain that the sacrifice was worth the ultimate goal.

Part of a compromise package, moreover, would undoubtedly involve

27. For further discussion of various alternatives, see Arend Lijphart, "The Northern Ireland Problem: Cases, Theories, and Solutions," *British Journal of Political Science*, 5 (January 1975), 83–106.

28. For a useful theoretical discussion of the problems of partition, see Ray E. Johnston, "Partition as a Political Instrument," *Journal of International Affairs*, 27, no. 2 (1973): 159–174.

the return of nearly complete political control to Northern Protestants. Ironically, such a new government, despite the retention of historic bigotries and hatreds, could be quite democratic. It could be much more responsive to the demands of Northern Irish citizens than the governments of the United Kingdom or the Republic. Also as part of a settlement package, extremist Protestant groups would be in a military position to demand high compensatory awards to comply voluntarily with any necessary movement of Protestants and the shrinkage of the Northern Irish state.

Catholics, on the other hand, would no longer have to fear repression or discrimination if they became part of an expanded Republic of Ireland. Also, their sense of national identity would be partially fulfilled, even though the island remained ununited. They would be a part of a political system where majority democracy is viable, with genuine opportunities through the electoral process for the alternation of political parties in control of the government. Even though concentrated in the northern areas of the nation, they could undoubtedly acquire over time a significant voice in the Irish government. Also to their advantage, the Republic of Ireland has significantly expanded its various welfare programs in recent years and has undergone rapid economic development.

Some members of Catholic extremist groups, who would be most likely to resist violently, might be bought off; they could be allowed to exact significant financial concessions for Catholics forced to vacate portions of Belfast and surrounding Protestant areas. Among the key concessions might be a major commitment to economic development of the new areas of the Republic. These payments might be exacted not only from the United Kingdom but also from the Republic of Ireland, which would have a strong financial as well as political and military incentive to avoid a confrontation with the IRA and other paramilitary organizations. The leaders of these organizations might profitably demand high-paying positions in the newly partitioned areas. These positions could involve political as well as administrative jobs, providing the extremist leaders with long-term roles in the policy process and possibly with crucial ego satisfactions.

From the British perspective, though short-term incentive payments, resettlement costs, and developmental assistance would be high, long-term expenditures and subsidies would ultimately decline. The poorest sections of Northern Ireland would no longer be the responsibility of the United Kingdom, damage payments from violence would eventually recede, and further reduction of British military forces could take place. The predominance of public housing and the small size of most businesses in Northern Ireland would mean the level of compensatory payments necessary for private property would be comparatively low. Additionally, some of the foreign and British companies incorporated into the Republic of Ireland by new borders might prefer the economic and financial conditions there.

The Republic of Ireland, despite heavy initial costs, would acquire a larger pool of labor (though this would aggravate unemployment in the short run) and greater physical size and diversity. In the long term this could enhance national prestige and economic power. With sufficient finesse, the Republic might be able to recover a considerable portion of repartition costs from the government of the United Kingdom, which has a more urgent and direct need to secure a peaceful resolution of the communal struggle. Also, the Common Market would be a logical source of funding and loans, and other assistance might be obtained from such countries as the United States and Canada. Various forms of assistance from the United Nations could also be utilized.

Politically, the Republic could claim a victory in securing the liberation of northern Catholics and in expanding the national territory. It would probably be necessary to abandon claims to the remaining areas. But the Republic could maintain for public relations purposes that eventually northern Protestants would see the wisdom of joining with the Republic in matters of common interest and eventually in seeking strong political ties. Extremist Catholic organizations such as the IRA could make similar claims, especially if their leaders were co-opted into new administrative structures in the Republic. The probability of significant political links actually developing, however, would be slight, and the more realistic among the Republic of Ireland's leaders would have to accept that this approach would mean a permanent abandonment of a small section of the island.

This brief list of advantages ignores a host of serious dangers and obstacles. Militarily, a smaller Northern Ireland would still be vulnerable to attack. Terrorism would be more difficult, but such tactics as rocket attacks by the IRA could be staged from the new Republic areas. Protestant extremists, however, could retaliate with terrorist attacks on Dublin or with attacks on areas surrounding the new state, thus generating popular animosity among Catholics against IRA terrorists and reducing their activities.

Perhaps more serious would be the prospects for continuing terrorist activity in Britain. Modern technology and a large Irish population in Britain could provide a means for continuing offensive operations should major terrorist organizations or factions reject repartition. Even though the great majority of Irish in Britain rejects terrorism, a small minority could severely weaken the London government's capacity to resist attack. Protestant resistance, moreover, could make peaceful resettlement unworkable. The Protestant expression "not an inch" reflects a very real attitude held by a sizeable portion of the majority in the North. At its worst, the process of resettlement, or perhaps the process of negotiating a new border, could touch off civil war and precipitate a holocaust.

Certain strategies, however, could minimize the risk. Resettlement might occur in stages, with United Kingdom and Northern Irish forces pulling back to locations successively closer to Belfast. The process could be further legitimized by the possible use of United Nations troops. Protestants voluntarily relocating would leave remaining Protestant resisters increasingly isolated, thus offering a further stimulus for relocation. Protestants wishing to remain, however, would have little to fear from the Catholic population or the government of the Republic. A more crucial problem would be the need to protect Catholics in Protestant areas, especially in Belfast. Relocating large numbers from the Catholic ghettos of Belfast probably would be the most difficult and costly part of repartition. Catholic ghetto residents surrounded by hostile Protestant working-class communities could become the victims of massacres. To prevent this, it would be essential to elicit the support or at least the compliance of the major Protestant loyalist organizations, including the paramilitaries.

A major problem with repartition stems from normative considerations: while both the Republic of Ireland and the United Kingdom are politically democratic, repartition would involve coercion of large numbers of people. Hopefully, such coercion would be nonviolent, but it might require official action, going against the first preferences of large sectors, possibly even a numerical majority, of the Northern Irish population. The majority of citizens in the Republic, moreover, seems to have little desire for such an alternative. Areas west of the Bann River already have high unemployment, and relocated Catholics would have to be given work or provided welfare services at a time when the Republic's economy suffers from serious unemployment and inflation. The original partitioning of Ireland in 1920, however, involved coercion of persons on both sides of the border, who were placed in political systems not of their choosing.

The argument that the majority in the Republic does not want the economic problems associated with resettlement must be balanced, among other things, by persistent claims by the Republic to the whole of Ireland. In any event, the normative problem could be mitigated by carefully structured local plebiscites and various resettlement provisions. An element of coercion would be inevitable in the establishment of a viable new border, but there has been a significant level of coercion ever since the founding of the political systems of Ireland.

However desirable, a consociational settlement in Northern Ireland that will endure over the long term may not be possible. Furthermore, violence could escalate into a "doomsday" situation in which repartition would occur as a consequence of armed conflict. Hence, decision makers in the United Kingdom and the Republic of Ireland would be well advised to develop contingency plans for the orderly resettlement of people and for a new agreed-upon border. More helpful still would be open discussion of repartition as a probable alternative for future policy. Acknowledging the enormous difficulties of resettlement, British and southern Irish leaders could argue that this alternative would be superior to repartition through civil war, and by means previously discussed they could attempt to elicit the support of key political figures in the North. Of course some northern Irish leaders would at first reject the idea of repartition. But its serious discussion might conceivably serve as an additional impetus for conciliation, and possibly for the evolution of a more workable consociational accord within the present state of Northern Ireland. If this last effort to achieve accord failed, repartition might then proceed on a planned basis through the use of strategies noted earlier. Once achieved, repartition would provide the foundation for a permanent solution to the tumultuous problems of ethnic conflict in Northern Ireland.

11

Scottish Nationalism, North Sea Oil, and the British Response *

MILTON J. ESMAN

In the 1964 British general election the Scottish National party (SNP) attracted 62,000 votes, 2.4 percent of the Scottish total. A decade later, in October 1974, the SNP polled 839,000 votes (30.4 percent), displaced the Conservatives as the second party in Scotland, and came within 6 percent of the dominant Labour party (see Table 11.1). From an examination

Table 11.1. Scottish vote in recent British general elections *

Parties	1964		1966		1970		Feb. 1974		Oct. 1974	
	% vote	No. of MP's	% vote	No. of MP's	% vote	No. of MP's	% vote	No. of MP's	% vote	No. of MP's
Conservative	40.6	24	37.7	20	38.0	23	32.9	21	24.7	16
Labour	48.7	43	49.9	46	44.5	44	36.6	40	36.2	41
Liberal	7.6	4	6.8	5	5.5	3	7.9	3	8.3	3
SNP	2.4	0	5.0	0	11.4	1	21.9	7	30.4	11

* Percentages do not total 100 because of votes for minor parties.

of political debates it is clear that the SNP, which stands for Scottish nationalism and independence, has seized the intellectual and political initiative and that the other parties in Scotland and the British government are spending much of their energies responding and adapting to this new challenge. Scotland is an open, competitive unit of the British political system where claimants to political power can freely propagate their views and organize for political action. Thus, voting returns, supple-

* An expanded version of this essay was issued by the Department of Politics of the University of Edinburgh in its *Waverly Papers Series,* Series 1, Occasional Paper no. 6 (April 1975). For their helpful comments on an earlier draft, I am grateful to James Cornford, James Kellas, Donald MacKay, John Mackintosh, John Davidson, Malcolm Slesser, Robert Shirley, Gianfranco Poggi, Neil MacCormick, and A. S. Halford-MacLeod.

mented by survey data, measure fairly accurately the movement of political preferences. These data demonstrate that a major shift in the configuration and the content of Scottish politics has occurred during the past decade. The purposes of this essay are to explain the emergence of Scottish nationalism as a major political force and to indicate what it portends for the future of Scotland and of Great Britain, of which Scotland has been both a constituent nation and an economic region since the Act of Union in 1707.[1]

English-Scottish Relations from the Union of 1707
until World War I

Since the union of the crowns in 1603 and the union of parliaments in 1707, relations between Scotland and England in the context of Great Britain have been peaceful except for the Jacobite rebellions in the eighteenth century. The most serious of these led to the brutal repression by English and Lowland Scottish forces of the Highland clans following their military support for the restoration of the Stuarts in 1745. By bringing order to an anarchic polity, the union stimulated both economic and intellectual development in Scotland. Since both countries have been predominantly Protestant and English-speaking, there have been no important religious or linguistic grievances.[2] Notwithstanding English threats and some hanky-panky at the Edinburgh Parliament, the terms of the Act of Union were acceptable to the elites of both nations. It protected the northern border of England from interference by hostile European powers, it insured a Protestant succession to the throne, and it opened the expanding English and imperial markets to hard-pressed Scottish industry and traders. It explicitly protected the major institutions of the Scottish nation—the Church of Scotland, Scots Law, Scottish education, and local government—and it guaranteed their continuity and legitimacy. Cognizant though they were of the relative disparities in power and wealth, the Scottish elites conceived the union not as an annexation but as an act of association—a prudential calculation that averted war with a more powerful neighbor and protected Scotland's vital interests, while afford-

1. For an excellent interpretive survey of modern Scotland, see James G. Kellas, *Modern Scotland* (London: Pall Mall, 1968). There are numerous good histories of Scotland.

2. The Gaelic language, which in 1707 was spoken by 30 percent of Scottish families, most of whom lived in the Highlands and Western Islands, lacked official sponsorship and was repressed during much of this period. It is now spoken by barely 1.5 percent of Scottish families, all of them bilingual.

ing her middle classes economic opportunities that would not otherwise have been available.

These opportunities, which Scotsmen began to exploit a generation after the union, included the chance to participate as individuals and as enterprises in the political and economic structures and in the intellectual life of the expanding British Empire. Though a distinctive Scottish political life disappeared, Scotsmen became prominent in both houses of the British Parliament and in the London-based civil service. Scottish manufacturing and mercantile firms and Scottish banking and insurance companies established themselves in the growing and affluent English market. Educated Scotsmen—doctors and engineers among them—who could not secure employment in Scotland because their numbers were in excess of Scottish needs, found profitable employment in England.[3] Above all, Scotsmen helped to build and maintain the worldwide British Empire. Wherever the empire extended, Scotsmen were active and conspicuous. Scottish names were prominent as settlers in North America and Australia and as soldiers, administrators, planters, traders, and investors in India, Malaya, China, Jamaica, and Africa. The profits of empire enriched Edinburgh, Glasgow, and much of the Scottish countryside. The age of empire was clearly an economic boon to Scotland, and Glasgow in the late Victorian period was perhaps the most prosperous city in the world.[4]

This was a period of steady acculturation to English norms. The Scottish nobility and gentry sent their offspring to English public schools to prepare them better to function in the political and intellectual life of an English-dominated Britain. The middle classes soon followed suit, as Scottish schools gradually became more English in their curriculum content. Scottish lads who wished to prosper and progress had to learn to participate in structures and in situations where the more "refined" En-

3. Scottish professional education was more readily available and was superior to the English, at least until World War I. The flow of Scottish professional graduates is documented by Donald MacKay in his *Geographic Mobility and the Brain Drain: A Case Study of Aberdeen University Graduates, 1860–1960* (London: Allen and Unwin, 1969). The subject is surveyed by Norman Furniss in his mimeographed paper, "The Development of Higher Education in Scotland: The Mixed Blessings of National Unification" (Indiana University, June 1974). Some Englishmen during this period believed that all doctors were Scottish.

4. The area of Scotland that did not participate in this prosperity was the northern region—the Highlands and Western Islands—the seat of the neglected and declining Gaelic culture. For these areas the nineteenth century was marked by poverty, neglect, unrest, and large-scale emigration to seek job opportunities in Glasgow and abroad. The Highland clearances in the nineteenth century displaced thousands of Highlanders for the benefit of English and Lowland Scottish landlords.

glish manners, style, and speech were required. The renowned Scottish scholars, scientists, and literary men wrote in the English language for English and international audiences. Since the elites had their eyes on England, a distinctive Scottish high culture failed to develop.

Though a popular culture survived, there were no institutions or media to feed it, and it stagnated. The Gaelic-speaking culture in the Highlands and Western Islands was officially ignored, and the number of Gaelic speakers steadily declined. Scotland tended to become an intellectual and cultural province or hinterland of English culture increasingly centered in London. Scottish intellectual, artistic, and literary life, as exemplified by the distinguished *Edinburgh Review,* contained little that was distinctively Scottish in style or substance.

Notwithstanding these integrative processes at the cultural, political, and economic levels, a distinctive national identity survived in Scotland and among Scotsmen. Many Scots were lost to the Scottish community through emigration to England or the empire, but those who remained continued to look upon themselves as a separate people, different from the English, attached to a territory where their ancestors had shaped a separate civilization, proud of a long history which became increasingly romanticized by Anglicized Scottish historians and literateurs, aware of a unique set of religious, legal, and educational institutions, and of distinctive accents and styles of speech and behavior that set them apart from other peoples, particularly from the English. Scotsmen were sensitive to their junior role in Great Britain, even as they successfully reconciled and compartmentalized their Scottish and British identities and loyalties.

Throughout this period Scotsmen complained of their peripheral political situation within Great Britain, of rule by a remote London-based Parliament, cabinet, and administration, which were ill-informed of Scotland's special needs and preoccupied with English and imperial concerns. This sense of political marginality contributed, along with an egalitarian ethos, to Scotland's solid and steady identification with the antiestablishmentarian Liberal party for three-quarters of a century before World War I, and to the Liberal party's sponsorship and support of the home rule movement. Home rule promised Scotland, as well as Wales and especially Ireland, a regional legislature that would permit self-government over a wide range of internal problems, but within the framework of the United Kingdom. Although home rule never materialized—indeed, British government and the British political parties became increasingly centralized during this period—Scottish opinion continued to identify with generalized strivings for governmental devolution as an expression of Scotland's distinctive national status and national needs.

Most Scots continued to perceive themselves as a nation voluntarily associated in the United Kingdom. To the London elites, however, Britain had become a single nation through an inevitable and desirable process of integration. From London's perspective, Scotland had become "North Britain," an economic region of the United Kingdom, and what passed for Scottish national sentiments were considered exotic and increasingly empty and irrelevant cultural residues and harmless symbols of an earlier stage of British development. These different perceptions (of Scotland as an associated nation, and of Scotland as an economic region) and the conflict inherent within them never became politically critical. Union had paid off for the majority of Scotsmen—for the gentry, the dynamic business community, the educated middle class, and even the urban industrial workers. Teachers, preachers, and lawyers in their protected Scottish enclaves of school, church, and law were well taken care of by the British arrangement. There were no elites available to mobilize the Highlands' crofters and the small farmers and craftsmen who benefited little from the union.

Moreover, British rule, in which Scottish politicians, administrators, and soldiers particpated, was benign, not exploitative. Scotland was not colonized, nor were English institutions imposed on Scotland, nor was the free expression of Scottish entrepreneurship or intellectual energies limited or threatened in any obvious way. The London government demonstrated a capacity and a willingness to respond, albeit slowly and reluctantly, to Scottish pressures. In 1885 the office of secretary for Scotland was created to provide a center in the London government for dealing with Scottish matters.[5] The Scottish Office was instituted with responsibility for administering a number of United Kingdom statutes in Scotland.[6] A decade later, in 1894, the Scottish Grand Committee was organized in the House of Commons, including all Scottish members of Parliament, with responsibility for reviewing all bills that concerned Scotland before they were acted upon in Parliament. Although the Scottish Office and the secretary for Scotland were components of the United

---

5. Technically the office was revived in 1885. It had been allowed to lapse in the eighteenth century.

6. H. J. Hanham, "The Development of the Scottish Office," in *Government and Nationalism in Scotland*, ed. J. N. Wolfe (Edinburgh: At the University Press, 1969), pp. 51–70.

Kingdom government, their very existence exemplified recognition by the United Kingdom center of the distinctive quality of Scottish problems, for which a decentralized pattern of public administration was considered useful.

For such reasons as these, Scottish nationalism did not become an important political force during the imperial phase of British history.

Hard Times for Scotland: From World War I until 1968

World War I was an economic disaster from which Great Britain has never recovered. While some economic historians trace the stagnation of the British economy to the first decade of this century, it was World War I that signaled the time of troubles for Britain. The heavy drain of manpower and resources left Britain economically and morally ex-hausted. The two interwar decades witnessed economic stagnation, caused at first by incompetent management of economic and fiscal policy, followed by the worldwide depression, which persisted until the outbreak of World War II in 1939.

Scotland was especially hard hit by the depression in its main market, England. There was little incentive to invest in modernization of the traditional coal, steel, shipbuilding, and heavy engineering industries, which had been the backbone of Scotland's economic power and prosperity. These industries gradually became obsolete and noncompetitive by international standards. The infrastructures of roads, housing, and public facilities were neglected during this long economic eclipse. Management had little incentive and few resources to innovate and modernize; the labor force, more than a third of which at one time or another suffered demoralizing unemployment, became equally conservative in protecting jobs threatened by technological changes, which alone could have insured the ultimate viability of Scottish industries.

World War II restored markets for Scotland's heavy industry, and the wartime industrial-dispersion policy brought important high-technology industries into the area. Postwar reconstruction abetted by the Marshall Plan sustained full employment, but after 1955 the secular decline was re-newed. Scotland's traditional industries, on which its remarkable prosperity during the Victorian age had been based, were no longer competitive. Shipbuilding, which enjoyed a worldwide boom after 1955, actually de-clined in the Clydeside's high-cost technologically backward yards, some of which survived only by government patronage and subsidies. Although Scotland, with the help of British regional subsidies, drew some high-technology and consumer-oriented industries, it was not an attractive site for new investment. Its militant, strike-prone labor climate (especially in the Glasgow area), its remoteness from major markets, and the neglected state of its public facilities provided few incentives for the location of new economic activity.

These trends were exacerbated by two factors. The first was the failure of the London government to join the European Economic Community, thus foreclosing the United Kingdom, including Scotland, from location by firms interested in penetrating the tariff wall enclosing the rapidly growing Common Market. The second was the increasing centralization of ownership and control in the British economy. London-based corporate headquarters, abetted by London-based financial houses, were expanding by acquiring regionally owned industries and bringing them under their own London-based managerial control. The centralization of manufacturing industries produced a parallel London-based centralization of the expanding service industries, of research, and of the trade unions. This process of economic integration and centralization occurred also in the public sector, which began its expansion with the post–World War II Labour government's nationalization of the coal industry. The net effect was the transfer of major economic decision making affecting Scotland to corporate headquarters in London and even in New York. It meant that while many Scotsmen in their individual capacities became important decision makers in these corporate headquarters, they were working in London and their context was the interest of their British and multinational firms, not the welfare of Scotland.

Scotland was becoming a branch-plant economy.[7] Ambitious Scottish managers and entrepreneurs had to leave Scotland if they were to operate on the scale that challenged their talents. Scotland was losing its entrepreneurial and managerial class as control of Scottish economic life passed out of Scottish hands. As government expanded into new areas, such as health and welfare, or took control of functions formerly determined by local authorities, including education and highway construction, or intervened directly in economic fields, such as agricultural marketing or industrial subsidies, public decision making involving Scotland became fur-

7. In a series of articles in the Edinburgh daily, the *Scotsman* (30 October–1 November 1973), John Firn, the Glasgow University economist, demonstrated that 59 percent of all Scottish industry, measured by employment, was in foreign hands. He found that the foreign-controlled industries also tended to be more modern, faster growing, and more profitable than the Scottish-controlled industries.

ther concentrated in the Westminster Parliament and in government departments in London. Scotland had become peripheral both economically and politically to the British center.

Beginning in the late 1950's and through the decade of the sixties, Scotsmen became more and more aware of the indicators of their malaise. With increasing integration and expansion of the electronic communications media, especially television, Great Britain as a whole became the reference point for Scottish comparisons. While living standards were gradually rising in absolute terms and there was little of the acute distress of the interwar years, Scotsmen knew that their unemployment rate was nearly double the British; that their mean per capita income was 10 to 15 percent below the British and a quarter below the Southeast (London) average, while living costs in Scotland were the highest in Britain; and that their amenities, especially housing, were far inferior to contemporary British or European standards and expectations. In the late 1960's and early 1970's, employment in Scotland actually declined by about 7 percent (Glasgow alone lost sixty thousand jobs), and the unemployment rate would have been significantly higher had it not been for a steady outflow of emigrants. Since 1950 Scotland has lost more than eight hundred thousand people, its entire natural population growth, through emigration—two-thirds to England, one-third overseas. Particularly painful to Scottish patriots and damaging to Scottish morale has been the emigration of Scotland's youth, especially its educated youth, because Scotland has not been able to offer them economic opportunities sufficient to keep them at home.[8]

During this difficult period the British center continued to respond to Scottish pressures. The Scottish Office was awarded additional responsibilities until virtually all domestic administration that did not involve the nationalized industries or economic policy was included in the Scottish Office under a cabinet-level secretary of state for Scotland.[9] The Scottish Office, which was installed in 1939 in its large new headquarters at Saint Andrew's House in Edinburgh, became the administrative center for Scottish affairs. In 1970 the Scottish Office and related Scottish depart-

8. For a recent survey of the Scottish economy, see D. I. MacKay and G. A. MacKay, *Scotland: A Growth Economy* (Edinburgh: Bell, Laurie, Robertson, 1974). An earlier and more complete analysis is Gavin McCrone, *Scotland's Future: The Economics of Nationalism* (Oxford, Eng.: Blackwell's, 1969).

9. The current activities of the Scottish Office are detailed in the second volume of *Written Evidence* (London: HMSO, 1969), submitted to the Royal Commission on the Constitution. The Office deals with the EEC Regional Fund on Scottish projects.

ments controlled and directed more than 10,000 civil servants, nearly all of them Scotsmen, in such fields as health, education, agriculture, housing, social services, conservation, fisheries, and even economic planning. While the Scottish Office represented administrative decentralization rather than policy-making authority, its senior civil servants and its secretary of state constituted a persistent and effective political lobby for Scottish interests at the center of the British system in London, a lobby that was shared by no other region in the United Kingdom.

On economic matters the United Kingdom's assistance to Scotland has always been based on its concept of Scotland as a region of Britain and in the context of regional economic policy premised on aid to economically depressed regions.[10] Since 1928, the United Kingdom's economic assistance program has gradually expanded. Financial incentives for industries to locate or to expand in "development areas" have combined more recently with licensing controls to prevent industrial and office locations and further expansions in the overcrowded London conurbation. The effect has been to steer new industries to the depressed regions. For most of this period, all of Scotland has been classified as a development area, and although it contains less than 10 percent of the United Kingdom's population (one-third of the land area), it has received about 40 percent of the funds expended for regional development. While British regional policy has not brought prosperity to Scotland, it has helped to initiate the restructuring of Scotland's obsolescent industrial base. It has been responsible for the location of new, modern industries and for decisions by established industries to remain in Scotland. Without these incentives it has been estimated that Scotland would have lost another fifty thousand jobs during this period.[11]

Because of its "unionist" commitment to the integration of all parts of the United Kingdom and its welfare-state orientation, the policy of the London government is to provide uniform standards of public services to all persons and all areas of the realm and, thus, to redistribute resources through the budget from more affluent to poorer regions. There has been an extended controversy about the balance of government financial flows

10. The United Kingdom's experience with regional policy is well documented. Among the leading studies are A. J. Brown, *The Framework of Regional Economics in the United Kingdom* (Cambridge: At the University Press, 1972); and Gavin McCrone, *Regional Policy in Britain* (London: Allen and Unwin, 1969).

11. Barry Moore and John Rhodes, "Evaluating the Effects of British Regional Economic Policy," *Economic Journal,* 83 (March 1973), 87–109. Their estimate for Scotland appears in the footnote on page 96.

into and out of Scotland. Scottish nationalists claim that Scotland pays more into the United Kingdom coffers than it receives in return, and many Scotsmen find it easy to sympathize with this argument. But if one accepts certain premises (for example, that Scotland receives a share of the benefits of United Kingdom defense expenditures proportionate to its population), then the weight of professional opinion is that the United Kingdom has been substantially subsidizing Scotland financially. A 1969 United Kingdom Treasury survey indicated that this subsidy exceeded one billion dollars a year, or 30 percent of public expenditures in Scotland. Per capita public expenditures in Scotland are one-third higher than the United Kingdom average.

The solicitude of the United Kingdom government for Scotland's depressed economy was insufficient to prevent a continuing decline in Scottish morale during this period, however. The prevailing mood was one of marginality and loss of control, of dependency on outsiders and resentment of that dependency. Even managers who retained their freedom of action were disinclined to take risks; workers and their unions were equally defensive, protecting their jobs, pensions, and subsidized substandard housing. Scottish cultural and intellectual life, even at the universities, became increasingly provincial, and little of distinctive Scottish quality remained. Although England was still an escape hatch for the discontented and the ambitious, the empire was no longer available for that purpose. Scotland and Scotsmen were no longer able to participate in a grand and proud imperial venture. The sun had set on the British Empire at considerable cost to Scotsmen. Scotland had become an economically deprived and peripheral region in a declining British polity.

But despite this pessimism and sense of resignation, Scottish national sentiment remained—rooted in centuries of common history; love of the land; the surviving institutions of church, law, and education; a common socialization and sense of community; a vigorous set of indigenous, Scottish-controlled communications media; a distinctive brand of humor; an active network of athletic leagues, which participate in international competitions; and well-established cultural organizations. A prominent political scientist could write a convincing treatise on the "Scottish political system" as a vital structure.[12]

A conspicuous outlet for the popular expression of Scottish nationalism

---

12. James G. Kellas, *The Scottish Political System* (Cambridge: At the University Press, 1973).

has been through professional football. Scotland traditionally fields a team in international football competition, and its fortunes are anxiously and proudly followed by Scots of all classes, religions, regions, ages, and sexes. Football matches between Scotland and England are said to be ritual reenactments of the Battle of Bannockburn in 1314, when outnumbered Scottish militia under Robert Bruce routed the invading hordes of Edward II of England.

The Politicization of Protest: 1968–74

As the Scottish economy resumed its decline after 1955, the ingredients of political protest were abundantly present, but not the structures or organizations to catalyze it. The established political parties were closely integrated into British structures and, indeed, were dependent affiliates or units of the British Conservative (or Tory), Liberal, and Labour parties. The Conservative and Unionist party was controlled by the Anglicized Scottish gentry, business interests, and associated professionals. All were committed unionists. The Labour party, no less unionist, was dominated by trade union officials with close ties to the British labor movement and by politicians who looked to Transport House, Labour party headquarters in London, for their rewards. They had no confidence that an independent Scottish economy could provide even as inadequately as Britain for the welfare of the Scottish working class. Indeed, they considered that political separation would lead to economic disaster. While the Scottish Trades Union Congress traditionally supported home rule within the United Kingdom, its leadership proclaimed that socialism, not nationalism, must be the salvation of the Scottish working class.

Home rule sentiment continued to command widespread Scottish support, but not the intensity of support that moved or threatened British statesmen. During the long struggle for home rule, the movement had several times approached success in Parliament, only to be diverted at the threshold by matters of higher priority to the British elites. United Kingdom politicians never felt that they had been penalized or had paid a significant political price for setting home rule aside at the crucial moment. They calculated that Scottish and Welsh voters supported the idea of home rule for symbolic reasons, but that the issue commanded neither enough emotional commitment nor sufficient priority to determine many votes in a general election. While in opposition, the Labour party regularly pronounced in favor of home rule, a virtuous antiestablishment posture. Once in office, however, the unionist bias of its leaders and of the civil servants who advised them was quickly and decisively asserted. In 1949 and 1950, the Scottish Covenant, a petition pleading for a Scottish "parliament with adequate legislative authority in Scottish affairs" and "within the framework of the United Kingdom," was signed by an estimated two million Scotsmen, but it was contemptuously disregarded by the Labour prime minister. Yet the Labour party won about the same percentage of Scottish votes in the next general election, 1951, as it had in the two previous contests. Home rule was a moral stance rather than a political priority for the great majority of Scottish voters. As Scotland's grievances began in 1955 to center increasingly on economic issues, the appeal of home rule was further attenuated, for there was little in legislative devolution that promised additional resources sufficient to relieve Scotland's economic distress or to make a practical difference in the Scottish standard of living or economic prospects.

A clear alternative was offered by the Scottish National party (SNP): national independence and the reassertion of control by Scotsmen in Scottish institutions over the political and economic destinies of the nation. The history of the SNP and of its predecessors dating back to 1928 has been thoroughly documented.[13] The early nationalists were mostly intellectuals and literary people concerned primarily with Scottish cultural redemption. They were fueled by a nostalgia for the past and by a pronounced anti-English bias. Many of them were Gaelic-language enthusiasts in a country in which the Gaelic-speaking enclave had fallen below 2 percent of the households, nearly all of which also spoke English. The movement was strong in dramatic rhetoric and exhortation, but weak in political organization. Like similar literary nationalist movements elsewhere, it experienced frequent schisms and internal conflicts of doctrine but little organizational discipline. Because it drew on national loyalties and grievances that had no other avenue of political expression, it experienced minor political successes including the election of its first member of Parliament in a wartime by-election in 1945. Yet it was not an important political force and never drew more than 1.2 percent of the vote in a general election.

In the early 1960's the SNP was taken over by a group of younger men who shared their predecessors' patriotic aspirations for a politically independent and an economically and culturally regenerated Scotland, but

---

13. For a recent history of Scottish nationalism before 1968, see H. J. Hanham, *Scottish Nationalism* (Cambridge: Harvard University Press, 1969).

who shifted the movement's emphasis from literature and language to practical politics.[14] They invested in party organization, in constituency politics, and in economic research; without disregarding cultural themes, they focused on economic issues, which they correctly perceived to be the main grievances and anxieties of Scotsmen in the 1960's. The youthful activists whom they recruited into the party were drawn from strata of Scottish life that had not previously been politically active. For the most part the new leaders were independent professionals and small businessmen unaffiliated with the gentry and business interests that ran the Tory party, or with trade unionists and university intellectuals who dominated Labour. The party's early mass support came also from groups that had few ties to the established parties—small businessmen, independent craftsmen, small-town nonunion workers, farmers, and fishermen—which prompted some observers to dub it a "Poujadist" party.[15] But it also gained support from working-class voters sensitive to the appeal of Scottish patriotism and especially from skilled workers and technicians, such as the residents of the new towns, who had moved away physically and psychologically from the Labour stronghold of Glasgow and who were reaching out for a new vehicle of political expression.

The main demand of the SNP is Scottish independence. This is the bedrock doctrine that gives the party its distinctive character and cohesion and the common faith that unites its diverse supporters. With independence, the party argues, great things are possible for Scotland, including the elimination of the economic deprivations, from which so many Scotsmen unnecessarily suffer, and the restoration of the elementary right of self-government and of national pride. Without independence and sovereignty, Scotland will continue to be governed by alien rulers and will remain a dependent and depressed province of a declining England whose governments have demonstrated little concern for Scotland's special needs. The SNP's manifestos touch every topic likely to appeal to prospective voters, from pension rights to natural-resource conservation, coal

14. A personalized history of this period in SNP affairs was written by party chairman William ("Billy") Wolfe. See *Scotland Lives: The Quest for Independence* (Edinburgh: Reprographia Press, 1973).

15. "Poujadism" refers to a short-lived French political movement in the 1950's representing the protests of small farmers, craftsmen, and shopkeepers who were being threatened by the modernization of the French economy. J. P. Cornford and J. A. Brand, "Scottish Voting Behaviour," in J. N. Wolfe, pp. 17–40. See also Roger Alan Brooks, "Scottish Nationalism: Relative Deprivation and Social Mobility" (Ph.D. diss., Michigan State University, 1973).

mine closures, teachers' salary claims, land-use planning, a Gaelic-language university at Inverness, and opposition to British entry into the European Economic Community (EEC).[16] The party's insistence on government intervention, economic planning, and extended welfare services has convinced some Tories that the SNP is leftist and socialist; its failure to support nationalization of industry has persuaded Labour spokesmen that it is really "Tartan Tory." Though there is an anti-English strain in most Scottish nationalists—as in many Scotsmen—the anti-English elements in the party's official statements are moderate by conventional nationalist standards; nor is there any sanctioning, even by inference, of political violence. The party doctrine commits the SNP to the achievement of independence by democratic electoral methods. Its social and economic positions are social-democratic, not revolutionary, and they are moderately stated, calculated not to frighten but to appeal to the patriotism of a broad spectrum of a people that feels comfortable with an orderly, middle-class style of politics.

As the British economy lunged and faltered with the stop-go macroeconomic policies of successive Tory and Labour governments in the 1960's, the reorganized nationalist party began to move. With very little funds, but with enthusiastic and active youthful members, the SNP emphasized political work at the constituency level with an intensity that the older parties could not match. In the 1966 general election, the SNP doubled its previous vote, and in a 1967 by-election, it won its second parliamentary seat. It scored its first major success, an important milestone in the party's development, in the municipal elections of May 1968 when it polled an astonishing 30 percent of the vote and demonstrated that it could draw votes from all classes of the population in all sections of the country. Not only did this performance elect a large number of SNP local councilors, but it provided a tremendous boost in morale and heralded a large increase in membership and in local chapters. Above all, it threw a scare into the ranks of the established parties, particularly the Labour party, which was in office at that time.

Scotland is very important to Labour, for it is the peripheral areas, Wales and especially Scotland, that regularly provide the Labour party with the seats it needs to win parliamentary majorities. The Labour es-

16. There are Gaelic-language enthusiasts in the SNP, which may help to account for its successes in Highland constituencies. Though the SNP favors special efforts to promote Gaelic culture, there is no question of transforming Scotland into a Gaelic-speaking nation. There is no language issue in Scotland.

tablishment in London took the 1968 municipal elections as a sign that all was not well in their Scottish fief and that some response was indicated. Already under pressure to consider some measures of regional deconcentration throughout Britain, the Labour government chose to regard the SNP vote primarily as a renewed demand for home rule.[17] On that shaky premise, it appointed in 1969 a Royal Commission on the Constitution to "examine the several functions of the central legislature and government in relation to the several countries, nations and regions of the United Kingdom" and to consider "whether any changes are desirable in these functions or otherwise in present constitutional and economic relationships."[18] The report of this royal commission, known as the Kilbrandon report after its second chairman, a Scottish law lord, was not released until 1973. It became an important factor in the subsequent evolution of Scottish nationalism.

While in opposition, the Conservatives established a party committee under their former (Scottish) party leader and prime minister, Sir Alec Douglas-Home, to look into the question of devolution. In its report, issued in 1970, the committee recommended a directly elected Scottish assembly with legislative powers over the functions administered by the Scottish Office. Yet, during their period in office from 1970 to 1973, the Tories failed to implement any part of this report.

The SNP had emerged during the 1960's as a convenient vehicle of political protest. It added a fresh element of excitement to the dreary landscape of Scottish politics, but there were few political observers who took it seriously. Third parties, not to mention fourth parties like the SNP, always had a difficult time in Britain's highly institutionalized two-party system. They could mobilize protest in by-elections and in local contests, which the voters knew would have little effect on important outcomes, but they could seldom make a respectable showing in general elections, which were serious business.

Beyond this structural feature of British politics, the SNP faced the uphill task of demonstrating the credibility of its main thesis, Scottish in-

17. Perhaps the most influential of a stream of arguments for deconcentrating the British government to allow greater regional impact on policy and to relieve members of Parliament and British administrators of the unnecessary burden of detail is found in the short volume by John P. Mackintosh, *The Devolution of Power, Local Democracy, Regionalism, and Nationalism* (London: Charles Knight, 1968). Mackintosh was Professor of Politics at Strathclyde University and is currently a Labour party member of Parliament.

18. United Kingdom, Royal Commission on the Constitution, vol. 1, *Report*, Cmnd. 5460 (London: HMSO, October 1973), p. iii.

dependence, to an educated electorate that was less than satisfied with the status quo, but that would not be committed to radical change by slogans alone and that harbored many deep and long-standing economic, familial, and sentimental ties to Great Britain. Two major issues were raised. The first was the security of a small state in a dangerous world. How could an independent Scotland with a small population within a relatively large territory protect itself? The SNP argued that if Norway and Ireland could manage on their own, Scotland could also, and at lower cost than its present tax contribution to the inflated and inefficient United Kingdom defense structure. But in the 1960's the Soviet threat was still manifest; there was the Berlin crisis in 1961 and the occupation of Czechoslovakia in 1968. Few Scots were convinced they could be as secure alone and independent as they were in Britain.[19]

More important were the economic risks of independence. How could an economically distressed country like Scotland, which depended on Britain for substantial current subsidies, for its main markets and trade connections, and for industrial investments, go it alone economically? The SNP argued that the British connection had become an economic disaster for Scotland. British monetary and fiscal policy was oriented to the state of the English economy, not to conditions in Scotland. Thus, deflation would be imposed when the English economy was overheated but at a time when Scottish industry was just beginning to feel its expansionary effects. The Scottish economy would never recover as long as its macroeconomic policy was governed by English needs. Until Scotland achieved political independence, it would be unable to shape economic policy suitable to Scotland's requirements. Moreover, with its whiskey, woolen, and farm exports, which earned substantial foreign exchange primarily for the benefit of the British (English) export-deficit economy, Scotland would have no balance-of-payments problem. English markets would not be lost to Scottish industry in the event of independence, for there would be a mutual interest in maintaining economic ties. Thus, the SNP argued, an independent self-governing Scottish economy would be economically viable, far preferable to its current deprived and dependent situation. But this line of argument was not sufficient to persuade Scottish workers that the factories in which they worked and produced primarily for English markets would not be closed if Scotland should sever its union with En-

---

19. A summary of this debate appears in John Erikson, "Scotland Defense Commitment: Some Problems of Cost, Capability, and Effectiveness," in J. N. Wolfe, pp. 71–91.

gland. Nor could Scotsmen drawing their civil, military, or individual pensions from funds controlled in London be assured that their interests would be protected in the event of separation. Businessmen who produced for the United Kingdom market asked what would happen if the United Kingdom were to impose tariffs on their products. The prospect of Scottish independence was not economically credible.

Although the Scots had serious economic grievances—of which the SNP never ceased to remind them—the prospect of independence for the weak and fragile Scottish economy seemed to pose unacceptable risks. While national sentiments remained vital and valuable to most Scotsmen in the late 1960's, they did not consider themselves an oppressed people. Their national aspirations were not repressed to the point that would justify a move toward independence no matter what the economic cost. This was the main vulnerability of the SNP position even to those who might have otherwise considered independence a desirable option. Its effect was to limit the SNP to a party of protest, which could flourish only in local and by-elections. When the chips were down, few Scotsmen were prepared to take their nationalism seriously enough to vote for the SNP. Although the municipal elections of 1968 had yielded an impressive protest vote of 30 percent, two years later, in the general election, the SNP lost two-thirds of that vote. If the SNP was to be more than a convenient vehicle of protest, it would have to break out of this impasse. Could Scottish independence be made economically credible?

From Protest to Rising Expectations: "It's Scotland's Oil"

In the early 1970's a dramatic new fact transformed Scottish opinion and Scottish politics—the discovery of oil in the continental shelf off Scotland's North Sea coast. The amounts were impressive—at least 3 billion tons and perhaps double that figure, enough to meet Great Britain's total annual requirements of 150 million tons for twenty to forty years.[20]

From the outset, the policy of successive London governments, Tory

20. Estimates of North Sea oil reserves increase steadily with exploration and new discoveries. Peter Odell of the Netherlands School of Economics estimates total reserves in the British and Norwegian sectors at from ten to eighteen billion tons. If the reserves are exploited to the feasible maximum, he estimates that despite high investment costs they could meet 75 percent of Western Europe's requirements from the early 1990's well into the twenty-first century. *Scotsman,* 7 November 1974, p. 1; 13 November 1974, p. 13; 14 November 1974, p. 7. Odell's estimates are considered overly optimistic by oil-industry and government sources.

and Labour, has been maximum and speedy exploitation, to get "British oil" out of the ground as fast as possible. The oil has been viewed as manna from heaven, a lifeline for the ailing British economy. It could liberate Britain from dependence on foreign sources of energy, which have been a chronic drain on its balance of payments. In 1974, after the escalation of prices by the Organization of Petroleum Exporting Countries (OPEC), Britain ran an external-payments deficit on current account of ten billion dollars, 5 percent of the British gross national product (GNP) and more than three-quarters of which could be imputed directly to energy imports. Both Tory and Labour governments have been compelled to resort to heavy external borrowing to avoid a drastic reduction in living standards and to buy time until the oil begins to flow. In these financing operations, they have been pledging as collateral future revenues from North Sea oil, which will be available in large quantities in the late 1970's. To the British government, the substantial taxes and royalties from North Sea oil will be an important supplement to the British exchequer. A portion could be allocated for the economic improvement of depressed regions throughout Britain, including Scotland, as an extension of Britain's long-standing regional economic policy. In addition, Scotland would benefit directly from an additional fifty thousand jobs, local procurement, and expanded public facilities resulting from the oil boom, although these would be concentrated in northern and especially eastern Scotland nearest the North Sea.[21]

The Scottish nationalists view the North Sea oil differently. Since it lies in the continental shelf of Scotland, it is "Scotland's oil," part of the patrimony of the Scottish people. It should, therefore, be developed and managed by a Scottish government for the benefit of Scotland. It should be exploited gradually at the rate perhaps of fifty million tons a year, enough to meet Scotland's needs and to permit substantial exports to England, earning as much in foreign exchange as Scotland could use effectively without causing internal inflation. At this rate the oil would last well over a century. A measured rate of closely controlled exploitation

21. Donald MacKay and his associates estimate that employment in Scotland resulting directly and indirectly from North Sea oil will peak at sixty to seventy thousand jobs and will begin to decline in the late 1970's. D. I. MacKay and G. A. MacKay, *The Political Economy of North Sea Oil* (Edinburgh: Martin Robertson, 1975). Far more important than the jobs directly created by the oil industry are the financial revenues (taxes and royalties) that, if wisely allocated by a political authority with substantial discretion over fiscal policy and expenditures, could finance the modernization of the Scottish economy and its infrastructure.

would avoid a boom and bust cycle, would protect the priceless Scottish natural environment, and would insure that opportunities to develop sources of supply for a dynamic high-technology industry would accrue to a renovated Scottish industrial system. Scotland could become the world center of expertise, engineering, and production of equipment for deep sea exploration and related marine technologies.[22] The revenues of North Sea oil would be used for the economic redemption of Scotland, to modernize its infrastructure, rebuild its decaying cities, restructure its obsolescent industry, improve public services, and provide amenities—in short, to make Scotland a dynamic, prosperous, and modern society.

But this quite possible future cannot be realized, according to the SNP, if Scotland remains a mere economic region of Great Britain. For as long as the British government controls the oil, its policies will inevitably be oriented toward meeting the desperate, immediate crises of a declining and decaying English economy. The benefits will be diffused over all of Britain. Scotland can expect to receive only a proportionate share, about 10 percent of oil revenues, and the administration of this share will be controlled by officials in London. The SNP sees conclusive evidence that the British government is not taking adequate steps to protect the Scottish environment, that it is not guaranteeing offshore procurement opportunities for Scottish or even British industry, and that it is mortgaging future oil revenues to finance its current external-payments deficit. Only if Scotland gains control of its oil can it insure that the oil will be used for Scotland's benefit, and only an independent Scottish government can gain that control.

In these terms the issue was presented in the early 1970's. Its effects were far-reaching. It provided, for the first time, economic credibility to the case for Scottish political independence, even though, as will be shown, a majority of Scots in 1974 were apparently not so convinced. Not only could Scotland manage economically on its own, so the argument ran, but Scotland in control of offshore oil could become one of the most prosperous countries in the world, as affluent as its neighbor Norway, which shares North Sea oil with Britain and has achieved one of the highest living standards in Europe. But if Scotland were unable to gain control of its oil, the benefits would be dissipated over the floundering

---

22. Ian Fulton argues that the "economic future of Britain lies off the ocean beds of the world" and that Glasgow's impressive engineering and craft skills should be converted, by oil revenues, to servicing deep sea operations. "Scottish Oil," *Political Quarterly,* 45 (July–September 1974): 310–322.

British economy, and Scotland would go down with England in economic decline as the poor man of Europe. The oil could redeem Scotland, but only if Scotland were free to manage it in Scotland's interest. Thus, the SNP slogan "Rich Scots or poor Britons."

Nineteen seventy-four was a milestone for Scottish nationalism as embodied by the SNP. It was the year of two general elections—two formal expressions of Scottish political opinion—and the year the SNP gained the political initiative in Scotland and became a major political force. The February election established the SNP for the first time as a serious factor in Scottish politics. It was the first general election in which the party polled a respectable vote and elected more than a single member of Parliament. Despite, or perhaps because of, the Labour government's sudden and strenuous efforts to accommodate what it diagnosed as Scottish grievances and aspirations, the SNP maintained its momentum eight months later in October, polling nearly a third of the total vote and displacing the Conservatives as Scotland's second party (see Table 11.1).

Where are these votes coming from and what is their political meaning? The figures in Table 11.2 indicate that the SNP draws substantial support (it registered about the same percentage gains) in each of the three major regions of Scotland. It contested every seat in October 1974 and was the only party in Scotland that polled at least 5 percent of the vote in every constituency it contested. It is weakest in the Glasgow region (Strathclyde) and strongest in the rural areas and the Highlands where the party gained a plurality of the vote. It also draws from all socioeconomic classes. The Dundee-based System Three (Scotland) poll, which in May 1974 correctly predicted the SNP's October vote, revealed that the SNP draws about 30 percent of the unskilled and semiskilled workers and 39 percent of skilled workers and technicians, but only 23 percent of professional, managerial, and other middle-class groups. The age stratification is more interesting: while the SNP drew support from only 20 percent of respondents over fifty-five and 30 percent between thirty-five and fifty-five, 40 percent of respondents under thirty-five expressed a preference for the SNP, more than for any other party. Among high school students, the percentage of SNP supporters is said to be even higher.

In the February 1974 election, the SNP attracted votes from both major parties but seemed to draw more from Labour than from the Tories. In October, however, its total gain of 8 percent came at the expense of the Tories, the Labour vote holding firm. While some of this switch represented tactical voting—Conservatives voting SNP to defeat the main enemy, Labour—more can be attributed to a growing conviction among middle-class Scots and nonunionized workers and their families that the enfeebled Conservative party can no longer adequately protect their interests and that these interests may be better served in an independent or autonomous (and prosperous) Scotland than in a deteriorating (and socialist) Britain. The commitment of the Labour government to progressive nationalization of industry, the militancy of the trade unions, and the progressive decline in the British economy as symbolized by the collapse of the pound sterling presage a further movement of Scottish middle-class support to the SNP.

Table 11.2. Regional distribution of Scottish votes (in percent)

Regions	Conservative	Labour	Liberal	SNP
Strathclyde				
1970	36.4	52.0	1.2	9.0
Feb. 1974	31.6	45.0	3.8	18.4
Oct. 1974	22.1	43.9	5.9	27.7
East-central Scotland				
1970	36.1	48.5	3.0	12.1
Feb. 1974	31.5	39.5	5.8	22.8
Oct. 1974	22.6	39.4	6.8	31.0
Rural Scotland				
1970	43.3	30.1	13.1	13.2
Feb. 1974	36.4	20.4	16.0	26.7
Oct. 1974	31.0	20.6	13.7	34.6

Source: Economist, 19 October 1974, p. 31.

The British establishment reacted to the growth of SNP support with an unprecedented set of promises calculated to appease Scottish discontents, accommodate Scottish demands, and thereby take the wind out of the nationalist sails. After four years of research and deliberation, including extensive hearings and specially commissioned research, the Royal Commission on the Constitution in October 1973 issued its bulky report, a 600-page volume representing the majority (which divided on several recommendations) and a 220-page minority memorandum of dissent.[23] The majority report accepted the long-standing home rule argument for substantial legislative devolution to Scotland and Wales. While specifically

23. United Kingdom, Royal Commission on the Constitution, vol. 1, *Report,* Cmnd. 5460, and vol. 2, *Memorandum of Dissent,* by Lord Crowther-Hunt and A. T. Peacock, Cmnd. 5460-1 (London: HMSO, October 1973).

rejecting both separatism and federalism, it recommended Scottish and Welsh assemblies directly elected by proportional representation and with substantial powers over all local activities, but without independent tax- ing authority or control over industrial or trade matters, since the unity of the United Kingdom as a political system would require centralized man- agement of the domestic economy and of foreign economic relations. Oil and oil revenues did not figure in the commission's recommendations, since this was too recent a factor to be taken into account. An indepen- dent exchequer board was to be established to determine the levels of fi- nancial resources that would be transferred in annual block grants to the Scottish and Welsh assemblies.

The royal commission, it will be recalled, was set up in 1969 by the Labour government in response to the SNP's unexpected surge in the 1968 local elections. In 1973 the perfunctory response of the Conserva- tive government and of the Labour oppostion seemed to presage the same treatment for this report that previous home rule proposals had experi- enced in unionist Whitehall and Westminster—neglect and oblivion. Then came the SNP election successes in February 1974, in which the Labour party lost 8 percent of its Scottish support and two important seats to the SNP, and emerged as a minority government. Immediately the Labour government set to the task of mending its political fences in Scotland to insure the support that was vital to the maintenance of its power in London.

In a White Paper issued three weeks before the October 1974 general election, Labour promised Scotland (and Wales) a directly elected as- sembly.[24] The Scottish assembly, from whose ranks a Scottish govern- ment or executive would be selected would be chosen by the familiar single-member-constituency system (by which Labour with 36 percent of the Scottish vote in October 1974 won 57 percent of Scottish seats in the House of Commons) rather than by proportional representation as pro- posed by Kilbrandon; Scotland would retain its current seventy-one seats

24. United Kingdom, *Democracy and Devolution Proposals for Scotland and Wales,* Cmnd. 5732 (London: HMSO, 1974). In June 1974 the Labour government had issued a "Green Paper," *Devolution within the United Kingdom: Some Alternatives for Discussion,* which set forth the seven alternative lines of action proposed by the majority and the minor- ity members of the Kilbrandon commission. Although the White Paper indicated that re- sponses from the general public were "disappointing," sixty Scottish organizations, includ- ing all the major institutions concerned with public affairs, had submitted written responses, the preponderance of them favoring the Kilbrandon Alternative A, which advocated a di- rectly elected assembly with substantive powers.

in Parliament, in contrast to the Kilbrandon recommendation that the number be reduced to Scotland's proper proportion within the United Kingdom of fifty-seven seats; and Scotland, again contrary to Kilbrandon, would retain its cabinet-level secretary of state. Block financial grants from London to Edinburgh would be determined annually by the British government, not by a nonpolitical board, as the royal commission had proposed. The assembly's powers over taxation, trade, industry, and other economic issues were left ambiguous, but it was clearly stipulated that no changes could be contemplated that would impair the "economic unity of the kingdom." Oil revenues would be allocated by London for the benefit of all depressed areas in Britain, including, but not limited to, Scotland. Thus, the Labour high command positioned itself to capitalize on home rule sentiment in Scotland, but only after an awkward struggle with the dominant faction of its Scottish executive, which publicly rejected devolution as "irrelevant" to the needs of the Scottish working class. Any concession to devolution, they feared, would strengthen the SNP and put Scotland on the "slippery slope" toward eventual separation. The national Labour party was forced publicly to compel its Scottish affiliate to reverse its position and accept legislative devolution for Scotland.

By promising a directly elected assembly, Labour successfully outbid the Tories who offered Scotland an indirectly elected body with even more ambiguously defined powers. This halfway promise may have contributed to the collapse of the Conservative vote in October, while Labour's eleventh hour conversion to devolution may have helped prevent a drift of Labour voters to the SNP, for the Labour vote in October held firm at 36 percent and the party actually picked up an additional Scottish seat.

While 80 percent of Scottish voters say that they favor some form of devolution, British politicians have suspected for years that they do not attach high priority to this issue. In a poll taken just before the October 1974 election, only 11 percent of the sample mentioned devolution as an important issue; inflation (70 percent), food costs (41 percent), housing problems (28 percent), labor relations (27 percent), wages (15 percent), the Common Market (15 percent), unemployment (15 percent), and crime (16 percent) all scored higher as priority concerns of Scottish voters.[25]

25. Sample survey, Opinion Research Center (ORC), reported in the *Scotsman,* 10 October 1974.

Nevertheless, today, in their present mood, the Scottish electorate is likely to punish any party that appears to be dragging its feet on devolution, for this has become an issue of Scottish pride. Consequently, since October 1974 all the parties have accepted, in principle, a directly elected Scottish assembly with legislative powers, and the Labour government has established a special task force to design a devolution package that would fulfill the party's pledge.

To supplement home rule pledges, the pork barrel was rolled out for Scotland prior to the October 1974 election. The British parties competed vigorously to offer additional and tangible economic benefits. Labour proposed a Scottish development agency, which would be allotted an unspecified share of North Sea oil revenues to rehabilitate the Scottish economy. The Tories matched this offer with a proposed Scottish development fund, similarly financed for like purposes. Labour committed itself to locate in Scotland the headquarters of the new British National Oil Corporation, to transfer the Offshore Supplies Office from London to Glasgow, to establish a drilling-technology center in Scotland, to transfer seven thousand civil service positions from the Ministries of Defence and Overseas Development to Glasgow, to double the regional employment premium, and even to make a special grant of two hundred thousand dollars to the Glasgow art museum to purchase a van Gogh painting. The Tories came forth with similar offers including the abolition of tolls on several major bridges and special protection for the inshore fishing industry. Never had Scottish voters been so assiduously courted by the major parties.

Thus has the British establishment demonstrated its willingness to respond to the SNP challenge by raising the ante in order to win Scottish votes and to keep Scotland in the fold. Oil and the SNP have substantially raised Scottish expectations and increased the price that London feels required to offer. Voting SNP has been paying off for Scotland. Even Scotsmen unconvinced about independence might vote SNP, so long as there is no realistic prospect of independence, in the expectation that this may extract additional benefits for Scotland from the British parties and from a British government eager to check the spread of the nationalist disease. In the current Scottish climate of rising expectations, the British parties face a cruel dilemma. If they appear to be niggardly, they can be punished by a voter switch to the SNP. If they are forthcoming, this only confirms the logic of voting SNP.

The consequence is that the center of gravity in Scottish politics has shifted to a more militant expression of Scottish self-interest. The only effective defense of the British parties against the SNP is to accommodate. Yet accommodation risks a backlash among English voters and members of Parliament against any significant devolution, which, in turn, would strengthen the position of the SNP.

What is the current state of Scottish opinion on issues involving relations with Britain? There are substantial survey data available. On the question of home rule, in October 1974 an equal proportion, about 20 percent each, favored maintaining the status quo and complete independence for Scotland, while the remaining 60 percent wanted more devolution short of independence.[26] This indicates that while 80 percent of respondents favor structural changes in the direction of greater devolution, at least a third of the 30 percent of the Scottish electorate which voted SNP in October 1974 was not committed to independence. It is clear, however, that devolution has little appeal in Scotland if it means a substantial economic sacrifice. A 1970 poll for the Kilbrandon commission revealed that only 12 percent of Scottish respondents, the bedrock nationalists, favored devolution if it meant that Scotland would suffer economically.[27] In an April 1974 poll, 91 percent responded that, if a choice had to be made, it was more important to improve living standards than to preserve Scotland's traditions and culture.[28]

On North Sea oil, Scottish opinion seems to be fluid, contradictory, and not yet fully formed. A poll taken a week before the October 1974 general election reported 59 percent agreeing with the statement that "the oil in the North Sea belongs to Scotland and tax revenues from it should be used for the benefit of the Scottish people." Sixty-eight percent, however, agreed that "the oil in the North Sea should be used to benefit all of Britain and not just Scotland alone"; and two respondents in three supported the cynical statement that "Scotland will probably get very little benefit from the North Sea oil discoveries; it will all go to the oil companies and the British government."[29]

Perhaps the most salient questions relate to Scottish estimates of their economic future. By nearly a two-to-one margin, respondents expressed

26. ORC poll in the *Scotsman,* 4 October 1974. These proportions have not fluctuated greatly in recent years, nor has there been a pronounced trend in favor of independence.

27. United Kingdom, Royal Commission on the Constitution, *Devolution and Other Aspects of Government: An Attitude Survey,* Research Paper no. 7 (London: HMSO, 1973), p. xx.

28. ORC poll, *Scotsman,* 13 May 1974.

29. ORC poll, *Scotsman,* 4 October 1974.

confidence that Scotland's economic future is more promising than the rest of Britain's, an expression of relative optimism and of rising expectations resulting from the oil boom. At the same time only 39 percent agreed (49 percent opposing) with the statement that "Scotland will soon be strong enough economically to be independent of the rest of Britain." [30] If this is an accurate reflection of Scottish opinion, the SNP has not convinced a majority of its constituents of the feasibility, let alone the desirability of Scottish independence. While Scotland is now mobilized politically to make demands on the British center and while it currently shares a mood of growing confidence and national self-assertiveness, a majority of the Scottish people have not decided that their interests will be served by independence.

Prospects: Accommodation or Confrontation?

No governing elite can accept with equanimity the dismemberment of the political system for which it is responsible. Most of them will resort to every weapon at their disposal, including, if necessary, violence and even civil war, to resist secession. Any conceivable British government can be counted on to use the resources and artifices of statesmanship to prevent the separation of the Scottish third of the United Kingdom. While this would be the case under any circumstances, it is especially true given Britain's utter dependence on North Sea oil.

As oil is essential to Britain's economic survival, Scotland is essential to the survival of Labour as Britain's party of government. The general package that the Labour government proposed in October 1974 is well within the capacity of the British government. Yet subsequent efforts to specify the devolved powers and the relationships between the proposed Scottish assembly and the London government have aroused intense controversy in British political circles. An English backlash has emerged, especially in the Conservative party, which has less stake in Scottish votes than does Labour. There have been sufficient expressions of doubt about the wisdom of devolution among a minority of Labour backbenchers to cause concern to the Labour government. This backlash appears to be based on unionist opposition to special treatment for Scotland and Wales and to constitutional changes which may threaten the unity of

---

30. Ibid. This contrasts with an ORC survey six months earlier (April 1974), in which 49 percent of respondents (36 percent opposing) agreed that Scotland would soon be strong enough economically to be independent. Whether this unexpected shift represents a sampling error or a genuine reassessment of Scotland's capabilities is not clear.

Britain. Although the Labour high command is sensitive to the need to appease Scottish opinion, it has been hesitant to relax London's controls over devolved powers and it has indicated no disposition to yield significant control over economic policy or to earmark any oil revenues for administration by the Scottish assembly. Any settlement that is limited to traditional home rule demands and that fails to provide the Scottish assembly with any control over oil revenues is likely to disappoint Scottish expectations and to strengthen the SNP. The achievement of a devolution package that can win a majority in the English-dominated British Parliament and still satisfy an increasingly demanding Scottish public will be an exacting test of the conflict-management skills of the Labour party leadership.[31]

Some form of legislative devolution to an elected Scottish assembly seems to be in prospect. If, in spite of devolution, nationalist and separatist sentiment should expand in Scotland, the London government would not be void of resources. If the SNP should win a majority of Scotland's seats in the British Parliament or a majority in the Scottish assembly, it still might not have a majority of the Scottish popular vote. London could then insist on a referendum.[32] By invoking delaying tactics, the British

31. To honor its 1974 campaign pledge promising devolution for Scotland and Wales, the Labour government, in October 1975, issued a White Paper, *Our Changing Democracy: Proposals for Devolution to Scotland and Wales* (Cmnd. 6348) containing detailed provisions for implementation and structural changes. It proposed a directly elected assembly for Scotland with legislative powers over many domestic activities, similar to those recommended by the Kilbrandon commission. It provided, however, for close political scrutiny over the exercise of these powers by the secretary of state for Scotland, a member of the British cabinet, with the right either to remand legislation to the assembly for further consideration or to veto legislation that he considers objectionable. No significant economic powers and no control over oil revenues were yielded to the assembly. The result was a storm of protest by all the major institutions of Scottish society, followed by spectacular SNP successes in local elections in both the Glasgow and Edinburgh areas, and, even more ominously for Labour, by the formation of a dissident Scottish Labour party. On 3 August 1976, the Labour cabinet issued a follow-up White Paper *Devolution to Scotland and Wales, Supplemental Statement* (Cmnd. 6585), which attempted to defuse the Scottish protest. While retaining the ultimate power of disallowance by the British cabinet, it eliminated the veto power of the secretary of state for Scotland and vested in the judicial committee of the privy council, Britain's highest court, the power to decide whether the assembly had acted within its powers. Judicial review of legislation, which is common in federal systems, would be an innovation in British government. The August 1976 White Paper increased the economic role of the proposed Scottish assembly by giving it responsibility for the proposed Scottish development agency, but did not provide additional financial resources.

32. The 1975 referendum on membership in the European Economic Community was an innovation in British government and may have established a precedent for future issues that are considered fundamental to the British Constitution. In 1976 there were proposals for

government could work for a reversal of sentiment or for a negotiated settlement short of secession.

There would also be opportunities for exploiting internal cleavages in Scotland. A substantial body of Scotsmen would, in any case, prefer to retain a British connection. This is probably true of the Irish Catholic minority of 15 percent concentrated in Glasgow. The Shetlanders, at the center of the North Sea oil deposits, might prefer their own independence or continued rule from London to government from Edinburgh, for they consider themselves less Scottish than Scandinavian. If Scotland is entitled to self-determination, their argument might run, would the Shetland Islands not be equally entitled to the same right, to opt for independence from Scotland or to remain British? [33] In extreme circumstances, any British government could be expected to resort to rough, confrontational tactics, from which it would desist as Scotland agreed to settle for less than independence. If all else failed, and despite reluctance to risk another Irish Republican Army (IRA) from the Scots, the British might feel compelled to resort to military intervention to maintain the territorial integrity of Britain and access to North Sea oil.

Between now and then the SNP could become the largest political party in Scotland. The Scottish middle class can be expected to move in greater numbers toward the SNP. The current inflation is hitting many of them severely, reducing their living standards in absolute terms. The difficulties encountered by both major parties in restraining the wage demands of the trade unions, and the acquiescence of the Labour government to union-sponsored measures that attack the remaining privileges of the middle class, have induced large numbers of them to reassess their political orientation. While they have been staunchly unionist in the past, and although the current swing of Conservative voters to the SNP may be more an expression of protest and a means of extracting benefits for Scotland than a vote for independence, current trends in British politics are likely to increase the appeal of the SNP to the Scottish middle class.

---

referenda from many sources, including former prime ministers Heath and Lord Home, to determine whether a majority of British voters or even of Scottish voters favored devolution as pledged by the Labour government (*Economist,* 25 September 1976, p. 21; and 2 October 1976, pp. 25–26).

33. This point was emphasized in a recent statement by Jo Grimond, the veteran Liberal party leader and member of Parliament for Orkney and Shetland (*Scotsman,* 13 December 1974). Recognizing this problem, the SNP has proposed substantial local autonomy for the Orkney and Shetland islands, similar to that of the current regime of the Faroe Islands in relation to Denmark.

Faced with the choice between an economically declining, socialist Britain and an independent or economically autonomous and relatively prosperous Scotland, which respects property rights, more middle-class voters are likely to turn to the nationalists.[34]

The SNP has demonstrated its ability to recruit working-class support, especially among nonunion workers in small towns and among skilled workers outside the Glasgow area. It has been more difficult for the party, however, to gain a broad-based following from among the Glasgow working class, which is critical to electoral outcomes in the Strathclyde conurbation, where nearly half the Scottish parliamentary seats are located. Glasgow is one of the most impoverished, chronically depressed, and economically declining metropolitan areas in Europe.[35] The psychology of the Glasgow working class is defensive, and the Labour party is the institution that traditionally protects its pensions, subsidized housing, and other economic interests. Thus, Glasgow remains a Labour stronghold.

The oil boom in the east of Scotland has not helped Glasgow, though there have been efforts to win major contracts for drilling and production platforms and components for Glasgow-based industries. The present Labour government is likely to persist in these efforts. Meanwhile, however, few Glasgow workers have ventured east to participate in the oil boom because of the high cost and shortage of housing, because of the absence of trade-union protection on the rigs, and because of attachments to family and neighbors in Glasgow. Most Glasgow workers remain skeptical about whether oil will produce any benefits for them or for the Glasgow area. While younger Glasgow workers may be open to an alternative to Labour's nineteenth-century cloth-cap socialism, most of this intensely class-conscious group have not been ready to forsake a known quantity for a party that looks and sounds middle-class and that might not be able to deliver social benefits equivalent to those now received from the British government.

Moreover, 30 percent of the Glasgow working class are Catholics of Irish origin. They are intensely loyal to the Catholic church, the Labour party, and their football team, the Celtic; they are suspicious of Scottish nationalism and fear that a nationalist regime would leave Catholics and

34. Recognizing this danger, Conservative party spokesmen keep reverting to the theme that the SNP is really a socialist party.

35. For an excellent journalistic analysis of the Glasgow problem, see ''The Two Nations: A Survey of Scotland,'' in the *Economist,* 29 September 1973.

persons of non-Scottish lineage marginal to a Scottish Protestant state.[36] Rumors of overtures by the Orange Order to the SNP, of a Scottish National Army (a Protestant version of the IRA), and of a militantly anti-Irish "Vanguard Scotland" regularly make their rounds in Glasgow's Irish Catholic neighborhoods at election time. While the SNP vote in the central industrial belt of the Strathclyde area has tripled since 1970 and Labour's has declined by nearly 20 percent, the SNP has never won a seat in a general election in this area, and the spread between the parties is still 16 percent.

In electoral terms, the main task of the SNP is to penetrate the Glasgow area. It is possible that the deeply class-conscious Glasgow working class will remain loyal at all costs to Labour and to British socialism. If, however, the Glasgow economy continues to decline in tandem with the rest of Britain, and if Glasgow shares in rising unemployment—which seems likely—while the rest of Scotland, propelled by the oil boom, prospers, more of Glasgow's workers and their families, especially the youth, can be expected to turn to the SNP in protest against economic adversity from which a Labour government has not been able to rescue them. Increasingly their standard of comparison will be eastern Scotland, and if oil can bring prosperity to the rest of Scotland, why not also to Glasgow? Would Glasgow's share of oil benefits not be greater under a Scottish government, as argued by the SNP, than under the British? If some of Glasgow's working-class discontents can be transmuted to rising expectations, the SNP seems likely to gain more working-class votes.

Barring serious mistakes by its leadership, the SNP is likely to continue to gain among all classes in Scotland. Yet, as the party becomes more prominent both in the London Parliament and in the proposed Edinburgh assembly, it may encounter unfamiliar vulnerabilities. It will be forced to take positions on social and economic issues that may divide its own heterogeneous constituency, antagonize potential converts, and expose it to concentrated political attack and even to coalition tactics by its unionist opponents.

The other Scottish parties will attempt to match or even to preempt the SNP by a vigorous articulation of Scottish needs and interests. When it comes to fighting for Scotland, the SNP in the future will no longer have

36. The communal cleavage in the Glasgow working class is reflected in their football loyalties. The Catholics of Irish origin support the Celtic club, while Protestants support the Rangers.

the field to itself. Once a Scottish assembly and executive are established, the British parties and the London government can be expected to react to nationalist demands with measures calculated to persuade the Scottish electorate that they are indeed responsive to its needs and aspirations, that the British connection will continue to benefit Scotland, and that a move toward independence would be foolish and costly. The risk, of course, is that these measures will appear too grudging and too late to keep pace with Scotland's rising expectations.

As the Scottish price rises, the United Kingdom government will endeavor to meet it by bargaining with Scottish members of Parliament in London and by negotiating with the Scottish assembly and its ministers in Edinburgh. On numerous specific issues, including annual block financial grants, the Edinburgh assembly, even if SNP-dominated, will find itself involved in bargaining relationships with London. It would be a rational strategy of the London elites to set up negotiating structures to deal with Scotland's claims through institutionalized bargaining. This would absorb the energies of Scottish politicians, including the nationalists, while providing both tangible benefits and symbolic recognition of Scotland's status as an associated nation. The SNP could thus be co-opted into an entangling network of bargaining relationships in London and Edinburgh, which could gradually erode its demands for independence and domesticate the party within a reformed British system. The 80 percent of Scots who do not now favor independence (some of whom nevertheless vote SNP) might be sufficiently pleased with the new arrangements, according to this strategy, to remain loyal to the United Kingdom. The decision of the SNP to accept the Kilbrandon recommendations for devolution and to participate in the Scottish assembly as a step toward eventual independence could be construed as a step toward co-optation.

There is another reason to suspect that institutional devolution could result in co-optation. Scottish national identity has meaning primarily in reference to the English "they." It is weak in positive cultural content and in cultural grievances. Despite the efforts of an earlier generation of literary and romantic nationalists, and despite the continuing concern of some SNP activists, the great majority of modern Scotsmen do not define their deprivations in cultural terms and cannot be mobilized emotionally or politically against the English on language or cultural issues. This is true of all classes, regions, and age groups.[37]

37. Unlike most modern nationalist movements, the SNP does not gain major support from students and young faculty members in universities. A substantial proportion of stu-

Thus, Scottish political nationalism differs in quality from that of the Catalans, the Bretons, the Welsh, or the French Canadians, to use only Western examples. It is not linguistically or culturally rooted. While dedicated Scottish nationalists and SNP activists have grand visions of a Scottish—even a Gaelic—cultural revival once independent statehood is achieved, their electoral appeals since the early 1960's have been primarily economic. As the polls have demonstrated, the SNP knows its constituents well, and the issues it has raised have struck home. This same economic and instrumental emphasis explains the emotional blandness, the dearth of passion, and the absence of violence in contemporary Scottish nationalism.

This bloodless quality may also explain the SNP's conspicuous success, for it is not perceived either by a broad spectrum of potential Scottish supporters or by the English "they" as an extremist or violent movement. This image facilitates the mobilization of support from among all classes, much of which would dissolve if the party were to become associated with "extreme" or "impractical" cultural issues, or with violence. It also makes the SNP a tolerable, though by no means a preferred, negotiating partner for the British establishment and its supporters in Scotland. Economic issues are usually negotiable, negotiation can lead to compromises, and compromises can lead to stable institutional patterns. Thus, it is not impossible that the moderate style and the pragmatic, instrumental quality of Scottish political nationalism—plus the aforementioned British strategy to co-opt the nationalists into a network of bargaining structures—will result in a set of negotiated arrangements that will leave Scotland much better off politically and materially, although short of the nationalist goal of full independence. The SNP and its supporters may lack the fanatical commitment needed to press for independence at the risk of violence if an attractive, intermediate, and peaceful settlement—one that leaves Scotland's prospects materially improved—should become available.

The performance of the economy of the United Kingdom has been the poorest of all the industrial countries since World War II, and its short-

---

dents and faculty members in Scottish universities are English. Students may be oriented to career opportunities in England, and faculty members may prefer to participate in a large and cosmopolitan British, rather than a smaller and more provincial Scottish, university network. My own judgment is that the absence of language and cultural issues makes Scottish nationalism uninteresting to young intellectuals; they cannot be "turned on" by prudential economic appeals.

term prospects, as has previously been indicated, are dismal. Associated with this economic stress is a bitter struggle for shares of income and intensified class conflict. Economic stress is putting heavy strains on political institutions. Decisions affecting the public are being preempted by pressure groups, while governments acquiesce in faits accomplis, further undermining confidence in the effectiveness of British political institutions.[38] These institutions and the vaunted British social discipline may be further strained as high levels of unemployment generate militant demands for higher and more inflationary levels of public assistance and even, perhaps, for the take-over of industrial establishments by unemployed workers.[39]

Four Scotsmen out of five today oppose independence and would prefer that Scotland remain in the United Kingdom. They are also concerned about their economic welfare. They recognize that the Scottish economy, already benefiting from North Sea oil, will soon have the capacity, even without North Sea oil revenues, to provide Scotland with a higher standard of living than is likely to be available in the rest of Britain. The SNP will persist in reminding Scotsmen that continuing membership in the depressed and declining British economy is depriving them of the even greater prosperity to which they are now entitled and that revenues from "Scotland's oil" could provide for an independent Scotland.

The success of the strategy of co-optation will depend not only on the health of the British economy, but also on the political skills and sensitivity of the London elites. In the challenge-and-response pattern of contemporary Scottish nationalism, the London elites of all political persuasions have been slow to respond and have lagged behind the development of Scottish opinion. Moreover, they are divided on the degree of devolution that should be conceded to Scotland and are fearful of English opposition. Their recent concessions to home rule might have been welcome in the 1880's or even in the 1950's, but are quite inadequate in the era of North Sea oil. Their information seems to underestimate the intensity both of economic expectations and of nationalist sentiment; substantive autonomy and especially the control of economic resources by a Scottish regional

38. The 1974 decision of the hospital-workers union not to treat private patients in government hospitals serves as an example.

39. The latter step might be avoided under a Labour government by effective nationalization, the government acquiring a controlling equity position by making cash investments designed to avert major closings (Burmah Oil and Leyland Motors are recent examples). The SNP opposes all nationalization of Scottish industries by the British government since this tends to increase London's control of the Scottish economy.

government appear to them to threaten both the effective operation of British institutions and the political and economic unity of the kingdom to which they are deeply committed. Unless the measures they ultimately adopt are more responsive to the present climate of Scottish opinion than those they have proposed, the result could be resentment in Scotland and polarization of opinion toward more extreme nationalist positions. The critical factor may be the willingness of London to yield the administration of substantial North Sea oil revenues to the proposed Scottish assembly.

Federal Region or Sovereign State?

Why did Scottish nationalism begin to make political waves only in the 1970's and not twenty, fifty, or one hundred years earlier? No single factor, not even North Sea oil, can explain a complex development of this scope and scale. Together, however, the following five factors seem necessary and sufficient to explain this phenomenon and its emergence at this point in history:

1. A deep-seated, territorially based national sentiment, which survived two and a half centuries of political union with a larger and stronger system. While ethnic definition and ethnic-group behavior can be regarded as contextual—a response to changing conditions—national sentiment and solidarity in Scotland have been so deeply rooted and persistent that they can be considered a given for the purposes of political analysis. For the political mobilization of regional interests, an ethnic base is useful, perhaps indispensable, both to activate domestic support and to claim legitimacy within the encompassing system.

2. Evidence of deprivation or discrimination in relation to the encompassing system or to other groups within it. Without real or perceived deprivations, there are unlikely to be politically salient grievances; without grievances, no protest. While numerous cultural and political grievances had been mooted in Scotland for many decades, they had been dampened by economic prosperity and by opportunities to participate in an expanding and glorious worldwide imperial venture. It was the contraction and disappearance of imperial opportunities accompanied by manifest economic deprivation in relation to England that triggered political protest in the 1960's.

3. The renewal of confidence—rising expectations. Deprivation could generate protest, but not on a politically significant scale until a credible alternative became apparent. Without a credible alternative, Scotsmen lacked the confidence essential to effective political mobilization on be-half of distinctive Scottish interests. Relative deprivation is a necessary but not a sufficient condition for political mobilization. For such mobilization to take place, there must exist either a profound threat to group values or aroused and well-founded hopes that the existing situation can actually be improved. Such a well-founded hope was supplied to a de-pressed and demoralized Scotland in a dramatic turn of fate by North Sea oil. The discovery of oil created the confidence and the rising expectations that were necessary for political revival.

4. Political organization. No social movement can become politically viable without organization. In Scotland that motive power was supplied by the SNP. Years of patient effort had built a struggling but durable or-ganization, which had been able to mobilize protest but not to become a major political force until protest could be converted to rising expecta-tions by "Scotland's oil." The rapid spread of this new confidence can be credited to the skillful propaganda of the SNP.

5. Declining effectiveness of the political center. The rising expecta-tions in Scotland have been accompanied by the declining performance, declining credibility, and declining prospects of the British economy and polity. Attachment to that system had been a source of opportunity, pros-perity, and pride to generations of Scotsmen. By the mid-1970's, it ap-peared to many Scots that Britain was becoming a burden to Scotland, a prospective drain on its resources, and an obstacle to the fulfillment of its legitimate expectations. Did this not vindicate the SNP argument that fur-ther association with a politically troubled and economically distressed Britain was no longer in Scotland's interest and that Scotland would be better off on her own?

The breakthrough of Scottish nationalism as organized by the SNP is still too near at hand and events are moving too rapidly to permit ade-quate evaluation. Scottish nationalism already exerts an important influ-ence on Scottish and on British politics. All the British political parties have been compelled to concede devolution, however vaguely and dif-ferently they define it, and to compete with each other in offering benefits to Scotland. The forthcoming Scottish assembly and Scottish executive, the most important structural change in Scottish government since 1707, will not only provide a large measure of self-government for Scotland, but also a forum for Scottish political expression and an institutional vehicle to pressure and bargain with the British center. In Britain's highly centralized governmental structure, a de facto federal enclave will emerge. North Sea oil and the SNP have radically altered the political terms of trade between England and Scotland. Whether as a federalized region or a sovereign state, Scottish relations with the English, the historical "they," have entered a new phase.

Note added in proof
Late in November 1976, the Labour government introduced into the House of Commons the Scotland and Wales Bill which incorporated its proposals for devolution as outlined in the White Paper of August 1976 (see note 31). On 22 February 1977 a motion to limit debate on this bill was defeated. The hostility of many English members of Parliament of all ideological persuasions to special treatment for Scotland has left the issue of devolution, at least temporarily, at an impasse.

12

Ethnic Political Conflict in South Tyrol *

PETER J. KATZENSTEIN

Contemporary Western European politics has recently been marked by an astonishing revival of ethnic political conflict. States that in earlier centuries had faced their crisis of national integration and that only a decade ago were involved in a process of supranational integration are now confronted with ethnic conflict and disintegration at the subnational level. Located in Italy, South Tyrol is the only area where developments have moved in the opposite direction.[1] In the mid-1950's and early 1960's, when ethnic conflicts hardly figured in Western European politics, South Tyrol was experiencing acute and increasing ethnic strife. It appeared entirely reasonable then to argue that "a lasting solution to the conflict seems to be neither imminent nor probable." [2] But over the next decade an attenuation of ethnic conflict occurred, which is remarkable in contrast to political developments elsewhere in Western Europe. The change in political and social conditions in South Tyrol was sufficiently dramatic to

* I would like to thank Sidney Tarrow for his excellent criticism of an earlier draft of this essay. I have also benefited from the critical comments and suggestions of Steven Baker, Milton Esman, Peter Gourevitch, Luigi Graziano, Gerhard Katzenstein, David Laitin, T. J. Pempel, and Gebhard Schweigler. Research for this essay was financially supported by the Western Societies Program of the Center for International Studies at Cornell University. I am grateful to Vincent M. Blocker, Ulker Copur, and Wallace Koehler, who assisted me in the collection and analysis of the data. Before publication in this book, the essay appeared in *Österreichische Zeitschrift für Aussenpolitik,* 16, nos. 4, 5 (1976).

1. Because it is better known in English, I have used the term "South Tyrol" rather than the legally correct "Alto Adige." The province of South Tyrol and the province of Trento constitute a special region, "Trentino–Alto Adige." For a description of the politics and language of place names in South Tyrol, see John W. Cole and Eric R. Wolf, *The Hidden Frontier: Ecology and Ethnicity in an Alpine Valley* (New York: Academic, 1974), pp. 17–18.

2. Leonard W. Doob, "South Tyrol: An Introduction to the Psychological Syndrome of Nationalism," *Public Opinion Quarterly,* 26, no. 2 (Summer 1962): 173.

lead a close observer of Central Europe to conclude that the conflict in South Tyrol had found a "permanent end." [3]

How can one account for the intensification and attenuation of ethnic political conflict in South Tyrol during the last two decades? Sociological and political analysis complement one another in explaining the two central aspects of the conflict, its trend and its timing. Sociological reasoning helps in making intelligible the increase in ethnic tensions in the 1950's and their gradual decrease in the 1960's. But an analysis that focuses exclusively on the demographic, social, and economic bases of ethnic political conflict leaves unexplained critical questions of timing. Why did ethnic tensions increase in the late 1950's and erupt into violence in the early 1960's? Why did that violence gradually diminish and ultimately stop in the late 1960's while a political compromise was being fashioned? These questions can only be answered by analyzing the interactions of political forces operating at three different levels. First, the South Tyrol conflict had an international dimension: it involved the Austrian government, which was acting under stringent domestic constraints. Second, the conflict was conditioned by the slow move toward regional reform in Italian national politics as well as by the universalization of clientelistic political practice in the 1960's. Finally, ethnic political conflict in South Tyrol was affected by the adaptation of German to Italian political practice at the provincial level.

The waxing and waning of ethnic political conflict in South Tyrol was the result of important social and political developments. During the last two decades, social and economic changes have led to a redefinition of South Tyrol's acute political problems. Ethnic issues no longer dominate economic ones. A corresponding shift can be discerned in the changing style of the province's politics, which now emphasizes symbolic aspects less than concrete ones. This change is, most importantly, traceable also in the substance of politics, which no longer centers on the politics of meaning but on the politics of interest.

The Historical Setting

In northern Italy irredentism has been a two-way street ever since the middle of the nineteenth century. [4] The very term irredentism goes back to

3. Elisabeth Barker, *Austria, 1918–1972* (Coral Gables, Fla.: University of Miami Press, 1973), p. 253.
4. An easily accessible historical overview is given in the most recent English-language source on South Tyrol. See Antony E. Alcock, *The History of the South Tyrol Question*

the Italian opposition to Habsburg rule in Venetia, Lombardy, and the Trentino. The defeat of the Austrian armies in northern Italy in 1859 and 1866 made it possible for Venetia and Lombardy to join a newly united Italy in 1870. But the Italians living in the Trentino—which then was part of the historic province of Tyrol—remained an integral part of the Habsburg Empire until the end of World War I.

In redrawing Europe's map in 1919 the victorious Allies chose in this instance geographical boundaries over historical and cultural ones. Although overwhelmingly inhabited by German speakers, South Tyrol was incorporated into an enlarged Italian state. With the rise of Italian fascism, the German speakers in South Tyrol faced a ruthless campaign of enforced acculturation. By executive decree and legislation, German presence and influence were repressed in all spheres of cultural, economic, and political life.[5] Brutally placed on the defensive, German nationalism forcefully retreated into the most remote valleys, which previously had been shielded by Catholicism against the spread of nationalist ideologies. A burdensome legacy of the Italian fascists' cultural repression of German speakers in South Tyrol has been the German-speaking people's continued distrust of postwar Italian policies.[6] But equally important for the future of South Tyrol were the economic policies adopted by the fascist government. Mussolini decided to construct a major industrial complex in the Bozen area in part because he wanted to increase the number of Italians in South Tyrol. Since the new Italian migrants settled only in and around the major cities, primarily Bozen and Merano, the ethnic conflict between Italians and German speakers also became a conflict between city and countryside, between workers and peasants.[7]

The second major event in the political history of South Tyrol was the

---

(London: Michael Joseph, 1970), pp. 3–77. For a recent bibliographical essay, see Harry F. Young, "South Tyrol: New Approaches to an Old Problem," *Canadian Review of Studies in Nationalism*, 2, no. 1 (Fall 1974): 132–143.

5. Dennison I. Rusinow, *Italy's Austrian Heritage, 1919–1946* (London: Oxford at the Clarendon Press, 1969).

6. This discussion neglects the psychology of nationalism in South Tyrol. See Leonard W. Doob, *Patriotism and Nationalism: Their Psychological Foundations* (New Haven: Yale University Press, 1964); Claus Gatterer, *Im Kampf gegen Rom: Bürger, Minderheiten und Autonomien in Italien* (Vienna: Europa Verlag, 1968), pp. 1277–1279; *Der Spiegel*, 26 August 1974, p. 12. See also Julian V. Minghi, "Boundary Studies and National Prejudices: The Case of the South Tyrol," *Professional Geographer*, 15, no. 1 (January 1963): 4–8; Lilyan A. Brudner, "The Maintenance of Bilingualism in Southern Austria," *Ethnology*, 11, no. 1 (January 1972): 39–54.

7. Alcock, p. 44.

agreement Mussolini reached with Hitler in 1939. It provided for the resettlement in Germany of all South Tyrolean German speakers who so desired.[8] Of the 80 percent who, for a variety of reasons, had opted in 1939 to emigrate to Germany, about one-third actually left during World War II. Twenty thousand of these migrants returned to South Tyrol after 1945, but the net population loss of German speakers in South Tyrol still amounted to about fifty thousand. As important as raw numbers was the qualitative impact of this demographic change. Those who had left for good were predominantly the young, urban residents and industrial workers or employees. Virtually all members of the urban middle class who did not own property also left. Besides unskilled farmhands, only the property-owning middle class and the vast majority of property-owning farmers stayed behind.[9] The net effect of the fascist policies was, therefore, to confine the German speakers in South Tyrol almost exclusively to the countryside and to decisively weaken the urban base from which they might otherwise have recruited their political leadership.

After 1945 no policy measures that seriously affected the relative balance between German speakers and Italians were taken. While the proportion of German speakers in South Tyrol had declined in the interwar period from 87 percent in 1921 to 72 percent in 1939, it stayed at a constant 63 percent between 1953 and 1971.[10] Unilateral Italian measures would, in any case, have been greatly impeded by the international obligation that the Italian government incurred in the Paris Agreement it signed with the Austrian government in September 1946. That agreement guaranteed far-reaching autonomy to South Tyrol in many spheres of economic and cultural life. The spirit, if not the letter, of the Paris Agreement was violated in 1948 when Prime Minister Alcide de Gasperi implemented the promised provincial autonomy for South Tyrol only within a larger region which also encompassed his native Trentino. The German speakers in South Tyrol thus found themselves in 1948 in one of Italy's "special regions," Trentino–Alto Adige. In this political setting they

8. Conrad F. Latour, *Südtirol und die Achse Berlin-Rom, 1938–1945* (Stuttgart: Deutsche Verlags-Anstalt, 1962).

9. Alcock, pp. 55–58, 210; Mathilde de Block, *Südtirol* (Groningen: J. B. Wolters, 1954), pp. 166, 221; Christoph Pan, *Südtirol als volkliches Problem: Grundrisse einer Südtiroler Ethno-Soziologie* (Vienna: Braumüller, 1971), pp. 78–79; Adolf Leidlmair, *Bevölkerung und Wirtschaft in Südtirol* (Innsbruck: Wagner, 1958), p. 76; Cole and Wolf, pp. 60, 270–271.

10. Leidlmair, pp. 39–40; *XI censimento generale della popolazione,* vol. 2, fasc. 17 (Rome: Istituto Centrale di Statistica, 1973), p. 157.

were again outnumbered by Italians and thus politically were not well protected.

The very limited jurisdiction of the provincial legislature in South Tyrol and the increasing unwillingness of the central administration in Rome to implement any of the important provisions of the Paris Agreement heightened frustrations. The German speakers regarded these Italian policies as little more than a dressed-up version of the repressive measures of the fascists. The death of de Gasperi removed the one Italian political leader who, deeply steeped in German culture, had enjoyed a minimum of trust in South Tyrol. The rightward shift of the Christian Democratic party (DC) in the 1950's furthermore seemed to confirm the worst suspicions of the German speakers.

The eruption of widespread terrorist activities in the late 1950's was an expression of the depth of South Tyrolean frustrations. The terrorism, in fact, provided the watershed in South Tyrol's postwar history. Terrorism in South Tyrol falls into two distinct phases. Until about 1962–63, attacks were planned by German speakers in South Tyrol with the support of nationalists in Austria and Germany. In the second phase, beginning in 1964, the attacks were planned abroad but enjoyed the active support of a radical fringe in South Tyrol. Before 1962–63, terrorism in South Tyrol was an expression of political frustration directed against objects; after 1962–63, it was an expression of political fanaticism directed against people. Before 1962–63, terrorism had the objective of accelerating a political solution that would bring either effective autonomy or self-determination. After 1962–63, terrorist activities served the objective of preventing any political arrangement between Austria and Italy that would fall short of guaranteeing the right to self-determination. In short, during the 1960's Adolf Hitler began to replace Andreas Hofer, the hero of Tyrolean political independence in the early nineteenth century, as the political mentor of terrorism in South Tyrol.[11]

---

11. Viktoria Stadlmayer, "Die Südtirolpolitik Österreichs seit Abschluss des Pariser Abkommens," in *Südtirol: Eine Frage des Europäischen Gewissens,* ed. Franz Huter (Munich: Oldenbourg, 1965), p. 526; Thomas O. Schlesinger, *Austrian Neutrality in Postwar Europe: The Domestic Roots of a Foreign Policy* (Vienna: Braumüller, 1972), p. 77. See also the public opinion polls reported in Werner Wolf, *Südtirol in Österreich: Die Südtirolfrage in der österreichischen Diskussion von 1945 bis 1969* (Würzburg: Holzner, 1972), p. 40; and Karl Heinz Ritschel, *Diplomatie um Südtirol: Politische Hintergründe eines Europäischen Versagens* (Stuttgart: Seewald, 1966), p. 327. In the light of these data the assessment of public sentiment given in Pan, *Südtirol,* p. 132, appears to be questionable.

Confronted with the choice between an all-out fight for self-determination and an insistence on the de facto implementation of provincial autonomy, the political elites in South Tyrol and in Austria opted for the latter. At the same time the gradual move of the DC to the left, manifested in its Opening to the Left in 1962, provided a new Italian willingness to accommodate many of the important grievances of the South Tyroleans. A tentative agreement worked out between Austria and Italy in 1964 granted the South Tyroleans many of their demands but was vetoed by the defensive and distrustful leadership of the South Tyrol Peoples party (Südtiroler Volkspartei, SVP). Five years later, however, an agreement was reached among the Italian government, the Austrian government, and the South Tyroleans, and by late 1974 about three-fourths of the provisions of that agreement had been implemented.

The Social and Economic Basis of Ethnic Political Conflict

Sociological reasoning helps in accounting for the trend in the escalation and de-escalation of ethnic political conflict in South Tyrol. Rapid demographic changes in the 1950's and 1960's correlate well with changes in ethnic strife. These demographic changes have had a great impact on the occupational structure of the province which, too, can be related to ethnic political conflict. Finally, South Tyrol has experienced a distinctive process of rural modernization which contributes to an understanding of political developments in the 1960's in particular.

Demographic Changes

During the last two decades demographic changes have correlated with both the increase and the decrease in ethnic conflict. In the early 1950's there was a widespread fear that a continuation of Italian immigration from the south would lead to a further erosion of the position of numerical superiority that the German speakers traditionally had enjoyed in the province. But by the late 1950's the higher birthrates in the backward German mountain areas, together with a decrease in Italian immigration, had begun to strengthen the position of the German speakers. Between 1961 and 1971 the proportion of German speakers increased on the average by 2.5 percent in every commune (see Table 12.1).[12]

12. The data in this section and in the tables are the result of a computer analysis of the Italian censuses of 1951, 1961, and 1971. The ninety-nine communes that had either unchanging boundaries or retraceable boundary changes since 1951 were assigned to four different groups according to their ethnic composition in 1961 and 1971: seventy-eight were

Table 12.1. Internal and foreign migration in South Tyrol by commune, 1951–71 (in percent)

Resident population	Total communes (N = 99)	Predominantly German-speaking (N = 78)	Moderately German-speaking (N = 11)	Mixed German- and Italian-speaking (N = 5)	Moderately Italian-speaking (N = 5)
Increase in proportion of German speakers (1961–71)	2.5	2.2	2.9	3.0	2.8
Proportion in other communes					
1951	4.6	4.4	5.3	5.5	4.4
1961	6.8	7.3	5.3	5.8	4.3
1971	6.0	6.4	4.3	5.1	4.1
Proportion abroad					
1951	0.8	0.8	0.7	1.1	0.4
1961	2.6	2.8	2.3	2.4	1.2
1971	1.6	1.8	1.3	0.9	0.6

Source: See note 12. Individual-level data are given in IX censimento generale della popolazione, vol. 1, fasc. 17 (Rome: Istituto Centrale di Statistica, 1955), p. 15; X censimento generale della popolazione, vol. 3, fasc. 17 (Rome: Istituto Centrale di Statistica, 1964), p. 89; and XI censimento generale, p. 157.
Note: N = number of communes.

In the 1960's South Tyrol's critical problems thus began to shift from ethnic to economic ones, and questions of ethnic identity gradually gave way to questions of economic and social reform.[13] As was true of many other rural areas throughout Western Europe, the scarcity of jobs became a critical problem. Although estimates of South Tyrol's job deficit vary considerably, new entries into the labor force may have exceeded annually by as much as 350 the number of new jobs created between 1959 and 1972.[14] Despite this rural underemployment, however, migration

predominantly German-speaking (80 to 100 percent); eleven were moderately German-speaking (69 to 79 percent); five were mixed German- and Italian-speaking (40 to 59 percent German-speaking), and five were moderately Italian-speaking (0 to 39 percent German-speaking). In five instances (commune census numbers 9, 28, 41, 44, 62), the proportion of the German-speaking population in 1961 and in 1971 would have resulted in the commune's assignment to different groups, but for this study the average for both years determined the assignment. Seven communes, each with a predominantly Ladinian-speaking population, were excluded from the analysis. Coding procedures and variable definitions are described in Peter J. Katzenstein, "Bolzano Ethnic Conflict Study: Final Code," unpublished paper (Ithaca, N.Y.: Cornell University, 1975).

13. Gatterer, pp. 1002–1003; Herbert Fiebiger, Bevölkerung und Wirtschaft Südtirols: Eine Darstellung ihrer Situation und ihrer Probleme (Bergisch Gladbach: Heider Verlag, 1959), pp. 26–27.

14. Manfred Kersting, Industrie und Industriepolitik in Südtirol (Innsbruck: Wagner'sche Universitätsbuchhandlung, 1973), p. 101.

data suggest that population movement, both within the province and from South Tyrol to the rest of Europe, correlated with the increase and decrease in ethnic political conflict: the proportion of the German-speaking population living in other communes and abroad increased sharply in the 1950's and diminished in the 1960's (see Table 12.1).[15] But this correlation between demographic change and ethnic political conflict leaves unspecified the direction of causation.

Occupational Structure

These demographic changes have had a strong effect on the occupational structure of the German-speaking population in South Tyrol. Although reliable occupational data by mother tongue do not exist before 1961, the available evidence strongly suggests that the proportion of the German-speaking population in the primary sector (agriculture and forestry) remained constant during the first half of the twentieth century. The rural character of South Tyrol in the early 1950's and the magnitude of change that has occurred since then is strikingly illustrated by the data presented in Table 12.2.[16] The shift out of the primary sector has amounted to about 15 percent per decade in the predominantly German-speaking communes as compared to about 10 percent for the other groups of communes. Change in the German-speaking countryside thus has been rapid.

The proportion moving out of agricultural occupations is distributed roughly evenly between the secondary (construction and industry) and the tertiary (service occupations) sectors. But in and of itself this description of change in South Tyrol's occupational structure does not explain why and how such change should affect ethnic political conflict. The traditional theory of nationalism offers at least two plausible hypotheses which focus on the move of the work force into the tertiary sector. These hypotheses emphasize the shift into the "high tertiary" sector and "professionalization," on the one hand, and into the "low tertiary sector" and "proletarianization," on the other.[17]

15. For more detailed data on emigration, see Lore Toepfer, *Die Abwanderung deutschsprachiger Bevölkerung aus Südtirol nach 1955* (Innsbruck: Wagner'sche Universitätsbuchhandlung, 1973), especially pp. 11–16, 40–42.
16. Ethnic data of questionable value are given in Franz Wahlmüller, "Südtirol auch ein soziales Problem," in *Südtirol: Versprechen und Wirklichkeit,* ed. Wolfgang Pfaundler (Vienna: Wilhelm Frick, 1958), pp. 278–279.
17. Gláucio A. D. Soares, "The New Industrialization and Industrial Employment in Latin America: Preliminary Comments" (paper delivered at the Seminar on Social Indica-

Table 12.2. Occupational structure of the economically active population of South Tyrol by commune, 1951–71 (in percent)

Sector	Total communes (N = 99)	Predominantly German-speaking (N = 78)	Moderately German-speaking (N = 11)	Mixed German- and Italian-speaking (N = 5)	Moderately Italian-speaking (N = 5)
Primary					
1951	61.4	67.4	42.9	27.4	42.2
1961	47.1	52.0	31.3	18.9	33.7
1971	33.3	37.0	19.9	13.5	24.7
Secondary					
1951	14.8	12.5	20.5	22.3	29.7
1961	20.8	19.3	25.0	24.1	31.1
1971	27.5	26.6	28.4	33.7	32.6
Tertiary					
1951	23.0	20.1	36.6	50.3	29.2
1961	31.3	28.7	43.7	57.0	35.2
1971	38.3	36.7	51.8	52.8	42.8

Source: See note 12. Individual-level data are given in Fiebiger, pp. 77, 85; Leidlmair, p. 76; *X censimento generale,* pp. 168–169; *XI censimento generale,* pp. 276–277; Alcock, p. 253; and Pan, *Südtirol,* pp. 102–105.
Note: N = number of communes.

Nineteenth-century Central European history supports the view that nationalist concerns are stronger in the middle class than they are among either aristocrats or workers. But the middle class itself is internally split. Political agitation is normally strongest among university students, school teachers, and white-collar professionals. What unites these socially diverse groups is their direct involvement in the production and distribution of information. The manufacturing middle class, involved in the production and distribution of goods, is normally much less interested in ethnic conflicts. Because members of the middle class involved in processes of information production and distribution are more easily moved by abstract concepts and ideologies and are less rooted in traditional loyalties, a disproportionate growth in their numbers should be related to observable swings in ethnic conflict.

The low tertiary sector includes low-skill service occupations. In contemporary Europe these occupations are normally the product of a periph-

tors of National Development in Latin America, Rio de Janeiro, May 1972), p. 6. Although James E. Jacob applies the distinction to the difference between the primary and secondary sectors, on the one hand, and the tertiary sector, on the other, I am also indebted to his "Socio-Economic and International Contexts of Linguistic Militancy in Twentieth-Century France," unpublished paper (Ithaca, N.Y.: Cornell University, 1974), pp. 21–23.

eral capitalism based in part on a backward retail sector and in part on a modern tourist economy.[18] Of primary importance in South Tyrol is the tourist industry, which offers workers only seasonal employment and low status and wages and which fosters their relative dependence on both proprietors and guests. This, it might be argued, has led to a new type of rural proletariat which is easily politicized. In nineteenth-century Central Europe ethnic political conflict was a primarily urban phenomenon. But with the growth of the low tertiary sector, the sociological conditions for the spread of ethnic strife to the countryside might have suddenly been established in the middle of the twentieth century.

Table 12.3. Tertiary sector occupations of the economically active population of South Tyrol by commune, 1951–71 (in percent)

Tertiary sector	Total communes (N = 99)	Predominantly German-speaking (N = 78)	Moderately German-speaking (N = 11)	Mixed German- and Italian-speaking (N = 5)	Moderately Italian-speaking (N = 5)
Total					
1951	23.0	20.1	36.6	50.3	29.2
1961	31.3	28.7	43.7	57.0	35.2
1971	38.3	36.7	51.8	52.8	42.8
High *					
1951	9.8	8.2	18.4	27.5	14.8
1961	9.7	8.1	17.7	30.2	13.3
1971	9.1	8.2	17.3	22.2	14.3
Low †					
1951	13.2	11.9	18.2	22.8	14.4
1961	21.6	20.6	26.0	26.8	21.9
1971	29.2	28.5	34.5	30.6	28.5

Source: See note 12; for individual-level data, see source for Table 12.2.
Note: N = number of communes.
* Transportation and communication, banking and insurance, public administration.
† Commerce, services (domestic and tourist).

The occupational classifications of the Italian census permit only a rough approximation of the distinction between a high and a low tertiary sector. But for a preliminary test the breakdown presented in Table 12.3 will suffice. The two parts of the tertiary sector were of about equal size

18. See, among others, Suzanne Berger, "The Uses of the Traditional Sector: Why the Declining Classes Survive," unpublished paper (Cambridge: Massachusetts Institute of Technology, 1973); Davydd J. Greenwood, "Tourism as an Agent of Change: A Spanish Basque Case," *Ethnology,* 11, no. 1 (January 1972): 80–91; and Davydd J. Greenwood, "Culture by the Pound: An Anthropological Perspective on Tourism as Cultural Commoditization," in *Hosts and Guests,* ed. Valene Smith (Philadelphia: University of Pennsylvania Press, forthcoming).

in 1951. But in marked contrast to the nineteenth century, the very high growth rate during the two decades after 1951 was restricted exclusively to the low tertiary sector. However, neither the absence of change in the relative size of the high tertiary sector nor the steady growth in the low tertiary sector can be easily related to the intensification and attenuation of ethnic political conflict which during the last two decades has occurred in South Tyrol.

Rural Modernization

The key to the puzzle may lie less in the quantitative than in the qualitative aspects of the change in South Tyrol's occupational structure. The German speakers in South Tyrol have not abandoned their rural life but have merely adjusted it to recent changes. The key factor in this process of adjustment lies in South Tyrol's inheritance laws.[19] Although between 1929 and 1954 the fascists suspended the traditional system of primogeniture, one of the bulwarks of German ethnic strength in South Tyrol's countryside, the values it had instilled were sufficiently strong to prevent a widespread division of German farms during that twenty-five-year period. During the last two decades the system has proved to have an astonishing capacity to withstand and assimilate great social and economic changes. Rural exodus, especially from the most economically backward German-speaking communes in the north, has been substantial. But the migration data presented in Table 12.1 demonstrate that this development has slowed during the 1960's, while the movement from the primary into the secondary and tertiary sectors has continued unabated. The magnitude of the industrialization in the countryside and the growth of a tourist-oriented economy are illustrated in Table 12.4.

The transformation of South Tyrol's countryside between 1951 and 1971 is indicated by the sharp drop in the absolute and relative numbers of family farmhands. At the same time there occurred a sharp increase in the relative number of employees and workers in the predominantly German communes. Since between 1951 and 1971 the relative number of dependent workers in agriculture who spoke German declined by 9 percent to only 10 percent of the total economically active population of German speakers, the increase in the relative number of industrial workers among German speakers was actually greater than the figures in Table

19. Udo Volz, *Die geschlossenen Höfe im Schnalstal* (Innsbruck: Wagner'sche Universitätsbuchhandlung, 1969); Leidlmair, pp. 131–136.

Table 12.4. Occupational groups of the economically active population of South Tyrol by commune, 1951–71 (in percent)

Occupational groups	Total communes (N = 99)	Predominantly German-speaking (N = 78)	Moderately German-speaking (N = 11)	Mixed German- and Italian-speaking (N = 5)	Moderately Italian-speaking (N = 5)
Self-employed					
1951	26.6	29.3	24.3	19.7	23.6
1961	26.5	28.1	23.8	18.1	25.1
1971	25.2	28.1	22.6	18.6	24.7
Family farm help					
1951	24.4	27.1	14.9	12.4	15.8
1961	15.7	17.2	11.0	7.4	9.7
1971	9.4	10.1	7.0	6.3	5.4
Civil servants and employees					
1951	5.8	4.6	10.2	12.7	9.2
1961	7.7	6.2	12.4	15.9	12.4
1971	14.1	12.2	21.0	24.2	19.3
Industrial and agricultural workers					
1951	41.8	39.0	50.9	55.2	51.4
1961	49.9	48.6	53.8	58.6	52.8
1971	49.6	49.6	48.4	50.9	50.6

Source: See note 12. Individual-level data are given in Leidlmair, p. 105; *X censimento generale,* pp. 179–189; and *XI censimento generale,* pp. 287, 297.
Note: N = number of communes.

12.4 indicate. These changes should be evaluated against the background of only a small decline in the number of self-employed German speakers in agriculture and a sharp increase in their relative proportion. Peasant farming as the backbone of the South Tyrolean countryside, by and large, has held its own during the last two decades, while almost thirty thousand family farmhands and agricultural workers have moved into the secondary and the low tertiary sectors.

The effect of the release of family farmhands and rural wage labor into new and better-paid positions in the secondary and tertiary sectors has been an adjustment in, rather than an abandoning of, rural life.[20] Primogeniture contributes to the continued high regard for farming held by most German speakers in South Tyrol. The increasing integration of the German valleys into a modern market economy prompts the typical German-speaking farmer to relinquish his sideline economic activities and

20. Cole and Wolf, pp. 19, 81, 88, 92–93, 279–280; John W. Cole and Phillip S. Katz, "Knecht to Arbeiter: The Proletarization Process in South Tyrol," *Studies in European Society,* 1, no. 1 (1973): 39–66.

to increase his landholding, if at all possible, rather than to move off the land altogether. Many members of the new working and service classes retain a link to agriculture through the assistance they frequently give to their relatives at harvest time. The astonishingly high proportion (30 percent) of part-time farmers reported in 1962 thus represents a mixture of mountain farmers who need sideline economic activities to make a sparse living and workers and employees who, for a variety of reasons, maintain some ties to the land.[21]

Many members of the new working class continue to live in the old village or nearby in newly built houses or small apartment buildings. Commuting to work has become a widespread practice. Although it is difficult to measure accurately how many German speakers commute from rural areas to industrial and tourist centers, one study has put the figure as high as 25 percent of the economically active population of German speakers.[22] The continued strength of ties to the land is reinforced by the striking gains, especially if measured in the increase of absolute income in the province, the tourist industry has scored in South Tyrol since 1945. The seasonal character of employment in the tourist industry and the geographic location of new tourist centers in increasingly rural and backward areas reinforce an occupational pattern that favors the preservation of some ties to the land.[23]

Since South Tyrol's agricultural orientation, reinforced by its Catholic religion, has inhibited the emergence of a class of radical nationalists concentrated in the tertiary sector, the persistence and adaptability of the province's agricultural way of life may well have moderated its ethnic political conflict. Sociological reasoning can thus offer a partial answer to the questions raised by the intensification and attenuation of ethnic politi-

21. Christoph Pan, ed., "Die Wirtschaftliche und Soziale Lage in Südtirol: Eine Meinungsumfrage durchgeführt vom Südtiroler Wirtschafts- und Sozialinstitut Bozen, im August/September 1960," *Schriftenreihe des Südtiroler Wirtschafts- und Sozialinstituts,* 1 (1962): 35. See also Volker H. Klepp, *Der Südtiroler Arbeitsmarkt* (Innsbruck: Wagner'sche Universitätsbuchhandlung, 1971), p. 70.

22. Kersting, pp. 78–80; Toepfer, p. 125.

23. Klepp, pp. 83–86; Helmut Klepp, *Das Beherbergungsgewerbe in Südtirol* (Innsbruck: Wagner'sche Universitätsbuchhandlung, 1968). This pattern of rural modernization has its economic costs. In comparison to the rest of Italy, South Tyrol's economic position has slipped badly during the last two decades. In 1954 it ranked twelfth among all Italian provinces, well above the national average. Productivity gains in South Tyrol's tourist economy during the next fifteen years were, however, only moderate. Despite significant increases in the absolute level of individual incomes, by 1968 South Tyrol ranked only thirty-ninth among all provinces, that is, well below the national average. See Kersting, p. 107.

cal conflict in South Tyrol. This discussion has examined three reasons in particular. First, demographic changes can be both a cause and a consequence of ethnic political conflict and are, thus, insufficient in and of themselves to account for the process of escalation and de-escalation. Second, changes in South Tyrol's occupational structure have been linear (the proportion of the work force in the secondary and low tertiary sectors has steadily increased at the expense of the agricultural work force), a fact that is not easily related to both the increase and the decrease in ethnic political conflict during the last two decades. Finally, South Tyrol's process of rural modernization helps one to understand the eventual decline of the conflict in the late 1960's, but it leaves unexplained why that conflict escalated in the late 1950's and early 1960's. To account for these critical considerations in the timing of the conflict, political factors must be included in the analysis.

Political Forces and Ethnic Political Conflict

Political forces are critical to a comprehensive analysis of ethnic political conflict in South Tyrol. These forces have operated at the international, national, and provincial levels. The international side of the South Tyrol conflict was conditioned by the success of the North Tyrol lobby in Austrian politics in the 1950's and by the displacement of the South Tyrol issue in Austria in the 1960's. Nationally, the shift of Italy's ruling DC away from the regional reform issue in the 1950's and, with its Opening to the Left, toward regionalization in the 1960's also had a strong impact on the conflict, as did the universalization of clientelistic forms of consensus formation in the 1960's. Finally, in the province, two distinct political processes—a clientelistic Italian one and a corporatist German one—differed over time in the impact they had on the political conflict.

International Forces: South Tyrol in Austrian Politics

Throughout Western Europe the intensification of ethnic political conflict in recent years has been greatest in countries experiencing the economic and psychological traumas that the loss of empire brought to these formerly hegemonic powers. The United Kingdom, France, the Netherlands, Belgium, and Spain bear out the empirical generalization that it took the colonial powers about one generation to withdraw from empire and another generation to adjust to the political, economic, and psychological effects of that withdrawal. The international aspects of the South Tyrol conflict support this generalization. Unlike the Western European states, Austria lost its empire not after World War II but after World War I. Throughout the interwar period Austrian concern for the fate of South Tyrol under Italian rule was of distinctly secondary importance compared to the Austrian desire for unification with Germany. Since unification between 1938 and 1945 did not bring the benefits the Austrians had expected, but war and defeat instead, it was only natural that the psychological and political commitments of the Austrians changed direction after 1945. Supranational and subnational questions became surrogates for national ones. Like the issue of association with the European Economic Community (EEC), Austria's foreign policy interest in South Tyrol represented a displacement of and a compensation for a disappointed German nationalism. Undoubtedly Austrian interest in South Tyrol was important for the development of a genuine Austrian national consciousness.[24] A step ahead of other Western European states, Austria has, after centuries of political prominence, now settled comfortably into a new role of political marginality within world politics. As a result, its interest and involvement in ethnic political conflict abroad have weakened.

Until the achievement of Austrian neutrality in 1955, all other foreign policy issues, including South Tyrol, were of subsidiary importance.[25] But from then on, a basic confusion over Austria's political objectives in South Tyrol—secession, self-determination, changes in the de jure autonomy statute, or an extension of de facto autonomy provisions—contributed for almost a decade to the intensification of the conflict over South Tyrol. An informal agreement between Austria's parties kept the country's South Tyrol policy out of partisan politics.[26] Because of Austria's low tolerance for political conflict, the coalition government of the Austrian Peoples party (Österreichische Volkspartei, ÖVP) and the Austrian Socialist party (Sozialistische Partei Österreichs, SPÖ) shaped government policy until 1966, on this issue as on many others, by increasingly substituting the appearance of political agreement for its reality. The political immobilism that resulted from Austria's consociational party

24. Wolf, p. 26; Stadlmayer, "Die Südtirolpolitik Österreichs," p. 476.

25. Basic factual information on Austrian policy can be found in a number of sources. Since 1960 the *Österreichische Zeitschrift für Aussenpolitik* contains regular reports, summaries, and articles. See also Heinrich Siegler, ed., *Österreichs Souveränität, Neutralität, Prosperität* (Vienna: Siegler Verlag, 1967), pp. 40–70; Hansotto Ausserhofer, "Der Südtirolkonflikt und seine Entspannung," *Beiträge zur Konfliktforschung*, 4, no. 3 (1974): 126–152. There are also regular reports in the journal *Europa Ethnica*.

26. Wolf, pp. 96–119.

system paralleled that of South Tyrol's corporatist one. The effect of this immobilism was an exacerbation of the ethnic conflict in South Tyrol.

Although the ÖVP was interested in good relations with the DC, its sister party in Italy, only a day after the signing of the Austrian State Treaty on 15 May 1955, ÖVP Chancellor Julius Raab reiterated that under the Paris Agreement of 1946 the Austrian government intended to fulfill its obligations to South Tyrol. Since the policy-making process was virtually handed over to the ideologically most committed actors in Austria, the North Tyroleans, an activist foreign policy was inevitable. Before 1955 the role of the Foreign Ministry had been weak on the question of South Tyrol. Expertise and commitment rested not with the national government in Vienna but with the state government of North Tyrol in Innsbruck.[27] The North Tyroleans were assured of an important institutional base in Vienna when in 1956 a new top civil service position was established in the Foreign Ministry for the South Tyrol problem in particular. That position was filled by ÖVP member Franz Gschnitzer from Innsbruck, since 1955 the head of the strongest South Tyrol lobby in Austria, the Berg-Isel Federation.[28] Within a few months after this appointment, Austrian policy shifted from cautious equivocation to strict opposition to Italy's South Tyrol policy. A year later Austrian policy also rejected the Italian view that South Tyrol was a legal issue which should be resolved by the International Court of Justice in The Hague and instead insisted it was a political issue which should be brought before the General Assembly of the United Nations.[29] Both changes can be traced back to policy shifts within the South Tyrol Peoples party (SVP), with the North Tyrolean state government and Gschnitzer serving as transmission belts.

The delegation of Austrian foreign policy to the most extreme faction of the North Tyrolean political elite—and thus to the SVP—was a product of the Austrian system of coalition government. The North Tyrolean branch of the ÖVP threatened to form an independent, regional party unless the Austrian government agreed to adopt a hard-line policy. Formation of such a party might have resulted in tipping the national balance of power in favor of the SPÖ. ÖVP Chancellor Raab gave in, therefore,

27. *Ibid.*, pp. 80–87; Alcock, pp. 231–233; Alexander Vodopivec, *Wer regiert in Österreich? Ein Politisches Panorama* (Vienna: Verlag für Geschichte und Politik, 1960), p. 199.

28. Alcock, pp. 274–275; Gatterer, p. 1022.   29. Alcock, pp. 280–281, 309, 326.

to electoral blackmail.[30] Although Socialist Bruno Kreisky became head of the Foreign Ministry in 1959, the domestic basis of Austria's South Tyrol policy did not change greatly. Since the SPÖ had a clear interest in using the South Tyrol issue as an electoral wedge into a staunchly conservative West Austria, Austria's foreign policy was activated further.[31] A new South Tyrol section was created in the Foreign Ministry, and Kreisky immediately labeled South Tyrol Austria's most pressing foreign policy problem.[32] Since the Italian government had remained cool to Austrian proposals for a reopening of bilateral negotiations, Kreisky succeeded in 1960 in bringing the South Tyrol question before the United Nations General Assembly. Although largely ineffectual in increasing Austria's leverage on Italy, this move proved to be a brilliant success in Austrian domestic politics. It portrayed Kreisky as an active and concerned champion of the South Tyrol cause as well as a statesman of international stature. At the same time, though, it also demonstrated to the political elites in North and South Tyrol how little support they could expect for their political grievances in an international forum.[33]

Under Kreisky, the role played by the political leadership of North and South Tyrol in Austrian foreign policy relating to South Tyral was subtly redefined. While their active participation in foreign policy making and implementation was somewhat curtailed, North and South Tyrol were given an absolute veto over Austrian policy. Kreisky, furthermore, was careful to include in this political arrangement not only party but interest group elites, such as the leaders of the Berg-Isel Federation.[34] Frequent consultations kept the domestic opposition against Kreisky's policy to a minimum. At the same time Kreisky used the rigidity of the radicals in North and South Tyrol as an implicit threat and a bargaining token in his negotiations with the Italian government.[35]

Reinforced by the Austrian public's infusion of a displaced German nationalist sentiment into the South Tyrol issue, the internal politics of Austria's coalition government led to a fundamental confusion over Austrian

30. *Ibid.*, p. 232; Barker, p. 246.
31. Alexander Vodopivec, *Wer regiert in Österreich? Die Aera Gorbach Pittermann* (Vienna: Verlag für Geschichte und Politik, 1962), pp. 280–281.
32. Wolf, pp. 51–52.
33. Alexander Vodopivec, *Die Balkanisierung Österreichs: Die grosse Koalition und ihr Ende*, 2d ed. (Vienna: Molden, 1966), pp. 280–281.
34. Wolf, pp. 42–44, 56, 92, 96, 133, 169.
35. Alcock, p. 389; Schlesinger, p. 73.

political objectives. In part that confusion resulted from the emptiness of Austrian political rhetoric. As was true of the political debate in South Tyrol, the language of nationalism in Austria emphasized symbols, not facts.[36] The resulting lack of precision was indispensable to the domestic politics of coalition formation. There existed, to be sure, slight differences between the ÖVP's emphasis of legal and historical aspects of the South Tyrol problem, on the one hand, and the SPÖ's emphasis of social and economic features, on the other, and these differences reflected, in part, corresponding ones within South Tyrol's SVP. But compared to the vast gap between the requirements of domestic political rhetoric and of foreign policy behavior, the effect of these domestic disagreements paled. Since the nationalist language of politics left the specific objectives of Austrian policy undefined, that policy for years remained immobilized between an insistence on change and an inability to specify the end result of that change.

Equally important to the confusion of Austria's political objectives was the large number and political heterogeneity of the actors involved in the formulation of Austrian policy. Most important in the early 1960's were the ÖVP chancellor, the SPÖ foreign minister, representatives of the South Tyrol lobby, professional diplomats, and the governor and party leaders of North Tyrol; omnipresent in the background was the leadership of South Tyrol's SVP. The Austrian government was politically incapable of setting one tune for so large a chorus; to the critical question of the nature of Austrian political demands on Italy, the chorus could respond only with a babble of voices.[37] In their hearts most Austrians, especially in North Tyrol, favored self-determination for South Tyrol; but political realism led political leaders, especially in Vienna, to demand assurances from Italy that it would offer a greater amount of autonomy to South Tyrol.[38] Since the domestic coalition that supported Austria's South Tyrol policy was so broad, it was inevitable that Austrian policy should vacillate between inconsistent demands. In the late 1950's Gschnitzer, for example, sought as undersecretary of state to formulate official government policy on South Tyrol's autonomy while speaking out as head of the Berg-Isel Federation in support of South Tyrol's right to self-determination.[39] The obfuscation of political objectives was expedient in Austrian domestic politics, but it reinforced a political immobilism in Austrian

---

36. Wolf, pp. 25–26.   37. *Ibid.*, pp. 50, 209–221.
38. *Ibid.*, pp. 168–169; Alcock, pp. 281, 356–359.   39. Wolf, pp. 58–59.

diplomacy that contributed to intensification of the South Tyrol conflict.

The important change in Austria's South Tyrol policy occurred in the early 1960's. The failure of Austrian policy was evident in the continuation of terrorist activity and in Austria's growing diplomatic isolation beginning in 1961. All quarters of Austria's political community were confronted with a fundamental choice between escalation and accommodation. The Austrian government increasingly appreciated the political costs of an active South Tyrol policy: Austria's hard-line policy on South Tyrol, which alienated Italy, contradicted its growing interest in an association agreement with the EEC, which required Italian acquiescence.[40] Austria's largest and most effective South Tyrol lobby, the Berg-Isel Federation, experienced a traumatic split in its leadership in 1961–62. For years the organization did not recover politically from the successful bid for power of a radical faction. The influence of more moderate spokesmen who had been direct participants in the Foreign Ministry and in the North Tyrolean government was reduced. These changes removed from government office all major advocates of South Tyrol's self-determination.[41] The successor of Undersecretary of State Gschnitzer, Ludwig Steiner, came from the Tyrol but was a nonpartisan diplomat with policy preferences that agreed with those of the national organization of the ÖVP in Vienna rather than with the regional one in Innsbruck.[42] These developments led, for the first time, to a clear restriction of Austrian political objectives. The Austrian government abandoned all calls for self-determination or for the granting of regional autonomy to the province of South Tyrol and restricted itself to demanding instead an extension of provincial autonomy within the existing region Trentino–Alto Adige which had been set up in 1948. This shift in Austrian policy, however, left untouched the right of veto of North and South Tyrol over any final Austro-Italian agreement. An agreement, which incorporated the recommendations of an Italian government report of 1964 and the now clarified Austrian political objectives, was actually reached in draft form in late 1964. But political immobilism in South Tyrol was still too great. The draft agreement faltered primarily on the veto of political elites in North and South Tyrol.[43] Because of this setback Kreisky's successor, ÖVP

40. *Ibid.,* pp. 28–29.
41. *Ibid.,* pp. 86–87; Vodopivec, *Wer regiert in Österreich? Die Aera Gorbach Pittermann,* p. 291.
42. Wolfgang Kos, "Österreichische Volkspartei und die Südtirol-Frage," unpublished paper (Vienna: Institut für Zeitgeschichte, 1972), p. 13.
43. Wolf, pp. 56, 222–223; Ritschel, pp. 479–505.

Foreign Minister Lujo Tončić-Sorinj, restricted his consultation of North Tyrol's political elite to the governor, and he limited any future veto by the South Tyrolean leadership to those parts of an Austro-Italian agreement that directly affected the living conditions in South Tyrol. On these questions significant gains were made both in bilateral negotiations between Austrian and Italian experts and in direct consultations between the SVP leadership and the Italian government. By 1967 virtually all substantive aspects of the conflict had been solved to the satisfaction of both governments and of the South Tyrolean political elite.

Foreign Minister Tončić-Sorinj also excluded procedural questions of international political and legal guarantees from the veto power of the South Tyrolean political leadership, thus completing the removal of the Austrian political barriers to a settlement of the conflict.[44] Since an irreconcilable clash between the Italian and Austrian positions threatened to torpedo the agreement on procedural grounds, the Austrian government now felt free to offer a method for supervising the implementation of the agreement which no longer was subject to the blocking power of the South Tyroleans. Foreign Minister Kurt Waldheim proposed a carefully designed timetable of reciprocal steps to be taken by the Italian and Austrian governments running parallel with the implementation of the agreement.[45] In 1969 a draft agreement between the two governments was approved by the two national parliaments, and by the end of 1975 about three-quarters of that agreement had been implemented to mutual satisfaction. For all intents and purposes the international aspect of the South Tyrol conflict had ended peacefully.[46]

National Constraints: South Tyrol in Italian Politics

The timing in the waxing and waning of ethnic political conflict in South Tyrol was shaped not only by international forces but also by de-

44. Wolf, p. 93.
45. Kurt Waldheim, *Der österreichische Weg: Aus der Isolation zur Neutralität* (Vienna: Molden, 1971), pp. 182–192; Heinrich Siegler, *Die österreichisch-italienische Einigung über die Regelung des Südtirolkonflikts* (Vienna: Siegler Verlag, 1970), pp. 3–4; Margit Minich, "Die österreichisch-italienischen Verhandlungen 1961–1966: I. Teil 1961–1963," unpublished paper (Vienna: Institut für Zeitgeschichte, 1972); Eva Charbusky, "Die italienisch-österreichischen Verhandlungen von Mai 1964–December 1966," unpublished paper (Vienna: Institut für Zeitgeschichte, 1972).
46. This outcome fits into a broader pattern of successful conflict resolution since 1945. See K. J. Holsti, "Resolving International Conflicts: A Taxonomy of Behavior and Some Figures on Procedures," *Journal of Conflict Resolution*, 10, no. 3 (September 1966): 282–291.

velopments in Italian national politics. These developments constrained the devolution of powers from the region of Trentino–Alto Adige to the province of South Tyrol, and this devolution was at the heart of the political solution by which the conflict was resolved in the 1960's. If South Tyrol had been the Italian government's prime focus of political attention, its ethnic troubles might have been solved more easily than actually was the case. But from the vantage point of Rome, South Tyrol's ethnic problems were part of the broader question of regional reform throughout Italy. As long as the Italian government, in the 1950's, was unprepared to move toward regionalization as a matter of state policy, little progress could be expected in the improvement of the political status of South Tyrol.[47] The gradual move toward regionalization which occurred in the 1960's removed an important obstacle barring a political solution to the South Tyrol problem. That move was conditioned by changes in Italy's party alignments as well as by the universalization of a system of mass patronage within the Italian system of government.

Why was the move toward the establishment of the Italian regions so painfully slow? The main reasons appear to have been the consolidation of the DC's grip on national power since late 1949 and the intensification of a cold war atmosphere throughout Europe. The Italian Communist and Socialist parties became strong and persistent spokesmen for regional reform because it promised to open an avenue to political power (the left could safely expect to capture at least three regional governments), and because the regions offered the Communists in particular a fertile ground for pursuing their alliance strategy with noncommunist, progressive forces in Italian society. Although the DC had both a federalist and a localist tradition, it opposed regionalization. Regional reform threatened to lead to an increase in the political power of the left, and throughout the 1950's the DC was strongly opposed to any such moves. It thus failed to propose legislation for the implementation of the regionalization program specified in Title V of the 1947 Constitution, and it enacted instead legislation that in fact modified the Constitution's provisions.

With the DC's Opening to the Left in 1962, this roadblock in the way

47. Peter Gourevitch, "Reforming the Napoleonic State: The Creation of Regional Governments in France and Italy," in *Territorial Politics in Industrial States,* ed. Luigi Graziano, Peter Katzenstein, and Sidney Tarrow (forthcoming); Sidney Tarrow, "Local Constraints on Regional Reform: A Comparison of Italy and France," *Comparative Politics,* 7 (October 1974): 1–36. On the historical origin of the special regions, see Ernst Weibel, *La création des régions autonomes à statut spécial en Italie* (Geneva: Droz, 1971).

of regional reform was gradually removed. The leftward shift of the Italian center of power permitted the progressive wing of the DC to forge a coalition with the Nenni Socialists who were strong advocates of regional reform. The coalition government failed during the next decade to enact any significant structural reform legislation other than on regional decentralization, which became a substitute for constructive reformism in other areas in Italian politics.[48] After intense parliamentary debate the first regional elections were finally held in 1970.

A striking degree of correspondence exists between the critical dates in the history of regional reform in Italian politics since 1945 and in the history of ethnic political conflict in South Tyrol. With the DC's rightward shift beginning in the late 1940's, demands both for regional reform and for South Tyrol's autonomy remained unheeded by the national government. Only in the early 1960's did the currents turn. In 1961, when the Opening to the Left was already in the cards, the important Commission of Nineteen—staffed jointly by members of the national, regional, and provincial governments, and by Italian and German speakers—was set up to resolve the South Tyrol problem. The long process of negotiation that followed the commission's report of 1964 led to the resolution of virtually all substantive disagreements between Rome and South Tyrol in 1967, the very year in which the regional reform legislation was debated at length and finally passed in the national parliament. The first steps in 1969–70 toward the implementation of the changes in South Tyrol coincided with the first general regional elections in postwar Italy.

A second development affecting the ethnic political conflict in South Tyrol has been the increasing use of patronage since the 1960's throughout the Italian system of government. Political clientelism in Italy is distinguished by the granting of special favors: jobs in the state bureaucracy and financial rewards.[49] The exclusion of the German speakers in South Tyrol from bureaucratic jobs has been a long-standing and well-documented grievance. For example, of the twenty-five hundred railway employees in the province in 1966, less than 10 percent were German speakers.[50] This figure is indicative of the magnitude of discrimination

48. Sidney Tarrow, *Between Center and Periphery: Grassroots Politicians in Italy and France* (New Haven: Yale University Press, 1977).

49. E. Gorrieri, *La giungla retributiva* (Bologna: Mulino, 1972), quoted in Luigi Graziano, "Clientelism and the Political System: The Sources of the Italian Crisis," in Graziano et al.

50. Quoted in *Europa Ethnica,* 23, no. 3 (1966): 123.

against German speakers throughout the public sector. Although estimates vary, most observers put the relative share of German speakers in the provincial bureaucracy at less than 20 percent.[51] A growing number of bureaucratic jobs were taken by the Italians who, in the 1950's and 1960's, were increasingly recruited not from Trento but from the south. The agreement that has been implemented since 1969 assures the German speakers of an ethnic proportion within the provincial bureaucracy. In the future, two-thirds of all civil service positions within the province will be reserved for German and Ladinian speakers. The six thousand positions thus promised will be added to the existing bureaucracy. Not a single Italian bureaucrat will lose his job.[52]

Industrial policy is the second major area in which clientelistic forms of consensus formation—jobs and money—have finally been extended to the German speakers in South Tyrol. Throughout the 1950's and 1960's the provincial government in Bozen was largely excluded from providing economic assistance to local governments or businesses. That exclusion was due in part to the magnitude of international movements of capital (perhaps as much as one-half of total investment in South Tyrol derived from foreign, mainly West German sources [53]) and in part to the Italian system of state capitalism, in which public or semipublic corporate giants, such as the gigantic state holding company (Ente Nazionale Idrocarburi, ENI) and the Institute for Italian Reconstruction (Istituto per la Ricostruzione Italiana, IRI), rely on central decision-making procedures above the provincial and regional levels. But the economic impotence of the provincial government resulted also from constitutional provisions. For example, legislation passed by the regional assembly in 1960 provided for the dispensing of about 400 million lire over a three-year period in direct subsidies to local governments in support of industrial development. Interest subsidies granted since 1963 supplemented this program by about 350 million lire per year, and in 1965 that legislation was broadened and the funds expended per year rose by an additional 250 million lire.[54] The provincial government's views on industrial policy were elicited, but the final decision was taken at the regional level where the German speakers were in a minority. Although there is no direct evidence of

---

51. Klepp, p. 75; "Memorandum der österreichischen Bundesregierung, vom 8: Oktober 1957," reprinted in Pfaundler, pp. 114–115; Pan, *Südtirol,* p. 123; Leidlmair, pp. 112–114; de Block, p. 180. Unfortunately I was not able to consult Olaf Weingart, "Die Besetzung öffentlicher Ämter in Südtirol" (Ph.D. diss., Innsbruck University, 1971).

52. Klepp, p. 75.   53. Kersting, pp. 58–70.   54. *Ibid.*, pp. 28–47.

the importance of ethnic considerations in the disbursement of funds, it is not impossible that such considerations may, at times, have had an undue influence. For example, the important interstate highway (Brennerautobahn) that traverses South Tyrol from north to south was constructed without a single subcontract being given to a German-speaking firm.[55]

Since 1969, however, the situation has changed greatly, and the provincial government is now, for the first time, in a position to allocate substantial sums for industrial development. The province now disburses more than one billion lire per year, virtually all of which either has been shifted from the regional to the provincial budget or is a subsidy from the national to the provincial government.[56] As a result of these changes the province's revenues have increased from eighteen billion lire in 1968, to thirty-six billion lire in 1972, and to about fifty billion lire in 1974.[57] South Tyrol thus has acquired an active interest in participating in the clientelistic politics of resource disbursement which appears to be so distinctive of contemporary Italy.

Local Incentives: Clientelism and Corporatism in South Tyrol's Politics

At the provincial level ethnic political conflict in South Tyrol during the last two decades has been shaped by the interaction of a clientelistic Italian political process and a corporatist German one. These two processes differ along a number of dimensions, some of which are briefly mentioned at the conclusion of this section; critical for this analysis, however, are differences in institutional structures, political objectives, and political strategies. In South Tyrol, clientelism can be observed in a decentralized group, the Catholic Employees Union (Katholischer Verband der Werktätigen, KVW) which focuses on social questions and follows a political strategy of association. Corporatism can be found in a centralized party, the SVP, which has concentrated on national problems and has been more inclined to follow a political strategy of dissociation. Since the early 1960s a slow process of adaptation of German political practices to Italian political incentives is evident, with a marked political shift taking place inside the SVP between 1962 and 1964.

---

55. Reinhild Bolz, *Die Brennerautobahn: Bedeutung für Südtirol* (Innsbruck: Wagner'sche Universitätsbuchhandlung, 1968), pp. 14–15.

56. Kersting, pp. 37, 110.

57. Helmuth Hartmeyer, "Das Paket," unpublished paper (Vienna: Institut für Zeitgeschichte, 1972), p. 8.

Especially in times of acute ethnic political conflict the KVW and the SVP have been held together by the central political actor in South Tyrol, the Catholic church.[58] As is true of other rural regions in Western Europe, the boundary separating religion from politics is not clearly marked in South Tyrol. In the immediate postwar years religious mass meetings drew crowds which in sheer numbers far exceeded political rallies. Recurrent mass pilgrimages which have taken place since then have often assumed an undisguised political character.[59]

As important as its popular appeal is the indirect influence the church has exercised in the political councils of both the KVW and the SVP. That influence has been used to moderate the political demands for reform on both ethnic and social welfare questions. Even at the height of nationalist agitation the church worked actively through the media and the educational system in the region to alleviate ethnic tension. The reorganization of the church's internal jurisdiction in 1964, which emphasized the distinctiveness of South Tyrol, was an indication of the willingness of the Catholic church to make institutional adjustments in the interest of ethnic accommodation.[60] But the fundamental reason why the church's influence has been so strong on both the KVW and the SVP has been the unrelentingly strong anticommunism in which these three organizations have shared at all times since 1945.[61]

The KVW. Although it is a lay organization and thus is formally independent of the church hierarchy, the KVW follows closely the social reform maxims of the church. "Fear of Communism was the mother of the KVW," and the church played the role of midwife.[62] The KVW was established in 1947 as a semiautonomous, South Tyrolean adjunct to the nationwide Italian Catholic Workers' Association (Associazioni Cristiane dei Lavoratori Italiani, ACLI). Since the objectives of the KVW were somewhat broader than those of a conventional union, its first important decision was to found the South Tyrolean Labor Union (Südtiroler Gewerkschaftsbund, SGB). For the first year a system of dual membership was set up; members of the KVW automatically became members of the

---

58. Gatterer, pp. 1310–1322.

59. Klaus Gruber, "Die Südtiroler Politischen Parteien" (Ph.D. diss., Innsbruck University, 1971), pp. 317–330.

60. Gatterer, pp. 1310–1311. See also the reports in *Europa Ethnica,* 20, no. 3 (1963): 128; and 20, no. 4 (1963): 171.

61. Gatterer, pp. 1319–1320; *Europa Ethnica,* 22, no. 2 (1965): 82.

62. Harald Johannes, *Die Sozialarbeit des K.V.W.* (Innsbruck: Wagner'sche Universitätsbuchhandlung, 1969), p. 15. See also Gatterer, pp. 989–993.

SGB and vice versa.[63] This decision led to dramatic gains in membership and a highly successful attempt to build an organization at the grass roots. The prime target of this organizing drive was the German-speaking rural wage labor, nine thousand of whom had joined the communist National Federation of Workers of the Land (Federterra), even though they continued to vote for the conservative party of the German speakers, the SVP. By 1952 the membership of the Federterra was approaching zero.

Since then the SGB has followed the conservative political strategies of the Italian Catholic labor movement. The political climate in South Tyrol has been hostile to the functioning of all unions, and in their relations with business the SGB leaders have remained defensive. Between 1954 and 1970 the general agreement negotiated between the unions and business remained unchanged.[64] The SGB has taken a stance against communist unions rather than against employers. Nationwide strikes, organized by the communist-led General Confederation of Italian Labor (Confederazione Generale Italiana del Lavoro, CGIL), are observed only in the large factories around Bozen; South Tyrol's strike statistics are thus among the lowest in Italy.[65]

The conservative strategy of the SGB has resulted in growing discontent among members of the German-speaking working class. Organizational density remains extremely low; only 10 percent of the German-speaking employees and workers in South Tyrol are organized by unions as compared to 40 to 50 percent in Italy and in North Tyrol.[66] Although union membership figures are notoriously unreliable in Italy, there can be little doubt that the SGB, after its early period of rapid growth, has experienced a prolonged period of decline in membership since the mid-1950's. Beginning in the early 1960's, an increasing number of German-speaking workers joined the communist-led CGIL; by 1964 it was already recruiting 15 to 20 percent of its membership in South Tyrol from among German speakers.[67]

63. Johannes, pp. 14–17, 27. In the public's mind the mutual identification of the two organizations lasted beyond the initial year. See Klaus Kassner, *Die Gewerkschaften in Südtirol* (Innsbruck: Wagner'sche Universitätsbuchhandlung, 1969), pp. 19–20.

64. Klepp, p. 92.   65. Kassner, pp. 59–60; Kersting, pp. 154–156.

66. Kassner, pp. 54–55; Pan, *Südtirol,* p. 107. These figures are influenced by the artisanal character of industrial employment opportunities for the German speakers in South Tyrol; but I contend that they also reflect the dissatisfaction of the German-speaking work force. See also Leidlmair, p. 254; Fiebiger, p. 124; and Gatterer, pp. 994–995.

67. Gatterer, pp. 993–994; Kassner, pp. 24, 50; Johannes, p. 34.

Although the fear of communism provided a strong ideological tie uniting the KVW, as an organization of the German-speaking population of South Tyrol, with the nationwide Italian ACLI, ethnic considerations were not entirely disregarded. Initially it was agreed that the leadership of the SGB should be based on a system of proportional ethnic representation at the middle level of the organization and on a system of ethnic parity at its top.[68] As long as ethnic political conflict in South Tyrol was dormant, this institutional solution looked attractive to the German-speaking leaders of the Catholic labor movement. But in the late 1950's, as the leadership of the SGB increasingly slipped into Italian hands and as nationalist agitation increased, the basis for an independent, Catholic, German union was laid in the minds at least of the German-speaking leadership. With the KVW adopting a neutral stand, an independent union was constituted in 1964 under the name of Autonomous South Tyrolean Labor Union (Autonomer Südtiroler Gewerkschaftsbund, ASGB).[69] This episode illustrates that the influence of the KVW is not unlimited; at the height of ethnic strife in the early 1960's, it could not stop the interference of ethnic concerns with its traditional economic objectives.

By all existing measures, though, the KVW is still the most powerful group in the province. In 1967 its membership of twenty-seven thousand—about 10 percent of the German-speaking population and about one-third of the German-speaking nonagricultural work force in South Tyrol—was considerably larger than the combined memberships of the SGB and the ASGB. Paying members, furthermore, represented more than 90 percent of the total membership as compared to only 40 percent in the SGB. In the late 1960's the KVW could count among its members 350 local councilors and one member each from the provincial and regional diets.[70] Public opinion also gives testimony to the prominence of the KVW in South Tyrol's group life: in a survey conducted in 1960 more respondents thought that social problems should be solved by the KVW than by unions, business, or unions and business combined.[71]

The importance of the KVW in South Tyrol results directly from its organizational objectives. Throughout the postwar years the KVW's interest has centered on the economic problems of the province. As early as 1956, for example, the KVW proposed to the SVP an economic develop-

---

68. Kassner, pp. 16–17.   69. *Ibid.*, pp. 49–52; Gatterer, pp. 1267–1268.
70. Johannes, pp. 37, 112–113, 118.
71. Pan, "Wirtschaftliche und Soziale Lage," p. 84.

ment plan for South Tyrol which was rejected outright by the party leadership. The formulation and implementation of social legislation is frequently subject to the intervention of the KVW.[72] But its major practical impact on the lives of the German-speaking population in South Tyrol derives from its exercise of a publicly licensed and subsidized legal counseling service which it provides free of charge for all South Tyrolean participants in Italy's social welfare system. This counseling service is typical of Italian politics and is a provincial adjunct to the nationwide counseling service offered by the ACLI. The number of cases that the KVW has handled each year has increased from six thousand in 1950, to twenty thousand in 1960, and to about forty-two thousand in 1967; in other words, in the late 1960's roughly 40 percent of all German-speaking employees and workers in South Tyrol relied on the assistance of the KVW.[73]

The practical effect of the KVW's work conforms with the conservative ideology of the organization's leadership. In 1947 the founder of the KVW attributed the glaring inequities in the administration of the existing social security programs to the absence of an effective organization speaking for the interests of employees.[74] Over the next two decades the KVW succeeded in having virtually all salaried and wage workers included under social security. Yet in the late 1960's, 70 percent of all pensions to which workers and employees were entitled in South Tyrol were at the minimum level, far below the requirements for survival.[75]

The KVW resembles an oversized broker acting on behalf of the particularistic grievances of individuals confronting the Italian welfare state. Although the KVW had focused much of its attention on the special problems of South Tyrol's wage and salary earners, it has retained close links with the business community for reasons of ideological affinity.[76] The KVW serves, in addition, as a critical institutional pillar supporting the cooperation between the German-speaking SVP and the Italian DC in the regional parliament in Trento. The strategic position the KVW thus occupies between labor and capital and between German speakers and

72. Johannes, pp. 34–37.
73. *Ibid.*, p. 44. The amount of social security benefits involved in these cases has increased from 60 million lire in 1950 to 395 million lire in 1960 and 1.6 billion lire in 1967.
74. *Ibid.*, p. 13.   75. Kersting, p. 135; Klepp, pp. 93–94.
76. Johannes, p. 28.

Italians assigns it a mediating role not only between the individual and the state but also within the political process of the province.[77]

The SVP. The increase and decrease in ethnic political conflict in South Tyrol was also affected directly by changes in the SVP. Numerically, the party's membership was very large: within months after the end of World War II the party counted more than fifty thousand members, and by 1947 the figure had risen to about sixty-five thousand. This was a threefold increase over the membership of the SVP's predecessor in 1921 and amounted to about one-half of the party's electorate.[78] The organization of the SVP was tightly knit and featured an effective, hierarchical chain of command. In sharp contrast to the KVW and the SGB, the SVP was organized from the top down; provincial organization was established first. Although the party was formed in May 1945, the first provincewide party congress was not convened until February 1947.

The SVP's organizational weakness at the grass roots is distinctive not only of the founding period, the immediate postwar years, but of the way the party has operated during the subsequent decades. Despite a tripling of the party's membership since the interwar period, the number of local party chapters has stagnated. Problems of recruiting party activists into local political life have been serious. Organizational malfunctioning, especially in the mountainous and rural parts of South Tyrol, have been attributable partly to the indifference of the party leadership.[79] The gap between the party's central and branch offices has been, at least in part, a reflection of the difference between the party leaders, who are drawn from the urban middle class, and the party's predominantly rural base.

The SVP prides itself in tracing its origins back to the end of World

77. This discussion has neglected the South Tyrolean Farmers League (Südtiroler Bauern Bund, SBB). Even though its potential for exercising influence should not be underestimated, the SBB has failed to become a political force of its own for a number of reasons. The heterogeneous economic base of South Tyrolean agriculture impedes united political action. Agricultural production is extensive and marginal (forestry and cattle-farming) in the north and intensive and export-oriented (orchards and vineyards) in the south. The split between the prosperous farmers with a regional political orientation and the marginal farmers with a local political outlook is reflected in the tensions that characterize the SBB. See Hermann Fabel, *Die bäuerlichen Standesorganisationen Südtirols* (Innsbruck: Wagner'sche Universitätsbuchhandlung, 1974).

78. Gruber, pp. 130, 230, 263; Wolfgang Pfaundler, "Das Südtiroler Volk und die Südtiroler Volkspartei," in Pfaundler, p. 465.

79. Gruber, pp. 130, 223, 230, 242, 264–266.

War I and the formation of the German Union (Deutscher Verband) which united all German parties with the exception of the small Socialist party.[80] But for an analysis of the party in the 1950's and 1960's a second historical source appears to be of equal importance. The Andreas Hofer Federation, which merged with the SVP in 1945, was an organization whose members in 1939 had rejected the option to return to Nazi Germany. From its beginning, therefore, the SVP membership did not include die-hard Nazis and extreme nationalists, most of whom had chosen to leave South Tyrol between 1939 and 1943. For about a decade after World War II the SVP followed a strategy of moderation. Its first program spoke of the need for South Tyrol's cultural autonomy but was equally explicit in its commitment to the use of peaceful and legal tactics.[81]

The measured tone of the SVP's political demands was maintained throughout the early 1950's. To be sure, the party focused its political attention on problems of cultural identity, education, and language policy in the schools and in the bureaucracy. Since the German speakers were a minority group in Italy, the SVP insisted on collective privileges which would assure the group's ethnic survival. Formal equality (*volle Gleichberechtigung*) was not enough. Instead the SVP demanded qualitative equality (*vollständige Rechtsgleichheit*), a kind of affirmative action program at all levels of Italian government.[82] But these demands were understandable in the light of what the German speakers viewed as the unfulfilled promise of the 1946 Paris Agreement and the ethnic discrimination to which they were subject.

Similarly striking, though, was the inability, or unwillingness, of the SVP leadership to recognize the importance of the social and economic changes then afoot in South Tyrol. SVP perceptions were skewed. Party leaders overlooked the high population growth in the German-speaking countryside, which was notable since the early 1950's, and disregarded the decline in Italian immigration from the south. They did so at least in part because they distrusted the statistics of the Italian government.[83] New social and economic problems looming at the horizon were thus neglected. Instead, an increasingly nationalist rhetoric captured the political

---

80. *Ibid.*, pp. 134–135, 157–206.
81. *Ibid.*, pp. 219–221, 226–228; Ritschel, pp. 203–206.
82. Pan, *Südtirol*, pp. 91–102.
83. De Block, p. 187; Gatterer, pp. 1000–1003, 1243; Alcock, pp. 216–217.

imagination of the SVP leaders. In vivid language they repeatedly warned that the German speakers in South Tyrol had begun their final "death march." [84] Although useful for maintaining party cohesion, the captivating image of the Germans marching—like lemmings headed for Lago di Garde—toward their extinction bore no resemblance to reality. It managed, however, to conceal for some time the sterility of the political strategy the SVP followed until the late 1950's.

That sterility was most clearly revealed in the SVP's persistent refusal to pursue an alliance strategy with other ethnically or territorially based autonomist political movements in Italy, some of which were located as nearby as Trento. The leftist coloration of these autonomist parties was antithetical to everything the SVP stood for and thus barred a coordination of political demands on the question of autonomy. [85] Instead, the SVP became a coalition party of the DC both in the regional government in Trento and in the national one in Rome. Such a strategy may have been understandable during the lifetime of Italy's first postwar prime minister, de Gasperi. He came, after all, from the Trentino and was basically sympathetic to the German speakers' cause. But when the DC, after de Gasperi's death, moved further to the right, away from regional reform measures which might have eased the plight of South Tyrol, the SVP did not alter its political course. The party's anticommunist imperative was deeply ingrained, and the ability to devise new political strategies was simply lacking. [86]

The failure in strategy led to sweeping changes in the party's leadership in 1957. The new leaders were drawn not from the liberal but from the nationalist segment of the urban middle class. They were younger and favored a more activist approach to South Tyrol's ethnic conflict. Unlike the old generation, they did not subscribe to a long-term perspective of eventually solving the problem of South Tyrol in a confederal Europe but favored instead short-term perspectives and Austrian assistance. The new leadership was politically unsophisticated and distinguished itself largely by the heavy emphasis it put on the importance of maintaining South Tyrol's German cultural identity. Maimed by fascist and Nazi indoctrination, the political imagination of the new party elite could interpret reality

84. Alcock, pp. 213–214.
85. Gatterer, pp. 1017–1021, 1349; Viktoria Stadlmayer, "Italiens Weg," in Huter, p. 584.
86. Alcock, p. 218; Gatterer, pp. 983, 1010–1011.

only through nationalist categories which fitted the vocabulary of *Volkstumpolitik* of the 1930's.[87]

The new party leaders instituted sweeping changes resulting in a radicalization of the party. In 1958 the minimum age for party members was lowered to fifteen years, thus opening to the party a new pool of committed activists;[88] many of the terrorist activities were carried out by men in their late teens and early twenties. In the regional parliament in Trento the SVP broke its alliance with the DC in 1959, and in the national parliament in Rome it started to withhold its support from DC cabinets in the early 1960's. As a result the influence of the party's leadership increased at the expense of the SVP members of the regional and national parliaments who, by and large, were advocates of a more moderate line.[89] Finally, as the SVP adopted a more radical posture on South Tyrol's ethnic problems, the party severed its institutional relations with the KVW and the SGB. Both organizations had been given voting rights in the party's executive committee in 1951. But the link was weakened in 1958 when these voting privileges were withdrawn.[90] The radicalization of the SVP was a result of the strategy of dissociation which it adopted after 1958.

Yet international and national constraints were sufficiently strong to make the party leadership waver between calling for a speedy implementation of the Paris Agreement of 1946, on the one hand, and pressing for international recognition of the right to self-determination, on the other.[91] Since the German speakers in South Tyrol were deeply split on this critical question, this obfuscation, initially, was politically expedient. But it encouraged the radical fringe of the party to move from word to action and to begin a wave of terrorism which increased from three acts in 1956–57, to eleven in 1959–60, and to thirty-three in 1961.[92]

The costs of this political strategy, measured both in human and political terms, were so great and the results so negligible that opposition was

---

87. Gatterer, pp. 983–984, 1021, 1262–1263; Stadlmayer, "Die Südtirolpolitik Österreichs," p. 495. The evidence available leaves unclear the extent to which South Tyroleans repatriated from Germany backed or actually constituted the new party leadership.

88. Gruber, p. 255.   89. *Ibid.,* p. 284; Ritschel, p. 293.

90. Gruber, pp. 252, 257–258, 279.

91. Alcock, pp. 301, 318, 358–359; Ritschel, pp. 316–317, 368–369, 384.

92. These are all the acts reported in the *New York Times, Facts on File,* and *Keesing's Contemporary Archives.* Although the total number in each period certainly was much greater, the rate of increase of terrorist acts reported in the American press is possibly a reflection of events in South Tyrol. See also Alcock, pp. 358–359.

activated within the party. Possibly encouraged by the Catholic church which traditionally had been opposed to the SVP on the issue of the political education of South Tyrol's younger generation, internal party conflict broke into the open in 1962. The conflict was spearheaded by the coalition that had been removed from the party's leadership in 1957. This Coalition for Reconstruction (Gruppe Aufbau) was heterogeneous and encompassed the old political guard; representatives of business, the unions, and the KVW; seventy mayors and vice-mayors; member of the provincial bureaucracy; and members of the regional and national parliaments.[93] These disparate spokesmen were united primarily by their recent fall from power within the party. But they also showed a growing recognition of the economic side of the ethnic conflict and, most importantly, a willingness to compromise with the Italians. Although the appeasers had a broad political base they did not intend to split from the SVP. Since their aim was to change the SVP's posture they encouraged the moves by which they were co-opted back into the mainstream of party life.

Judging by the magnitude of the shift in the SVP's political stance after 1962, the effect of the appeasers within the SVP must have been great. The party began to shift away from the policy of self-encapsulation which it had adopted after 1957. For example, the major aim of the changes in the party statute in 1964 was to increase grass-roots support of the party. For the first time the party confronted seriously the economic aspects of the South Tyrol conflict. In 1966, four years after the internal party conflict had broken into the open and ten years after the KVW had made the first move toward economic reform, the SVP members of the provincial diet proposed an economic development plan for the province.[94] Most importantly, perhaps, the conflict within the party's ranks accelerated the move toward a redefinition of what was considered an acceptable political solution to the South Tyrol problem. Although the possibility had been mentioned by several party leaders before, it was in response to the findings of the Commission of Nineteen in 1964 that the SVP leadership for the first time acknowledged that a de facto extension of South Tyrol's autonomy within the existing regional framework would constitute an acceptable political solution.[95] Once this had been conceded by the provincial political leadership, it remained a matter of time until developments

93. *Ibid.,* p. 360.   94. *Europa Ethnica,* 23, no. 4 (1966): 174.

95. Waldheim, p. 179; Alcock, pp. 360, 397–398; Josef Pasteiner, ''Die Entnationalisierungspolitik in Südtirol,'' unpublished paper (Vienna: Institut für Zeitgeschichte, 1972).

in Austrian and Italian politics were sufficiently intermeshed to bring about a final settlement of the conflict. The change in provincial policy brought about by the Gruppe Aufbau is thus unmistakable. It is summarized best by the different approaches taken by the party's leader Sylvius Magnago in the early and in the late 1960's: in 1962 Magnago was still pleading in his speeches for the primacy of symbolic—in his words "pure"—politics; by the late 1960's he was emphasizing economic and social issues instead.[96]

Clientelism and Corporatism. During the last two decades ethnic political conflict in South Tyrol has been shaped by the interaction of two different political structures and processes. In an instructive comparative case study, John Cole and Eric Wolf have recently described the divergence of a German and an Italian village, situated in the same valley in South Tyrol, in social and political organization despite their convergence in ecological and economic structures.[97] Divisible inheritance in the Italian village and a system of primogeniture in the German village leave their traces on family and interpersonal relations. The Italian family consists of a web of equivalent, cross-cutting ties, and interpersonal contacts emphasize the principle of reciprocity. The German family, on the other hand, divides kinsmen into lineal units, and interpersonal relations are marked by the principle of balance. In sharp contrast to the German village, in the Italian village labor exchanges and social calls are frequent, and involvement with the outside world is high. The social universe in the Italian village is viewed as coterminous with the relations among past kin and potential future kin. In the German village the social universe if constructed from separate, lineal family units welded into different public associations. Core values such as hierarchy and orderliness exist, therefore, outside the network of kin relations in the German village, while in the Italian village values such as equality and casualness are an integral part of the kinship system. In the Italian village political relations are personalized and political conflict is de-escalated and made private. In the German village political relations are organized and political conflict is escalated and made public. The structure of Italian political

---

96. *Europa Ethnica,* 20, no. 1 (1963): 35; Joachim Rössl, "Innere Auseinandersetzungen in der SVP und Bildung neuer Parteien," unpublished paper (Vienna: Institut für Zeitgeschichte, 1972), p. 10; Kersting, p. 185.

97. The distinctions made in this paragraph can be found in Cole and Wolf, pp. 8, 10, 19, 169, 242–245, 262, 265, 278; and in Eric R. Wolf, "Cultural Dissonance in the Italian Alps," *Comparative Studies in Society and History,* 5 (1962): 1–14.

organizations emphasizes the principle of equality, and the Italian political process resembles a circle composed of equivalent social and political units. German political organizations are hierarchical, and the German political process approximates a wheel with different spokes converging in one center.

Only further research can establish whether these differences in local political life are also found at the provincial level. But the preliminary data presented here suggest a number of striking differences between a clientelistic Italian political process and a corporatist German one. The Italian process is reflected in a decentralized group, the KVW, which focuses on individual, concrete, and divisible political objectives. The German process is expressed by the SVP, a centralized party, which concentrates on collective, symbolic, and indivisible political goals. Adhering to a strategy of association, the KVW acts like a broker, while the SVP's stance as an advocate makes it pursue strategies of dissociation. In its pursuit of a politics of interest, the KVW attempts to resolve economic questions in an instrumental manner. In its quest for a politics of meaning, the SVP addresses ethnic questions in an ideological style.

For two reasons these distinctions are overly sharp. Ideal types are always abstractions from data that will never fully agree with them. Throughout the last two decades, for example, the SVP's anticommunism has moderated its political demands and has made them often compatible with those of the KVW. On the other hand, when in 1964 the ASGB was formed, the KVW was evidently powerless to prevent the intrusion of ethnic considerations into its chosen field of social and economic reform.

The distinctions between an Italian and a German political process are exaggerated for a second reason. Since the early 1960's South Tyrol has witnessed a gradual adaptation of German to Italian political practice. The centralization of German party politics, for example, has weakened. From the late 1940's to the mid-1960's various minor parties were founded both to the SVP's right and left; they failed with great regularity.[98] But since the mid-1960's, a number of these splinter parties have proven their staying power. By the early 1970's three minor political parties existed which competed with the SVP for the German-speaking vote.[99] The trend toward decentralization is reflected also in the internal political conflicts and shifts in ideological orientation which the SVP ex-

98. Rössl; Gatterer, pp. 869–870, 892, 1265–1266, 1348.
99. Hans Michael Roithner, "Innere Auseinandersetzungen in der SVP und Bildung neuer Parteien," unpublished paper (Vienna: Institut für Zeitgeschichte, 1972).

perienced in the 1960's. In the face of this shift from political monism to incipient political pluralism, the SVP has exhibited an electoral staying power typical of Italian politics. In South Tyrol the total proportion of votes cast for the SVP in the national elections of 1953 and 1972 declined from 59.9 to 58.9 percent, while the SVP's average vote in South Tyrol's communes increased from 78.8 to 80.9 percent.[100] Finally, the agreement of 1969 may encourage the spread of a system of party-directed mass patronage in South Tyrol which Luigi Graziano regards as typical of Italian politics in the 1960's.[101] Since Italy's system of clientelistic politics is distinguished by the instrumental support it generates and by a great capacity to diffuse conflict, the process of adaptation of German to Italian political practice now underway in South Tyrol has contributed to the attenuation of ethnic political conflict.

Ethnic political conflict in South Tyrol has been shaped by two types of forces, one social, the other political. Demographic, social, and economic changes make intelligible the demise of ethnic political conflict. The improved ethnic strength of German speakers, the stabilization of migration flows, and the growth of industrial and service employment in the countryside have led to an adaptation of the province's rural way of life which has proven conducive to the attenuation of ethnic political conflict. But these nonpolitical forces do not explain the turning points in the process of escalation and de-escalation of ethnic political conflict. Changes in Austrian and Italian politics in the early 1960's were critical for reversing what since the mid-1950's had been a process of escalation. The impact of these political forces operating at the international and national levels required, furthermore, a change in the province's politics. Without the adaptation of German to Italian political practice, which was observable in South Tyrol's politics in the 1960's, the German speakers would have continued to emphasize the importance of the ethnic question.

One central conclusion can be drawn from the foregoing: ethnic political conflict in South Tyrol has been shaped by both social and political fators. Sociological analysis is helpful in determining the trend of the

100. Individual-level data for 1953 are given in Alcock, p. 493; 1972 election returns are reported in a letter from the president of the provincial cabinet sent to me on 17 July 1974. Procedures for calculating election data by commune are explained in note 12 above.

101. Graziano, ''Clientelism and the Political System.''

conflict; political analysis is indispensable to an understanding of timing. An analysis of only one or the other factor fails not only to do justice to the evidence of this particular case but to the complexity of contemporary ethnic politics throughout Europe.

13

Does the Consociational Theory Really Hold for Switzerland? *

JÜRG STEINER and JEFFREY OBLER

Recently, Brian Barry offered a useful critical discussion of the con-sociational democracy school.[1] This school was initiated, independently, by Arend Lijphart and Gerhard Lehmbruch to explain why such socially segmented societies as the Netherlands, Austria, Switzerland, and Belgium have remained politically stable.[2] Barry argues that the propo-nents of this school have used the key concepts of "accommodation" and "consociational democracy" in confusing, misleading ways. For Barry, accommodation (or its more obscure synonym, consociationalism) is a descriptive term meaning agreement or settlement. Political accommo-dation means the capacity of political actors to settle their differences in an amicable fashion. But Lijphart, so Barry charges, uses political ac-commodation and consociational democracy as theory-laden terms: as used by Lijphart, consociational democracy is not a concept but a theory which encompasses a wide range of complex, related propositions. In its simplest terms, the theory Lijphart implies when he uses the term con-sociational democracy can be summarized along the following lines: in a consociational democracy there are several self-contained, internally co-hesive, and socially isolated blocs which mirror social class and religious, linguistic, and/or ethnic differences; these blocs are led by a small group of leaders who command the loyalty of their followers and who are willing and able to resolve conflicts among the blocs in a peaceful fashion

* Financial support for this project came from the Swiss National Science Foundation.

1. Brian Barry, "Political Accommodation and Consociational Democracy," *British Journal of Political Science,* 5 (October 1975): 477–505.

2. Arend Lijphart, "Consociational Democracy," *World Politics,* 21 (January 1969): 207–225; and Gerhard Lehmbruch, "A Non-Competitive Pattern of Conflict Management in Liberal Democracies: The Case of Switzerland, Austria and Lebanon," in *Consociational Democracy: Political Accommodation in Segmented Societies,* ed. Kenneth McRae (Toronto: McClelland and Stewart, 1974), pp. 90–97.

by employing various consociational decision-making devices; this accommodation among the elites accounts for the low levels of hostility among the blocs and for the stability of the political system. As Barry understands the way Lijphart employs the term, a system can be considered a consociational democracy only if it conforms to all of the above cited attributes; and, by definition, any "consociational democracy is necessarily stable and successful in mediating conflicts." [3] We believe that Barry's complaint is justified; the term consociational democracy is used interchangeably and confusingly as both a descriptive term (describing the form of decision making) and a theoretical term (theorizing why certain kinds of political systems are stable). In this essay consociational *decision making* refers to the descriptive meaning of the term, while consociational *theory* refers to the theoretical meaning.

Barry raises some questions regarding the application of consociationalism, in both its descriptive and theoretical senses, to Switzerland. [4] He doubts that decision making in Switzerland is "preponderantly" consociational, and he argues further that the consociational theory cannot account for the political stability of Switzerland. [5] We agree partly, but not fully, with Barry's assessment of the Swiss case. The first part of this essay deals with consociationalism in the descriptive sense; the second part treats it in the theoretical sense.

Consociationalism in a Descriptive Sense

Although Switzerland is one of the smallest of the European democracies, it is one of the most socially diverse societies in Europe. The Swiss have language differences: about 75 percent speak German; 20 percent, French; about 4 percent, Italian; and 1 percent, Romansch. [6] The Swiss are split along religious lines: the population is about equally divided between Protestants and Catholics. Finally, the Swiss are divided by socioeconomic differences similar to those of other highly complex, industrialized societies. Linguistic, religious, and socioeconomic cleavages crosscut one another to create a complex set of subcultures. Yet, as has been noted so often, Switzerland is one of the most stable polities of Europe, and hostilities among these subcultures have been most often

---

3. Barry, p. 480.

4. In his own words, Barry's analysis of Switzerland is "based mainly" on Jürg Steiner, *Amicable Agreement versus Majority Rule: Conflict Resolution in Switzerland* (Chapel Hill: University of North Carolina Press, 1974).

5. Barry, p. 488.   6. This breakdown excludes foreigners.

minimal. This stability, which will be examined more carefully in the second part of the essay, has been attributed to the willingness of Swiss political leaders to accommodate, or, in other words, to the existence of consociational decision making. But Barry has questioned whether the Swiss decision-making process is preponderantly consociational. In this section this point is considered.

The most outstanding and incontestable sign of elite accommodation is the composition of the collegial Swiss executive, the Federal Council, which is elected for the full legislative period of four years without possibilities of a vote of nonconfidence. The Federal Council includes members of the four major political parties; the Christian Democrats, the Free Democrats, and the Social Democrats each have two representatives on the council, and the Swiss People's party has one representative. This allocation of positions on the council is roughly proportional to the parties' share of the popular vote. Given the size of the Federal Council, no other party is entitled to a seat based on its share of the popular vote. The practice of having all or most major parties represented in the council has a long tradition in Swiss political history. The last step was taken in 1959 when the Social Democrats were accorded a proportionate share of seats. Efforts are also taken to have the ''appropriate'' mix of linguistic, religious, and cantonal representatives. If one of the three largest parties, for example, has already nominated a French-speaking candidate, its second candidate must almost necessarily be German-speaking. A balanced distribution of linguistic, religious, and cantonal affiliations is sought not only within each party but also for the Federal Council as a whole. Hence, in the allocation of positions on the Federal Council efforts are made to include individuals who represent not only the largest parties but also the various subcultures in Swiss society.[7]

This spirit of accommodation mirrored in the distribution of seats on the Federal Council may spill over into the formulation of public policy. Indeed, numerous studies of Swiss decision making underline the willingness of Swiss political leaders to compromise in order to avoid conflict. Paolo Urio's study of the so-called Mirage affair is especially useful, for it shows how consociationalism can succeed even when an issue fosters considerable conflict.[8] Urio relates how the federal government, in

7. For a good description of the elections of the Federal Council, see Erich Gruner, *Die Parteien in der Schweiz* (Berne: Francke, 1969).
8. Paolo Urio, *L'affaire des Mirages: Décision administrative et contrôle parlementaire* (Geneva: Editions médecine et hygiène, 1974).

preparing to purchase one hundred French Mirage fighters, made several mistakes which inflated originally anticipated costs. The bungling nurtured suspicion; there were even complaints that the Parliament had not always been told the truth. Opposition to the proposed purchase was vigorous. At one point tensions became so great that the Social Democrats demanded the resignation of the Free Democratic federal councilor responsible for national defense. Despite these difficulties, the Swiss political leaders managed to come up with a solution whereby fifty-seven of the proposed one hundred fighters were purchased. Accepted almost unanimously by Parliament, this solution represented a compromise between those who insisted on the purchase of one hundred planes and those who wanted to renounce the whole deal. Although elite accommodation prevailed, the compromise ironically meant that the Swiss had to pay more for each of the planes bought from France.

But such compromises are common also among political systems that are not normally considered consociational. Moreover, there are several features of the Swiss decision-making process that do not conform to the consociational model of decision making. First, the Swiss parties that are partners in the Federal Council do not formally agree to support an articulated set of policies. Until 1967, policy issues were never formally discussed by the Swiss coalition partners. For the legislative period 1967–71, the Federal Council, for the first time, formulated a paper containing "guidelines" for governmental activities. These guidelines were not nearly as formal as platforms developed in other political settings. They were negotiated not by the government parties, but rather by the federal councilors after they had been elected for a four-year term. The guidelines were not binding: after four years the legislature discussed a report issued by the Federal Council on the fulfillment of the guidelines; but the legislature had no sanctions to indicate their satisfaction with the report. After the 1971 election, the government parties themselves agreed on a set of policies to be implemented in the coming session; but these policies were formulated in such a general and vague way that their actual significance was minimal. After the 1975 election, the government parties gave up the idea of writing an agreement on policy goals. The Federal Council, however, again formulated guidelines for its governmental activities. The point here is that no specially articulated consensus on Swiss public policy exists among the major national political parties. Any agreement that emerges takes place on a rather ad hoc basis.

Second, while there is agreement concerning the party distribution in

the Federal Council, there is no agreement among the major parties concerning the particular individuals who should be elected to the Federal
Council. The candidates are presented to the Federal Assembly (both
houses of Parliament meeting in a joint session) by the individual parties
and not by the government coalition as a whole. There have been quite a
few cases when the candidate supported by a particular party was *not*
elected by the Federal Assembly. This usually happens because the party
nominates a candidate from one of its extreme factions and, therefore, the
other parties do not consider the nominee acceptable. In 1959, for example, the Social Democrats nominated Walther Bringolf, fully aware
that his communist past might present problems. Indeed, Bringolf did not
get the absolute majority of the votes in the Federal Assembly. The other
parties proceeded to elect Hanspeter Tschudi, a more acceptable Social
Democrat.

Third, just as the Swiss political leaders avoid conflict through compromise, there are instances when compromises are not reached and decisions either are made through nonconsociational means or are not made at
all. Disagreement among Swiss political leaders is not uncommon. Since
the deliberations and votes in the Federal Council are secret it is not possible to ascertain the degree of consensus among the councilors. But parliamentary sessions are open, and therefore the disagreement within and
among parties as well as the conflicts between Parliament and the Federal
Council are visible. One example of conflict between the Federal Council
and Parliament, which took place in the winter of 1966–67, is described
by Peter Gilg.[9] The federation was confronted with the delicate task of
bringing its financial affairs back into balance. In the Federal Council a
compromise was reached: the tax on stock dividends would be retained,
and in return for this a 10 percent increase in income and sales taxes was
scheduled. In the parliamentary deliberations a number of members of the
three bourgeois government parties opposed the stock dividend tax; consequently it was abolished despite the recommendation of the Federal
Council. As a countermove, the Social Democrats opposed the increase
in income and sales taxes, which led to the fall of that part of the government compromise, too. Such independent actions of the Parliament are
not uncommon in Switzerland.

Fourth, the existence of a referendum procedure also undermines the

9. Peter Gilg, "Parteien und eidgenoessische Finanzpolitik," *Schweizerisches Jahrbuch für Politische Wissenschaft,* 9 (1969): 41–74.

consociational character of the decision-making process. Many key policy issues in Switzerland are decided through the referendum; and by its very character, the referendum is an institution that permits a majority to impose its solution on the minority. The referendum is essentially a process of mass and not elite decision making; and the consociational theory is explicitly concerned with elite and not mass decision making. Yet it is also true that the referendum is important for the resolution of conflicts among the government parties; if no solution can be found in the Federal Council or in Parliament, the conflict is often settled through the referendum. Over the question of health insurance, for example, the Social Democrats were so far apart from the other coalition parties that no solution within the government was feasible. Hence, the issue was resolved by the referendum.

The preceding discussion suggests that since the Swiss decision-making process includes consociational as well as nonconsociational elements, it is not a simple matter to categorize the Swiss system according to the conventional typologies offered by proponents of the consociational school. This leads to consideration of a more subtle and comprehensive typology of decision making. The basis is a recent study undertaken by Jürg Steiner on the decision-making process in the Free Democratic party of the canton Berne. From January 1969 to September 1970, 111 of 119 party meetings held were observed. (These were meetings of the executive committee, of the parliamentary group, of the central committee, and of specialized committees dealing, for example, with educational questions.) During these 111 meetings, open disagreement among the participants was articulated 466 times. These 466 conflicts were taken as units of analysis. It was then asked in how many cases conflicts were regulated by either majority rule or consociationalism.

At first, the study seemed to strongly support the commonly accepted notion that Switzerland is, in a descriptive sense, a consociational democracy. Only 12 percent of the conflicts were regulated by the majority principle. Surprisingly, however, there were also relatively few cases that corresponded to consociationalism, defined as a situation in which all participants who have expressed an opinion finally agree on a common solution. This agreement may be expressed in a formal vote, orally, or just in a gesture.[10] Thus, consociationalism does not necessitate the consent of all participants, but only of those who have expressed an opinion. Even

10. Another expression used for consociational decision making is amicable agreement.

applying this relatively broad definition, only 21 percent of all the decisions could be classified as consociational.

What about the remaining 67 percent of the cases? Thirty percent were relatively easy to classify as nondecisions: at the end of the discussion no decision had been made. In one-quarter of these cases the president of the meeting postponed the decision explicitly in his summary. Much more often—in three-quarters of the cases—the discussion passed to the following agenda without any final action; thus, the decision was implicitly postponed. Should the nondecisions be considered consociational? There was certainly an explicit, or at least an implicit, agreement that no decision should be made. But this agreement was limited to a matter of procedure and not to the substance of the issue. The consociational literature is vague as to whether nondecisions should be considered consociational. Here they are treated as a special category.

Thirty-seven percent of the cases to be classified—those that were not considered decisions by majority rule, consociational decisions, or nondecisions—at first appeared to constitute a nonclassifiable, residual category. But it appears now that these cases can be subsumed in a meaningful way under the coined phrase ''decisions by interpretation.'' These decisions are characterized by the fact that one or a few of the participants interpret the essence of the discussion, and that this interpretation is tacitly accepted by the other participants. Such an interpretation can be made by the president of the meeting in his final summary or by the secretary in the minutes of the meeting. A decision by interpretation can also be made in such a way that a few key actors interpret tacitly what the decision of the group is and then direct the discussion so that the decision is implicitly made. An example taken from the parliamentary group will serve to illustrate decisions by interpretation:

Of thirty-nine members of the group, thirty-two participated at this particular meeting. Member A proposed that in the future the important parts of discussions in German be translated into French. At that time 25 percent of the parliamentary group were French-speaking; the other members were German-speaking. Hitherto, each member had spoken in his native language, the German-speaking members in a special Bernese dialect. Member B opposed the proposal of A as too cumbersome and put forward the alternative that the Bernese dialect be replaced by High German. Three more participants responded, all supporting A. At that point the president summarized and interpreted the essence of the discussion in the sense that the proposal of A had won. Member B remained silent, neither supporting A nor asking for a vote of the whole group. If B had supported A, the decision clearly would have been consociational; had he asked for a vote, it obviously would have been majority rule. But B chose neither of these two alternatives, tacitly accepting the interpretation of the president.

No claim is made, of course, that the decision making in the Free Democratic party of the canton Berne is representative of all Swiss parties, or even of Switzerland as a whole. The study nevertheless demonstrates the difficulties of classifying political decision making as either majoritarian or consociational. It has already been argued that to locate nondecisions on a continuum from majoritarian to consociational is difficult, if not impossible. The difficulties are even greater in locating decisions by interpretation on such a continuum. One may be tempted to classify these decisions as tacit consociational, since no opposition is made when the essence of the discussion is interpreted. But the tacit acceptance of an interpretation does not necessarily mean the vanishing of the opposition. In the Free Democratic party, in such situations, the opposition often surfaced again at a later meeting. Are decisions by interpretation, then, tacit majoritarian decisions in the sense that the minority accepts its defeat without a formal vote? There are two objections against such a classification. First, it is often unclear who holds the numerical majority, since all participants rarely speak up. Second, the tacit acceptance of an interpretation may in many cases mean that the opposition has given up; but there may be reasons why the consent is not openly expressed.

The proposal here is to treat majoritarian decisions, consociational decisions, nondecisions, and decisions by interpretation as four different categories which cannot be located on a single continuum. Given these four categories, Switzerland could hardly be characterized as a consociational democracy. But it probably would not be a majoritarian democracy either.[11] What then? Evidently a more detailed typology containing more than one dimension should be developed. This necessitates, of course, a modification of the consociational theory. It is no longer sufficient to formulate the theory in terms of more or less consociationalism or majoritarianism.

---

11. This judgment is based on an analysis of the published case studies of decision making in Switzerland; see Steiner, *Amicable Agreement*.

Consociationalism in a Theoretical Sense

The first part of this essay has not answered clearly the question to what extent Switzerland is a consociational democracy in a descriptive sense. The problems of classifying decision making as either consociational or majoritarian have been revealed, and the conclusion has been drawn that a more subtle and comprehensive typology is needed. Only if consociational decisions are conceptualized in a broad way as simply the residual category of majoritarian decisions, can Switzerland probably be described as preponderantly consociational. Even if such a broad definition is assumed, the theoretical question still remains whether consociational decision making is indeed the *cause* of the low hostility among Swiss subcultures. For the sake of theoretical exploration it is *assumed* in this section that Swiss decision-making practices are preponderantly consociational. To assess the relevance of the consociational theory to the Swiss case, first the extent of subcultural segmentation must be considered; second, the level of hostilities among the subcultures; and, third, the role that the decision-making pattern might have on the degree of hostilities.

Subcultural Segmentation

If Switzerland were relatively homogeneous, the consociational theory would not be applicable because the problem that it seeks to explain would not exist. The question of whether Switzerland is highly segmented subculturally may appear rhetorical, for the Swiss speak four different languages and practice two major religions. Such diversity should qualify Switzerland a priori for membership in the theoretical universe with which the consociational theory is concerned. But the matter is not so simple; indeed, there are authors, such as Raimund Germann, who claim that Switzerland has become a relatively homogeneous country.[12]

It is important to differentiate conceptually between cultural diversity and subcultural segmentation. Cultural diversity means simply that the members of a political system differ with regard to cultural attributes, such as language and religion. The people sharing the same cultural attribute may or may not develop a sense of identity that distinguishes them from other members of the system. Here subcultural segmentation is referred to only if such feelings of self-identification exist. Possible indica-

---

12. Raimund Germann, *Politische Innovation und Verfassungreform: Ein Beitrag zur schweizerischen Diskussion über die Totalrevision der Bundesverfassung* (Berne: Verlag Paul Haupt, 1975).

tors are responses to attitudinal survey questions, frequency of interactions among the members of a subculture, and organizational ties within a subculture. The concept of cultural diversity often is not carefully distinguished from the concept of subcultural segmentation; we agree with Hans Daalder who critically notes that "demographic variables are often assumed to be of attitudinal importance, with little investigation of the degree to which this is actually true." [13] Switzerland has, of course, a strong cultural diversity with regard to languages and religions. The formula of Douglas W. Rae and Michael Taylor could be used to compute the degree of cultural diversity in an elegant and formal way.[14] But this is not the point in the present context. In connection with the consociational theory, it is not the level of cultural diversity, but the level of subcultural segmentation that is of interest. Here the data situation is much more difficult.

The Department of Political Science at the University of Geneva has recently conducted the first broad, systematic analysis of Swiss cleavages, based on a national survey sample of the Swiss electorate in 1972.[15] These data reveal interesting political differences among the groups formed by Swiss linguistic, religious, and class cleavages. For example, 30 percent of the French-speaking Swiss and 16 percent of the German-speaking Swiss consider themselves primarily members of their linguistic group rather than members of their canton or nation. Although there are no linguistic parties, language differences, as demonstrated by Henry H. Kerr, have a bearing on voters' preferences; controlling for religion and class, he found that French-speaking Swiss are more sympathetic to the parties of the left than are German-speaking Swiss.[16]

The survey did not establish the degree to which the Swiss consider themselves members of their religious group. But clear differences in partisan choice were revealed; practicing Catholics tend to support the Christian Democrats, while nonpracticing Catholics and Protestants are more

13. Hans Daalder, "The Consociational Democracy Theme," *World Politics,* 26 (July 1974): 615.

14. Douglas W. Rae and Michael Taylor, *The Analysis of Political Cleavages* (New Haven: Yale University Press, 1970).

15. So far the following works have been published: Henry H. Kerr, Jr., *Switzerland: Social Cleavages and Partisan Conflict,* Sage Professional Paper in Contemporary Political Sociology, vol. 1 (Beverly Hills, Calif., 1974); Ronald Inglehart and Dusan Sidjanski, "Dimension gauche-droite chez les dirigeants et électeurs suisses," *Revue Française de Science Politique,* 24 (October 1974): 994–1025; Dusan Sidjanski et al., *Les suisses et la politique* (Berne: Lang, 1975).

16. *Switzerland.*

likely to vote for the other major parties—the Free Democrats, the Social Democrats, and the Swiss People's party. A link between social class and partisan choice was also established; not surprisingly manual workers vote most often for the Social Democratic party.

The three cleavages crosscut one another. Both the relative importance of the cleavages as well as their cross-cutting structure vary considerably from one canton to another. For many issues the cleavages are politically salient at the cantonal rather than at the national level. For example, in Fribourg, a predominantly Catholic canton, Protestants form a cohesive subculture with their own interests, identities, and organizational ties. They take an active part in cantonal politics especially on the question of the religious orientation of the schools. In the national arena, however, many of the Protestant Fribourgeois identify more as members of their canton than as members of their religious group because religious issues are not particularly salient in Swiss national politics. There are many impressionistic studies of Swiss subcultures.[17] But as yet nobody has undertaken a systematic study to determine the precise number and relative strengths of the subcultures at the cantonal and national levels. For now it can only be stated that the Swiss subcultural structure is extremely complex; a great number of actors engage in subcultural confrontation in the cantonal and national arenas.

The Geneva survey also offers age-cohort data which allow an assessment of how groups' identities and partisan choices have varied over time. These data suggest that the ties between the individual and his linguistic and religious group may have declined; this, in turn, may indicate a more general decline in the degree of subcultural segmentation. Among younger, and especially Catholic, voters, religion and religiosity are less salient considerations in their party preferences. Language differences, which were particularly important for the generation that reached political maturity during World War I, are likewise a less prominent determinant of political choice. The impact of class differences, on the other hand, has remained fairly constant over several generations. The survey also revealed that the sense of national identity among the Swiss has become more prevalent. Among French speakers, for example, only 31 percent of the oldest age cohort, but 55 percent of the youngest, think of themselves primarily as Swiss.

17. For an older but still valuable source, see Hermann Weilenmann, *Pax Helvetica oder die Demokratie der kleinen Gruppen* (Erlenbach Rentsch Verlag, 1951).

Is Switzerland still highly segmented subculturally or has it become a relatively homogeneous country? There is no easy answer because no yardsticks exist; there is no simple formula for computing subcultural segmentation similar to the one Rae and Taylor have developed for cultural diversity. The reason for this lack of a commonly accepted yardstick is, of course, that it is much more difficult to measure the level of subcultural segmentation than the level of cultural diversity. If one wanted to determine, for example, whether subcultural segmentation was greater among Dutch Catholics than among Swiss Catholics, simple attitudinal survey questions would not be sufficient; one also would have to consider the interaction patterns and the organizational links within the two subcultures. It would be even more difficult to compare, for example, the Austrian *Lager* with the Swiss language groups, since the social basis of the subcultures would be different.

In view of these difficult problems of measurement, more precision than is actually possible cannot be expected. The best solution in this situation seems to be a well-informed expert judgment, along the lines of Val Lorwin's elegant analysis.[18] This method raises, of course, problems of reliability, but it may better fulfill the criterion of validity. Without pretense of too much precision, the conclusion here is that among the European democracies Switzerland ranks neither with the very homogeneous nor with the very segmented systems. Thus, Switzerland seems a marginal case for the application of the consociational theory; it is certainly not a hard test for the theory.

Hostility

The dependent variable of the consociational theory is the level of hostility among the various subcultures. Based on the data of the *World Handbook of Political and Social Indicators,* hostility is very low in Switzerland by international comparison: between 1948 and 1967, domestic violence caused no deaths in Switzerland; only fifteen other nations had such an impressive record.[19] Further, since 1967 no deaths have occurred in Switzerland for political reasons. According to the *World Handbook* there were seven armed attacks and four riots in Switzerland

18. Val R. Lorwin, "Segmented Pluralism: Ideological Cleavages and Political Cohesion in the Smaller European Democracies," *Comparative Politics,* 3 (January 1971); 141–175.

19. Charles Lewis Taylor and Michael C. Hudson, *World Handbook of Political and Social Indicators,* 2d ed. (New Haven: Yale University Press, 1972).

from 1948 to 1967, figures which are also very low by international comparison.

The absence of subcultural hostility has been taken so much for granted that no one has bothered to conduct an in-depth study of the subject. The *Année Politique Suisse,* which, among other things, provides annual summaries of linguistic and religious affairs, has reported sporadic hostilities; but the overall impression one draws from this source is that subcultural peace prevails. [20]

In this context it is important to note that a frequent precondition of hostility, *relative deprivation,* is remarkably absent among Swiss language groups. Harold Glass has demonstrated that the minority language groups do not feel more deprived than the German-speaking Swiss. [21] This is an interesting finding because one may expect that the stronger leftist tendencies in the French-speaking area would indicate a higher sense of deprivation.

The Jura problem represents the most notable exception to Swiss tranquility, and it has precipitated most of the limited violence that has ruffled the Swiss over the past decades. [22] The Berne canton comprises a German-speaking majority and a predominantly French-speaking minority in the Jura districts. [23] The French-speaking minority is further divided between the predominantly Catholic Jura districts to the north and the predominantly Protestant Jura districts to the south; the German-speaking part of the canton is overwhelmingly Protestant. Since the late 1940's, the French-speaking Catholics in particular have actively sought greater autonomy and even independence from the Berne canton as a means of freeing themselves from what they consider the political and economic hegemony of the German-speaking majority. To attract attention to their cause, the Jura separatists have occasionally resorted to violence and sabotage. Though modest in contrast to subcultural strife in the United States or Northern Ireland, this violence has been frightening for the Swiss, who are so accustomed to order and civility.

The approach here so far has been to consider only manifest hostility.

20. *Année Politique Suisse,* University of Berne Publications in the History and Sociology of Swiss Politics (Berne, 1965–1976).

21. Harold E. Glass, "Subcultural Segmentation and Consensual Politics: The Swiss Experience" (Ph.D. diss., University of North Carolina at Chapel Hill, 1975).

22. For a good analysis of the Jura question see, Hans Peter Henecka, *Die jurassischen Separatisten: Eine Studie zur Soziologie des ethnischen Konflikts und der sozialen Bewegung* (Meisenheim am Glan: Verlag Anton Hain, 1972).

23. At present the French-speaking minority is about 15 percent of the canton.

There is, of course, also the structural approach. In recent lectures at the University of Zurich, Johan Galtung argued that Switzerland has a high level of structural hostility; by this he meant a great degree of social inequality.[24] Galtung has certainly referred to an important problem, but we prefer to distinguish conceptually between hostility and social inequality. This does not indicate disinterest in the problem of social inequality. On the contrary, in the concluding section it is argued that consociational decision making may contribute to inequalities; this tendency may in the long run also increase the level of manifest hostility. Separating and not blurring these various concepts should help with the clarity of the analysis.

Causal Relationships

Assuming that Switzerland is sufficiently segmented subculturally for the consociational theory to apply, that its decision making can be broadly characterized as consociational, and that structural hostility is excluded so that Switzerland appears to be a relatively peaceful country, is the consociational theory necessarily supported? The answer seems to be no. To be sure, the consociational theory would give a plausible explanation for the Swiss situation but certainly not the only plausible one. One could also argue that consociational decision making is not the cause but the consequence of a low level of hostility. According to this interpretation consociational decision making would be a simple epiphenomenon. One would be left with the task of looking for other causes of the low hostility. There are some that are immediately apparent. The high economic development of Switzerland may satisfy the demands of the various subcultures to such an extent that no strong feelings of relative deprivation have arisen. It may also be important that the three major languages have about the same international prestige. This is, for example, not the case in Belgium, where the uneven international pretige of the two major languages is said to have contributed to many of the current problems.[25] A third cause for the low hostility in Switzerland may be that the load on the central system is not very heavy. Because of the federal structure, many of the tricky problems faced by a subcultural country are dealt with primarily at the cantonal and even at the local level. Neutrality,

24. Summer semester, 1971.
25. Jeffrey Obler, Jürg Steiner, and Guido Dierickxs, "Decision-making in Smaller Democracies: The 'Consociational' Burden," Sage Professional Paper in Comparative Politics (Beverly Hills, Calif., 1977).

too, removes many problems from the central political arena. There are, therefore, other plausible explanations besides consociational decision making for the low level of hostility in Switzerland. This does not, of course, exclude consociational decision making as an explanatory factor. But it indicates that the simultaneous appearance of consociational decision making and a low level of hostility does not necessarily mean that the latter is a consequence of the former.

The problem of causality may be further elucidated if a closer look is taken at the hostility that occurred in connection with the Jura problem. Its evolution is compatible with the classical formulation of the consociational theory. The Bernese cantonal government has tried for years to solve the problem in a consociational way. For example, it invited the separatists to participate in an expert committee. The hope was that this committee would find a solution acceptable to all participants. But the separatists again and again rejected such invitations. When the consociational method failed, the Bernese government tried to use the majority principle to find a solution. A constitutional amendment in March 1970 opened the way for a whole series of referenda. In the first referendum, in June 1974, a slight majority of the Jura population decided to form their own canton. But under the constitutional amendment, the districts that opted against a canton Jura were given the opportunity to indicate in a second referendum whether they wanted to stay with the canton Berne. In March 1975, the southern Protestant districts decided to remain with the canton Berne. In September 1975, some border communities decided in still another referendum whether they wanted to change. In a last step a national referendum will have to decide whether Article 2 of the federal Constitution, which enumerates the cantons, shall be changed by adding the canton Jura.

This majoritarian procedure with a whole series of referenda has not brought the Jura problem closer to a solution. Hostility is even on the increase; there is a strong possibility that the solution that has emerged from the referenda will be further contested, for many separatists say openly that they will never give up their claim to the southern districts.

From a theoretical view one may argue that the development of the Jura problem fits the consociational theory. That the leaders on both sides have not firmly chosen a consociational strategy could explain why the hostility has not decreased. But there is also another perspective: perhaps a consociational strategy has not been possible because hostility is too high. There are ways to explain the high hostility without referring to the lack of consociational decision making. It may be important that the northern Jura, where the separatists have their stronghold, is in several ways in a minority position within the canton Berne. Unlike the southern Jura, the northern Jura is clearly in a minority position not only linguistically but also religiously. Futhermore, the northern Jura is economically among the weakest regions of the canton. This minority position could explain why feelings of relative deprivation and even hostility have developed in the northern Jura.

The general discussion of the possible causal relation between consociational decision making and the level of hostility is further complicated because some observers claim that in the long run consociational decision making may contribute to malaise and even hostility. This argument is most forcefully put forward by Raimund Germann.[26] According to his view, consociational decision making is very damaging to the innovative capacity of a political system, since the process is very slow and the most conservative group always has a veto power. Germann also complains that elite cooperation prohibits the citizens from casting instrumental votes, for they are unable to replace one set of leaders with another. The lack of innovation and meaningful political participation, according to Germann, causes frustrations on the part of the citizens. These frustrations may ultimately lead to the outbreak of violence. Germann argues that if Switzerland would shift to a two-party system, modeled after the Anglo-Saxon pattern with periodic changes in power, its innovative capacity would be bolstered, and Swiss citizens could play a more efficacious political role. To foster the development of a two-party system organized around class divisions, he proposes a new electoral system, a full time parliament, and restrictions on the use of referenda. Germann does not fear that the introduction of a competitive, majoritarian system would jeopardize subcultural concord, since, in his view, the growing homogeneity of Swiss culture precludes the danger that greater political competition would turn one subculture against another.

There are some empirical data that can be used in support of Germann's thesis. In a recent national survey Ronald Inglehart and Dusan Sidjanski have found diffuse frustrations among the Swiss population.[27] These frustrations were also expressed in some recent referenda in which proposals supported by all major parties were defeated or only barely accepted. Max Imboden, too, noticed growing frustrations; as early as 1964

---

26. *Politische Innovation.*   27. "Dimension gauche-droite."

he spoke of a "Helvetian Malaise," an expression that has been widely used since then.[28] An obvious argument against linking this "Malaise" with consociational decision making is that in countries without consociationalism, such as France and Italy, frustrations may be even greater. In such comparisons, however, many variables are not held constant. Thus, it may be that the level of frustration in France and in Italy might be far greater if these countries were to practice consociational decision making.

The strongest support for Germann's thesis comes from Austria.[29] During the time of the great Conservative-Socialist coalition from 1945 until 1966, complaints increased that the system was not innovative enough and that the citizens did not have sufficient means for effective political participation. In Austria, too, there was more and more talk of a developing malaise. Since the dissolution of the coalition in 1966 and the change to one-party governments, the level of frustration seems to have decreased.

Germann's thesis, however, is less supported by recent developments in the Netherlands. Like the Austrians, the Dutch changed in the middle of the 1960's from a consociational to a more competitive system. Before this change there were also many complaints about the lack of innovation and means for effective political participation. But after the change, frustrations did not decrease; on the contrary, they increased.

Conclusions

In the title of this essay the question is posed whether the consociational theory really holds for Switzerland. The theory is certainly not clearly rejected. It appears to be a plausible explanation for the relatively low hostility in Switzerland. But several reservations are in order.

1. The theory needs further conceptual clarification. The theoretical universe to which the theory is supposed to be applicable must be clarified. What is meant exactly by strong subcultural segmentation? Also, the two key variables of the theory, consociational decision making and hostility, need to be more clearly defined in the literature.

2. In the relation between consociational decision making and hostility, the latter should not be treated as a dependent variable only. It seems likely that the two variables are in a feedback process: the more consocia-

28. Max Imboden, *Helvetisches Malaise* (Zurich: EVZ Verlag, 1964).
29. See Obler, Steiner, and Dierickxs.

tional decision making prevails, the lower the level of hostility; and the lower the level of hostility, the more consociational decision making prevails. It is sometimes assumed that this feedback process can be initiated if only the political leaders are willing to do it. But there may be situations in which hostility at the mass level is too high for the leaders to make such a move. This may be the case in the Jura, and even more so in the Austrian First Republic, in Cypus, and in Northern Ireland. We agree with Hans Daalder that in such cases of high hostility an "intelligent choice by particular elites at a critical juncture of a nation's history" is not a sufficient condition for the implementation of consociational decision making.[30] Hostility must first be reduced through other means. As the Austrian experience in 1945 suggests, such means may be dramatic changes in the international system. Thus, consociational decision making is not a solution for a very hostile situation. But if hostility can be decreased through other means, consociational decision making may well contribute to its further decrease.

3. The positive feedback process between more consociational decision making and less hostility may break down in the long run. Consociational decision making seems to have the tendency to reduce the innovative capacity of a political system and render effective political participation difficult at the mass level. These two effects may cause frustrations and, ultimately, even the outbreak of new violence.

4. If a low level of hostility is taken as a value goal, the final conclusion is to recommend that after a certain time the consociational decision-making model be changed into a more competitive one. A decrease in the intensity of subcultural identification, which will probably result from consociational decision making and low hostility, should facilitate a change to a more competitive system. For Switzerland, Raimund Germann may be right that subcultural identification has decreased so much that a change to a more competitive system would not provoke hostilities among the subcultures. But there are other difficulties which are linked to the institutional setting. A multi-party system with low party discipline and a strongly developed referendum would make it difficult for a competitive-majoritarian system to work. Coalition building would be complicated and a governmental coalition, once in office, would not have a secure party basis. Most seriously, a numerically strong opposition would

30. Daalder, p. 618.

always have a good chance to defeat major governmental policies in a referendum.[31] Raimund Germann is well aware of these problems, and he appropriately argues that a change to a competitive system would also necessitate a restriction of the referendum, greater discipline and centralization among the parties, and a replacement of the multiparty system with a two-party system. Germann is realistic enough to see that in terms of practical politics such changes are nearly impossible in the near future. The expert committee in Switzerland that is currently preparing a total revision of the federal Constitution has already explicitly rejected a change to a competitive system. Thus, for the time being Switzerland is "stuck" with the consociational decision-making model.

Overall, we are not too optimistic about the long-range consequences of consociational decision making. The conclusions of this essay are accordingly framed in a more moderate tone than that of Lijphart, who claims that the politics of accommodation "is a normative model that is more appropriate than the pluralistic model for the world's many highly divided societies aspiring to democratic rule." [32] It appears, however, that the competitive model, too, faces severe difficulties, even in countries such as Great Britain. Thus, the consociational decision-making model may in many cases be the lesser of two evils.

31. For further elaboration, see Jürg Steiner, "Coalition Formation in Switzerland" (forthcoming in a volume about coalition formation by Yale University Press).

32. Arend Lijphart, *The Politics of Accommodation: Pluralism and Democracy in the Netherlands,* 2d ed. (Berkeley: University of California Press, 1975), Preface.

14

Some Causes of Political Change in Modern Yugoslavia

SUSAN BRIDGE

As Axis armies retreated from Yugoslav lands in 1945, communist-led guerrillas known as Partizans consolidated power in their wake. Much of the country the guerrillas took charge of had been leveled materially, and the situation in some regions was desperate. Worse, a historically divided population emerged from the confusions of war and the moral complexity of long foreign occupation more bitterly divided along political and ethnic lines than ever before.

The victorious communists declared their intention to include Yugoslavia's several major nationalities in postwar government on an equal footing. They also endorsed broadly democratic values, albeit in language indistinguishable at the time from that of their Soviet mentors. These two principles of governance—ethnically based or "consociational" representation and social democracy—have continued to be central themes in official pronouncements for the past thirty-plus years. The official rhetoric has not been empty: gradual changes in the actual conduct of politics in this period have moved the Yugoslav system significantly closer in practice to these two elusive ideals.[1]

---

1. *Consociationalism* as described by Arend Lijphart and summarized in Milton Esman's introduction to this volume is a political arrangement characterized by principles of representation and of elite behavior that are intended to facilitate conflict management in an ethnically divided society. As used in this essay, consociationalism and democracy are conceptually distinct though not mutually incompatible modes of political decision making. *Democracy* refers to norms of political behavior that permit a general population routinely (and thus typically in an institutionalized fashion) to require political elites to make important policy decisions in accordance with mass preferences. Both consociationalism and democracy are matters of degree, as the terms are used in this essay. A given political system may have some but not all features that conform to the consociational model, and consociational practices may exist by themselves or in combination with other procedures. Similarly, the degree of influence a general population can exercise over elite decision making varies widely. Several authors note that consociationalism by its nature compromises democracy at

Beginning in the early 1970's, however, the long-term trend toward consociational democracy was in some respects reversed. In 1971, communists divided publicly over what the relationship of the Croatian republic to the Yugoslav federation should be. In 1972, alleged nationalists in several republics were expelled from the Party (used here to refer to the Communist party, renamed the League of Communists in 1953). Soon afterward there followed a campaign against left liberals ("anarcho-liberals") within the Party, and Yugoslav politics has taken on a more authoritarian aspect ever since. The turmoil had not abated by late 1976, but the conflict had shifted throughout Yugoslavia to differences over a broad range of economic and political matters. Several trials of pro-Soviet communists ("cominformists") have been held recently, and more seem likely.

The Yugoslav case is of singular interest to students of politics in ethnically divided societies. Viewed from the perspective of the existing literature, recent events are not easy to explain. For two decades before the 1971 crisis, Yugoslav politics had been conducted in a manner that was both increasingly consociational and increasingly democratic. Presumably this evolution should have resulted in a more finely tuned system for aggregating political preferences and for conflict management when those preferences differ greatly.

Why, then, was the long-term trend reversed? And what are the prospects for consociationalism and democracy in Yugoslavia now?

No attempt is made here to relate the past three decades of Yugoslav political history in all its uniqueness and controversial complexity. The intention is to identify and discuss certain aspects of the Yugoslav experience which, it will be argued, are relevant to other times and places. Furthermore, an interest in policy making has led to a decision to concentrate on variables over which political leaders have a significant degree of control: variables that are, in the narrow sense, political.[2]

---

least to some extent. In fact, elites who manage political conflict among ethnic groups according to consociational principles may represent those constituent ethnic groups in a democratic fashion, or they may not. One way of characterizing the Yugoslav dilemma is as a search for a viable mix of democracy and consociationalism.

2. Eric Nordlinger notes that "the mainstream of the recent literature emphasizes attitudinal and socio-economic explanations at the expense of political ones, it is concerned almost entirely with the maintenance of democratic institutions rather than their emergence, and it deals primarily with clearly successful or unsuccessful democratic regimes while paying little attention to those that hang in the balance." Eric A. Nordlinger, *Conflict Regulation in Divided Societies*, Harvard University Center for International Affairs Occasional Paper no. 29 (Cambridge, January 1972), p. 2.

While social scientists have discovered a multitude of important relationships between socioeconomic variables and political outcomes, the socioeconomic characteristics of any polity are relatively intractable. Too often they function as the social scientist's surrogate for the enervating "burden of history," which dooms human beings in the present to unhappy reenactments of the past. Focusing explanation on socioeconomic variables to the near exclusion of politics permits professional observers to conclude that the actors are more helpless than in fact they may be.

In this essay, particular attention is given to the effects over time of three political factors: the *structure* of formal political representation, the *scope* of political institutions in society, and the *sequence* in which democratic procedures and consociational procedures are introduced. None of these three is treated prominently in the literature on consociational democracies or on communist systems. To the extent that they do prove to be important influences on the conduct of politics, this knowledge might be used to insure more desirable outcomes.

An Overview of the Yugoslav Case

Historically, a commitment to socialism has carried with it an instrumental commitment to a political system of broad scope. Since 1946, a large number of Yugoslavia's important social, economic, and cultural choices have been made within the public sector. Furthermore, the network of institutions that can legitimately organize preferences regarding these choices is preemptive: that is, debates are channeled exclusively through governmental assemblies, the Party, and ancillary organizations that operate under the aegis of the Socialist Alliance, which is the Party's popular front.

Because the range of social, economic, and cultural decisions that is mediated through Party and government is so great and because alternative channels for organizing the expressions of preferences are not available, the stakes in Yugoslav politics have been—and continue to be—extraordinarily high. The effects of scope are further amplified by two practices that screen out minority preferences at each level of representation: organization by single-member district in both Party and government, and vestiges of democratic centralism.[3] Constituent groups in the

3. Leninist norms for policy formulation and implementation within a disciplined revolutionary party are referred to, in summary fashion, as democratic centralism. According to these norms, policy is formulated democratically as the result of discussions within all the basic units, or cells, of a given communist party, but once formulated it becomes binding on

Yugoslav political process stand to gain or to lose a good deal more than do their counterparts in Western European and Canadian politics.

But if the scope and the preemptive nature of political institutions help explain some of the intensity of Yugoslav politics, the structure of these institutions has been decisive in determining what "issue packages" are of strategic importance on that country's political agenda today.[4] All the official institutions for the aggregation of political preferences are structured in a nearly identical manner, vertically by geographic unit. Several hundred communes are grouped into six republics, which in turn form the federal government; an intermediate provincial level exists between the commune and the republic in two culturally distinctive parts of Serbia (see Map 4). The communist-led founders of modern Yugoslavia intended this organization of political life within Party and government hierarchies to give major ethnic groups, which cluster geographically, formal political representation as nationalities.

In broad outline, then, Yugoslav politics has been conducted for the past three decades through preemptive, vertically structured institutions whose power to make social choices is great. Within this general framework, there have been three major reorganizations—in 1953, in 1963, and, after three years of heated debate and intense bargaining, again in 1974.

Each of these reorganizations has recorded a new concordat among the politically powerful about who shall get what, when, and how. One scholar's observation of American politics holds for Yugoslav politics as well: "The grand strategy of politics has concerned itself first of all with the structure of institutions. The function of institutions is to channel conflict; institutions do not treat all forms of conflict impartially, just as football rules do not treat all forms of violence with indiscriminate equality."[5] *In Yugoslav politics, the structure of institutions prevents the expression with indiscriminate equality of preferences within the communist-dominated establishment.* Some combinations of preferences are

all members and is strictly imposed by central leadership. In practice, these norms have frequently been tantamount to the suppression of debate in party forums at all stages of policy formulation.

4. The term "issue packages" is from Seymour Martin Lipset and Stein Rokkan, eds., *Party Systems and Voter Alignments: Cross-National Perspectives* (New York: Free Press, 1967).

5. E. E. Schattschneider, *The Semisovereign People: A Realist's View of Democracy in America* (New York: Holt, Rinehart & Winston, 1960), p. 72.

Map 4. Republics and autonomous provinces of Yugoslavia. The Socialist Federal Republic of Yugoslavia has six constituent republics: Bosnia-Hercegovina, Croatia, Macedonia, Montenegro, Serbia, and Slovenia. Serbia includes on its territory two autonomous provinces, Kosovo and the Vojvodina.

more likely than others to become important at the federal level by dint of the way institutional channels work. These patterns—particularly the systematic bias in favor of aggregation by ethnic groups—have been, in part, a deliberate accomplishment; yet clearly not all the consequences were intended.

Party and Government in the Early Postwar Years

In the immediate postwar period, the most important fact of political life was the centralized solidarity of the communist-led Partizan guerrillas and those who had joined them. This horizontal political cleavage dominated all others for many years. Yet in retrospect it seems clear that the major changes in Party composition and the vertical organization along territorial lines of daily politics within both Party and government prepared the way for the resurgence of ethnic politics that shook the Yugoslav system to its very foundations twenty years later.

Beginning in 1946 and spurred by the traumatic break with the Soviets in 1948, the wartime leadership began to transform the Party from a cadre to a mass organization. The Party was enlarged severalfold in all locales by the new recruits.[6] In terms of life experience and political inclinations, the rank and file soon began to resemble the general population far more than did the top leadership. As the Party membership grew and became more diverse, the old conspiratorial norms began to give way to direct public action. By the early fifties, the nature of the bond among Yugoslav communists was already very different than it had been just a few years before, and the ideological gap between Party and society had been narrowed considerably.

The 1946 Constitution legitimized two principles by which the general population was to be represented in government. One resembled that version of traditional parliamentary democracy in which voter opinion is expressed according to place of residence, and the other affirmed the consociational principle: the Federal People's Assembly was composed of a Federal Council elected by citizens voting as Yugoslavs, and a Council of Nationalities, in which citizens were represented as members of a constituent nationality. Legislation had to be passed by both chambers. *Both* kinds of political identity within government, as within the Party, were expressed through vertical, territorially based hierarchies. Thus the first of the two distinctive characteristics of consociationalism, political representation of individuals according to ethnic identity, was deliberately adopted in one house of the Federal People's Assembly. Insofar as ethnic divisions coincided with territorial divisions, the principle of aggregation of preferences by ethnic groups was also reinforced by procedures in the second house and in the Party (see Figure 14.1).

While the former Partizans who held top posts in Party and government were willing to honor nationality distinctions as long as they were peacefully expressed, they, like political theorists in the West, assumed that these ancient political identities would soon be replaced with more modern ones. Yet with the passage of time, the territorially based, vertical

6. Dušan Bilandžić, *Borba za Samoupravni Socijalizam u Jugoslaviji, 1945–1969* (Zagreb: Institut za Historiju Radničkog Pokreta Hrvatska, 1969). Bilandžić's figures indicate that by 1953 about 80 percent of the Party's membership were postwar recruits.

Arrows = strength of democratic inputs
Arrows' slant toward center = prominence of consociational institutions at federal level
Density of shading = relative authority at each level of organization

Federal-level politics

Republican-level politics

Communal-level politics

Figure 14.1. Democratic inputs and consociational institutions in Yugoslav politics, 1946–52. From 1946 to 1952, representation in the Party and the government was territorially based and so tended to be ethnically based; explicitly consociational institutions were fairly prominent at the federal level. Political authority was highly centralized in federal institutions, and democratic inputs from below were relatively unimportant in decision making at each level.

structure of the institutions they had built militated strongly against the very evolution they had hoped for.

Politics under the Constitutional Law of 1953

From the early fifties Marshal Tito and many if not all of his close associates talked and acted as though they expected to accomplish a radical grass-roots democratization of Yugoslav society within their lifetimes. Moreover, during the fifties and the sixties, these leaders committed enormous organizational resources to, and invested considerable psychological energy in, introducing successive institutional arrangements whose net effect *was* democratic. Constitutions and constitutional laws in postwar Yugoslavia have a special meaning in this context. These documents are rather like political programs: they are compromises among the political leadership, endorsing some features of the conduct of politics in the present, rejecting others, and serving as guidelines for intended future political change.

The Constitutional Law of 1953 gave official expression to the expectation that political differences would increasingly divide Yugoslavs along class lines rather than by nationality. Again there were two chambers in the Federal People's Assembly, but now only one-half of one of them was officially elected according to the nationality principle, while the other half was elected by the citizens at large. The second chamber was elected by workers in socially owned enterprises. All three kinds of representation—the voter as ethnic group member, the voter as citizen, and the voter as producer—were grouped by commune and by republic.

Although after 1953 most agriculture was in private hands, the scope of political decision making remained immense in every other sphere of Yugoslavia's modernizing society and burgeoning economy. To ease some of the enormous administrative burdens of planning, the federal government undertook a partial decentralization.[7] In principle, considerable political and economic authority devolved to republics and communes under the 1953 Constitutional Law; and, in fact, over the next ten years republics and communes gradually became more important decision-making and patronage-dispensing centers (see Figure 14.2).

A new role was announced for the enlarged Communist party. The Party—renamed the League of Communists to symbolize this new role— was no longer to influence Yugoslav politics in a conspiratorial manner from behind the scenes. Policy preferences were to be thrashed out among Party members at their meetings. Members were then to work publicly to convince other citizens in open forums—in the legislative branches of government, within trade unions, in neighborhoods, and at places of work—that their recommendations should be accepted. The Party in its new incarnation would not command, but would be obliged to educate and to persuade.

During the fifties this widely advertised new relationship between Party and society was routinely honored in the breach. Despite varying degrees of compliance, the official norms slowly did modify practice. The Party remained enormously influential as a personnel pool from which people were drawn for important jobs. Particularly in the more highly developed areas of the country and at the enterprise level, however, the Party's direct participation in social and economic decision making diminished.

The Party itself began gradually to function as an institutional channel for communicating political preferences up through its hierarchy, as well as for disseminating political preferences down from the top as it tradi-

7. For an analytical summary of economic decentralization, see Nicholas R. Lang, "The Dialectics of Decentralization: Economic Reform and Regional Inequality in Yugoslavia," *World Politics,* 27 (April 1975).

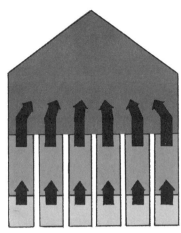

Arrows = strength of democratic inputs
Arrows' slant toward center = prominence
    of consociational institutions at federal
    level
Density of shading = relative authority at
    each level of organization

Federal-level politics

Republican-level politics

Communal-level politics

Figure 14.2. Democratic inputs and consociational institutions in Yugoslav politics, 1953–62. Between 1953 and 1962, representation in the Party and the government continued to be territorially based and so tended to be ethnically based; however, explicitly consociational institutions became less prominent at the federal level. Political authority was decentralized somewhat to the republican and communal levels, and democratic inputs from below became somewhat more important in decision making, especially at the communal and republican levels.

tionally had done. While democratic centralism continued to be the official norm for decision making during this period, emphasis shifted, almost imperceptibly at first, from authoritarian centralism to a tentative and circumscribed but politically meaningful stress on democracy within the Party.

Party membership rose, fell, and rose again in the decade following 1953. The advantages of being a paid Party functionary changed, and changed unevenly across the country. Not illogically, being a local Party or government official was most important in those communes where the federal government subsidized social and economic modernization most heavily.

By the beginning of the sixties, a complex pattern of political cleavage had evolved within both Party and government structures. For their part, conservative leaders in the communes guarded their entrenched status jealously. Among these local elites frequently were former Partizans determined to insure themselves the influence they felt was their due; in some areas official veterans' organizations exerted pressure on Belgrade to pursue policies favored by the local political machines of which they were a part.

The principle of equal treatment of Yugoslavia's nationalities, together with the way representation was structured, came gradually to mean that political preferences of any sort would gain added weight when linked to the nationality issue. Being a spokesman for nationality sentiment was effective on a wide range of issues as long as one proceeded with a modicum of discretion. Managers and other locally based modernizers used both the nationality issue and the central establishment's own slogans advocating workers' self-management to increase the autonomy of their enterprises, and thus their own freedom to maneuver. The various challenges to the center had a misleading appearance of unity. Although the preferences of these disparate groups were mutually incompatible, all sought "decentralization" in one guise or another. The result was that in some ways their activities reinforced each other.

The scope of government did more than just intensify political disagreements because so much could be won or lost: indirectly, the very size of the public sector did much to enhance the credibility of Belgrade's critics. As socialists, Party and government elites had publicly assumed responsibility for everything from combating infant mortality to increasing labor productivity and building an infrastructure worthy of a modern state. As was bound to happen given the magnitude of the undertaking, numerous programs fell short of the mark. Grievances, which in many other societies would be directed at a variety of institutions, were focused on the overburdened center.

Similar political dynamics may be observed in other socialist states, and the difference is becoming one of degree in the welfare states of Western Europe and North America. As the scope of these political systems has increased—invariably faster than their organizational ability to deal with the tasks undertaken—disaffection with the system itself has become a frequent and not illogical response. It seems likely that the recent resurgence of opposition by ethnic minorities to central authority in industrialized countries is related to the abrupt and continuing expansion of the scope of government in these states since World War II. When a government proves incapable of acquitting itself effectively of the responsibilities it has publicly assumed, discontent may remain unorganized for some time in the population at large. But circumstances such as marked differences in living standards among culturally distinctive regions will cause discontent to center around the ethnic question.

In 1960 the Yugoslav government embarked on a course of modest de-etatization. Whatever the merits of this kind of response to the problems of central management in an increasingly complex socioeconomic system, the reform faltered when repercussions from Western Europe's 1961 recession reached Yugoslavia. The centrally based modernizers found their position further weakened. By then the several groups of adversaries within the communist establishment each had sufficient organizational strength and ideological rationale to prevent any one course of action from prevailing decisively. Immobilism threatened. Equally ominous was the fact that—largely because of the structure of institutions—complicated political cleavages were oversimplified and increasingly expressed as differences among nationalities.

The Political Compromise of 1963

The political compromise institutionalized in the 1963 Constitution and in related electoral laws was complex. Its broad effect was to increase democratization in traditional, parliamentary terms *but to weaken the consociational principle at the federal level.*

Like the Federal People's Assembly set up ten years earlier, the new Federal Assembly had three sorts of constituents. The first was the citizenry at large; one representative was elected directly to the senior Federal Chamber by the inhabitants of several contiguous communes. The second set of constituents was the communal assemblies, in which workers from socially owned enterprises were doubly enfranchised; the communal assemblies sent representatives to the Federal Assembly's three functional specialized chambers.

The third set of constituents—and significantly the least powerful within the new federal structure—were republican and provincial political elites. Republican and provincial assemblies sent representatives to the new Chamber of Nationalities, which sat as a minority component within the Federal Assembly's Federal Chamber. While all legislation was passed by the Federal Chamber in tandem with one of the other three specialized chambers, representatives sent by republican and provincial governments had only 70 of the 190 votes in that pivotal body.

Explicitly consociational representation in government at the federal level thus became a *less* prominent feature in Yugoslav politics in 1963 than it had been previously (see Figure 14.3). The consociational principle was further diluted because federal officials could deal directly and individually not only with the republics and provinces, but also with the

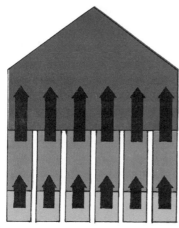

Arrows = strength of democratic inputs
Arrows' slant toward center = prominence
of consociational institutions at federal
level
Density of shading = relative authority at
each level of organization

Federal-level politics

Republican-level politics

Communal-level politics

Figure 14.3. Democratic inputs and consociational institutions in Yugoslav politics, 1963–66. From 1963 until mid-1966, representation in the Party and the government continued to be territorially based and so tended to be ethnically based; however, explicitly consociational institutions were virtually nonexistent at the federal level. Political authority was somewhat further decentralized to republican and communal levels, and democratic inputs from below became somewhat more important at all levels.

communes that composed them. Yet there was no important forum where republics and provinces could deal directly and multilaterally with each other and with the federal government. The vertical channeling of preferences by territorial unit (and so more or less by nationality) remained the most salient feature of political representation up to the republican level; but at the federal center, ethnic preferences had virtually no formal voice.

At the same time, under the 1963 compromise, representation at the federal level moved much closer to a contemporary liberal version of the democratic ideal. Direct rather than indirect elections were now held for the most important body in the federal legislature, on the basis of electoral districts of approximately equal size. In addition, during the sixties, it became increasingly common at all levels of government for more than one candidate to stand for each seat.

The 1963 Constitution also signaled a shift in economic decision making from local Party and government elites to workers' councils in the enterprises. Two years later, in 1965, this officially sanctioned change was put into practice in earnest with Yugoslavia's dramatic and dislocating turn from central planning to market socialism. Direct subsidies from the federal government to uneconomic enterprises were stopped. While considerable indirect power was still exercised through fiscal controls, the central elite's role in economic decision making was greatly simplified.

This abrupt reduction in direct political control of the economy did not affect communities across Yugoslavia uniformly. Hardest hit by far were conservative, locally based communists employed in Party and government hierarchies in Bosnia-Hercegovina, Macedonia, Montenegro, and some of the poorer parts of Croatia and Serbia. It was in these places that obtaining and distributing benefits from the federal government had been a vital part of the political economy. (The federal government had traditionally distributed these benefits on the basis not only of need but of political allegiance, the major criterion of allegiance being the degree of local support the Partizans had received during World War II and immediately thereafter.) These same conservative communists suffered yet another blow when their most powerful ally at the federal level, Alexander Ranković, was dismissed as head of the political police and expelled from the Party in disgrace.

The reform-minded communists who dominated politics at the federal center were confident that, given the chance, the general population would endorse their liberal policies. They resolved to use a democratized electoral process to reduce the presence of conservative opponents in the legislative branches of government at all levels. Just before the 1967 elections, a wave of constitutional amendments increased the power of elected bodies at the federal level. The main focus was on the directly elected Federal Assembly. Because nominating procedures were extremely complex, competition was limited to politically well informed groups—in effect, only communists became candidates in important races. Reforming communists at the center encouraged like-minded competition against less "progressive" communists. Elections were more hotly contested than ever before at all levels of government.

The process of democratization in Yugoslavia during this period is reminiscent of the pattern of events that characterized the partial democratization of some Western European countries in the late nineteenth and early twentieth centuries. Conflict within an entrenched political establishment led to a widening of the effective franchise when groups *within* the establishment, who expected to benefit from such a change, introduced more democratic procedures as a strategy to weaken powerful opponents.

The 1967 election results showed that the central reformers had miscalculated; anticentrist candidates were nominated and elected in far greater numbers than expected. There were several reasons for this. Local officials oversaw nominating procedures, and many contests were won or lost in the nominations process; the same groups were responsible for printing ballots, and being first on the list is an advantage in Yugoslavia just as it is elsewhere. In some instances where contests were expected to be close, unofficial but formidable organizations sprang up to get out the favorable vote. The general population, as well, had grievances against the central government: the abrupt economic reforms of 1965 had led to sudden increases in unemployment, inflation, and general economic uncertainty. They were widely resented. Prosperous Slovenia and Croatia also suffered the dislocations of breakneck modernization, and resentment was deepened there by federal fiscal policies that amounted to progressive taxation by republic to finance federal government services benefiting the poorer republics disproportionately. Pursuing political ends through a democratized electoral system was a tactic introduced in Yugoslavia by liberal communists at the federal center. By the 1967 elections this style of competition had been adopted in some degree by communists of all colorations.

The Erosion of the 1963 Compromise

One of the first fruits of increased procedural democracy in the 1967 elections was the conscious reintroduction of consociational features in federal-level institutions. Immediately following the elections, the new federal parliament passed a second wave of amendments further broadening its own powers and changing its structure. The Chamber of Nationalities was upgraded. For the first time in its history, this chamber, in which representation was on a classically consociational basis, began to exercise its right to sit separately from the Federal Chamber (see Figure 14.4).

In a similar mood, Croatia and Slovenia took advantage of their right to differentiate the structure of representation within their own republican governments. In both cases the aggregation of popular sentiment directly to the republican level was streamlined, and these two republican assemblies became even more important political arenas than they had been previously.

The invasion of Czechoslovakia had immediate political repercussions in Yugoslavia in the last half of 1968. Party membership had stagnated and aged since the early sixties; now it shot up by at least 15 percent.

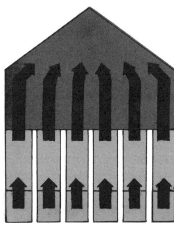

Arrows = strength of democratic inputs
Arrows' slant toward center = prominence of consociational institutions at federal level
Density of shading = relative authority at each level of organization

Federal-level politics

Republican-level politics

Communal-level politics

Figure 14.4. Democratic inputs and consociational institutions in Yugoslav politics, 1966–69. From about mid-1966 to early 1969, representation in the Party and the government continued to be territorially based and so tended to be ethnically based; explicitly consociational institutions began to be reintroduced at the federal level at the end of this period. Political authority was gradually decentralized further to republican and communal levels as the economic reforms of 1965 took hold, and democratic inputs from below became much more important at all levels.

Most of the new recruits were in their twenties, energetic, unorthodox even by Yugoslav communist standards, and anxious to defend their country against aggression if need be. The presence of the new members and the continuing drama in Czechoslovakia reinforced sentiment for democratization in Slovenia and Croatia—the republics most immediately vulnerable to armed attack.

At the December 1968 Party congresses in Slovenia and Croatia, leadership composition changed radically. An astronomical 80 percent of Slovenia's top Party leadership elected that month were young communists who had never held positions of great power in the Party before. Many of those who had helped shape the Yugoslav federation over the previous two decades no longer held official posts. An intelligent and ambitious triumvirate in their forties acceded to key positions in the Croatian Party, with influence second only to that of their powerful patron, Vladimir Bakarić, who had headed the Croatian Party since Partizan days.

Also in December 1968, a new draft of the Party Statutes at the federal level proposed two important departures from past practice. One, affirming the legitimacy of maintaining minority views as long as the will of the majority within the Party was not actively obstructed, strengthened institutional safeguards of democratic procedure within the Party. The second, proposing that republican-level Party organizations for the first time have their own statutes, formalized consociational principles and strengthened Party elites at the republican level vis-à-vis those at the federal center. When the Yugoslav Party's Ninth Congress met in March 1969, the final version of the new Party Statutes included a third major change, the creation of a powerful Executive Bureau not anticipated in the December draft. With this innovation, the consociational principle was institutionalized at the very pinnacle of the Yugoslav Party hierarchy: regardless of vast differences in the size of their respective populations, the six republics were represented by two members each and the autonomous provinces were represented by one member each. Tito himself presided over the Executive Bureau, bringing its total membership to fifteen.

The status of Party organizations within the Yugoslav National Army was the subject of an important controversy at this time. All army units are composed of a mix of officers and recruits drawn from throughout Yugoslavia. At issue was the proper relationship of the army's ethnically heterogeneous Party organizations to the ethnically more or less homogeneous Party organizations in the republics and provinces on whose territory they were stationed. The continuing radical decentralization of virtually all of society's institutions and the need to prepare for events that might accompany an eventual succession crisis made the issue particularly sensitive.

The December 1968 draft of the Party Statutes had envisaged rather close coordination between Party units in the army and local, provincial, and republican Party organizations, and would, in effect, have allowed the army's Party organization to act as a political coordinator for the federal center. The Statutes as adopted the following March indicate that mandatory close political cooperation with the army's Party organizations was successfully resisted by representatives of republican-level Party organizations. The army's representation in federal Party bodies is similar to that of a pan-Yugoslav "republic." It sends one representative per thousand members to Party congresses, just as the provinces and republics do, and it sends half as many additional delegates to these congresses as are sent directly by each republican-level Party organization.

In late 1968 and early 1969, further changes in the structure of representation in the federal government were introduced. In December 1968, the relative power of the Federal Assembly's three constituencies—the republican and provincial elites, the communal assemblies, and the general population—was dramatically altered. The Chamber of Nationalities, elected by republican and provincial assemblies, replaced the Federal Chamber as the senior of the five chambers. The directly elected Federal Chamber was sharply downgraded. While the latter change reduced the influence of representatives elected by the population at large, the political context in which this took place clearly indicates that this as such was not the purpose of the change. Rather, the intention was to discourage direct institutionalized access through federal institutions to the communal level, bypassing the republics and provinces (see Figure 14.5).

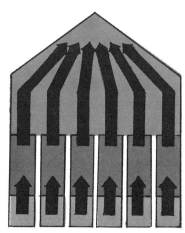

Arrows = strength of democratic inputs
Arrows' slant toward center = prominence of consociational institutions at federal level
Density of shading = relative authority at each level of organization

Federal-level politics

Republican-level politics

Communal-level politics

Figure 14.5. Democratic inputs and consociational institutions in Yugoslav politics, 1969–72. From 1969 to mid-1972, representation in the Party and the government continued to be territorially based and so tended to be ethnically based; explicitly consociational institutions were elaborated at the federal level. Political authority was further decentralized, notably to the republican level, and democratic inputs from below became very important at all levels.

Previously, most members of the Federal Assembly were responsible only to individual communal assemblies or to the voters at large in given electoral units. Now, the republican and provincial assemblies were interposed squarely between the federal government and the local constituencies: no federal legislation on any subject could be passed without the formal consent of the members of the Chamber of Nationalities who were elected and subject to recall by majority votes in joint sessions of the chambers of their respective republican and provincial assemblies.

The apportioning of votes in the Chamber of Nationalities was radically different from that in the Federal Chamber it replaced as senior chamber. Now an equal number of delegates, twenty, were chosen by each of the six republics regardless of population, and ten delegates were chosen by each of the two autonomous provinces. Thus, in the most powerful chamber of the Federal Assembly, just as in the top Party forum, some ethnic groups were accorded a greater percentage of the votes than they had of the total population (see Table 14.1).

Table 14.1. Distribution of population and of votes in the Yugoslav Chamber of Nationalities by republic/province

Republic/province	% of total population	% votes in Chamber of Nationalities
Bosnia-Hercegovina	17.0	14.30
Croatia	23.0	14.30
Macedonia	8.5	14.30
Montenegro	3.0	14.30
Serbia	40.0	14.30
Vojvodina	10.0	7.15
Kosovo	5.0	7.15
Slovenia	8.5	14.30

Another change further heightened the sense that the April 1969 election results might do much to shape Yugoslavia's future. Previously, half the delegates to the Federal Assembly had stood for election to four-year terms every two years. The staggered replacements had limited the effect that turnover could have in any one election year. Beginning with the 1969 election, all members of all chambers were to be elected simultaneously every four years. The political complexion of the new, highly consociational system of representation would be determined through the electoral process. In the nominating procedures and at the polls, Yugoslav communists used the election as one stratagem of several in a pitched battle among themselves over their widely differing policy preferences.

When the ballots had been counted, one knowledgeable observer wrote:

It is even difficult to say whether the elections of April 1969 should be judged a step forward in "democratization," as the regime claims, or a step backward in comparison with the last parliamentary elections, in 1967. . . . Among the more obvious contradictions was the fact the voters were offered a choice of two or more candidates for a majority of the seats to be filled, far more than ever before. At the same time, the nomination process was more complicated and strictly controlled than in 1967.[8]

These anomalies were more apparent than real. The complexity of the nomination procedures once again guaranteed that by and large only members of the political establishment stood, but competition among these nominees was frequently fierce.

No one group won a clear victory throughout Yugoslavia, but nationalist candidates were nominated and elected from many districts in Croatia and Slovenia. By the time the results were in, competitive elections had acquired important new opponents from among their original promoters: the liberal, modernizing communists at the federal center who had set the pace for Yugoslav politics during the sixties could no longer doubt that there was indeed a large reservoir of popular resentment against their policies, which their opponents had been able to tap.

By June 1971, the new Federal Assembly had passed twenty amendments to the Constitution. Two others followed. A twenty-three-member collective State Presidency was established, composed of representatives from each republic and province apportioned according to the consociational principle. As had been the case in the Chamber of Nationalities since December 1968, delegates to this powerful new body were chosen and subject to recall by the republican and provincial assemblies they represented. As the dean of émigré Yugoslav observers wrote when the texts of these changes were first published, "The latest draft amendments practically amount to a new Constitution." [9]

Croatia: Crisis and Repercussions

Formal decentralization of political power was invoked to secure a greater measure of actual political decentralization. Members of the Croat and Slovene leaderships, aided by some leaders from Serbia and Macedonia, led a movement to create still more institutional vehicles for further decentralization.

The change in the locus of political decision making, confirmed by the 1971 amendments to the Constitution, was substantial. But the amendments were also vague; ambiguity on key points was apparently necessary

8. Dennison I. Rusinow, *Yugoslav Elections, 1969: Part I,* American Universities Field Staff Report, Southeast Europe Series, 16, no. 5 (1969): 2.
9. Slobodan Stankovic, "Constitutional Changes in Yugoslavia," Radio Free Europe Bulletin (Munich, 8 March 1971).

in lieu of genuine compromise. Party membership and to some extent the general public were kept informed of the nature of disagreements on given issues by those leaders who felt their case would be strengthened in doing so. Good press coverage further heightened tensions and increased the number of people involved.

Many believed the conflict over where power should rest within the Yugoslav federation might soon be unmanageable. Differences that once again threatened to immobilize the Yugoslav system were endowed with increased legitimacy as they were channeled through a more democratic electoral system to institutions at the federal center. Paralysis threatened Party as well as government: the Party's new Executive Bureau, in which republics and provinces were represented according to the consociational principle, became yet another central forum in chronic deadlock, as did the recently created State Presidency.

The showdown began in late 1971. The first phase ended with the expulsion from Party and government posts of a number of prominent and popular young Croat politicians. By mid-1974, personnel changes and expulsions from the Party had changed the political physiognomy of virtually every republican-level Party and government in the federation. These dismissals, student demonstrations, bitter exchanges among intellectuals, and other dramatic events in late 1971 and early 1972 are emblazoned in many memories as Croat resistance to economic stagnation imposed by a Serb-dominated central government. But contrary to numerous impressionistic accounts, economic growth rates had remained respectable within Croatia just as they had throughout Yugoslavia.[10] The issues are not reducible to Serb-Croat animosity.

Tensions probably reached the flash point first in Croatia for a number of reasons. For one, even though Croatia like Slovenia had fared quite well as the result of the 1965 introduction of market socialism, the reforms underlined the limited voice these republics had in central decisions. Because they were relatively prosperous, Croatia and Slovenia were required to pick up the tab for the central reformers' miscalculations. This was most resented when it took the form of requiring that a large portion of hard currency earnings from abroad be forfeited to federal treasuries. Perhaps in part because they were not quite as well-to-do as the Slovenes, the Croats were pained by the prospect that this policy slowed the steady rise in their standard of living.

10. Lang, pp. 329 ff.

Second, when the widespread unpopularity of the 1965 reforms became apparent, central authorities sought to place politically reliable personnel in key positions throughout the country. In Croatia these personnel
were often from the Serb minority, which accounts for about 15 percent
of Croatia's population. Serbs in Croatia, faced with genocide at the
hands of Croat fascists in World War II, had turned in great numbers to
the Partizans and had tended to be favored in personnel matters ever
since. Since Slovenia, by contrast, is ethnically homogeneous, personnel
identified by the central authorities as politically reliable in that republic
were Slovenes.

Third, and again in contrast to Slovenia where the standard of living is
uniformly high, Croatia has two ethnically Croat and extremely poor
regions within its boundaries: the barren Dalmatian hinterland, and Sla-
vonia on the Hungarian border. It was politically expedient and not difficult to persuade these populations that the blame for their economic
backwardness lay not in Zagreb, but in Belgrade.

The decisive factor, however, was probably leadership style. Vladimir
Barkarić's three young protégés—Míko Tripalo, Savka Dabčević-Kučar,
and Pero Pirkar—were inclined to encourage still further democratization
of political and cultural life within Croatia. There is no reason to doubt
that they approved of democratization as a matter of principle, but very
likely they were especially enthusiastic because they felt that mobilizing
popular sentiment against federal economic policies in general, and
against Serbs in particular, strengthened their position when they
bargained with other republican-level elites over sensitive economic and
political issues.

By mid-1971 it was apparent that the preferences of these three strong-
willed young leaders for association among the Yugoslav republics constituted something close to loose confederation. More importantly, their
sense of urgency in this matter led them to seek to quicken the pace of an
already rapid political evolution. They met resistance at the center and
lost crucial support from more cautious decentralizers in other republics.
To this they responded by seeking popular backing within Croatia, but
they did so in the simplest and most dangerous manner:

In seeking wider support in this political struggle for decentralized power, the
Croatian new guard began to play with Croatian national sentiment, historically
the easiest and surest way of arousing mass enthusiasm while also frightening
one's negotiating partners with the implicit threat that nationalist forces may get
out of hand if one's demands are not met. . . . To many the Matica [publishing

house] began to look increasingly like the nucleus of a new, nationalist political party outside and challenging Communist control. . . .

This development, combined with the Croatian leadership's increasingly rigid negotiating positions in disputes with the Federal center and their toleration of nationalist "excesses," which terrified the non-Croatian minorities with recent memories of Ustase atrocities in multi-national Croatia, frightened off Croatia's former allies in other regions. Their consequent isolation then forced the Croatian leadership into ever more exclusive dependence on mass popularity inside Croatia, based more on their appeal to national than on their appeal to socialist allegiance.[11]

The group's earlier mentor, Bakarić, disassociated himself from these tactics.

In November 1971, Tripalo, Dabčević-Kučar, and Pirker found they could not end a strike at Zagreb University organized by militant extra-Party groups they themselves had helped mobilize. They were swiftly called to task and relieved of all formal political authority by a coalition of anxious fellow communists from other republics and from the center. Tito took personal charge of the proceedings.

Bakarić, the skillful and liberal communist who had dominated Croatian politics for a generation, remained head of the Croatian Party. He had worked patiently during the sixties for the kind of decentralization that did, in fact, take place—that is, the institution of formal and informal consociational procedures, in which power was shifted steadily from the center to the republican-level governments. But Bakarić did not question the value to Croatia of the Yugoslav federation, and he maintained strong horizontal ties with communists of the older Partizan generation in other republics and at the federal center.

Others fared less well. In the course of 1972 and 1973, Party members in all republics known to favor further radical decentralization ("nationalists") or to be especially tolerant of preferences aggregated from below ("anarcho-liberals") were removed from positions of power. Some particularly energetic and popular leaders were dismissed in Serbia and in Macedonia. Critics associated with the Marxist humanist publication *Praxis,* now centered at Belgrade University, were soon under fresh attack. Some blatantly autarkic economic practices pursued by republican-based banks in Croatia, in Slovenia, and in Serbia were curtailed. By the end of 1972, the importance of horizontal loyalties among communists at

11. Dennison I. Rusinow, *Crisis in Croatia: Part I,* American Universities Field Staff Report, Southeast Europe Series, 19, no. 4 (1973): 4.

or near the top of Yugoslavia's political establishment had been forcefully reasserted across the country, as had the value of discipline (in contrast to procedural democracy) in Party and government organizations.

The Attempted Consolidation

Elections scheduled for the spring of 1973 were canceled, and the 1969 Federal Assembly's tenure was extended a year. A new constitution—the fourth since World War II—was hammered out. This latest constitution changes the organized expression of political preferences at the base in two ways. The first is structural. The new set of institutions is called the "delegate system." While constituencies are still territorially based, all, with a negligible exception at the subcommunal level, are *functionally defined working groups*. For the first time, these include the private peasants.

New nomination and election procedures within the new constituencies are the second fundamental change. The "delegate system," intentionally reminiscent of the Paris Commune, is constantly and pointedly contrasted by its proponents with classic parliamentary democracy. A delegate's mandate, in contradistinction to that of a classic representative, is very

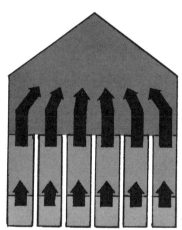

Arrows = strength of democratic inputs
Arrows' slant toward center = prominence of consociational institutions at federal level
Density of shading = relative authority at each level of organization

Federal-level politics

Republican-level politics

Communal-level politics

Figure 14.6. Democratic inputs and consociational institutions in Yugoslav politics, from 1972. Since 1972, representation in the Party and the government has continued to be territorially based and so has tended to be ethnically based; explicitly consociational institutions have been retained and strengthened at the federal level. Political authority has been recentralized to some extent, and democratic inputs from below have become less prominent in politics at all levels.

limited. Delegates are not professional politicians; rather, they are expected to resemble their constituents as closely as possible, and they continue to draw the same pay as they did in the job they held before they were elected.

The radically consociational features introduced into the Yugoslav political system from 1969 through 1971 in the form of amendments to the Constitution were retained and even appear to have been strengthened. Very broad powers were given the nine-person State Presidency, composed of one delegate from each republican and provincial assembly plus that body's own president. By early 1976, Yugoslavia's communists, on the one hand, had reaffirmed their commitment to consociationalism among ethnic elites and, on the other, had drastically modified and attenuated the pressures from below to which these elites can be subjected (see Figure 14.6).

Conclusions

The structure and procedures that have characterized Yugoslav political institutions since World War II have produced, with the passage of time, a more explosive combination of issues than other institutional arrangements would have done. By the late sixties, the major issues dividing Yugoslavs—market socialism, federal subsidies to poor locales, reinvestment policy, the organization and function of the army, the role of the Party, and ultimately the nature and importance of political democracy—came increasingly to the federal agenda as issues dividing Yugoslavs by nationality.

That differences among Yugoslavia's communists began to be summarized primarily as nationality differences was both misleading and dangerous. It was misleading because a considerable range of preferences existed among communists within each of the constituent republics, and this was strikingly true of Croatia. Yet both the preemptive nature of channels for political representation and their vertical structure militated against this being even approximately reflected in federal forums. As noted earlier, the vestiges of democratic centralist habits and the fact that representation in Party and government was largely by single-member districts further reinforced these patterns.

While no system of representation can summarize complex underlying cleavages intelligibly at the national level in a modern state without considerable distortion, the structure of institutions in postwar Yugoslavia inhibited the expression of political preferences along any *but* ethnic lines. At the same time, the broad scope of the public sector insured that feelings, however imperfectly expressed, would run high.

Encouraging the organized expression of political preferences as differences among nationalities over a period of years without also making institutional provision for mediation of such differences in top Party and governmental councils immobilized central decision making and was, finally, seriously destabilizing. Not until 1969 were forums introduced at the federal level that were adequate by reason of composition and mandate to mediate political differences in the manner in which they were being aggregated—that is, as differences among republics. By 1972, when consociational institutions were fully elaborated in both Party and government, they were thrown into deadlock by the nature and intensity of the demands from below to which the rapidly democratizing political system exposed political leaders.

Procedural democratization of political life in Yugoslavia had been underway in earnest throughout the country since 1965. First at the communal, provincial, and republican levels, then at the federal level, in Party organizations as well as in government, political leaders found themselves increasingly answerable to constituents who were more and more assertive. A common response to these democratic pressures was to reflect them, to become more assertive at the next level of organization.

Consociational democracy as an ideal type is distinguished from other democratic arrangements in *two* ways. First, of course, political preferences are aggregated by ethnic groups. Second, the democratic principle itself is attenuated to allow representatives of the component groups a free hand in trading one compromise for another in behind-the-scenes bargaining. A combination of explicit rules and informal practices insulates representatives at the highest level from short-term, issue-specific accountability to those they represent.

The Yugoslav case suggests the following about the genesis of such complex political arrangements: if democratization *precedes* the introduction of consociational decision making, especially in a highly charged atmosphere, then conflict management among elites representing largely ethnic constituencies is likely to be unsuccessful. Popular pressure will not permit the infinity of compromises on major and minor issues that must be the essence of elite behavior in such a polity. By implication, if the introduction of consociational decision making precedes democratization, as it did in Belgium, Holland, and Switzerland, then the habits of bargaining and compromise—without which consociational institutions cannot function—are far more likely to become part of the political culture of all constituent groups.

What does this augur for the future?

The political concordats of the past few years were negotiated in the certain knowledge that Yugoslavia's charismatic leader, Tito, would soon cease to be active in politics. The assumption among the politically powerful has been that official norms spelled out in Party Statutes, in various laws, and in the Constitution will be important during the transition period. Even if the use of force should figure prominently in Yugoslav politics at some point—for example, if the army should move publicly to back an incumbent government against domestic opposition—existing channels and norms within Party and government are still likely to determine much of how issues are shaped, what kinds of constituencies make up the polity, and what the norms for decision making on disputed issues will be.

The turn to more authoritarian governance increases the likelihood of general political continuity in Yugoslavia in the next few years. Those who hold the ultimate political vetoes—as in any polity, those who control the police and the army—have demonstrated that they are willing to intervene as needed to prevent rapid, unplanned political change. Moreover, it has been made clear to domestic actors that collaboration with groups abroad who are unfriendly to Yugoslavia's communist establishment—whether anticommunist nationalists or interfering Soviets—is taken seriously and is dealt with severely.

The return to authoritarian rule in Yugoslavia makes it more likely that fundamental questions concerning the conduct of politics will be dealt with serially, rather than all at once. Democratization in the classic sense, in general, and the institution of competitive elections and traditional parliamentary procedures, in particular, have been halted or reversed throughout Yugoslavia since 1972. But if the analysis put forward in this essay is correct, one important precondition for the eventual development of democratic institutions, which did not exist in the early 1970's, can now gradually be established. That precondition is the successful use over a number of years of explicitly consociational procedures among Party and governmental elites representing ethnically based constituencies.

CONCLUDING OBSERVATIONS

15

Perspectives on Ethnic Conflict in Industrialized Societies *

MILTON J. ESMAN

The subject of the foregoing essays has been the renewed prominence and increasing salience of ethnically based political conflict in countries of the contemporary Western world. Unlike newly independent, postcolonial countries, those examined in this volume have stable and well-established political systems. There has been time to cultivate allegiance to the symbols and structures of the state and to gain long experience in dominating and absorbing minorities and in operating institutions designed to regulate intergroup conflicts.

During the two decades following World War II, many academic observers and politicians relegated ethnic particularism and solidarity to the status of vestigial phenomena in modern societies and thought that modernization, economic rationalization, intellectual enlightenment, and political integration were destined to cause their decline and eventually their disappearance. What can account for the failure of scholars and politicians to anticipate the recent emergence of ethnic militancy? How and why have ethnic solidarities, once described as *primordial,* become an important dimension in the politics of *advanced* societies? What explains the new legitimacy of ethnic politics?

The essays have addressed these questions and three others in particular:

1. What techniques of mobilization and politicization are employed by various ethnic movements, and what new forms of social and political organization have appeared to spearhead these movements?

2. What are the methods by which the governmental and political elites of established states attempt to respond to, and manage the claims of, emergent and dissident ethnic minorities?

* I am grateful to Val Lorwin for his meticulous and very helpful comments on an earlier draft of this essay.

3. How are ethnic conflicts within established states converted into international issues?

The essays have been concerned primarily with the political expression and consequences of ethnic solidarity and ethnic conflict within existing political systems, rather than with the processes of ethnogenesis. There has been consensus among the authors on a working definition of ethnicity. It has both objective and subjective attributes: objective cultural properties expressed in language, religion, historical experience, or common institutions; and the subjective awareness of identity, belonging, solidarity, and common interests. Though it has an objective base, ethnicity is contextual in its manifestations; boundaries, intensities, and issues for any group may shift over time in response to changing experiences and problems. Ethnic solidarities derive meaning only in "we-they" relational terms. Thus, ethnic solidarity is mobilized and politicized through grievances in reference to the encompassing political system or to rival ethnic groups, which are perceived both as different and as competitive or threatening. Because of contextual variations and distinctive circumstances, it is difficult to theorize about ethnic pluralism or conflict even in industrialized societies which have many features in common. Yet, from the essays in this volume, a significant number of propositions can be adduced which help to explain and clarify the ethnic dimension of contemporary politics in the Western world and specifically the questions posed above. Only long-established, geographically concentrated groups which claim a territorial homeland are dealt with in this book. In this essay the term *ethnoregional* is used to designate these groups.

Why Now?

Why should the prosperous and peaceful period following the post–World War II reconstruction of Europe which was completed about 1955 witness the escalation of grievances and demands expressed and politicized in ethnic terms? Several factors have converged to produce this phenomenon.

The first is the greatly expanded role of modern government. The classical economists' night-watchman state of the nineteenth century has been superseded by the service state which is heavily engaged in social, economic, and cultural policies and programs. The modern state now claims from one-third to one-half of national income which it expends or transfers for economic development, social welfare, and national security. The centralized welfare state has appropriated functions previously

performed by private organizations or by local authorities or which were not performed at all. It is a conspicuous and ubiquitous presence in the lives of its subjects; increasingly it claims support and allegiance in terms of the demands to which it responds, the needs it fulfills, and the services it provides. Its expanding activities foster the expectations of organized constituencies as the state becomes society's universal problem solver. As the state regulates, invests, and provides services, it stimulates demands which begin to overtax its capabilities. The benefits and costs of its multifarious activities are distributed differentially among classes and among regions. Having stimulated expectations, central governments become at the same time the focus of demands and the target of grievances. Of critical importance, in the context of this volume, is the fact that some regions are the homelands of distinctive ethnic groups.

Perversely, these grievances originate from economically advanced as well as from economically retarded regions. The latter (Scotland and Britanny, for example) blame their deprivations on the neglect of a central government dominated by another ethnic group, while the relatively richer regions (such as Croatia and Catalonia) complain that their hard-earned prosperity is being drained by a hostile central government for the benefit either of a parasitical bureaucracy or of preferred but undeserving regions dominated by other ethnic groups. Economic grievances emerge when regions are neglected, but they are not stilled when regions are assisted because the assistance seldom proves sufficient to meet rising expectations once groups are politicized along the ethnic lines. In addition to economic grievances, cultural grievances are frequently invoked by ethnic activists to demonstrate the injustices perpetrated by an indifferent or hostile central government. Most commonly invoked of these grievances is systematic discrimination against regional languages in government, education, mass media, and economic activity.

Since World War II there has been a rapid process of industrial rationalization. The size and scale of industrial enterprises have increased because of economic growth, merger, and acquisition. This has tended to concentrate economic control, especially in expanding and dynamic industrial sectors, in a relatively small number of large corporations, financial houses, and public enterprises. Especially in Britain and France, the headquarters of these firms tend to be located either in or near the capital city or abroad. The expansion of public sector enterprises has reinforced this process. Peripheral regions lose what influence they had previously been able to exercise over economic decisions, which pass to

rapidly expanding corporate headquarters or offices of government enterprises in the capital cities. Investments and job opportunities become concentrated at the center. Research, product development, and similar high-income employment opportunities for professionally and technically trained youth are located at or near corporate headquarters. Peripheral regions are increasingly reduced to economic backwaters disadvantaged by stagnant economic structures, producing lower income levels, higher unemployment, inferior public facilities and amenities, and substantial net emigration.

The communications revolution has greatly enhanced regional and ethnic perceptions of grievances. The mass media, especially radio and television, have completely penetrated the peripheral regions. There is considerable uniformity in the messages they convey, and these tend to reflect conditions, culture, and life styles of the increasingly affluent center. This makes it easy, indeed inevitable, for people in the regions to compare their conditions with the international "consumerist" norms purveyed by the media, and with the conditions that prevail at the center and presumably are enjoyed by the dominant ethnic group. Reduced costs of travel have made it possible for regional people to observe the differences in conditions firsthand, and their impressions are confirmed or accentuated by what they observe of tourists visiting their regions. The obvious control of the media by the center—obvious because of the language spoken and the topics treated—may aggravate cultural grievances even in relatively prosperous regions. All such evidence of relative deprivation becomes grist for the mills of the new generation of ethnic activists.

Where do ethnic activists come from? Although hard data on this subject are limited, it seems that the activists originate primarily from groups that have benefited from the post–World War II expansion of higher education but that are frustrated by limited career opportunities in the peripheral regions or by a sense of ethnic discrimination. They seldom belong to the traditional liberal professions or to the public bureaucratic structures; nor are they involved in industrial management or in trade unions, the institutions primarily related to class struggle and class ideology. Many appear to be underpaid teachers suffering both from declining social prestige and low incomes. Too well educated and articulate to accept an unsatisfactory status quo, they are alienated from the main occupational structures, which are not responsive to their social or economic aspirations. They are therefore searching for a new rationale and for new

channels of political expression. Many of them discover this outlet in the new relevance of a previously dormant feeling of ethnic solidarity, combining countersystem protest and a challenge to established elites with the rediscovery of a rich history that rejects the well-worn religious and class-based issues of the immediate past in favor of a fresh organizing principle.

The momentum of the ethnoregional political movements, especially in the United Kingdom, has been increased by the declining legitimacy and effectiveness of the postimperial center. The economic opportunities as well as the psychic rewards of empire, in which metropolitan ethnic minorities participated and benefited, are no longer available. Moreover, expanded and more secularized educational experiences have, in large measure, demystified the centralized state, its symbols, and its apparatus, especially among the youth. Institutions are judged increasingly by pragmatic criteria of performance; many educated young people find them deficient when evaluated in terms of new aspirations for economic equality, group participation, and cultural authenticity. The legitimacy of all inherited institutions in the West—religious, economic, and political—has diminished during the past decade. The ethnic activists who propound new principles and alternative structures for political legitimacy and allegiance have capitalized on this general diminution in the legitimacy of inherited institutions. Ethnic political movements appeal especially to educated youth, many of whom find that ethnic identification and solidarity fill the political space previously occupied by religious and class loyalties.

A supporting theme among some ethnoregional militants has been rejection of the increasingly impersonal and remote technocratic and bureaucratic structures of government and industry. Such militants believe that the remoteness of these structures has resulted in a loss of community, in insufficient opportunities for participation in decision making, and in a general sense of alienation and anomie. To them, the ethnic group in its homeland provides a basis for rebuilding community on a scale that permits genuine participation and attention to human values. Often this theme is combined with concern for the environment, which is considered threatened by industrial and commercial development; the centralized bureaucratic government, controlled by a remote ethnic "they," is considered an abettor of such development. Some ethnic activists glorify the small state as politically more democratic, socially more humanistic, and economically more efficient than large centralized sys-

tems. While the "small-is-beautiful" theme and related critiques of technology and bureaucracy based on loss of community are vigorously pro-
pounded by intellectual elements in the ethnoregional movements, these
critiques have not exercised a significant mobilizing appeal among
broader strata of ethnic constituencies.

Two international developments have facilitated the struggle of ethnic
activists. The first has been the reduced prospect of war and the declining
fear of military pressure by the Soviet Union. None of the ethnoregional
movements in the West would be inclined to welcome the Soviet Union
as its liberator, but "detente" during the past five years has improved
prospects for small states and has made the risk of generating internal dis-
cord in established states more tolerable. Second, ethnic activists have
been encouraged by the examples of small European polities (such as
Norway, Switzerland, and the more recently independent Ireland and
Iceland) that seem to be doing well on their own; their existence refutes
the belief that small states inherently lack the economic scale and the security resources to survive in a dangerous, competitive world. A further
demonstration that independence—not to mention greater autonomy
within existing state structures—is both a feasible and justifiable aspiration has been provided by the achievement of independence during the
past two decades by former colonial states, many of which are smaller
and much poorer than European ethnoregional groups. Third World rhetoric is not uncommon in the propaganda of some ethnic activists in Western countries.

Tactics of Ethnic Mobilization

Essential resources of every political movement are leadership, normative appeal (doctrine), and organization. What can be generalized about
these factors among contemporary ethnoregional movements in Western
Europe and Canada?

Reference has already been made to the social origins of ethnic activists. As in most protest movements, a substantial component of the
ethnoregional movements consists of relatively well educated persons,
including teachers and technicians, whose economic rewards, social recognition, or opportunities for the exercise of power and influence fall
short of their expectations. Reacting against the material and psychic
frustrations of marginality, these activists initially take the greatest risks
in shaping ethnoregional movements and in building organizations designed to promote their objectives. When they experience some success

in mobilization within their region, they become a counterelite to the established elites, who are linked to the political and economic structures of the centralized state. In competing for support from the same ethnoregional constituency, the counterelite are likely to clash over fundamentals, especially over the proper relationship of the region to the political center. As the enthnoregional movement expands and draws additional support from more diversified sources, the leaders of the movement who agree on the ultimate goals of independence or autonomy may begin to differ over appropriate intermediate goals, tactics, and timing, since they must decide whether to use violence or peaceful electoral politics, and whether to place an emphasis on cultural, economic, or political issues. Some activists insist that true national redemption is possible only if it is combined with major changes in the distribution of social and economic power. The leaderships of ethnoregional movements are seldom monolithic even when ultimate political goals are agreed upon. Like other dissident social movements dominated by true believers, ethnoregional movements are vulnerable to fission on esoteric ideological grounds. When the objectives of the movements begin to gather public support, leaders whose skills are primarily expressive begin to yield to leaders with pragmatic political and organizational abilities. The movements then become vulnerable to a different threat—competition from established political groups who find it expedient to embrace some ethnically based symbols and demands in order to neutralize the appeal of ethnoregional movements and to co-opt parts of these movements' growing constituencies.

Ethnoregionalism is endowed with a strong normative resource, based on the continuing legitimacy of the concepts of popular sovereignty and self-determination, on the diminishing appeal of traditional patriotism, and on the demystification of the centralized state. Indeed, so compelling are the normative claims of ethnic self-determination that nowhere in contemporary Europe have regional grievances been successfully politicized except where they enjoy an ethnic base. Thus, while economic conditions in northern England have been as bleak as those in neighboring Scotland, they have not resulted in the organization or expression of politically significant grievances. There is even evidence of attempts to invent or rediscover an ethnic base for regional claims (Occitania, for example) in order to legitimate them externally and enhance their capacity to promote internal mobilization.

Some ethnoregional movements aim for greater autonomy and more equitable participation within an established state, while others insist on full independence. In the latter case, they must attempt to undermine their potential constituents' practice—a practice reinforced by generations of education and political socialization—of reconciling ethnic identities and loyalties with allegiance to the centralized state, that is, of attempting simultaneously to be a good Breton and a loyal Frenchman, a good Quebecker and a loyal Canadian. To break these psychic links, the leaders of ethnoregional movements must highlight grievances and deprivations and must emphasize the impossibility of redressing these grievances within the existing political framework. Thus, they must attempt to polarize loyalties and to force a political and moral choice between the established state and the ethnic group—between, for example, "rich Scots or poor Britons." The individual must be persuaded that his interests are linked with the power of his ethnic group and that the latter requires some form of political self-determination. Thus, constituents may be torn between preference for independence on political and cultural grounds and fear that independence would exact an unacceptable economic price. Such a dilemma appears to be restraining the movement for independence in Quebec.

An effective mass appeal must be oriented to grievances, economic or cultural. Where there is an imminent threat to a vital interest of the ethnic minority (such as the survival of the Basque language proscribed by the Madrid regime), ethnic protest may be mobilized at a politically significant level. In most cases, however, grievances alone are insufficient to mobilize protest at a level that threatens existing arrangements. To be effective, grievances must be associated with rising expectations, with credible hopes for personal and group improvement. Unless there are plausible rising expectations, activists will be unable to generate politically significant mass support because of fear that structural changes would worsen already unsatisfactory conditions. The effects of credible rising expectations are dramatically illustrated by the burgeoning support of the Scottish National party following the discovery of North Sea oil. Given the necessary combination of grievances associated with relative deprivation, of rising expectations, and of an organizational vehicle to mobilize support, the task of the ethnic elites is to convince their constituents that the realization of these rising expectations is incompatible with existing structural and constitutional arrangements. When a substantial number of constituents (the threshold is perhaps 20 percent) are convinced of this incompatibility and are prepared to vote or otherwise to act on that premise, the ethnoregional movement ceases to be a mere nuisance and begins to be a real problem for the maintenance of the polity.

The activists in some contemporary ethnoregional movements have demonstrated a leftist strain in their rhetoric, in contrast to the rightist language that characterized several similar movements in Western Europe and Canada prior to World War II. The struggle for socialism, they proclaim, is an essential complement to the struggle for national liberation. The concepts of "internal colonialism" and "proletarian nations" taken from recent Third World experience have been appropriated by some ethnoregional activists to emphasize their antiestablishment orientation in social and economic as well as political terms. While leftist rhetoric may be useful in dramatizing ethnoregional grievances at the early stages of mobilization, its political valence in contemporary Western societies is limited. In all of the ethnic homelands there is a property-owning peasantry and a substantial urban middle class who are repelled by the rhetoric of any movement that appears to threaten property rights. Ethnoregional political movements in the industrialized West, which aspire to cross the threshold into political significance, emphasizes, therefore, the theme of unity and common interests within the ethnic community they are attempting to activate. They mobilize vertically and their appeal is inclusive of all class and occupational groups. This diminishes the effectiveness and the utility of leftist rhetoric or of any threat to property rights, which would divide an ethnoregional constituency and alienate substantial groups of prospective supporters. State interventions to enhance economic development, improve social welfare, or protect the environment are, of course, common elements in the manifestos of ethnoregional movements, primarily because they offer substantial and widely diffused benefits at little apparent cost.

The tactics employed by ethnoregional movements depend on the resources the movements can mobilize and the opportunities available to them for expression—the latter a function of the response of the political center to the ethnoregional challenge. Mass demonstrations and violent tactics have the advantage of drama for a movement that is struggling for attention; violence attracts attention and contributes to consciousness-raising among prospective militants and sympathizers. But except where the center responds only repressively and affords no opportunity for the peaceful expression of grievances (Spain and the Basques, for example), violent tactics soon alienate more constituents than they attract. As movements gain broad support, the proponents and practitioners of violence lose their audience, which they are likely to regain only if the center resorts to repressive methods or refuses to accommodate ethnoregional claims. The more successful movements (for example, the Scottish National party and the Parti Québécois) rely on political organization and propaganda and employ primarily peaceful, though sometimes militant, tactics of persuasion. The practice of working "within the system"—of seeking and accepting national and local office—may, however, tempt activist leaders who aspire to independence to risk co-optation and to accept compromises short of their ultimate goal.

Although they proclaim their groups' sacred right to self-determination, the leaders of ethnoregional movements frequently are prepared, in the interest of group cohesion, to limit individual freedom. They are especially concerned with stemming the drift of some of their fellows into the more prestigious ethnic "they." This drift may occur through language acculturation (the Québécois in Montreal and the Flemish in metropolitan Brussels are prime examples of the phenomenon); and such acculturation is regarded both as an affront to group dignity and as subversive to group maintenance. On language issues ethnoregional groups usually insist on the principle of territoriality, which allows little room for ethnic minorities residing within their territorial domain to exercise the right of self-determination, and which leaves little opportunity for resident members of the dominant regional group voluntarily to drift away. This insistence on territorial monopoly, however, compromises the ability of ethnoregional groups effectively to champion the rights of fellow ethnics residing as a minority in the homeland of another group. In contests between individual freedom of choice and the promotion and protection of the collectivity, ethnoregionalists choose the collectivity and define it territorially. When they attain political power within their homelands, nationalists are seldom tolerant of the rights of minorities in their midst.

Conflict Management by the Political Center

Elites at the political center are primarily concerned with maintaining the boundaries of the system for which they are responsible. This objective is greatly facilitated by an ethnically homogeneous population. By fostering acculturation and eventual amalgamation or assimilation and by refusing to countenance cultural or institutional pluralism, central elites seek to build a homogeneous nation. Ethnic pluralism is tolerated and eventually legitimated only when ethnic groups demonstrate a refusal to accept either assimilation or subordinate status and when the central elites are unwilling to pay the price in conflict and violence that enforced assimilation or structural subordination may bring. Ethnoregional demands are thus a challenge—an unwelcome challenge that elites at the center would prefer not to have to cope with, but to which they find it necessary to respond.

The first response to this unwelcome challenge is usually studied *neglect,* denial of official recognition, and a refusal to take ethnoregional demands seriously, in the hope that they will die down or go away. Ethnic activists frequently resort to acts of violence to overcome this neglect. If ethnoregional demands survive the pain of neglect, they next evoke *ridicule* from the center and its political and intellectual allies. The objectives of ridicule are to discredit ethnic spokesmen as crackpots or fanatics, to define ethnic claims as nonissues, to forecast the disastrous economic consequences of separation, and to undermine confidence in the movement by depicting its language and culture as backward, unable to survive on its own, and unworthy of international recognition. This form of ridicule can be both sophisticated and effective. It poses or it has posed a heavy psychological burden for ethnoregional groups such as the Breton, the Québécois, and the Flemish whose indigenous languages and cultures had indeed stagnated in recent centuries. The eventual consequence, however, is to sensitize members of the dominated ethnic community to their identity and their grievances.

When neglect and ridicule fail—though frequently they succeed in delaying the mobilization of ethnoregional demands—central governments must resort to tactics of either *repression* or *accommodation,* and sometimes to a combination of the two. Repression usually involves outlawing or limiting the activities of political or even cultural organizations, banning publications, harassing or imprisoning ethnoregional leaders and activities, refusing to legitimate the use of local languages, and excluding minority representatives from positions of political authority (such as in Northern Ireland).

While such repressive practices are not unknown in the contemporary west (the French government's banning of Breton and Corsican separatist organizations serves as an example), regimes usually take accommodative measures first in the hope that the need to consider coercive sanctions can be obviated. There are essentially two methods of accommodation that central governments can adopt: concessional and structural. Concessional tactics involve the recognition of regional claims of economic deprivation and the provision of subsidies or financial assistance to foster economic development. Assistance is provided through a variety of fiscal devices and incentives or by direct public investment in the regional infrastructure or enterprises. Where grievances are more cultural than economic, central governments tend to accept the use of ethnoregional languages in public schools, in local and regional governments, and, for limited purposes, even in the structures of the political center. Such concessional forms of accommodation do not require changes in the distribution of power within unitary states.

Where concessional tactics do not suffice, regimes are compelled, usually with great reluctance, to resort to structural adjustments that allow for more regional autonomy or for federalism. The effect of such structural changes is to devolve to ethnoregional groups control of regional or provincial units of government. Such devolution legitimates regional jurisdiction over official language and education, and over social services, public employment, language use in economic enterprises, and even some elements of economic policy. Devolution of power can vary with issue areas. Disputes between center and region in federalized polities (Canada, for example) frequently have to do with the degree of control each will have over particular policy areas and with the distribution of fiscal resources. Central elites in unitary systems, however, are slow to concede regional autonomy, fearing that separatist appetites will not be satisfied with concessions, but instead will grow with eating. The crisis provoked by Croat nationalism in the early 1970's following the relaxation of central controls in the structurally federal Yugoslav system is the kind of evidence that confirms such fears. Whether to accommodate or to reject ethnoregional demands for autonomy thus becomes a painful strategic choice for central elites. One choice risks secession, the other violence.

Initiation of the process of devolution to ethnoregional authorities does not negate the importance of representation at the center, because the center, even in federalized systems, has an important symbolic role, exercises important powers, and controls important resources. Usually, devolution is accompanied by proportionality, formal or informal, in the center's political, bureaucratic, judicial, and military offices, and by recognition of regional languages for official use in all branches of government. In some situations, where the size of competing groups approaches equality (for example, Belgium), proportionality may yield to parity, with the formal or informal practice of mutual veto or concurrent majorities.

Proportionality is usually linked with consociational politics, a theme which is explored in several essays in this volume. There is some ambiguity about the precise meaning of "consociational." Some believe that it has been stretched to include all instances of elite accommodation in maintaining segmented political systems. The *spirit* of consociational politics is agreement among elites to take seriously and to consider mutually legitimate the aspirations, grievances, and vested interests of their respective constituencies and to attempt to compromise differences within the prevailing political framework. The objective is to preserve the existing polity while averting mutually destructive confrontation and violence by arrangements that produce peaceful coexistence and even intergroup cooperation. This contrasts with the orthodox democratic principle of majoritarianism which frequently leaves minorities (for example, Catholics in Ulster) permanently powerless to influence public policy on their own behalf.

The *practice* of elite accommodation may take many forms, some of which cannot be reconciled with earlier and more rigorous definitions of consociational politics. These definitions postulated political organization along vertical ascriptive lines, with each ethnic organization being controlled by an elite which forms a governing cartel with the elites of parallel groups; the legitimacy of these elites and the compromises worked out within the cartel are accepted by the deferential or politically passive mass membership of these organizations. There have been extended critiques of this model which will not be reviewed here except to note that the necessary conditions in the original model—including the autonomy of elites and the existence of a deferential, passive mass—seem to be too severe to explain or prescribe ethnic conflict management in most contemporary industrialized states.

Elite accommodation at the center can, however, be expressed in a variety of practices, including proportionality and the unremitting search for compromise solutions which leave no group a loser. It can occur in a variety of structures including multiethnic coalition cabinets, political parties with balanced ethnic representation, and proportionally staffed government agencies. Thus defined, elite accommodation is indeed instrumental to consensual conflict management and a clear alternative both to assimilationist policies and to majoritarian practices. It remains essential even when some of the burden of conflict has been lightened by devolution to ethnoregional federal or quasi-federal units.

Where ethnic groups are regionally based, some form of regional autonomy incorporating or verging on federalism is the most likely method of accommodative conflict management. Elite accommodation at the center is a necessary condition to the successful practice of federalism, since it reduces pressures for secession. Accommodation is facilitated by the security that autonomy affords ethnoregional groups in their homelands and by the reduced agenda of issues with which central elites must deal. Elite accommodation does not eliminate ethnoregional demands or ethnic conflict on economic or cultural issues, but it does provide a set of processes and rules for consensual management of these conflicts. Except in Ulster where geographic separation of the ethnic parties seems unlikely to occur prior to British withdrawal, and except for the recent immigrant groups which have not been dealt with in this volume, the combination of regional autonomy and elite accommodation at the center offers the most likely general formula for maintaining ethnically segmented political systems with a minimum of coercion in the face of growing ethnoregional demands.

It is not clear whether federal structures and elite accommodation contribute to low levels of hostility among competing ethnoregional groups or whether an underlying lack of hostility makes these structures and practices workable. Yugoslavia seems to demonstrate the first possibility, Belgium the second. Federal systems seem to have the capacity to mitigate interethnic hostility and to provide flexible patterns for regulating relations with the center. Switzerland, Yugoslavia, and Canada have depended on federal structures and practices to manage ethnoregional conflicts with the help of elite accommodation at the center and have done reasonably well. Britain may be moving in that direction in order to accommodate Welsh and especially Scottish nationalism. The fact that regional separation has not been an issue in post–World War II German politics—even though Bavarians, for example, have as proud and distinctive a sense of identity as Bretons or Scots, and Bavaria was an independent kingdom only a century ago—may be attributed, in some measure at least, to the devolution of power and the political elbow room provided by the structure of the German Federal Republic.

International Implications

The classical reason that ethnic pluralism has been feared and deprecated by statesmen is that the grievances of ethnoregional minorities leave their states vulnerable to interference by outsiders and prospective enemies. This is especially true if minorities identify sympathetically with, or are fragments of nations that control, a contiguous state, for this establishes the conditions for irredentist politics. While irredentism was an important source of conflict in Western European politics prior to World War II, it is not at present a major factor, principally because of the low levels of interstate hostility following World War II. Austrian claims to the South Tyrol have been settled by an international treaty and are no longer an element of friction. Neither the Dutch nor the French attempt to capitalize on the language cleavages in Belgium. Nor do Germany, France, or Italy interfere in Switzerland; nor does Germany incite the Alsatians. Nor do ethnic groups in these segmented countries invite outside assistance. Although de Gaulle blatantly encouraged *le Québec libre,* his lead has not been followed by subsequent French politicians, and their aid has not been solicited by Quebec separatists. Additionally, the struggle of the Basques whose homeland spans national borders has not produced tensions between France and Spain because both share a common interest in retaining the status quo.

The only active irredentist situation in Western Europe is in Ulster which the Republic of Ireland and the Irish minority in Ulster claim as Irish territory. The most hopeful effort at settlement of this bloody and intractable communal conflict was embodied in the Sunningdale Agreement of 1974 which would have replaced a defunct majoritarian system with the structures of a consociational regime. An important reason for the failure of this formula was inclusion of a provision, at the insistence of the Republic of Ireland and the Northern minority, that a Council of Ireland be created to establish an all-Ireland forum for the discussion of common problems. The proposal for creation of the council seemed to imply an ultimate union of Ireland. This destroyed the credibility of the Sunningdale formula in the eyes of a majority of Ulster's Protestants and led to the formula's repudiation. Until the conflicting populations can be territorially separated, regional autonomy will not be available as a conflict management process; and as long as the irredentist issue is kept alive, there can be no consociational regime.

Several trends in the international environment have encouraged and facilitated the reassertion of the solidarity and claims of ethnic minorities in the economically advanced and well-institutionalized polities of the Western world. These include the withering of empire; the disappearance of its psychic and material rewards, in which the ethnic minorities participated; and the subsequent demystification and decline in the legitimacy and, in some cases, the effectiveness of the centralized state. These trends have been reinforced by the success of small European nations in securing and maintaining independent statehood and by the attainment of independence by poor and backward colonial peoples. Ethnically based disturbances of the status quo now seem less risky, and the feasibility of independence has been enhanced by a perception of reduced external threats, especially the danger of Soviet subversion and invasion. These contextual factors have had more influence on the emergence of ethnoregional movements than have more specific events or trends in international relations, including European integration.

The most important post–World War II development in European affairs has been the movement toward economic integration which has made a European political union at least plausible. The ''Europeanist'' movement and the prospect of a European community to whose institutions the sovereignty of the old centralized states could be transferred encouraged many of the continental ethnic minorities (though not the Scottish or the Welsh nationalists) to look to the emergent Europe to rescue them from the total control of unitary states dominated by the ethnic ''they.'' Intellectuals among them envisaged a ''Europe of regions'' or a ''Europe of ethnic groups'' linked to the supranational European community with which they would share an interest in curbing and reducing the role of the centralized states. Some powers would be transferred to the community, others would devolve to reinvigorated regional governments, many of them defined by ethnic boundaries. The new Europe would thus foster the political and cultural redemption of the old ethnic communities. This dream was shared by many Europeanists including individual Eurocrats in Brussels.

This vision, however, has been shattered by experience. The institutional manifestation of an integrated Europe, the European Economic Community (EEC), like all international organizations, is tightly controlled by its members and these are the traditional states. They have made it clear that they will not permit their creature or any of its organs to promote the dismemberment of their domains by encouraging or legitimizing ethnoregional aspirations. Regional assistance is tolerated as long as it is focused on promoting economic growth or reducing economic disparities and as long as the areas affected are designated as economic regions, not as ethnic homelands. Moreover, EEC officials are permitted to deal with regional economic problems only through the organs of member states.

Within the EEC, it has been recognized that rationalization of European industry has penalized many peripheral areas. To help its members foster growth in economically retarded or troubled regions and to show its "human face," the EEC has established the Regional Fund. The Regional Fund is relatively small, however, and its resources do not flow directly from the EEC to the regions but only through the agencies of member states in support of their national policies for regional development. Thus the institutionalized version of the European movement and of European integration has disappointed early expectations; it has not proved a useful resource in the struggle of ethnoregional groups.

Outcomes?

Ethnic particularism never died nor was it ever entirely dormant in the modern industrialized First World. Flemish protest divided the Belgian polity during the interwar years. Basque and Catalan demands for autonomy were features of Spanish republican politics in the 1930's. French Canadian nationalists maintained their defensive struggle for autonomy in their Quebec homeland. At the apogee of empire, the United Kingdom was preoccupied with Irish nationalism, and an insurrection culminated in the separation of most of Ireland.

But for the most part, the economic and psychological opportunities and benefits of empire and of European world supremacy, the economic growth this supremacy fostered, and the central governments' assimilationist policies (which opened the ranks of privilege and prestige in business, the professions, and government to ethnic elites) sufficiently satisfied most elites who possessed the ability and the motivation to mobilize grievances in ethnic terms. Grievances for the masses tended to be articulated in class and religious terms and to be channeled into class and confessional structures through labor unions, peasant organizations, and political parties. The nationalism of established states was the dominant ideology; ethnic particularism was considered backward and even subversive. The evident diminution of ethnic solidarity and ethnic conflict in Western Europe at a time when such conflict was threatening to shatter the Habsburg and Romanoff empires persuaded most Western politicians and observers, academicians among them, that ethnic problems were a mark of reactionary political systems. In the enlightened West, they thought, ethnic pluralism was fading. Modernization, economic integration, and nation building inevitably would cause it to disappear. Conservatives, liberals, and Marxists agreed—though for different reasons—that the retrograde and disruptive phenomenon of ethnic particularism deserved to be speeded to the ash heaps of history.

For reasons already outlined, during the past fifteen years ethnic awareness and solidarity have been infused with new vitality and legitimacy, contrary to most observers' expectations. Assimilationist pressures have been reversed; ethnoregional identity is being asserted and even celebrated with renewed vigor; ethnic identity has become a source of pride rather than shame to members of minority groups. Consequently ethnoregional interests have been politicized to the point that statesmen can no longer afford to neglect them.

In my essay on Scotland, I proposed five conditions that seem necessary and sufficient to explain the recent resurgence of Scottish nationalism. Modified slightly, they can be generalized to explain and predict the politicization of ethnic solidarities elsewhere in the First World. The conditions are:

1. Group identity based on such objective properties as distinctive language, history, or institutions and the perception of solidarity and common interests associated with these shared properties.

2. Grievances based on perceived political, economic, or cultural deprivations or discrimination in relation to the encompassing system or to other ethnic groups within it.

3. Rising expectations resulting from credible prospects that the existing situation can be improved. Grievances alone cannot generate ethnic mobilization and mass support on a scale that is politically significant—although they may lead to violence and disruption—except where a major interest of the community, such as its language, is felt to be in immediate danger. Grievances in most cases, therefore, must be accompanied by plausible prospects for improvement in the cultural status or economic conditions of the ethnoregional community.

4. Declining authority and effectiveness of the political center, undermining its moral claims on the allegiance of peripheral groups and reducing the economic and psychic satisfactions it is able to deliver. The poor performance of the center vindicates the claims of ethnoregional elites for autonomy and self-determination. One reason that the various French peripheral groups, in contrast to the British, have succeeded in becoming only nuisances, but not threats, to the Paris regime is that the latter has been more effective in its economic and social management.

5. Political organization to articulate ethnoregional goals and group interests, to mobilize support and participation, to contest elections, and to seek political power.

That the first four conditions now prevail in many industrialized states facilitates the emergence of organizations to mobilize support and to politicize ethnoregional demands. But while it is possible to explain the emergence of ethnoregional movements, it is not possible to predict their outcomes. Their future depends as much on the conflict management resources of the political center and on the skill of their elites in using them as on the mobilizing abilities of the peripheral contestants.

At present the balance favors the central elites. There is no evidence of majority support for secession or separation in any of the cases covered in these essays. For a variety of sentimental and economic reasons, large numbers of those who vote for secessionist parties, and even of those who countenance the activities of terrorist groups, do not now insist on secession, though most of them and the majority of their coethnics want economic improvement, cultural concessions, and various measures of regional autonomy. In the absence of overwhelming support for secession, the central elites command impressive capabilities to accommodate moderate ethnoregional claims and to repress their extreme or violent manifestations within existing frameworks and state boundaries. The price they must pay is to abandon the goal of a homogeneous population and the policy of assimilation and to legitimize and transact with political spokesmen of ethnoregional movements. This will probably result in increased regional autonomy through institutional or de facto federalism and in economic and cultural concessions to ethnoregional demands, as outlined earlier.

As the recent moves toward a Belgian settlement indicate, relaxation of rigid centralized control can be accomplished without impairing the external boundaries of existing states. Settlements of this kind are likely in most of the cases treated in this volume, because interethnic hostility, except in Ulster, is not so intense as to preclude working compromises shaped and implemented by accommodative political elites. Central elites in Britain, France, and Spain have been reluctant to recognize and accept the legitimacy of ethnoregional demands in contrast to the Belgian, Swiss, Canadian, and Yugoslav elites who have had more experience in managing such conflicts. They may yet prove unable to accommodate even moderate demands because of ineptitude or insensitivity aggravated by majority resistance to ''unreasonable'' concessions. This could lead to the radicalization of ethnic minorities, provoke cycles of violence and repression, and eventuate in guerrilla warfare or in successful independence movements. But so great are the advantages the centers hold, so limited the popular support for secession, and so satisfying the possibility of forms of autonomy short of independence that the prospects favor compromises within existing state boundaries.

These compromises, however, cannot be final settlements. Ethnoregional cleavages will persist. Ethnoregional political movements and the governmental structures they control will remain cultural and economic interest groups; they will use their political resources to assert their claims and to promote and protect their interests. The ethnic dimension of politics, along with class, occupational, and corporatist cleavages, will be part of the agenda of industrial and postindustrial societies for the indefinite future.

Contributors

William R. Beer is Assistant Professor of Sociology at Brooklyn College of the City University of New York.

Suzanne Berger is Lecturer in Political Science at the Massachusetts Institute of Technology.

Jacques Brazeau is Professor of Sociology and Vice Dean of Graduate Studies at the University of Montreal.

Susan Bridge is Assistant Professor of Government at Wesleyan University.

Edouard Cloutier is Professor of Political Science at the University of Montreal.

Walker Connor is professor of Political Science and Faculty Exchange Scholar at the State University of New York at Brockport.

Milton J. Esman is the John S. Knight Professor of International Studies, Professor of Government and Public Administration, and Director of the Center for International Studies at Cornell University.

Davydd J. Greenwood is Associate Professor of Anthropology at Cornell University.

Peter J. Katzenstein is Assistant Professor of Government at Cornell University.

Arend Lijphart is Professor of International Relations and Chairman of the Department of Political Science at the University of Leiden.

Jeffrey Obler is Associate Professor of Political Science, University of North Carolina at Chapel Hill.

Lawrence Scheinman is Professor of Government and Director of the Peace Studies Program at Cornell University.

David E. Schmitt is Associate Professor of Political Science at Northeastern University.

Donald V. Smiley is Professor of Political Science at York University in Ontario.

Jürg Steiner is Professor of Political Science, University of North Carolina at Chapel Hill, and Visiting Professor at the University of Geneva.

Aristide R. Zolberg is Professor of Political Science and the College at the University of Chicago and Co-Chairman of the Joint Committee on African Studies of the Social Science Research Council–American Council of Learned Societies.

Index

**ETHNIC CONFLICT IN
THE WESTERN WORLD**

Designed by R. E. Rosenbaum.
Composed by Vail-Ballou Press, Inc.,
in 10 point VIP Times Roman, 2 points leaded,
with display lines in Helvetica.
Printed offset by Vail-Ballou Press on
Warren's No. 66 text, 50 pound basis.
Bound by Vail-Ballou Press
in Joanna book cloth
and stamped in All Purpose foil.

Library of Congress Cataloging in Publication Data
(For library cataloging purposes only)

Conference on Ethnic Pluralism and Conflict in Contemporary Western Europe and Canada,
Ithaca, N.Y., 1975.

Ethnic conflict in the Western World.

Essays originally presented at the conference sponsored by the Western Societies Program of
the Center for International Studies at Cornell University.
Includes bibliographical references and index.
1. Minorities—Europe—Congresses. 2. Canada—English-French relations—Congresses.
3. Nationalism—Europe—Congresses. 4. Nationalism—Canada—Congresses. I. Esman,
Milton Jacob. II. Cornell University. Center for International Studies. Western Societies
Program. III. Title.
D1056.C66   1975   301.5'92   76-28012
ISBN 0-8014-1016-9